MILLENNIUM

5

First published in 1998
jointly by

Gracewing
2 Southern Ave.
Leominster
Herefordshire HR6 0QF

Millennium Romae Editrice
1 Largo Angelicum
00184 Roma
Italy

ISBN 0-85244-387-0

Printed by Tipolitografia Pioda sas
Via Monserrato, 156 - 00186 Roma

Fabio Giardini

Pray without Ceasing

Toward a Systematic Psychotheology of Christian Prayerlife

Gracewing.

Millennium Romae

PARCERE SUBIECTIS ET DEBELLARE SUPERBOS

TABLE OF CONTENTS

PREFACE

Writing about prayer involves the risk that a concentrated effort to make some sense of one's own personal prayer experience may easily produce the equivalent of a spiritual autobiography. Quite often the spiritual itinerary mapped out by Christian authors does follow the paths they themselves have actually travelled. No wonder, then, that writings about prayer contain so many differing interpretations and explanations, for these can be expected to vary as much as the life-experiences of their authors.

Even though the writer on prayer cannot help but draw stimuli and insights from his or her own experiences at prayer, "theologians of prayer" must also present objective and universal reasons in support of their conclusions. Aware of this we will strive to make our reflections on prayer as objective and universal as possible, while at the same time allowing its experiential character to emerge.

Christians often pray without asking questions about prayer. Their prayers are daily exercises: obligations to be fulfilled before one finds the leisure to reflect upon the complex processes and elusive nature of prayer. We may even justify that unreflective attitude with a pragmatic statement – after all, it is more necessary to pray than to know what prayer is all about! But those who really desire to become prayerful persons need the clarity and security found in a knowledge of what genuine prayer is.

Between the experience of prayer and the reflection upon it there is such a close inner connection that their separation, when it occurs, is detrimental to personal sanity and the real development of both. Given this interconnection between the life of prayer and theological reflection on prayer, we could not well dispense with theologians of prayer.

If we are convinced of the usefulness and even necessity of theological reflection on prayer we cannot help but become involved with many of its problems, especially with regard to the specific nature of prayer itself.

Two fundamental questions can be asked about prayer. What are people doing when they pray? Why is doing that "praying"? These questions open out upon two vistas of prayer-research: one descriptive, the other interpretative. Descriptions of prayer will assemble as many aspects, elements and stages of prayer as possible, contenting themselves with a commonsense meaning of prayer. Interpretations will thrust to the heart of the matter and seek to take hold of prayer's very nature. This last task requires an essential and systematic definition, the development of technical terms, and their clear explanation.

Although all forms of prayer are interlaced with one another, their great variety and complexity make a broad spectrum of *definitions* of prayer possible. Many such definitions have emerged in successive periods of Christian spirituality. Prayer is variously proposed as to think, to meditate, to gaze on, to contemplate the mystery of God, etc. Each and every act, stage, and form of prayer can have its own proper definition, especially suited to itself.

Most writers who today attempt to define prayer, besides mentioning its most obvious act, "speaking with God," usually also emphasize the spiritual loving attitude that every genuine act of prayer should involve. Sometimes the depth and permanence of this attitude is also pointed out.

The common thought of different definitions of prayer is that prayer is the actualization of a relationship we have with God. In such a relationship one can note a shift of emphasis between a view of prayer, which works within a model of relationship between God and the human person as between the Most High and his lowly servant; and another view of prayer seen as a relationship between the Father and his children, of God the beloved and his lovers. This change of models of prayer is not only a dilemma within the history of spirituality; it can be also a personal event occurring at certain moments of the spiritual growth of the praying Christian.

Also the distinction between acts and attitude helps to clarify the life of prayer, within which they are necessarily interconnected. Acts and attitude differ from each other in the life of prayer not only quantitatively but qualitatively, as much as points differ from lines in Euclidean geometry and are irreducible to one another. For just as a thousand points cannot make a single line, thousands of acts of prayer cannot make the attitude of prayerfulness.

Given the complexity of the life of prayer the term "prayer" admits of different meanings.

- In a general sense, prayer is an all-inclusive word which can refer to the whole *life* of prayer.
- In a *categorical* sense, prayer means particular kinds and acts in the life of prayer, all of which can be put into diverse terms.
- In a *transcendent* sense, prayer means a fundamental permanent *attitude* and dynamic orientation of the prayerful person. This sense embraces whatever in prayer is neither general nor can fit into any of its categories. It "transcends" all categories while at

> the same time pervading all of them through and through. Paradoxically, what is transcendent lies both above and within everything it transcends.

"Transcendent" in this context designates whatever inheres in the deepest part of self, which can also be termed the transcendental self, insofar as it covers that stratum of the human person which goes beyond all specifically articulate thoughts, affections, feelings, etc. At that level of spiritual depth (or height, which here is the same) the human person has a particular spiritual character of "self-transcendence," a dynamic power which drives him or her towards the infinite and eternal, and prevents such a one from finding complete satisfaction in anything finite and temporary. At that level the human person is placed before God; and when divine grace is added, the person can enter into direct communication with the transcendent God.

This last meaning of prayer can be fittingly expressed by the word *Prayerfulness.* Taken in this sense, prayerfulness refers to the vital core of the life of prayer, to the purest essence of prayer; while, on the other hand, one's entire life of prayer with all its acts and exercises should be the embodiment of that prayerfulness in words and gestures, in images and feelings, in ideas and reasonings.

Bearing in mind the multiplicity of the life of prayer we realized that an essential clarification of it required a study – in orderly succession and systematic interconnection – of its principal component elements (chapters I-IV), kinds and acts (chapters V-VIII), integration and growth (chapters IX-X), and transcendent attitude (chapters XI-XII).

* * *

ACKNOWLEDGEMENTS

In writing this book I was helped by many people. Large audiences of students who attended classes at the University of St. Thomas in Rome, and many groups of retreatants who listened to spiritual conferences in Italy, the United States, Ireland, and the Philippines, responded in various ways to my ideas on prayerfulness and inspired me to clarify and develop them. Friends and colleagues with whom I discussed the subject also helped by stimulating me to correct and enrich the book in many ways. Brevity prevents the mention of all their names. But one name cannot be passed over in silence. For this book could simply not have been written and published without the very valuable cooperation of Sister Mary Dominic Yanker, O.P., of the Dominican Monastery of Mary the Queen in Elmira, New York. She was always generous with encouragement, suggestions, and editorial observations, as she keyed the manuscript into the computer. Therefore I dedicate this book to her, and through her to all Christians who yearn, as she earnestly does, for an ever growing loving awareness of God's presence in prayer.

Fr. Fabio Giardini, O.P.

CHAPTER I

BODY, SOUL, AND SPIRIT IN PRAYER

[1]Life experience comes before reflection. But reflection enables one to better realize and rightly appreciate life experience. Reflection on life experience

> "Takes advantage of what one knows, utilizes for the sake of new knowledge already actually possessed. It is to help oneself with what one already knows in order to reach knowledge of what one does not yet know."[2]

By understanding, discerning, and evaluating their own life experiences, people get to know themselves and mature as persons.

The same holds true also of prayerlife, prayer experiences, and praying people. What we call "prayerlife" is an extremely complex and variegated, many-sided and multi-layered human activity. Any listing of its aspects, forms, grades etc., could never pretend to be exhaustive.

In order to gather data from prayerlife an initial commonsense notion of prayer may suffice. But a clarifying interpretation requires a thrust toward the heart of the matter to take hold of prayer's essential core and basic components.

A first convenient manner of reflecting on Christian prayer life is to distinguish its most basic components, describing them separately and together in the unfolding of prayer.

---

[1] Names printed in all capital letters and abbreviations in parentheses and footnotes refer to the corresponding works in the ABBREVIATIONS and BIBLIOGRAPHY found at the end of the book.

[2] SIMON, pp. 136-137.

i. *Basic Components of Christian Prayerlife*

> "The OT distinguishes between true and false prayer in the following manner. True prayer is of the heart, i.e., *it involves the whole person and means that a man comes before God with his whole being and in an attitude of humble submission.* (Jr 29:12 ff).
>
> False prayer, by contrast, is offered merely 'with the lips', i.e., a man merely utters (or simply repeats) words and phrases with no self-surrender or offering of his 'heart' and life to God, except perhaps as a pure formality, with no intention of fulfilling the will of God as revealed, e.g., in his commandments (Is 1:15f; 29:13; Am 5:23f)."[3]

This teaching of the OT carries on into the NT too. Doubtless, Christians ought to pray to God with their whole person.[4] But for the sake of clarity we will distinguish in Christian prayerlife a body, a soul, and a spirit.[5] Of course, Christians ought to pray neither with their bodies split off from their souls nor without their spirit. As an activity in which the whole Christian self is supposed to be involved, prayer should be directed by the spirit, performed by the body, and mediated by the soul.

Accordingly, a spiritual, a psychic, and a corporeal component can be distinguished in Christian prayerlife. We will term these components "the spirit", "the soul", and "the body" of prayer.

---

[3] DNNT, vol. III, p. 844. Emphasis ours.

[4] ŠPIDLÍK [2], p. 195: "La prière est un acte vital, et pour que l'oraison soit intégrale, el faut que l'homme entier y participe avec toute sa personne."

[5] We follow rather freely the Pauline distinction: "May the God of peace make you perfect and holy: and may you all be kept save and blameless, *spirit, soul and body,* for the coming of our Lord Jesus Christ." (I Th 5:22-23), even though this "passage does not imply a trichotomy of personality" in Rm 7:7-25 *(mind, flesh,* and "I"); Ga 5:16-24 (where personality as needing to be sanctified by God. Cf. Dt 6:5": PORTEOUS, p. 429 b. Paul, however, developed what has been called "the triangle of personality" in Rm 7:7-25 *(mind, flesh,* and "I"); Ga 5:16-24 (where *mind* is replaced by *spirit)";* McCASLAND, p. 434 a. The early Christian tradition uses the same threefold distinction: IRENEUS, p. 1144 and ŠPIDLÍK [1], p. 46ff.

a. Body and soul of prayer

The *body* of prayer is the corporeal, visible side of it. It includes many different postures and gestures: standing, stretching and lifting up one's hands, bowing, kneeling, prostrating, etc., plus looks, gazes, words, sighs, groanings, songs, tears, etc., which accompany the activity of prayer. They are often mentioned in the sacred Scripture.[6] Just as an example –

> "Ezdra blessed Yahweh, the great God, and all the people raised their hands and answered, 'Amen, Amen!'; then they bowed down and, face to the ground, prostrated themselves before Yahweh... The people were in tears as they listened to the words of the Law".[7]

A contemporary author still suggests quite similar postures of the body –

> "In adoration as in meditation, the position of the body calls for attention. We can kneel, focusing our eyes, heart, and attention upon God. Or we can prostrate ourselves full length on the ground. Or we can stand perhaps bowing profoundly from the waist, slowly and rhythmically, as in the eastern orthodox custom."[8]

As the human body is always in some place and time, so also "the body of prayer" has its places and times. Nothing is really prescribed about the time and the place of Christian prayer, as, in principle, any place and time may be good for prayer.[9]

However, suggestions and indications about the places more suitable for prayer can be found in the sacred Scripture. For instance, besides confirming that the Temple of Jerusalem is "God's house of

---

[6] For the many postures of prayer recorded in the Scripture see SMITH, p. 866a.

[7] Ne 8:66-7, 9. All our quotations of the sacred Scripture are from JB.

[8] LEECH, p. 59.

[9] "De temporibus orationis nihil omnino praescriptum est, nisi plane omni in tempore et loco orare." TERTULLIAN, 23. In EA, n. 47, p. 23.

prayer";[10] Jesus exhorts his disciples to enter into their private room and shut the door in order to pray there in secret to their Father in heaven:

> "Be careful not to parade your good deeds before men to attract their notice; by doing this you will lose all reward from your Father in heaven... When you pray, go to your private room and, when you have shut your door, pray to your Father who is in that secret place, and your Father who sees all that is done in secret will reward you."[11]

Jesus himself withdrew at times from the crowds, to secluded and lonely places (the wilderness, the mountains, the countryside, etc.) to pray.[12]

Some Fathers interpreted these actions of Jesus as if He intended to teach Christians not only to seek a quiet place to pray without distractions,[13] but also to practice faith in God's omnipresence, which enables Him to hear and see all His children, even when they pray in remote or hidden places.[14]

Concerning the time of prayer we read in Mark that the night was a favorite one with Jesus.[15] Accordingly, Christians, too, should often get up from bed during the night and praise God, for those who have the Word of God abidingly vigilant within themselves do not need to sleep all night long.[16] Virgins consecrated to God were especially exhorted to

---

[10] Cf. Lk. 19:46 = Is. 56:7.

[11] Mt 6:1, 6.

[12] Cf. Mk 1:35; Lk 9:28; etc.

[13] Cf. ORIGEN, 31, 4: "Potest (Christianus) etiam, quo suas quisque preces quietior et minus distractus absolvat, certum ac definitum in privatibus aedibus, si spatium sit, eligere locum, ut ita dicam, sanctiorem, ibique orare...". In EA, n. 105, p. 55.

[14] Cf. CYPRIAN, 4: "Magisterio suo Dominus secrete orare nos praecepit, in abditis et semotis locis, in cubiculis ipsis, quod magis convenit fidei, ut sciamus Deum ubique esse praesentem, audire omnes et videre, et majestatis suae plenitudine in abdita quoque et occulta penetrare." In EA, n. 159, p. 77.

[15] Cf. Mk 1:35; 6:46.48; 14:7.

[16] Cf. CLEMENT OF ALEXANDRIA, 2, 9, 79, 1-2 and 81, 4: "Ita ergo dormitandum est, ut facile excitemur... Quocirca saepe etiam noctu e lecto

get up and sing hymns to God in the middle of the night, for at that same hour the Lord Jesus rose from the dead and praised with hymns His heavenly Father.[17]

In their daily prayers early Christians adopted the times of the devout Jew

> "The devout Jew prayed three times daily – in the early morning at the time of the temple sacrifices, at 3:00 P.M. when the evening sacrifices were offered, and at dusk when the lamps were lit. Threefold daily prayer is mentioned by the Didache (8);[18] at each of the three times the Christian is to recite the Lord's Prayer...
>
> Further hours of prayer were gradually added until a daily round of six periods of private devotion was established by the time of Hippolytus (*Apostolic Tradition* 36). It is from these hours that the daily offices later developed."[19]

After reminding us that the third, the sixth, and the ninth hour were times of prayer,[20] Tertullian cannot help writing that these three daily times of prayer are the minimum demanded of Christians who are to adore the Father and the Son and the Holy Spirit.[21]

---

exsurgendum est, Deusque est laudandus... Non enim oportet eos, qui inhabitantem et vigilantem intus habent Logon, tota nocte dormire." In EA, n. 78 and 79, pp. 35-36.

[17] Cf. ATHANASIUS, 20: "Media nocte excitaberis et hymnis celebraberis Dominum Deum tuum. Ea ipsa hora resurrexit Dominum noster ex mortuis et Patrem suum hymnis celebravit, quae iniunctuum nobis est, ea ipsa hora hymnos Deo dicamus." In EA, n. 226, p. 119.

[18] Cf. also ORIGEN, 12, 2: "quae solet oratio vocari non minus quam ter quaque die fieri debet." In EA, n. 106, p. 54.

[19] RICHARDSON, p. 893b. Remember that the Brahman must say certain prayers three times a day, and the Muslim five times.

[20] The sixth and ninth hour of the day were chosen as times of prayer by the early Church. Cf. Ac 3:1; 10:3.9.30.

[21] "Ne minus ter die saltem adoremus, debitores trium Patris at Filii et Spiritus Sancti, exceptis utique legitimis orationibus, quae sine nulla admonitione debentur ingressu lucis et noctis.": TERTULLIAN, 25, In EA, p. 23

Naturally, the places, times, and various postures, gestures, etc., of prayer recorded in the sacred Scripture[22] and the early Christian writings, are all ordained to embody, express and symbolize the inner thoughts, volitions, affections, fantasies, emotions, and attitudes of the praying Christians, which constitute "the soul of prayer".[23]

The body and soul of prayer are united in prayerlife like the body and the soul in the human person. They may be distinguished from one another for the sake of analytical clarity, but they should never be separated in Christian prayer. For the body of prayer contains and expresses the soul of prayer, while the soul of prayer enlivens and gives spiritual content and significance to the body of prayer.

> "A vital prelude to prayer is the attainment of control of the body. It is very important, for example, to find a physical posture which helps and does not hinder, our practice of prayer. In the west we tend to neglect the question of the posture, and our prayer suffers accordingly.
>
> There is no position which is always right for prayer. Sitting on a hard chair, kneeling perhaps with the help of a prayer stool, standing – all these can be valuable. It is important to find the posture which helps us.
>
> The use of the hands needs some attention, for the hands can be a major source of distraction. They can be occupied by holding them together, by holding them open with the palms upwards on the knees, by raising them to the skies.
>
> Breathing also matters, and the use of breathing in prayer is an important aspect, again much neglected in the west."[24]

But, although the body can contribute a great deal to the soul of prayer, Christian masters very early stressed that the activity of the soul is more important in prayer than whatever the praying persons can do with their bodies.

---

[22] For more about places and times of prayer mentioned by the sacred Scripture, see SMITH, p. 865b-866a.

[23] Remember that in the sacred Scripture "*nephesh* (soul) can represent the totality of feeling (Ex 23:24). The *nephesh* hungers and thirsts; is greedy; is satisfied; feels joy, sorrow, love, hatred, hope, despair, etc.... It is used as the subject of emotions in Mk 14:34; Lk 1:46; Jn 12:27.": PORTEOUS, p. 429a.

[24] LEECH, p. 40.

> "Do not pray by outward gestures only, but bend your mind as well to the perception of spiritual prayer with great fervor... Whether praying along with the brethren or alone, strive to make your prayer more than mere habit. Make it a true inner experience."[25]

But they also remind Christians that singing Psalms, as the monks are wont to do, is expedient to dispose their soul to pray well.

> "The singing of the Psalms quiets the passions and calms the intemperance of the body. Prayer, on the other hand, prepares the spirit to put his own powers into operation... Psalm-singing is an image of wisdom which is many-sided; prayer is the prelude to immaterial and uniform knowledge."[26]

Lay Christians, who cannot sing psalms as the monks do and reach through this prayer practice the "immaterial and uniform knowledge" mentioned in the preceding quote, are given the following advice.

> "Even if you are not able to do this (= praying) with your heart, at least with your mouth you should earnestly and diligently repeat those things which belong unto the Passion (of our Lord Jesus Christ), because when a thing is often spoken with the mouth it does in the end impart warmth and fervor into the heart...
>
> (And eventually produces perfect prayer, which is) devout, pure, constant, humble and fervent, uttered with the mind and the heart and all the

---

[25] EVAGRIUS, ch. 28, p. 59; ch. 41, p. 61. Several quotations of the same contents from early Greek Fathers can be found in ŠPIDLÍK [2], pp. 86-87. The traditional Christian teaching about this point is clearly explained by Aquinas: "As Damascene says, *since we are composed of a twofuld nature, intellectual and sensible, we offer God a twofold adoration* (*De Fide Orthodoxa,* 12, PG 96, 1133), namely a spiritual adoration consisting in the internal devotion of the mind, and a corporeal adoration, consisting in exterior humbling of the body. Moreover, because in all acts of religion the external act is referred to the internal act as to the more important, exterior adoration is performed because of interior adoration: in other words, the bodily signs of humility which we perform increase our desire of submitting ourselves to God, because we naturally proceed from things of sense to things of mind." (II-II, q. 84, a. 2 co., BLACKFRIARS, vol. 39, p. 107).

[26] EVAGRIUS, ch. 83, p. 69; ch. 85, p. 69.

> strength of the soul and the feelings of the body, asking and imploring with most ardent desire."[27]

The two ancient monastic rules most often followed in the western Church during the Middle Ages demanded of the monks that they pray while "entertaining in the heart what the lips are reciting"[28] and "moving the mind in harmony with the voice".[29] The ability of doing precisely that is still asked of God in our Liturgy of the Hours.[30]

The same union of lips and mind in prayer is demanded of lay Christians in a homily of St. John Chrysostom –

> "Many enter the church, recite a myriad of lines of prayer verses and then go out, not knowing what they said: they move their lips but do not listen to what they say.
>
> You yourself do not pay attention to your prayer and want that God should heed it? 'I knelt down' – you say. That's true, but your thoughts flew away."[31]

About the union of body and soul in prayer, a medieval spiritual author makes a distinction, at the same time realistic and consoling,

---

[27] ANGELA, II, ch. vi, p. 60; ch. vii, p. 63.

[28] "Hoc versetur in corde, quod profertur in ore; et nolite cantare, nisi quod legitis esse cantandum": *Rule of St. Augustine,* ch. 3. The text of St. Augustine's Letter 211, 7, PL 33, 960 of which the *Regula* is derived has "voce" instead of "ore": cf. EA n. 701, p. 358. Seemingly the sources of the Augustinian norm are – "Go on singing and chanting to the Lord *in your hearts* (Ep 5:19)." "With gratitude *in your hearts* sing psalms and hymns and inspired songs (Col 3:16)." Cf. also Rm 10:8-10: "If your lips confess that Jesus is Lord and if you believe in your heart that God raised him from the dead, then you will be saved." (v. 9).

[29] "Sic stemus et psallendum, ut mens nostra concordet voci nostrae": *Rule of St. Benedict,* ch. 19 in EA n. 1387, p. 647. Cf. TERTULLIAN, 17. In EA, p. 23: "Deus non vocis, sed cordis auditor est, sicut conspector." Also "Abba Elias said: Unless the mind sings with the body, the labor is in vain..": YUSHI, p. 60.

[30] Prayer at Vespers, Tuesday of the fourth week, in LITURGIA, vol. III, p. 949: "Ut ea semper meditemur in cordibus, quae tibi labiorum vocibus profitemur."

[31] EA, n. 362, p. 225-226. Translation ours.

between Christians who live in a "contemplative" environment and those who live in an "active" one.

> "The prayer of the people who are busied with active works is made of two words, for they often form one word in their hearts, through thinking of worldly affairs, and pronounce another with their mouth, of the psalm sung or said. However, if their intention is true, their prayer is still good and worthy of reward, even if it should lack savor and sweetness.
>
> But the kind offered by a contemplative is made of only one word, for it is formed in the heart, so it sounds whole in the mouth: as if it were only one thing that both forms and pronounces... (In this case) the body is nothing but an instrument and a trumpet of the soul, on which the soul blows sweet (notes) of spiritual praises to God."[32]

The body and soul, i.e., the "outer" and "inner" sides of prayer, are variously combined by praying Christians to form a good many different spiritual and bodily postures and gestures.

A recent Document of the Holy See summarizes the ancient Christian teaching about the use of the body in prayer stating that, since praying Christians should strive for God with their whole being, various bodily postures can help to recollect the soul and to dispose the spirit to prayer.[33]

A number of bodily postures and gestures of prayer are described in a noteworthy thirteenth-century work entitled, *The Nine Ways of Prayer of Saint Dominic,* which derives from the previous medieval monastic tradition and sums it up. Its unknown author declares in the prologue that he wants to say something about how Dominic used to pray, i.e., by bowing deeply, prostrating, taking the discipline, genuflecting, standing erect, standing with arms outstretched, standing erect with arms and body stretched heavenward, sitting to read, praying while walking.

All these postures were for Saint Dominic –

---

[32] HILTON, II, ch. 42, p. 291.

[33] "In oratione homo totus Deo attingere debet et ideo etiam suum corpus positionem debet assumere aptiorem ad animum secum colligendum. Haec positio symbolice exprimere potest orationem ipsam.": CDF: *Letter,* n. 26.

> "A way in which the soul uses the various members of the body to foster its own loving ascent to God... This manner of praying stirs up devotion, the soul stirring the body, and the body in turn stirring the soul. Praying in this way used to make Saint Dominic dissolve utterly into weeping, and it so kindled the fervour of his good will that he could not contain it: devotion showed quite plainly in his bodily members."[34]

Aquinas explains that certain postures and gestures of the body can powerfully dispose the soul for prayer; and that, in turn, when the prayer of the soul reaches a certain intensity, it bursts out into bodily expressions. This teaching drawn from St. Augustine, is often used in his treatment of religious acts.[35]

Also St. Ignatius of Loyola, in a note of "additional directions" placed at the end of the First Week of *The Spiritual Exercises,* writes:

> "I will enter into the meditation, at times kneeling, at times prostrate on the ground, at other times supine, or seated or standing, always seeking what I desire."[36]

Bodily postures and gestures are useful insofar as they symbolize and foster the inner attitude of the praying soul. The same posture or gesture can also serve different acts of prayer.[37]

But not any kind of bodily actions and sensations can symbolize genuine Christian prayer. Certain of those actions and sensations rather hamper or destroy Christian prayer altogether, in a way analogous to how idolatry drives away genuine religious worship.[38]

---

[34] NW, pp. (11)-(12). Emphases ours. See also the reflections of BOLAND.

[35] Cf. BOLAND, p. 180, note 13.

[36] SE, p. 61.

[37] For example, St. Dominic used to sit in order to read the Holy Scripture prayerfully. But sitting can also be used to dispose oneself to the practice of quiet contemplative prayer.

[38] Cf. "Si symbolismus (corporis) inadaequate ac non recte intellegatur, *idolum* prorsus fieri pereclitatur et ideo impedire elevationem spiritus ad Deum. Vivere inambitu orationis totam realitatem proprii corporis ut symboli admodum difficilius est, cum id in quemdam *corporis cultum* possit degenerari, atque inducere ad omnes

At any rate, even though body and soul do give an indispensable contribution to Christian prayerlife, they alone cannot bring about the union with God at which Christian prayer ultimately aims.

b. Spirit of prayer

A specific contribution of the *spirit* of prayer must be added to the contributions brought by body and soul to prayerlife, if Christians want to encounter God directly by their prayers. Implying precisely that, an ancient Christian master of prayer writes –

> "Let the virtue that deals with the body be a pledge of the virtues of the soul, and those of the soul a pledge of those dealing with the spirit, and these latter a pledge of immaterial knowledge."[39]

One may wonder about the real difference between "spirit" and "soul" as components of the human person and what these two terms are supposed to mean.

In the new Testament,

> "The spirit of man is that aspect of man through which God encounters him, that dimension of the whole man wherein and whereby he is most immediately open and responsive to God, that area of human awareness sensitive to matters of the spiritual realm.
>
> Often in talk about this area of encounter, it is not clear whether the language refers to the spirit of man or to a particular force to be experienced through this dimension of his being, or to a spirit or power from without ...
>
> Life in the Spirit in general terms means to let his (= the believer's) character be moulded by God according to the pattern of Jesus Christ ... something which by attentive openness to God he allows the Spirit to produce through him."[40]

---

sensationes spiritualibus experientiis subrepticie adaequandas.": CDF: *Letter,* n. 27. Emphases ours.

[39] EVAGRIUS, ch. 132, p. 76.

[40] DNTT, vol. III, pp. 693-694 and 702.

Moreover, Vatican II uses the biblical concept of spirit in its summary of Christian anthropology. In fact, according to the Council the human being is not just union but *unity* of body and soul.[41] And the soul about which the Council is here speaking includes the soul and the spiritual soul, which is otherwise known as the spirit.

> "By his power to know himself in the depths of his being *(interioritate sua)* he (= man) rises above the whole universe of mere objects. When he is drawn to think about his real self (quando convertitur ad *cor*) he turns to those deep recesses of his being (ad *hanc profundam interioritatem* redit) where God who probes his heart (*corda scrutatur:* cf. I Kg. 16:7; Jer. 17:10) awaits him, and where he himself decided his destiny before God. So when he recognizes in himself *a spiritual and immortal soul (animam spiritualem et immortalem)...*, he grasps what is profoundly true in this matter."[42]

In other words, human persons rightly recognize their "*spiritual* and immortal souls" in those innermost "depths" or "deep recesses" of themselves, which the sacred Scripture calls "the heart". Such *spiritual* souls are the innermost cores of the human being where persons decide their destiny before God.

As it clearly appears by comparing this teaching with the summary of biblical theology reported above, the "*spiritual* soul" is identical to "the (human) spirit" and distinguished by and large from the soul.

To understand the foundation of this distinction we have to remember that the soul plays two essentially complementary roles within the human being. On the one hand, it penetrates into and gives life to the body. On the other hand, it transcends the same body, which it vivifies, driving and steering the person towards the transcendent ultimate goal, which is God.

Because it is and acts within the body, the soul is conditioned by the body and operates within the latter's space and time limits. But insofar as it transcends the body, the human soul is not restricted to the

---

[41] GS, n. 14: "Corpore et anima unus, homo", FLANNERY, p. 914.

[42] *Ibid.,* FLANNERY, p. 915. Emphases ours.

body and it is called "spirit",[43] or "spiritual soul", as Vatican II puts it. It is that "part" of the human soul which is directly acted upon by the Holy Spirit when Christians act and pray as God's adopted children.[44]

This is the teaching of St. Paul -

> "Paul's analysis of personality, one element of which is man's spirit, enables him to present his idea of the Christian fellowship in the Holy Spirit. According to Rom. 8:9-17, it is the spiritual nature with which God has endowed every man that makes possible for the Spirit of God to dwell in man. It provides a basis for the continuing conversation between man's spirit and the divine Spirit which comes to dwell within him."[45]

Christian theologians acknowledge the existence of *the spirit* and of the *spiritual life* in the human person.[46] Of this "extreme interior spirit" St. Teresa of Avila was experientially aware, but she said that she did not know how to explain it for lack of learning.[47]

---

[43] Cf. ST, I, q. 97, a. 3: "The rational soul is both soul and spirit. It is called soul in virtue of what it has in common with other sorts of soul, which is giving life to the the body... But it is called spirit in virtue of what is proper to itself and is not common to other sorts of soul, namely its having an immaterial intellectual power." (BLACKFRIARS, vol. 13, p. 143).

[44] Cf. Rm 8:16; Ga 3:3; 5:13; I Co 3:1-2.

[45] McCASLAND, p. 434a b.

[46] "Man leads a double life. One is outward according to the world of body and senses; the communion or intercourse with God and the angels (...) is not here. The other is inward, according to the life of mind and spirit; it is here that we have intercourse with God and the angels, though imperfectly in our present state (...) yet perfectly in man's true home" (ST, II-II, q. 23, a. 1, ad 1um, BLACKFRIARS, vol. 34, p. 7-9). According to CHENU, "le *spiritus* est la faculté du divin".

[47] *Castillo Interior,* VII, 1, 7, p. 568: "Cada día se espanta más esta alma, porque nunca más le parece (que todas tres Personas) se fueron de con ella, sino que notoriamente ve... que *están en lo interior de su alma; en lo muy muy interior, en una cosa muy honda, que no sabe decir cómo es, porque no tiene letras,* siente en sí esta divina companía." Emphasis ours. See also Ibid. 2, 10; p. 575: *"Este centro de nuestra alma, y aun de creer,* que pienso, hermanas, por no saberme dar a entender, no os dé alguna tentación de no creer lo que digo." Emphasis ours.

Given the difficulty that we all have to figure out what the human spirit really is, the following imaginative clarifications can be enlightening.

> "There is a root or depth in thee, from whence all the faculties come forth, as lines from a centre or branches from the body of the tree. This depth is called the Centre, the Fund or Bottom of the soul. This depth is the unity, the eternity. I had almost said the infinity of thy soul; for it is so infinite that nothing can satisfy it or give it any rest but the infinity of God."[48]

Following the sacred Scripture, Thomas Merton terms this "root or depth... Centre, Fund or Bottom", *the heart,* and understands it as

> "The deepest psychological ground of one's personality, the inner sanctuary where self-awareness goes beyond analytical reflection and opens into metaphysical and theological confrontation with the Abyss of the Unknown yet Present."[49]

This deepest psychological ground is such a determining factor of spirituality that, according to Evelyn Underhill,

> "Spiritual life is simply a life in which all that we do comes from *the centre,* where we are anchored in God: a life soaked through and through by a sense of his reality and claim, and self-given to the great movement of his will."[50]

It is at this profound spiritual depth, usually called *the spirit,* where Christians receive the Divine Persons' indwelling presence, enjoy Them and respond to Them by faith, hope, and charity.

As we ought to pray to God with our whole person, prayer has to be not only an activity of the body vivified by the soul and of that "part"

---

[48] William Law, *The Spirit of Prayer,* quoted by GRIFFITHS, p. 98. The same deepest ground of the human soul is called *Gemut* by Eckhart and Tauler, *substancia del alma* by John of the Cross, etc.

[49] MERTON, p. 33. This concept of "the heart" is common among the early eastern Fathers. Cf. BOUCHET, especially pp. 179 and 184.

[50] UNDERHILL [3], p. 36.

of the soul which is immersed in the body, but also of the other part of the soul that transcends the body and is called spirit.

This spirit was sometimes imagined as located at the summit of the soul.[51] Of course, the imagination can hardly figure out a "depth" which, at one and the same time, is also a "summit". But the juxtaposition of "depth" and "summit" is not nonsense language to those who are willing to use paradoxes in order to catch at least a glimpse of such mysterious reality.[52]

Our spirit, which delves into bodily and psychic experiences, which occurs, as it were, at the sensory surface of our being, can be imaginatively situated in the depths of our personality. But, insofar as it yearns and strives for God who "dwells in heaven", it rises above the whole universe of creatures, and can be sensibly located at the summit of the same personality.

Accordingly, the prayer produced at that spiritual summit can be considered as a "peak experience". Not in the sense, though, of being particularly exciting or emotionally intense, but because it is the actual expression of that participation in the Divine Life which God grants to his adopted children.

That is why the prayer of the human spirit is essentially made up of the response which it gives to God through its exercise of the theological virtues infused by the Holy Spirit. Hence the ancient Fathers of the Church and modern spiritual theologians can say that the Holy Spirit uses our spirit to love God and "breathe" prayer to the Father.[53]

---

[51] Cf. ŠPIDLÍK [2], pp. 346-347. See also - "the spirit is the higher part of the soul and the part which has relations with God and receives his communications.": CROSS [1], III xxvi, 4, p. 424.

[52] E.g., "by his power to know himself in the *depths* of his being man rises *above* the whole universe of objects". GS, n. 14, FLANNERY, p. 915.

[53] Cf. ŠPIDLÍK [2], p. 52. Cf. CRUZ, *Cántico Espiritual B,* 38, 3, p. 1102: "Ama el alma a Dios con volundad y fuerza del mismo Dios, unida con la misma fuerza de amor con que es amada de Dios; la cual fuerza es en el Espíritu Santo, en el cual está el alma allí transformada." The Scriptural foundation of this theological insight is Rm 8:26-27.

c. *Union of body, soul, and spirit in Christian prayerlife*

Those who practice the prayer of the spirit do not need to express it in a showy and noisy way, as, e.g., lifting up the eyes, stretching out the hands, talking aloud, etc.[54] They may be standing or kneeling or sitting still, with their eyes closed and hands clasped or maintaining a recollected expression while concentrating on Christ and the Divine Persons who abide within the depths of their heart or spirit.

A contemporary author well-known for promoting "centering prayer", which is a prayer generally elicited from the spirit, writes –

> "I think that for most of us Westerners the best posture for prayer is to be comfortably settled in a good chair – one that gives firm support to the back, but at the same time is not too hard or stiff. As the author of *The Cloud* says, 'simply sit relaxed and quiet...'.
>
> Most important, the body should be relaxed... Settling down in our chair and letting go, letting the chair fully support the body, is sacramental of what is to take place in the prayer. In centering prayer we settle in God, let ourselves go, let him fully support us, refresh us... It is good, too, if we close our eyes during this prayer."[55]

Actually, this prayer ascends towards God along the inner pathways of the spirit, entering into direct contact with him – as we have

---

[54] Cf. TERTULLIAN, 17: "Cum modestia et humilitate adorantes, magis commendabimus Deo preces nostras, ne ipsis quidem manibus sublimius elatis, sed temperate et probe latis, ne vultu quidem in audaciam erecto. Nam illi publicanus, qui non tantum prece, sed et vultu humiliatus et atque dejectus orabat, iustificatior phariseo procacissimo discessit. Sonos etiam vocis subiectos esse oportet, aut quantis arteriis opus est, si pro sono audiamur? Deus autem non vocis, sed cordis auditor est, sicut conspector." In EA, n. 45, p. 23. Cf. CYPRIAN, 4. "Sit autem orantibus sermo precatio cum disciplina quietem continens et pudorem. Cogitemus nos sub conspectu Dei stare. Placendum est divinis oculis et habitu corporis et modo vocis. Nam, ut impudentis est clamoribus strepere, ita contra congruit verecundo modestis precibus orare." In EA, n. 159, p. 77. In ch. 6 of his book also Cyprian refers to the parable of the pharisee and the tax collector.

[55] PENNINGTON [1], p. 11.

already said – through the theological virtues which directly reach God in himself.[56]

In conclusion, the body of prayer includes all the physical external activities of prayer. The soul of prayer comprises all the psychic interior activities of prayer. The spirit of prayer involves the innermost vision, direction, and purpose that vivifies the prayer of the adopted children of God.

By identifying Christian prayer with "contemplation" *(theoria),* several early Greek Fathers suggest an analogous threefold distinction of prayer on the grounds of its sensory, mental, and spiritual objects.[57] The body of prayer is the presupposed sensory foundation of all prayerlife. The soul of prayer enlivens the body of prayer with a natural prayerfulness. The spirit of prayer imbues both the body and soul of prayer with the supernatural prayerful believing, hoping, loving infused by the Holy Spirit into God's adopted children.[58] In fact the body and soul of prayer would fall short of the filial response praying Christians ought to give to their heavenly Father, unless they are perfected by the spirit of prayer.

ii. *Growth of Prayerlife's Components*

Besides clarifying the basic elements which compound the life of prayer, the preceding distinctions can also help to chart the territory and mark on it the most common itinerary praying Christians have to follow if they want to become mature persons of prayer.

---

[56] "Man is created towards God...*by the exercise of his interior faculties,* namely believing, hoping and loving" (Cf. St. Augustine, *De Civitate Dei,* X,5; ST, I-II, q. 99, a. 3, co., BLACKFRIARS, vol. 29, p. 39) "They are called theological virtues because *God is their object,* inasmuch as they direct us rightly to him" (I-II, q. 62, a. 1, co.; BLACKFRIARS, vol. 23, p. 139). Emphases ours.

[57] Cf. ŠPIDLÍK, [2], pp. 196-197.

[58] Cf. for instance, 1 Co 15:45 wherein the life which the "soul" *(psyche)* gives the human person is mortal in contrast with life eternal give by the "spirit" *(pneuma).*

a. Growing in prayer's body and soul

Whoever wants to become a mature person of prayer must first develop a healthy body of prayer, in a way analogous to the child who must first develop a strong body to become an adult. For unless the body of prayer grows enough to support the soul of prayer, one can hardly expect any mature prayer life to thrive. This is carried out by praying with all corporeal postures and gestures, gazes and words, etc., which each one may find expedient to his or her own exercises of prayer.

But to be genuine, the bodily expressions of prayer must be quickened by the phantasies, thoughts, reflections, emotions, affections, volitions, etc., which make up the soul of prayer. For only by joining this soul of prayer to his or her body of prayer can the praying person perform true human acts of prayer.

b. Growing in prayer's spirit

When both the body and soul of prayer have grown to a development beyond which it is impossible or unadvisable to strive, the question about what spirit of prayer should be active and developing in those who want to reach perfect Christian prayerlife becomes urgent. Sure enough, such a question is more consequential than that concerning what acts or exercises Christians should practice when they pray.

A question of this kind cannot be answered by saying that one should pray *more,* adding other acts and exercises of prayer to those which one is already wont to practice. This question brings to the fore the necessity of praying not more but *better,* i.e., of animating one's usual acts and exercises of prayer with more faith, hope, and charity.

In other words, it is not the quantity but the quality of prayer that is at issue here.

> "The value of prayer is found not merely in its *quantity,* but also in its *quality.* This is made clear ... by his (= Christ's) saying: 'When you pray do not do a lot of empty chattering' (Lk 18:10 and Mt 6:7)."[59]

---

[59] EVAGRIUS, ch. 151, p. 80. Author emphasis.

And the quality of Christian prayer especially depends on, yet is virtually equivalent to the intensity of the spirit of prayer, i.e., to the interlacement within the ongoing process of prayerlife with the theological virtues.

Christian spiritual masters claim that the convenient amount of vocal and mental prayer practiced each time people pray should be proportioned to the praying persons' capacity of keeping their attention and devotion alert.[60] For, exercises of vocal and mental prayer should not be prolonged beyond the moment after which attention and devotion become virtually impossible.[61]

The spirit of prayer is deeper than the body and soul of prayer, for it penetrates and abides in the most profound recesses of the praying person. It is also more enduring than the soul of prayer, since it can subconsciously operate not only during formal acts of prayer but also when those acts are over.[62]

It is quite hard to pinpoint the spirit of prayer, which lies hidden in the deepest recesses of the praying person and is virtually identical with prayer-in-the-Spirit,[63] as difficult to grasp as the Holy Spirit himself who "breathes" in us this form of prayer.

c. *Christian prayerlife's patterns of growth*

The pattern of growth of the body and soul of prayer is quite different from that of the spirit of prayer. The body and soul of prayer grow through the repetition of acts of prayer. The spirit of prayer grows instead through the increase of infused theological virtues.

Christians have a natural ability to develop their "bodies and souls of prayer" by frequently exercising them. But the spirit of prayer is essentially supernatural, i.e., beyond the natural capacity of Christians,

---

[60] ŠPIDLÍK [2], pp. 98-100.

[61] Cf. ST, II-II, q. 83, a. 14, c. In this article Aquinas refers to and comments upon St. Augustine's *Letter to Proba,* ch. 9-10.

[62] About this point see GIARDINI [1].

[63] Cf. Rm 8:14-16; Jn 4:23-24.

who cannot therefore produce or increase it. The Holy Spirit pours the spirit of prayer, as well as the theological virtues, into the hearts of praying Christians and makes it grow endlessly[64] within them, even though not without their free cooperation.

iii. *Impeding and Surpassing the Growth of the Body and Soul of Prayer*

a. Against the growth of the body and soul of prayer

As the body and soul of prayer grow through their repeated exercise, all that hampers or impedes the exercise of these components of prayer makes their growth difficult or even stops it. Sickness and sinfulness are the most common causes which impede the exercise and growth of the body and soul of prayer.

Bodily indispositions and bad humors caused by various illnesses and unfavorable circumstances of the praying persons not only make the activity of prayer toilsome and painful but also hamper or prevent those who would like to pray from performing physical gestures and/or psychic acts of prayer. Because the "instruments" necessary for the activity of prayer, i.e., the human body and psyche, are temporarily or for a long time unfit for that purpose.

Sinfulness is another major impediment to the body and soul activity of prayer, because when these components of the human person are employed in a sinful behavior, they acquire a vicious disposition which contrasts with the same person's dealing with God in prayer.

---

[64] What GREGORY OF NYSSA (I, n. 7-8) writes about the endless qualitative growth of Christian perfection can be applied also to the spirit of prayer, which is the prayerful expression of the very core of Christian perfection: "Whoever pursues true virtue participates in nothing other than God, because he is himself absolute virtue. Since, then, those who know what is good by nature desire participation in it, and since this good has no limit, the participant's desire itself necessarily has no stopping place but stretches out with the limitless... (So) the one limit of virtue is the absence of limit."

b. Beyond the growth of the body and soul of prayer

Christians can be prevented from obtaining satisfactory results from their bodily and psychic activity of prayer by the very transcendence of God who is the goal and object of prayerlife. The praying activity of the body and of the soul cannot reach God as a friend of the praying person unless they are elevated to the supernatural level by the spirit of prayer.

In other words, no use of the human body and psyche in prayer can produce acts that are able to reach God directly and in himself. Acts of the body and soul of prayer can certainly put praying Christians on their way towards God, but the very nature of those acts do not lead praying Christians into a direct contact with the infinitely transcendent Being of God, which is, as it were, situated beyond the limits of their natural range of action.

Particularly at the threshold of the higher grades of contemplation, praying Christians have the bewildering experience that whatever the body and psyche working together, do to strive toward God does not in any way succeed in reaching God in himself. On the contrary, it is hopelessly sidetracked into a spiritual blind alley.

No further progress on the way of prayer is then possible unless praying Christians surrender their whole prayerlife to the Holy Spirit. In fact, only when the Holy Spirit's *élan* and promptings are willingly and docilely received by praying Christians through that "opening" of their soul to God which above was termed "spirit", the same Holy Spirit is allowed to pour into them the "spirit of prayer" or "prayer-in-the-Spirit", which enables them to encounter God directly.

Here is how John of the Cross explains this grade of prayer, which he calls "purgative aridity, night of senses, contemplation" –

> "[It is a prayer] in which *the sensual part of the soul* has fallen low, and is weak and feeble in its actions, by reason of the little pleasure which it finds in them: but the *spirit,* on the other hand, is ready and strong. For the cause of this aridity is that God transfers to *the spirit* the good things and the strength of the *senses,* which, since the soul's natural strength and senses are incapable of using them, remain barren, dry and empty.
>
> For *the sensual part* of the man has no capacity for that which is *pure spirit* and thus, when it is *the spirit* which receives the pleasure, the *flesh* is

> left without savour and is too weak to perform any action. But *the spirit,* which all the time has been fed, goes forward in strength, and with more alertness and solicitude than before, in its anxiety not to fail God."[65]
>
> "God now begins to communicate Himself *to the soul, no longer through senses,* as He did aforetime, by means of reflections which joined and sundered its knowledge, *but by pure spirit,* into which consecutive reflections enter not; but He communicates Himself to it by an act of simple contemplation, to which *neither the exterior nor the interior senses of the lower part of the soul can attain.*"[66]

At this point of the growth process of prayerlife only "the spirit of prayer" infused by the Holy Spirit mysteriously works in praying Christians, while their soul - John calls it "exterior and anterior and interior senses of the lower part of the soul" - of prayer must be kept quiet and silent lest their activity hamper the infusion of this prayer by the Holy Spirit.

> "The way in which they are to conduct themselves in this night of senses is to devote themselves not to reasoning and meditation... *What they must do is merely to leave the soul free and disencumbered and at rest from all knowledge and thought... contenting themselves with merely a peaceful and loving attention toward God,* and in being without anxiety, without the ability and without the desire to have experience of Him or to perceive Him. For all these yearnings disquiet and distract the soul from the peaceful quiet and sweet contemplation which is here granted to it."[67]

c. *Towards a complete understanding of Christian prayerlife*

We hope that the preceding distinctions and clarifications can give a primary understanding of the major components of Christian prayerlife. But, all our analyses have been too general to satisfy the desire of comprehending the many intricacies of the whole prayerlife. The clarification should, therefore, be pushed forward.

---

[65] CROSS [2], I, ch. 9, § 3-4, p. 65. Emphases ours.

[66] *Ibid.* § 8, pp. 67-68. Emphases ours.

[67] *Ibid.* ch. 10, § 4, pp. 70-71. Emphasis ours.

The soul of prayer occupies a central position between the body of prayer, on the one hand, and the spirit of prayer, on the other. In the gradual transition from the development of the body of prayer to living out the spirit of prayer, the soul plays, as it were, the role of go-between. Hence, any further clarification of the basic components of prayerlife must especially focus on the activity that the soul exercises in prayerlife.

As the human soul uses its cognitive and affective powers, which are concretely called *mind* and *heart,* to produce all its activity, the activity of the human soul in prayerlife, too, flows from and is the result of the human mind and heart, by whose activities prayerlife is carried out.

Accordingly, another study about the manifold specific activities which mind and heart contribute to Christian prayerlife appears to be necessary in order to progress towards a complete understanding of Christian prayerlife. Such a study has been already published by this author elsewhere.[68]

---

[68] See GIARDINI [2] and [3].

CHAPTER II

THE MIND'S ATTENTION IN PRAYER

As it was pointed out in the foregoing chapter, Christians are to pray to God with their "whole being". God however is pure spirit. Hence prayer must be mostly performed by the mind and heart i.e., by the immaterial knowing and loving elicited from these two human powers.[69]

So, in order to explain Christian prayer one must describe the various ways mind and heart work when Christians pray. In our attempt to give such an explanation we will use the term *attention* to mean the "activity of the mind" and the word *intention* to mean the "activity of the heart."

Of course, prayerlife as a whole and at every stage of its long growth process is a manifold and various combination both of the mind's attentions and of the heart's intentions. But a clear understanding of these two distinct spiritual components of prayerlife demands that we consider them separately. In this chapter we will deal only with the major kinds of attention in prayer.

i. *The Major Kinds of Attention in Prayer*

---

[69] Cf. JOHN PAUL II [1]. n. 37, p. 105: "Among all other earthly beings, only a man or a woman is a 'person', *a conscious and free being,* and precisely for this reason, the 'center and summit' of all that exists on earth" (GS, n. 12, FLANNERY, p. 913). "Sacred Scripture teaches that man was created 'to the image of God', as able to *know and love his Creator.*" In our time Catholic theology has extensively developed and strongly emphasized these anthropological elements. Karl Rahner, for one, has taken them as the foundation of his theology, understood as "a doctrine of man *before God,* as precisely openness to God." Cf. HILL, p. 131f. Author's emphasis.

It is a matter of spiritual experience that prayer cannot be performed without attention.[70] But attention is exercised in many ways, takes different forms, and reaches various levels of consciousness. Perhaps it is not an over-generalization to say that, among the many kinds of conscious attention which are possible in prayer, the most important are *active* attention, *receptive* attention, and *ecstatic* attention.

These kinds of attention mark the major steps of the knowing process involved in Christian prayerlife.

Progressing through these kinds of attention praying Christians achieve a double cognitive growth. a) They increase their realization of God's presence and b) they explore the extent of their consciousness.

a. Active attention

In prayer attention is actively paid to God by focusing one's mind on Him. An ancient Christian master of prayer insistently exhorts to do precisely that:

> "Stand resolute, fully intent on your prayer. Pay no heed to the concerns and thoughts that might arise the while. They do nothing better than disturb and upset you so as to dissolve the fixity of your purpose...
>
> Strive to render your mind deaf and dumb at the time of prayer and then you will be able to pray... Undisturbed prayer is the highest act of the intellect (*nous*= mind).
>
> A great thing indeed – to pray without distraction: a greater thing still – to sing psalms without distraction."[71]

St. Teresa of Avila contends that

---

[70] About the need of attention in prayer see ST, II-II, q. 83, a. 13 and the comments on it by PINCKAERS, p. 269-275.

[71] EVAGRIUS, ch. 9, 11, 34, 69, pp. 57, 60, 85.

> "If a person does not *think of whom he is addressing,* and what he is asking for, *and of whom he is asking,* I do not consider that he is praying at all, even though he may be constantly moving his lips."[72]

A modern author clearly explains that the focusing of consciousness on God in prayer is

> "Steeping our awareness in the great fact that *He* exists, that we are in *Him*, that in *Him* we live and more and have our being."[73]

When Christians sustain their active attention to God in prayer by carefully considering and pondering God's Mystery, they make what has been traditionally called *meditation.*[74]

During the past centuries spiritual master have variously described this exercise of prayerlife.

> "Meditation is the busy application of the mind to seek with the help of one's reason for knowledge of hidden truth...
>
> Meditation busily applies itself to this work [of reasoning]. It does not remain on the outside, is not detained by unimportant things, climbs higher [than reading], goes to the heart of the matter, examines each point thoroughly."[75]
>
> "Consideration [a synonym for meditation] is an intense application of the mind to enquire, or the intention of the mind as it seeks for truth."[76]
>
> "Meditation, which is much discursive reflection with the intellect, is an admirable and very meritorious prayer."[77]

---

[72] *Interior Castle,* I, 1, trans. by E. Allison Peers, vol. II, pp. 203-204. Cf. *The Way of Perfection,* XXII, I: XXVI, 2-3.

[73] BOASE, p. 10. Cf. pp. 13, 16, etc. Emphasis ours.

[74] Mary, the mother of Jesus, is an outstanding model of treasuring within her spirit and pondering God's works and words. Cf. Lk 2:19, 51.

[75] GUIGO II, II, p. 82: V, p. 83.

[76] St. Bernard, *De Consideratione,* II, 2. Quoted in GUIGO II, *Introduction,* p. 26.

[77] ST. TERESA OF AVILA, *Interior Castle,* VI, 7, 10.

> "Meditation is a discursive action wrought by means of images, forms and figures that are fashioned and imagined by the said senses [i.e., the two 'interior bodily senses which are called imagination and fancy'], as when we imagine Christ crucified, or bound to the column...or when we imagine God seated upon a throne with great majesty."[78]
>
> "[Meditation is] the attentive thought voluntarily repeated and entertained in the mind, arousing the will to holy and salutary affections and resolutions."[79]

Contemporary authors particularly stress the deepening of faith effected by discursive meditation. Actually this form of prayer serves also the will and the heart by moving them to love God.

> "Meditation is a reflection on a mystery of faith which will establish it more firmly in our mind and soul... (causing) a growth in faith and a much clearer insight into a particular divine mystery."[80]
>
> "Discursive prayer (= meditation) helps one to assimilate the various truths and principles of the Christian life... (Through it) basic truths and principles of the Christian and spiritual life have a better chance of taking a deeper hold of a person."[81]
>
> "The aim of Christian meditation is to make our minds and senses familiar with the truth of revelation so that this contact may move our hearts."[82]

In recent years the words *meditation* and *contemplation* have been used somewhat interchangeably.[83]

> "In meditation we use our understanding, our reasoning, to come to a deeper knowledge of the God we are drawn to love. In contemplation we seek the same knowledge, but by the use of our imagination – 'reliving' imaginatively the events of the Lord's life, and seeing ourselves, with our own

---

[78] CROSS, [1], II, XII, 3, p. 215.

[79] DE SALES, VI, 2, p. 272.

[80] RAGUIN, p. 30.

[81] CARTER [1], p. 33.

[82] VAN KAAM AND MUTO, p. 53: cf. p. 55.

[83] HALL, p. 9.

> concrete personal history, as parts of those events... The signs of the Gospels become real in our own lives via meditation and contemplation... Meditation and contemplation are just the beginning of the Christian life of prayer."[84]

But the writer of these words, who is a Jesuit, is aware that

> "John (of the Cross) means by contemplation an immediate experience of God as he is in himself, as contrasted with a mediate, indirect experience through our own thoughts and feelings (which he calls meditation[85])."[86]

So that,

> "Contemplation can be used either in the active, acquired, Ignatian sense, or in the Carmelite sense, as a passive, infused way of praying."[87]

Someone terms the Carmelite contemplation "deep meditation":

> There is "discursive meditation" and "deep meditation", which is "the quiet contemplative prayer that leads to deeper states of consciousness."[88]

Others according to whom "meditation" enters into the unconscious mind at the very ground of our being, give "meditation" the meaning attributed by the Carmelite school to contemplation, namely a significance

> "more or less equivalent to what the mystics of the Eastern Church called the 'prayer of the heart' – at least in the general sense of prayer that seeks its roots in the very ground of our being, not merely in our mind and our affections."[89]

---

[84] GREEN [2], pp. 40-41.

[85] See above note 9.

[86] *Ibid.* p. 112.

[87] *Ibid.* p. 12.

[88] JOHNSTON, p. 111-112.

[89] MERTON, p. 34.

More explicitly,

> "Meditation goes beyond the conscious mind into the unconscious. In meditation I pass beyond my thoughts which reflect my body consciousness. I discover my ground in the Word, my real self which exists eternally in God and with God...as a thought of God, a word of God."[90]

Apparently, the ground for extending the meaning of meditation from a discursive form of prayer, which aims at feeding active attention to God's mystery, to another form of prayer, which "leads to deeper states of consciousness beyond the conscious mind into the unconscious", is the experience that active attention in prayer little by little gives way to receptive attention.

> "(There is) a broad feature that tends to be manifest in the progress of most of those who follow the life of prayer. It is the gradual transition both in prayer and in the rest of life from a state in which the human activity and effort preponderate to a further stage in which prayer and life seem to become a matter of acceptance rather than of effort."[91]

Such a transition occurs when praying Christians go beyond the prayer that they themselves cause into a prayer which happens to them, because it is infused into them by God.[92] To put it another way, one passes from a form of prayer generally called meditation and understood as

> "Something *we* do, *our* activity of analyzing the gospel and making applications to our own life situation and resolution as to how we would serve Christ better" to a prayer which "becomes less and less what *we* do and more and more what *God* does in us."[93]

---

[90] GRIFFITHS [2], p. 35-36.

[91] BUTLER, p. 121.

[92] Cf. *Ibid.*, pp. 122-124.

[93] GREEN, [2], p. 11. Author's emphasis. Cf. "The call of God is not so much to do something as to allow something to be done in us...the problem and the challenge which confront the one who prays are ultimately not to do but to surrender... It is letting go, hanging loose, floating free...": p. 100-101.

At this moment of the growth process of Christian prayerlife active attention yields to and is replaced by receptive attention.

b. Receptive attention

To give up active attention in order to progress in prayer may be especially difficult for Christians who are used to the hectic activity of contemporary society. In order to facilitate their willingness to do that, we stress that the present kind of attention is receptive and not absolutely passive, i.e., not so opposite to active attention that the praying mind which enters into it is exclusively acted upon by its object.

Here is how a philosopher describes receptive attention by and large:

> "What happens when we look at a rose? What do we do as we become aware of colour and form? Our soul is passive and receptive. We are, to be sure, awake and active, but our attention is not strained; we simply 'look'– in so far, that is, as we 'contemplate' it and are not already 'observing' it (for 'observing' implies that we are beginning to count, to measure and to weigh up). Observation is a tense activity; which is what Ernest Jung meant when he called seeing an 'act of aggression' (*Blatter und Steine,* p. 202, 1934).
>
> To contemplate, on the other hand, to 'look' in this sense, means to open one's eyes receptively to whatever offers itself to one's vision, and the thing seen enters into us, so to speak, without calling for any effort or strain on our part to possess it. There can be hardly a doubt that that, or something like it, is the way we become sensorially aware of a thing.
>
> But what of knowledge, the mind's spiritual knowledge? Is there such a thing as a purely receptive attitude of mind in which we become aware of immaterial reality and invisible relationships? Is there such thing as pure 'intellectual contemplation' – to adopt the terminology of the schools? In antiquity the answer given was always yes."[94]

---

[94] PIEPER, p. 24-25. He reminds us that intellectual knowledge is held by Immanuel Kant to be exclusively discursive, not intuitive; and therefore it always involves active intellectual effort, yet "hard work". But the influence of Kant is today not so exclusive, since, according to HILL, p. 311, there is in our society a Western fascination with an "Eastern attitude in which consciousness stands open and receptive towards reality as it 'gives itself' as a gift."

Some kind of receptive – and not merely passive attention – must be practiced in prayer for several good reasons.

1. It would not be attention at all unless it were willingly practiced by the praying Christian and integrated into his or her free and conscious activity.[95]

2. In order to be receptively attentive, the praying person must

> "Banish the countless distracting thoughts that plague his mind and prepare himself for God's action."[96]

3. There are moments in prayerlife when Christians must actively surrender their minds to God's action, as the following description makes clear:

> "Sometimes we were so absorbed in His (= God's) presence that words would not come at all, and whole hours passed in silence. There is nothing in those hours of making the mind a blank and waiting for ideas to come as it were 'out of the blue'. But rather communion of this kind *demands that every part of the mind and will be actively and joyfully handed over to the Lord for Him to use. There is nothing passive about it, but the most active cooperation possible."*[97]

During the active attention of discursive meditation, praying Christians try to grasp the Divine Mystery and keep it under their reason's control. But, as the Divine Mystery begins to reveal itself, it proves infinitely beyond the power and reach of human reason. When praying Christians receive such a revelation the only way they have to acknowledge the Divine Mystery is

---

[95] Cf. BUTLER, p. 70, and DALRYMPLE, p. 27.

[96] CLOUD, ch. 26, p. 83.

[97] HURNARD, p. 43, quoted by GREEN [2], p. 95. Emphasis ours.

> "To become 'passive', but with a passivity that is infinitely receptive."[98]

So, praying Christians give up active discursive attention and let their attention become receptive and intuitive.

> "We cease trying to master God in our lives and allow him to master us. The gift of contemplative prayer is God's way of taking care of our lives and opening us up in readiness to receive his love and so be transformed."[99]

In fact, when we pray by exercising our usual mental power our whole prayerlife is seemingly reduced by the active attention which we can draw from our own reason. But when we plunge into the depth of our mind, we discover that it functions more like a planet, which shines at its best only when it is in position for receiving the light of the sun.

This receptivity is not, however, to be understood as if all that the preceding activity of the mind had brought to praying Christians should be discarded. Receptive attention really adds new vistas of the Divine Mystery without obliterating the previous understanding of it obtained by discursive meditation.

A very fine imaginative description of how this can happen in receptive attention is given by Simone Weil:

> "(Receptive attention) consists of suspending our thought, leaving it detached, empty and ready to be penetrated by the object.
>
> It means holding in our minds, within reach of this through, but at a lower level and not in contact with it, the diverse knowledge we have acquired which we are forced to make use of.
>
> Our thought should be, in relation to all particular and already formulated thoughts, as a man on a mountain who, as he looks forward, sees also below him, without actually looking at them, a great many forests and plains.

---

[98] GRIFFITHS [1], p. 169. In another of his books this author praises "the active inactivity or action in inaction *(wei-wu-wei)*, which gave to Chinese culture its immeasurable refinement": GRIFFITHS [2], p. 92.

[99] DALRYMPLE, p. 31. See the articulate description of such transformation at pp. 20-27 of this book.

> Above all our thought should be empty, waiting, not seeking anything, but ready to receive in its naked truth the object which is to penetrate it."[100]

Apparently, the servant in the Gospel parable, who is exhorted to be vigilant and waiting in patience for his Master to return[101] is supposed to be practicing an attention quite similar to that described in the preceding passage. Such is the receptive attention to be practiced in prayer, and which another author identifies with the "vigilance" recommended by Jesus:

> "When Jesus asked his disciples: 'watch and pray' (Mt 26:41) he meant that vigilance is inseparable from prayer, is impossible without prayer; neither can be realized without the other. What the New Testament commends is more precisely *vigilance in and through prayer.* Only with prayer vigilance becomes spontaneous, easy, effortless, like the flow of water from the spring."[102]

That vigilant receptive attention in prayer is quite similar to the *hesychia* (stillness) of the Eastern Christian spiritual masters, i.e., that

> "Intuitive, non discursive awareness in which we no longer form pictures in our mind's eye or analyseconcepts with our reasoning brain, but feel and know the Lord's immediate presence in direct personal encounter."[103]

Or, in other words,

> "The prayer of silence: praying and waiting and open to receive the light that will surely come, a silence charged with longing and expectation, a

---

[100] WEIL, p. 72. The reader will better grasp the meaning of this passage if he or she bears in mind the distinction between *pensée pensée* and *pensée pensante* made by the French philosopher Maurice Blondel. The word *pensée* always translated in this passage as "thought" really means *pensée pensante* which in English would be better put as "thinking".

[101] Cf. Lk 12:35-37 = Mt 24:45-51.

[102] DUJAT, p. 113. Author's emphasis.

[103] WARE, p. 184.

> silence which discloses an inner emptiness which we long for God to fill. It is a void which cries out for the light of his presence."[104]

In the sequence of the Teresian grades of prayer receptive attention begins with recollection *(recogimiento),* which is

> "A preparation for being able to listen. So that instead of striving to engage in discourse, one tries to remain attentive and aware *(attentos a ver)* of what the Lord is doing within one."[105]

Seemingly both active and receptive attention in prayer are alluded to in the Bible by the simile of "knocking at the door". In active attention it is the praying person who does the knocking.[106] In receptive attention the Lord Himself is doing the knocking,[107] and He complains when we do not listen.[108]

Here is what we should do when the Lord knocks at our door:

> "On hearing Christ's voice, we open the door to receive him, as it were, when we freely assent to his promptings and when we give ourselves over to doing what must be done. Christ, since he dwells in the hearts of his chosen ones through the grace of his love, enters so that he might eat with us and we with him (cf. Rv 3:20). He ever refreshes us by the light of his presence insofar as we progress in our devotion to longing for the things of heaven. He himself is delighted by such a pleasing banquet."[109]

Today a good number of authors term "opening" and "listening" to God receptive attention in prayer.[110] The need of being attentively

---

[104] RAGUIN, p. 12.

[105] *Interior Castle,* IV, 3, 4.

[106] Cf. Mt 7:7-8.

[107] Cf. Rv 3:20.

[108] Cf. Is 50:2; 65:12; 66:4; Jr 7:12.

[109] St. Bede, *Homilies,* XXI, CCL 122, 151, quoted in LITURGY, III, p. 1419.

[110] Cf. GREEN [1], LEECH, p. 3; BORROWS, p. 79; NOUWEN [2]; GROESCHEL.

open or listening to God when we pray is based on two complementary truths of Christian theology.

1) The former concerns God's way of dealing with us.

> "Being open to God in prayer, listening to him, asking him what he would have us to do, is based on the very basic truth that God is the one who takes the initiative in Christian life... to be open to God in prayer means to make ourselves receptive to his love for us... In prayer God desires our openness: he wants us to listen, he wants us to allow him to reveal to us himself more and more."[111]

2) The latter is about the theological meaning of human "subjectivity".

> "Subjectivity is always a transcendence which listens, which does not control, which is overwhelmed by mystery and opened up by mystery. It exists only by opening itself beyond itself, and, to put it in biblical language, it is in its origin and from the very beginning the experience of being known by God himself."[112]

An author distinguishes two ways of receptive attention or listening to God in prayer. The former consists in the expectation for what God may tell us through the Scripture: the latter is contented with welcoming God, enjoying his presence as that of the beloved.

> "(There is in prayer) a silence which is a kind of waiting and listening for what God may tell us through the words of Scripture, through our own hearts... [And there is another] silence of being in God's presence without asking for or expecting anything, but just being there."[113]

---

[111] CARTER [2], p. 13.

[112] RAHNER [1], p. 58. Cf. VON BALTHASAR, p. 33: "God created us as spiritual creatures, and so we are 'hearers of the word'."

[113] BONDI, p. 98.

The active and the receptive attentions in Christian prayerlife have respectively certain analogical links with the Divine Word and the Holy Spirit.

Actually, through prayer's attentions Christians try to contact God either by means of inner words or by silently listening to him. The former is an attempt to respond to the mystery of the Word made flesh. The latter is yielding to the Holy Spirit who prompts sighs and groanings which cannot be put into words.

So, through the latter approach to God, praying Christians are led to realize

> "That neither the sublimity of their thoughts nor - even less - the subtlety of their methods of prayer gives them access to God. As the intensity of the divine light increases, they see the uselessness of all their learning... God himself, after he has given us some inkling of what he is, at once wants us to realize that he is quite beyond our full comprehension. This is a basic truth for anyone who seeks to find God by prayer... If we accept the mystery of his absence, we shall draw near the enigma of his nature."[114]

The "prayer of attentive silence" carried out by receptive attention

> "Is the first step toward spiritual rapture, and this rapture or ecstasy is the product of faith working in the depth of our being. We begin to learn what faith means for us the moment we turn away from ourselves and keep silence before God. Silence is the beginning of ecstasy."[115]

So, receptive attention gradually becomes ecstatic attention.

---

[114] RAGUIN, p. 32-36 passim. About the "negative" (apophatic) knowledge of God in prayer see St. Gregory of Nyssa, *De Vita Moysi,* PG 44, 376 d: 377 a: *In Canticum Canticorum Homiliae* XI, PG 44, 1000 c. Pseudo-Dyonisius, *De Divinis Nominibus,* PG 3, 872 a:, *De Mystica Theologia,* PG 3, 997 b.

[115] RAGUIN, p. 11.

c. *Ecstatic attention*

Ecstatic is the highest level of attention reached in prayer when the praying mind is so absorbed by the object of its consideration that any attention to other objects, even the attention of the thinking mind to itself, disappears.[116] When it experiences ecstasis the praying mind "stays out" (this is the root sense of the Greek word *ek-stasis)* of itself, wholly focusing on the object of its contemplation.[117] This kind of attention involves two aspects, which are interrelated as the two sides of the same coin.

1) The *self-forgetfulness* of the thinking subject, so that one can speak of an "egoless attention". All activity such as thinking, imagining, emoting, that serve to define oneself, become suspended; yet, awareness remains open, clear and vibrant. The self disappears from the mind's screen and is no longer in the power seat directing reality.[118]

2) The *absorption* of the thinking subject in the intriguing, arresting, overwhelming known object.

> "Reality engulfed you so powerfully and suddenly that you only senses global oneness with all around you."[119]

---

[116] Cf. Tertullian, *De Anima,* ch. 45: "Ecstasin dicimus, excessus mentis, et amentiae instar." In EA, n. 67, p. 30. ST, II-II, q. 175, the whole question.

[117] As by ecstatic attention praying Christians are also driven deep into themselves (Cf. St. Augustine, *Sermones,* 12, 4, 4: "Intus in animo Deus loquitur...spiritu hominis assumpto, quam Graeci ecstasim vocant." in EA, n. 291, pp. 312-313). Some authors call this kind of attention *"en-stasis"* (i.e., "staying-in").

[118] In Zen Bhuddism egoless attention is the perfectly concentrated way of doing anything. Cf. HERRIGEL, p. 40-42.

[119] Gerald May quoted by MALONEY [2], p. 78, who adds: "This is what classic writers of mystical life call infused contemplation." Cf. the description of "natural ecstasy" given by William Wordsworth in his famous *Lines Composed a Few Miles Above Tintern Abbey*, 13 July, 1798: "I have felt a presence which disturbs me with the joy of elevated thoughts: a sense sublime of something far more deeply interfused, etc."

So, by ecstatic attention to a fascinating and subduing object the mind loses all the control that in the preceding kinds of attention it exercised - although differently in active and receptive attention - over its object. In ecstatic attention the object forcefully draws the mind to surrender totally to it.

That is precisely what happens in prayer when the mind of the praying Christian is so held by the divine presence that it is unable to think and to pray discursively, but is

> "So totally aware of the divine presence that one can hardly even identify his own self in the dazzling light of this Presence.[120]

Here is how Teresa of Avila describes ecstatic attention and interprets it as the praying Christian's special "participation in Christ's death to the world":

> "The faculties are *truly asleep* to the things of the world and of ourselves. During the time that the union (with God) lasts, the soul is left as though without its sense, for it has no power to think even if it wants to. It is like one who in every respect has died to the world so as to live more completely to God...
>
> The soul is so separate from the body that it doesn't even know if it has life enough to breathe. At least, if it does breathe, it is unaware that it is doing so: *it is so stunned!"* [121]

The "admirable heavenly and super-human saying" of St. Anthony the Great reported by John Cassian undoubtedly refers to the ecstatic attention of "perfect prayer":

> "As long as a monk understands that he is praying he has not yet attained perfect prayer."[122]

---

[120] LE SAUX, p. 31.

[121] *Interior Castle,* V, 1, 3. About the words which we have emphasized, remember that also the ancient Greek Christian theologians called ecstatic prayer "sleep" and "sober intoxication". Cf. ŠPIDLÍK, 277-279.

[122] CASSIAN, *Collationes,* IX, 31, 808 b: "non est perfecta oratio in qua monachus, vel hoc ipsum quod orat intellegit." Cassian qualifies this dictum

In fact, in the ecstatic attention of "perfect prayer", God so engages and absorbs the mind that praying Christians cannot turn in reflection upon themselves and lose awareness that they are praying at all.[123]

Another surprising, yet paradoxical description of ecstatic attention in prayer is given by St. Isaac, who speaks of perfect prayer in terms of "prayer outside prayer". This has been interpreted as the praying mind going forth from itself and plunging into God.[124]

To resolve the apparent contradiction of "prayer outside prayer" it is necessary to take the word "prayer", used twice in the phrase, in two different senses, both similar enough, though, to be expressed by the same word.

The more common use of the word "prayer" appears at the end of the phrase. There it means an act employing mental and vocal words to approach God discursively. But beyond all the verbal strivings of such discursive prayer praying Christians attain to a prayerful silent stillness of their mind. This is what is meant when the word "prayer" is used at the beginning of the phrase.

So, "prayer outside prayer" is that form of prayer in which the praying mind has reached a quiet, intuitive, single-pointed concentration in God, beyond all the images, words and concepts used and needed by beginners to be attentive when they pray.

> "This is the purest of pure prayer: the prayer which looks for no visual image, uses neither thoughts nor words: the prayer wherein, like a

---

"admiranda sententia, coelestis et plusquam humana sententia." Translation ours. CHADWICK, p. 229, translates: "St. Anthony uttered his heavenly, inspired, saying on the end of prayer: 'That prayer is not perfect in which the monk understands himself and the words which he is praying'... I hardly dare to add anything from my own slender experience."

123 "This attention (to the end of prayer, actually to God) is sometimes so strong that the mind forgets all other things, as Hugh of St. Victor says *(De Modo Orandi)*, II, PL 176, 976)." (ST, II-II, q. 83, a. 13, co., BLACKFRIARS, vol. 39, p. 85).

124 Cf. EVDOKIMOV, p. 218.

> spark leaping from a fire, the mind is rapt upward, and, destitute of the aid of the senses or anything visible or material, pours out its prayer to God."[125]

In conclusion, there is a form of prayer in which the presence of God absorbs the attention of the mind so overwhelmingly that it does not advert at all to the fact that it is praying. The attention of the mind is carried out in this form of prayer without self-awareness and without conceptualizing and reasoning about its object.

This attention is called *samadhi* in Hinduism, and it is described as,

> "The absorption of the mind in the object of its contemplation, when all sense of distinction of subject and object disappears.[126]

Buddhist meditation aims at the same kind of attention.

> "Although at the beginning of any Buddhist meditation there is the concept 'I am meditating' or 'I am mindful', if the right path is followed, then this sense of 'I-ness' and 'mine-ness' becomes less marked, or rather its bases in mind and body become less identified with 'myself', until this concept dissolves away completely and not-self (or not-soul, as *anatta* may also be translated) is seen with penetrative wisdom."[127]

To sum up, in prayerlife

— *active* attention is the mind's focusing on and thinking of God: the proper *human* way of paying discursive attention to God;

---

[125] Cassian quoted by PENNINGTON [2], p. 28. This form of prayer called also *oratio ignita* by Cassian seems to be the "pure prayer" of which Evagrius Ponticus writes. Cf. ŠPIDLÍK, pp. 254 and 281-282.

[126] GRIFFITHS [2], p. 140.

[127] Bhikku Khantipolo, *On Mindfulness,* in ASIAN, p. 289. While the peak-experience of Bhuddist meditation seems to be the ontological dissolution of the illusory self, Christian self-forgetfulness is psychological.

— *receptive* attention is the mind's opening up, waiting on and for, silent listening to God: a somewhat *superhuman*[128] way of paying intuitive attention to God;

— *ecstatic* attention is the mind's total self-forgetful absorption into God's Mystery: an entirely *transhuman* surrender of the whole human mind to God.

So, the whole growth process from active through receptive to ecstatic attention is a progressive giving up of the praying mind's control over its object.

Prayer's *active attention*, which reaches its climax in discursive meditation, is an attempt at grasping and "controlling" the divine truth.

By prayer's *receptive attention* the same divine truth is left free to reveal itself in whatever way it pleases, to the self-conscious praying mind, docilely open to such revelation.

At the stage of the mind's *ecstatic attention* the divine truth entirely overpowers the praying mind, which is driven out of its own self-consciousness and wholly subdued by and absorbed into the Divine Truth. At this point the Divine Truth is the sole and overwhelming center of the whole praying mind's attention.

It is worth noticing that the praying mind begins to practice inner silence when in receptive attention it gives up its attempt to control its object, although it maintains its own self-consciousness. But whereas the mind's silence involved in receptive attention is still self-conscious, the innermost silence of ecstatic attention reaches perfect self-forgetfulness.

So, the ultimate goal of all kinds of the mind's attention in prayer is to lead praying Christians to center entirely on God, and in this way clear the mind of all thoughts, ideas, images, discourses, etc., which

---

[128] *Superhuman* is not equivalent to *supernatural.* The purely receptive vision or *intellectus,* included in the human capacity of knowing besides the active effort of discursive thinking or *ratio* which is properly human, was regarded by the ancient Greek and Middle Ages philosophers as "a sort of participation in the simple knowledge which is proper to higher beings, of whom it is said that they possess the faculty of spiritual vision. (Aquinas, *De Veritate,* q. 1, a. 1, co.). Therefore *vita contemplativa* is said to be "non proprie humana sed superhumana" (CG, lib. III, cap. 112), although it is not the noblest *supernatural* mode of knowing possible to the Christian. About this see PIEPER, p. 27 and pp. 40-41 and 44.

would be harmful and useless or inconvenient for achieving perfect union with him.

The three kinds of attention in prayer can be illustrated by the analogy of the successive stages involved in interpersonal communication and union. As a matter of fact, an interpersonal relationship gradually progresses from the mutual speaking/listening stage toward a so silent union of the partners that they do not need to talk at all.

> "Remember the common experience of being with a spouse or a close friend at the end of a long day of talking or working on a project or doing chores. You know each other. You have just shared a common experience. Sometimes you want to talk about it, but sometimes what you need is not to talk at all, but just be quiet together. Words seem too much. They only ride on the surface of the deep way you are together at that moment."[129]

The different kinds of attention may receive some further clarification by being compared to the rungs of a ladder mounted by the praying Christians' increasing concentration upon God, until they finally reach the climax of total ecstatic surrender to him.

In fact, these three kinds of prayerful attention somehow correspond to the three traditional stages of the growth process toward Christian perfection by and large. *Active* attention belongs to the purgative stage of beginners; *receptive* attention to the illuminative stage of proficients; *ecstatic* attention to the unitive stage of perfects.[130]

ii. *Attentiveness, Awareness, Ecstasis*

All attention adds intellectual light to the mind. The forms of this light are as many as the kinds of attention. We have so far described the

---

[129] BONDI, p. 100.

[130] The three major kinds of attention are used to describe the growth process of "centering prayer" by PENNINGTON [3], especially pp. 389-392.

most important kinds of attention in prayer. Now we turn to explore the forms of light these kinds of attention produce in the mind during acts of prayer.

The mental light of attention can be *sharp, soft* or *dazzling*. We term "attentiveness" the sharp mental light; "awareness" the soft mental light; and "ecstasis" the dazzling mental light. We will first explain the difference between attentiveness and awareness.

a. The difference between attentiveness and awareness

Attentiveness is the light which shines in the mind when it actually focuses on particular object, so as to clearly know it. Awareness is the light with which the mind glows when it perceives in a diffuse manner without focusing on anything in particular, so as to be cognizant of something without distinctly knowing it.

Attentiveness and awareness can be taken as synonyms when we stress the similarity of the cognitive experience they equally involve. But we distinguish them from one another when we wish to point out the different modes of knowing produced by each one of them in the mind.[131]

Doubtless, it is clarifying to take attentiveness as focused attention and awareness as diffuse attention and so distinguish them from each other.[132] But making too clearcut a distinction could amount to an oversimplification, for in the flow of knowing they endlessly shade off into one another. The borderline between them is rather nebulous and ill-defined.

Yet psychological experience and analysis allow us to make these distinctions. Some people are more sensitive to the stimuli caused by distinct objects of knowledge. Other people better perceive the field

---

[131] See the differences between "conscious" and "aware" in FERNALD, p. 135.

[132] The late Ambrose McNicholl claimed that "attentiveness" mostly looks at the *structure* (essence, form) of the object, whereas "awareness" grasps the *existence* of it with only a confused and blurred perception of its contents. Cf. HILL, p. 215.

within which those objects are situated. Seemingly, men score better in focused attention, women in diffuse attention.[133]

Two English idioms refer to these two different kinds of attention. We can speak of what is in the "forefront" of our minds (that to which we give explicit and focused attention) and what is in the "back" of our minds (of which we are only implicitly and diffusedly aware).

As a matter of psychological fact, we may be well aware of whatever is within our field of vision, yet have our attention narrowly focused on some particular point. We are aware of all kinds of sounds in the background while we pay attention to someone's words. We are aware of the sounds but they fail to gain our complete attention.

These examples make at least one point clear - the total experience of knowing includes a "center" to which the mind is directly attentive and a "margin or halo" around that center. The mind does not pay direct attention to that halo, but is certainly aware of its contents.

> "Even when the mind is fully conscious, all objects of consciousness are not present with equal clearness. Our field of consciousness is so limited that we can only grasp a small amount at "the center" with full attentiveness. The rest remains "on the margin of consciousness" as an object or "horizon" which is only sensed along with what is thought and can only be brought explicitly to mind by means of further reflection."[134]
>
> "A brief reflection will enable us to recognize that our consciousness involves concentric circles of awareness. We have a center of attention that is surrounded by areas of awareness which are more or less intense and gradually reach a fringe where there is scarcely any explicit awareness... A center of attention and a context of conscious awareness."[135]

---

[133] The Jungian *animus* and *anima* are construed as "focused consciousness" and "diffuse consciousness" respectively. See NEUMAN, pp. 21f. MALONEY [1], p. 76, applies this distinction to Christian prayerlife: "The *anima* is open, receptive, waiting expectantly for new richness in order to absorb it and become more its true self. The *anima* describes the prayer of the heart."

[134] SPLETT, p. 4166.

[135] WRIGHT, JOHN, p. 168-169.

This experience has a physiological foundation in the human eye, whose functioning is closely related to the mechanism by which the brain maintains both attentiveness and awareness.[136]

> "In the eye the surface of the retina is not uniform. Only a minute patch, about one third of a millimeter wide, in the center of the retina, has a grain fine enough to receive and transmit an image in great detail. This patch contains special light sensitive cells or cones with separate individual nerve fibres leading to the brain.
>
> Around this patch are groups of other cones, and the more sensitive but sparser and less discriminating rods, which have a common nerve fire only for each bunch as their link with the brain.
>
> This arrangement therefore provides a high capacity for perception of detail in the very limited centre of the scene to which the eye is directed, with very poor discrimination but greater sensitivity elsewhere."[137]

A few further details. Attentiveness leads us to critical thinking. It attempts to grasp the essential significance of the object in focus by forming a clear concept of it, and setting that concept within a broader context of meaning. Awareness involves immediate cognitive contact with a certain reality, short of discursive thinking, although not without some sort of intuitive judgement about the reality present. In other words, the mind does not need to have a clear concept of what the person is aware of. It suffices to be receptive or perceptive of the known reality. A conceptualization, rational organization or reflective judgement of it are not necessary.

So, attentiveness works by forming ideas and organizing them into some frame of reference through inner discourse. It is conceptual, discursive and systematic. Awareness, by contrast, does not require clearly expressed ideas, does not organize particular knowledge within a broader context of meaning, and does not develop in logical reasoning.

---

[136] Keep in mind that more than sixty percent of our brain cortex is linked with the eyes.

[137] WALTER, WILLIAM GRAY, pp. 79-80.

It is a non-conceptual, non-discursive, non-systematic, pervasively intuitive intellectual alertness.[138]

What the mind knows through attentiveness is reflectively and explicitly understood. What we know through awareness is non-reflectively and implicitly "sensed" or experienced. This differentiation can be traced back to and grounded on the distinct roles played by an intellectual image of an object known either through attentiveness or through awareness.

If we receive an imprint of an image but do not produce a concept from it, then we perceive and are aware of the object but do not really understand it. But if we elaborate on the image received, re-casting it into a freshly moulded concept, then we are explicitly attentive to the object and really understand it.

b. Attentiveness and awareness in prayerlife

If we now apply the distinction made between attentiveness and awareness to prayerlife, we can say that attentiveness is the result of active attention of the mind in prayer, while awareness is the fruit of receptive attention by which one opens up self to some experience of God simply by waiting for and listening to him in patient docility. In this sense an author writes,

> "The real prayer goes on like an undercurrent, like something a person sees out of the corner of his eye without fully turning to look at it. There are moments in prayer when we do in some dim way know that we are responding to God without words or ideas or images, but if we turn to look at it or try to objectify it we are back in unknowing."[139]

---

[138] Actually, one can distinguish between "reflecting" and "thinking without even realizing it", a "passive pre-reflective thinking, which at times can reach even deeper than our reflective moments and our uncontrolled mental wandering." NOUWEN [1], pp. 66-67.

[139] BOULDING, p. 16. An instance of awareness which dissolves when it changes into attentiveness may be found in the narrative of the two disciples of Emmaus in Lk 24:31-32.

Granted the obvious and continuously shifting blend of these different kinds of attention, a sort of circular movement may occur during acts of prayer. What is at first reflectively understood can become blurred and experienced only through a vague awareness lingering in the mind. Or, what was sensed only through diffuse awareness can become an object of attentive reflection and be clearly understood when the mind focuses sharply on it. Scholastic theologians used their own terms for these changes in focus during prayer. They spoke of actual and virtual attention."[140]

> "Actual attention is present when those who pray have complete awareness of what they are doing here and now: virtual attention is that which is had at the beginning of prayer and extends throughout prayer without being retracted, although there may be involuntary distractions."[141]

This "actual attention" is obviously equivalent to the active attention we consider the source of attentiveness, which is in this text "complete awareness". And "virtual attention" is similar to what we term awareness. It can be assumed that a certain amount of our attention has soaked through to the deeper levels of the mind. If actual attention is dissolved by involuntary distractions with which the surface layers of the mind teem, still the residue of attention left at deeper levels can continue to inspire and guide prayer; provided, of course, that the person keeps on praying.

In that case, prayers

---

[140] Virtual is the attention/intention that is still working in the person as the result of a previous conscious and free choice, even though that choice is no longer explicitly present to the same person's spirit. "We are not expected always to be thinking of our last end whenever we desire or do something in particular. The force of our first intention with respect to it persists in each desire of any other thing, even though it is not adverted to. For example, in walking somewhere one does not have to be reminding oneself of one's destination at every step." (ST, I-II, q. 1, a. 6, ad 3um, BLACKFRIARS, vol. 16, p. 25). This distinction can be used also to differentiate the kinds of attention practiced in the life of prayer. "The cause of prayer is the desire of charity, and this desire ought to be with us continually, either actually or virtually." (Cf. *Ibid.*, II-II, q. 83, a. 14, co., BLACKFRIARS, vol. 39, p. 89).

[141] AUMANN, p. 317.

> "Have their first value from the intention which governs them, and if through human frailty attention fails, the first value remains."[142]

It is worth noting that repeated assaults of involuntary distractions present a great challenge not only to beginners in prayer. The so called "prayer of quiet" reached by proficients swarms with distractions. At one level of the psyche, the imagination runs wild, while at a deeper level one is

> "Virtually attentive to God's presence, making no effort to chase the distractions, letting them come and go, while peacefully enjoying the deep awareness of God's presence."[143]

Given the continual swinging between attentiveness and awareness and the diversified blending of these two kinds of attention occurring in the praying mind, spiraling upward and downward movements alternate between these two kinds of attention through the dynamism of prayerlife.

What was before reflectively grasped by explicit focusing of attentiveness is then vaguely sensed by an awareness lingering in the mind. This is spiralling downward. What was before sensed by a diffuse awareness later on becomes an object of attentive reflection and is clearly understood by the mind focusing sharply on it. This is spiralling upward.

c. *The unself-aware insightfulness of ecstatic prayer*

Now that we have explained the difference between attentiveness and awareness called forth by active and receptive attention, we can compare them with the effect of ecstatic attention in prayer; that is, "unself-aware insightfulness". What we are trying to say by the paradoxical and rather abstract words placed between quotation marks in the preceding phrase, is that when praying Christians attain to the stage of ecstatic attention, they become totally unself-aware while at the same

---

142 BOASE, p. 9.

143 JOHNSTON, p. 38: cf. p. 119.

time are granted a profound contemplative insight into the Mystery of God.

A distinction made by Bernard Lonergan may help to clarify the issue. In the act of knowing Lonergan distinguishes "conscious awareness", namely, the consciousness a person has of him or herself while he or she is knowing, from "intentional awareness", namely, the consciousness one has of the object while he or she is knowing. As he puts it,

> "Whenever operations are performed, the subject is aware of himself operating, present to himself operating, experiencing himself operating. By these operations one becomes aware of the object. This psychological sense is what is meant by the verb, intend, the adjective, intentional, the noun, intentionality."[144]

Using the above distinction we can say that the unself-aware insightfulness of ecstasy occurs in prayer whenever the conscious awareness Christians have of themselves while praying is entirely absorbed by the dazzling light of God and the only consciousness remaining is an overwhelming intentional awareness of him

Why in this stage of Christian prayerlife the dazzling of the human mind by the divine light occurs is explained by John of the Cross.

> "We must here assume a certain doctrine of the philosopher (i.e., Aristotle), which says that, the clearer and more manifest are Divine things in themselves, the darker and more hidden are they to the soul naturally.
>
> Just as the clearer is the light, the more it blinds and darkens the pupil of the owl; and, the more directly we look at the sun, the greater is the darkness which it causes in our visual faculty, overcoming and overwhelming it through its own weakness.
>
> In the same way, when the Divine light of contemplation assails the soul, which is not yet wholly enlightened, it causes spiritual darkness in it; for not only does it overcome it, but likewise it overwhelms it and darkens the act of its natural intelligence.
>
> For this reason Saint Dyonisius and other mystical theologians call this infused contemplation a ray of darkness – that is to say, for the soul that is not enlightened and purged – for the natural strength of the intellect is

---

[144] LONERGAN, pp. 7-8: cf. p. 15.

> transcended and overwhelmed by its great supernatural light.... This illumining ray of his [= God's] secret wisdom causes thick darkness in the understanding."[145]

So, all self-awareness produced by active and receptive attention in prayer and sustained through attentiveness and awareness is overshadowed by the light of the divine object in which the mind is immersed, and as it were, drowned. At any rate, such drowning is anything but the loss of attention. Rather it is the mind reaching its most sublime climax of attention to God. It is the total transformation of the mind into sheer attention!

The ecstatic mind becomes utterly un-self-aware during this act of prayer. It disappears into its own attention to God, as a pane of glass becomes invisible when the sun shines on and through it. The ecstatic has no perception of self at this moment, but has not lost all attention. He or she has overstepped both active and receptive attention in perfectly self-forgetful, intimate, cognitive union with the Lord of all attention. All other forms of attention are replaced and substituted for in this ego-less union.[146]

All kinds of attention so far analysed belong to the scope of the conscious mind. But modern psychology has discovered another region of the human mind which lies beyond what we commonly call consciousness. We can assume therefore that the mind in prayer pays also some attention to God, which comes from that less known region of its psyche. What kind of attention is it?

iii. *Unconscious Awareness in Prayer*

The attention of the mind in prayer not only reaches out toward its object, God, but also expands into the deep, unconscious layers of the

---

[145] CROSS [2], II, 5, 3, p. 100-101.

[146] "I know, in confidence, – writes Henri le Saux [Abhishiktananda] – the anguish of true Christian contemplatives when the 'I' has vanished by which they had up until then addressed God.": quoted by DUPUIS, p. 75. Of course, such a vanishing of the "I" is psychological and not ontological.

praying subject. Just as the different ways of reaching its object cause particular forms of consciousness, so the expansion of attention into the deep layers of the mind creates a new level of awareness.

The various kinds of attention we have examined above are different forms of consciousness exercised in prayerlife. The new level of awareness which we here hope to clarify belongs to another genus of human consciousness. This genus, because of its implicitness and depth, is somewhat paradoxically qualified as unconscious; even though it is situated within the realm of consciousness.

> "The unconscious is part of the conscious being: *the conscious being possesses and has an unconscious because the unconscious is a property and a creation of the conscious...* It is considered as a region of the psyche that has its limits fixed by the conscious being, which contains it and thus marks off its boundaries as unconscious. The conscious contains the unconscious as another 'self'."[147]

Only a few English words are available to describe the vastly complex activity of the human mind. All of them signify what occurs within the realm of conscious and explicit attention, in the first place. No exclusive terms are available for describing what may happen below the level of conscious and explicit attention. To discuss these realities we are obliged to add negative - as un-conscious, un-aware, un-attentive, etc., - or explicative qualifications to the vocabulary at hand.[148]

But even after we coin new terms, what happens below the level of explicit consciousness cannot be easily expressed. The negative and explicative qualifications added to terms coined to signify explicit consciousness, hardly express a direct grasp of what happens below the level of it. They only point to and hint at that, like signposts which do show the direction but do not take the wayfarer to the place where he or she is going.

---

[147] RULLA, p. 92. Emphasis ours.

[148] Explicative modifications are in VAN KAAM, vol, III, p. 233, who employs such unusual and far-fetched words as pre-focal, infra-focal, trans-focal, pre-vocal, infra-vocal, trans-vocal, and so forth.

For this reason authors often resort to metaphors to suggest insights into those profound regions of the mind rather than trying to present definitions composed of essential characteristics.[149]

a. The idea of unconscious

The best way to describe the diffused awareness below the conscious level of the mind is to qualify it as unconscious. In this sense we speak of unconscious awareness and attempt to explain what role this kind of awareness plays in prayerlife. What do we mean by unconscious?

The field of consciousness can be restricted to whatever we are directly aware of.[150] But it can also be extended to include what escapes most awareness.

> "When we speak of consciousness we should think of a continuum extending from relatively deep unconsciousness at one end and extraordinary sensitivity at the other. The continuum passes from coma to sleep to drowsiness to alertness to hyperalertness.[151]

Human consciousness is an exceedingly variegated phenomenon! It includes all inner happenings we are directly conscious of and also that part of the functioning mind of which we have no explicit consciousness. Apparently, by far the greater part of our mind is "below the waterline, submerged in what we may still call the unconscious."[152]

---

[149] For instance, HASSEL [1], p. 816, who describes the level of "unconscious awareness" in prayer as an "underground river, ocean floor of life experience, background music of all activity", etc. The metaphor favored by Christian mystics – "a small murmuring stream within you", like a brook murmuring in the heart", etc., can be traced back to the Bible. Cf. JOHNSTON, [1], p. 94.

[150] ASSAGIOLI, p. 18.

[151] BENSON, p. 104-105.

[152] WALTER, p. 147.

> "This unconscious has been defined as the opposite of psychological consciousness, that is, of all that a man explicitly knows of himself and deliberately wills of his own accord. Thus it includes all those areas of the human being which do not directly impinge on consciousness, but nevertheless, unknown to him, influence his attitude and decisions."[153]

Some psychologists speak of the "sub-conscious", which takes in the whole field of psychic experience that is not present to the actual consciousness of the individual. Insofar as this subconscious lies below the threshold of actual consciousness, it can also be called the "sub-liminal."[154]

More precise working distinctions might be introduced:

> "The conscious level is an awareness of the person which is immanent in the act of seeing, hearing, imagining, having insights, etc. The subconscious, rather, takes in that field of psychic experience which is not present to the actual consciousness of the individual.
>
> The subconscious, in its turn, is formed by the preconscious, which includes those memories which may be recalled to awareness by a voluntary evocation such as a reflective effort, an examen of conscience, introspection, meditation, etc.; and secondly, the subconscious is formed by the unconscious, which includes those psychic contents which can be brought to awareness only by means of professional means, not by voluntary evocation of the subject him/herself."[155]
>
> "The preconscious is conscious, although outside the field of direct attention or, in other words, it is implicitly rather than explicitly conscious."[156]

Some concluding remarks about the whole idea of the unconscious are in order. A psychologist contends that the unconscious is,

---

[153] HOSTIE, p. 151a.

[154] *Limen* in Latin means threshold.

[155] RULLA, p. 481.

[156] *Ibid.,* p. 90.

> "Neither provable nor refutable. Its scientific merit depends not on provable validity, but on its organizing qualities and heuristic value. It is not an observable fact, but provides a conceptual framework useful for study and understanding of human behavior."[157]

But, according to another one,

> "Research proves by inference two important facts: the existence of the unconscious as an active force, and of the unconscious repression... The existence and the influence of experience unconsciously lived has been proved by an abundance of research."[158]

The unconscious should be thought of not only as a vast repository of personal psychic experiences but also as a wellspring of psychic energy which in many ways influences human conscious and deliberate activity, particularly the spontaneous and undeliberate actions, such as memory lapses, slips of the tongue, abrupt emotional reactions, etc.

> "We affirm that the unconscious exists as a psychogenetic force; that it is strongly active in the life of normal persons, and of each and every person, so much so that it permeates many of their actions; further, that its influence is persistent and shows striking resistance to change."[159]

The distinction between a center of consciousness and its unconscious margins, or between knowing below the water-line and above it, is somewhat arbitrary, because the lines of demarcation fluctuate. However, as great a researcher as C.G. Jung insists that we imagine the unconscious as a rich and large root system which nourishes the tiny plant of consciousness sprouting visibly from it.[160]

In the same vein, a poet wrote that conscious thinking is like a pebble rippling the surface of the unconscious mind. The unconscious,

---

[157] ROBINSON, pp. 10-11.

[158] RULLA, pp. 83 and 114. See also pp. 78-116.

[159] *Ibid.*, p. 79.

[160] JUNG [1].

then, is quite a convenient name for all those powers, parts, qualities of the human psyche that, at any given moment, escape the knowledge of the conscious person.

Modern psychology has good reasons for acknowledging a range of psychic life below and beyond the center of direct explicit and attentive consciousness, and for naming it the unconscious. It has often forgotten, however, to mention that there it finds, side by side, the most animal instincts of human beings, their least explicable powers, and their most spiritual intuitions, the best and the worst, the most savage and the most spiritually refined parts of their personalities.[161]

Such a complaint, however, cannot be made against Jung and Jungian psychologists, for they not only have strongly criticized Freud's idea of the exclusively animal unconscious, but have reversed the materialistic primacy assumed by S. Freud of the sexual over the spiritual. In fact, they contend that in dreams the spiritual yearnings of the person for union with God are more frequently expressed through sexual imagery than sexual drives through spiritual imagery.

The unconscious has been and still is much studied by modern psychologists. But the ancients had some grasp of it too. The *memoria sui* of which St. Augustine, for one, writes about[162]

> "Does not mean at all the sense faculty of recall but something closer to self-consciousness or continued presence of self. Augustine would appear to be suggesting *an underlying structure and dynamism of the soul that is conscious but preconceptual.*"[163]

In any case, there are Catholic theologians today who use the idea of the unconscious to explain Christian life.

> "It is not only our manifest and conscious actions which determine our ethical-moral [and spiritual] state: on the contrary, as today's depth-psychology has shown, half-conscious and subconscious motives hidden in

[161] UNDERHILL [1], p. 52-53, 67.

[162] Cf. *De Trinitate,* IX, 4 PL 42, 963.

[163] HILL, p. 56 and note 12. Emphasis ours.

the profound reaches of the self determine the overall dimension of a life and form the total Christian character."[164]

In systematic outline, then, we sum up the major layers of consciousness:

I. *Conscious* refers to whatever the waking self directly or reflectively knows and is attentive to or aware of.

II. *Unconscious* or *subconscious* in a broad sense refers to whatever is actually beyond a direct and reflective grasp of the cognitive faculties, but which influences attitudes and decisions. The psychic contents of the unconscious are both animal and spiritual. The spiritual unconscious could also be called *superconscious,*[165] which fits especially the supernatural grace and virtues granted to the Christian by the Holy Spirit.

Within this wide realm we distinguish

a. the *pre-conscious* or *subliminal* which can be recalled to consciousness by ordinary reflective self analysis:

b. *deep unconscious* or *unconscious in a strict sense* which requires psychotherapeutic techniques to be brought to consciousness. C.G. Jung and Jungian psychologists distinguish within the deep unconscious both the *personal unconscious* of one's forgotten or repressed memories, and *collective unconscious,* which contains the vast symbolic heritage common to the whole human race.

b. The unconscious in prayerlife

We can now use this concept of the unconscious to explain the unconscious awareness of the mind in the life of prayer.

---

[164] SCHMAUS, p. 243.

[165] E.g., WILBER, p. 3.

During formal acts of prayer, different kinds of attention permeate a person's consciousness in diverse ways or on different occasions. But this does not make a person prayerful all the time. One's unconscious must be soaked with the awareness of God's presence before one can be continually prayerful. For want of a better term, we call this form of response to God subconscious awareness.

We are pointing to that residue of conscious attention which remains active in one's subconscious after the acts of prayer. That residue pervades the entire life of the prayerful person. We call it awareness because, similar to conscious awareness, it is a non-conceptual, non-discursive, intuitive, diffused mode of perceiving God, and, consequently, lacks conscious expression. We qualify it as subconscious because it resides in the unconscious region of the mind, even though from there it radiates its sense of God's presence into the entire life of the prayerful Christian.

This assumption of subconscious awareness may be an intriguing supposition. It could help to explain how and why we can pray unceasingly. But is such awareness open to experiential proof? It would be rather anachronistic to ascribe to earlier epochs of Christian spirituality a clear and explicit idea of this subconscious awareness which the development of modern psychology has allowed us to delineate. And yet, we have reason to hold that such subconscious awareness has been witnessed by many spiritual masters and authors of the past.

Lack of accuracy in the terms used seems to indicate that these writers have stumbled upon prayerful subconscious awareness without being able to reach a clear grasp of it. In presenting some of these testimonies, ancient and modern, we hope that they will ring truer if read while bearing in mind the explanations given above about the subconscious awareness.

Eastern Christian mystics seem to be aware of a spiritual state which fits our description of subconscious awareness.

For instance Simon the New Theologian describes,

> "*A state of awareness which remains with us all the time.* The abiding state can be recognized by feelings of peace and joy, by surrendering to the gentle inspiration of the Holy Spirit, by a subtle persuasion of God's all-

pervasive presence. This state of *general awareness* is strengthened and clarified by the peak experiences we have during ecstatic prayer."[166]

Because he wishes to popularize Eastern teaching on prayer, Archbishop Anthony Bloom writes quite often on subconscious awareness in the life of prayer. He acknowledges that

> "Prayer is essentially standing face to face with God, consciously striving to remain collected and absolutely still and attentive in his presence."

But he then adds:

> "Prayer only makes sense if it is lived. Unless they are lived, unless prayer and life become completely interwoven, prayer becomes a sort of polite madrigal which we offer to God at moments when we are giving time to him."

Consequently, it is necessary that

> "The *awareness of God* grows within you to such an extent that whether you are with people, listening, speaking, or whether you are alone working, *you will still be able to pray.*"[167]

Also Western contemporary spiritual authors mention subconscious awareness in prayer.

Basil Hume, according to whom to pray in general is "to try to make ourselves aware of God and in that awareness to respond to him",[168] writes that

---

[166] WIJNGAARDS, p. 66. Emphasis ours.

[167] The last three quotes are from BLOOM [1], p. 93; cf. pp. 57-58 and BLOOM [2], p. 35. Emphasis ours.

[168] HUME, p. 126.

> *"We are simply aware of God when there is an awareness of God in the very depth of our being,* a response which is not necessarily translated into words, images or ideas."[169]

Thomas Merton teaches that contemplatives, i.e., true persons of prayer, seek to penetrate the ultimate ground of what they believe, hope and love by way of a deepening of their religious awareness in the discovery of a dimension of life and reality beyond that of the empirical self. This deep religious consciousness has God as its proper object; it is

> *"God-consciousness.* Not concentration on an idea or concept of God, still less on an image of God, but *a sense of presence, of an ultimate ground of reality and meaning,* from which life and love could spontaneously flower."[170]

This description is very close to an unconscious awareness imprinted in the depth of the spirit[171] by the repetition of the acts of prayer.

In a conference on prayer, Henri J.M. Nouwen speaks first of a sense of the presence of Christ which can become explicit in the acts of prayer. But then he recognizes,

> *"A quiet presence of which I am only indirectly aware.* In the beginning I hardly noticed the difference. Slowly, however, I realized that I could carry Christ, the image of God, within me and let him affect not only by reflective thoughts but my daydreams as well."[172]

David J. Hassel situates subconscious awareness at the fourth level of his model of the human psyche.

---

[169] HUME, p. 35. Emphasis ours.

[170] ASIAN, p. 349. Emphasis ours.

[171] Merton calls that "the heart". For what he understands by heart, see above, ch. I, note 49.

[172] NOUWEN [1], p. 81. Emphasis ours. Remember that the unconscious is at work especially in daydreaming.

> "The fourth level is like a great underground river which, underlying the upper levels quietly nourishes them, sustains them in their storms and blisses, acts as the continuity underneath their sometimes rapid fluctuations of irritation – pleasantry, pain – pleasure, sorrow – joy...
>
> *The fourth level is never explicitly conscious in itself* but only by way of contrast with the top levels. It is not simply experiential, but *implicitly experiential.*[173]

Dennis Edwards explains how the subconscious – he qualifies it "pre-conceptual" – awareness of God can coexist with daily occupations.

> "In the everyday experience of God, an object in the world, such as a friend, is *the center of conscious attention* and love, while the mystery of God is experienced in a *pre-conceptual way as a horizon* of this experience of a friend."[174]

In Christian prayerlife the subconscious awareness of God consists chiefly in an awareness afforded by the theological virtue of faith. In fact, it can be identified with that

> *"Obscure awareness of God in Christ* which alone can account for the certainty which faith can give, in a form that is pervasive, not merely something in the back of the mind, nor yet always in the forefront of the mind, but, as it were, *just below the surface*, ready to emerge when it has a chance. A man who has faith always knows that he has it – that is, *he is aware that he has a certain attitude of mind in regard to Christianity even when he is not adverting to it."* [175]

This is why some spiritual authors recommend the prayer of sheer supernatural faith. Quite often,

---

[173] HASSEL [2], p. 9. Emphasis ours.

[174] EDWARDS, p. 100. Emphasis ours.

[175] TRETHOWAN, p. 80. Emphasis ours.

> "the God of whom the worshipper had said, 'He is here' remains silent and hidden. Then the prayer supported by faith alone must go into this silent darkness and maintain itself there."[176]
>
> "On certain occasions we may be aware of God's presence, more often dimly so, but there are times when we can place ourselves before him only by an act of faith, without being aware of his presence at all."[177]
>
> "It does not matter whether or not we are aware of anything: we believe that our being always prays, and that is enough for a believer."[178]

These passages are good examples of the ambiguity which the term "awareness" allows. At first sight they seem to stress the lack of any "awareness" of God's presence in the prayer of faith. But, on second reading it clearly appears that they hardly say that, since by "awareness" they only mean the conscious perception of some experiential sign of God's presence.

In reality, by declaring that an attitude of deep faith is in any case present and active in the prayer of faith, not only do they not exclude from it the subconscious awareness of God's presence, but, on the contrary, they imply it. In fact, without such subconscious awareness faith would not be possible at all. And since it is faith which after all characterizes this form of prayer, without faith's subconscious awareness of God's presence this prayer of faith simply could not be.

This special awareness through faith has been insightfully described by Leonard Boase.

> "By the Prayer of Faith we mean a raising of the soul to God in which the knowledge or thought-factor is not merely supernaturalized but experienced as such. It is *a communion with God in which the soul is aware of His reality and of His presence by a sort of 'sixth sense' or 'telepathy'*, which is specifically different from the kind of certainty that it exists attained by logical demonstration.

---

[176] GUARDINI, p. 23.

[177] BLOOM [1], p. 58. Emphasis ours.

[178] WOLFF, pp. 62. This author paradoxically claims that "we always pray, everyone always prays. For our being always cries out something to God and God always hears us, even when that cry comes out from the hearts of 'unbelievers' who have no desire or reason to pray to God.": p. 17.

> It is a certainty different also from the assent of faith given by Christians in everyday conditions: but it differs from this not specifically, but because *the same certainty of faith has moved, so to speak, into the sensitive focus of consciousness.*
>
> Hence there is no sharp break in the development of this prayer out of the less experiential 'acts of faith' with which the prayer of Christians ordinarily begins. There is instead *an imperceptible brightening and intensifying of the soul's assurance that God is there, until it becomes a knowledge immediate and direct,* resembling in immediacy the knowledge given by the senses.
>
> The soul *'feels' aware of God's presence,* as the eye is aware of light or of objects visible in the light. It was to suggest this immediacy that we used the expression like a 'sixth sense' above; not, of course, to be understood literally."[179]

Such Prayer of Faith is substantially the same thing as what St. John of the Cross calls the "Night of Sense", the first part of the Dark Night of the Soul. It differs from that only because St. John of the Cross envisages the Night of Sense as a relatively short prelude, whereas, according to L. Boase,

> "It would seem, whatever the reason, that among the many who persevere in mental prayer in these days, a great proportion are destined to walk most of their lives along the sloping hillsides wherein faith has strengthened into experiential awareness *that* God exists. The Prayer of Faith is their appointed lot it seems."[180]

The following exposition of the Prayer of Faith appears to fit best what we have termed the subconscious awareness of faith in the life of prayer.

> "It is not possible to combine vocal prayer with commonplace occupation beyond an occasional ejaculation. It is not possible to combine meditation with daily tasks, unless they are routine manual labor of the simplest kind. But the special value of the Prayer of Faith is just *because it is functioning on a different plane, it is quite compatible with other occupations.*

---

[179] BOASE, pp. 74-75. All emphasis ours.

[180] *Ibid.*, p. 77.

> Hence it is that the lives of the saints are studded with allusions to the fact that their prayer was *uninterrupted and continuous.* It was certainly not that they were getting eight hundred and fifty-three ejaculations into a common or garden of five minutes. It was that their souls, by *a window of consciousness above the level of ordinary awareness,*[181] *were unintermittently gazing towards God."*[182]

c. *Unconscious residues of conscious attention*

We showed above that different kinds of conscious attention practiced during the exercises of prayer bring forth different intellectual lights in the mind of the praying person. Now we contend that certain residues of those lights sink and remain in the deepest recesses of the prayerful Christian's mind to constitute the subconscious awareness of God's presence. Those residues are special forms of the firm belief involved in theological faith, and pervade the praying Christian's existence.

In particular,

I. The practice of *active attention* in prayer causes in the unconscious level of the mind a firm belief that God is very real, more than whatever else we assume as unquestionably real: for instance, the external world, other people, our very being, etc.

After all, the very aim of discursive meditation, by whose exercise active attention to God in prayer is methodically developed, is that God's mysterious reality may take a stronger and deeper hold on the praying Christian's mind.

II. The practice of *receptive attention* in prayer extends the preceding firm belief of God's realness to all things, persons, and events encountered by prayerful Christians in daily living. It is as if the real

---

[181] About these words, remember as we said above, that subconscious awareness can also fittingly be termed superconscious, when it means the awareness caused in the Christian by supernatural faith.

[182] *Ibid.,* pp. 83-84. All emphasis ours.

God were the sun, shedding light on all objects, so that prayerful Christians can always bask in his light.

III. The practice of *ecstatic attention* in prayer, in which God's realness and light absorb the praying mind so much that it becomes unself-aware, brings forth an all-pervading and total self-submission of the mind to God's overwhelming truth.

It seems to us that the following description of those who have reached constant prayer includes the residues of the three lights with which the practice of the different kinds of attention in prayer infuses the unconscious of praying Christians.

> "For them the depths of the universe will always open up to Heaven, and what is human is never seen separately from what is divine. They are always in a state of prayer, linking everything to its source and to its final destination... Everything human is always related to God, though in no way ceases to be human. Far from it. Such people express, by their general attitude, their relationship with God and the rapture it gives them.
>
> If we have to reach this state of being continually at prayer, it is important to gain by faith a vision of the world which embraces its hidden realities. This kind of prayer remains difficult to achieve, for it counts upon the integration of our world and the world of faith, and that is something that cannot be achieved without a long experience of the depths of the spiritual life."[183]

d. Subconscious and deep unconscious faith-awareness

We would suggest that the distinction made above between the subconscious and the deep unconscious can be used analogically of faith-awareness in prayer. It may explain some puzzling aspects here.

The theological virtue of faith involves two essential dimensions. The first, termed in Latin *fides qua,* is the infused habitual disposition to promptly assent to whatever has been revealed concerning the Mystery of God. The second, called the *fides quae,* is the very Mystery of God

---

[183] BOASE, pp. 83-84.

itself, to whose revelation the theological virtue of faith enables the believer to assent.

Most of the time the entire virtue of faith remains hidden in the unconscious level of the mind, at its roots. The believer can, however, make conscious and explicit acts of faith, bringing faith into action, anytime he or she wishes. For this reason, the virtue of faith should be more precisely situated in the subconscious level of the mind, for subconscious spiritual materials can be rather easily recalled to consciousness.

The same is not true of the Mystery of God which is not only the specific object of faith but also abides in the innermost spiritual depths of the believer. That abiding Mystery can never be brought to full consciousness in such a way as to be explicitly and adequately understood. Even during the most perfect acts of attention or with the most profound insights one can attain during formal exercises of prayer, the heart of the Mystery escapes conceptualization.

This is why the Mystery of God must be somehow situated in the deep unconscious. The deep unconscious is in fact characterized by an inability to raise its contents to the light of consciousness, through ordinary means of psychological introspection. Analogously, the Mystery of God abiding in our depths will emerge into an explicit, clear and conscious knowledge of God in the Beatific Vision, when the extraordinary *lumen gloriae* will, in Heaven, substitute for our ordinary *lumen fidei.* Maria Boulding describes our earthly experience of God's unknowability as follows:

> "We do not know all of this [viz,. our mysterious sharing through Christ in the life of the Holy Trinity] clearly in the time of prayer. We pray in faith and darkness and what awareness we have of the indwelling God is global and unanalyzed.
>
> But it may help if we know that our prayer is Trinitarian independently of any clear perception of ours. The Holy Spirit is sharing the authentic prayer of sonship in us at a level we cannot directly perceive or control."[184]

---

[184] BOULDING, p. 30.

At the level to which the last words of this passage refer we cannot perceive any contact with the Mystery of God.

> "It is in His image that God has made and is still making us. When I look towards the Creator in prayer I know and I am known, love and I am loved, because I am like Him. *This is a fact far deeper than any perceptual awareness of it I may happen to have.*"[185]

This is a good description of the deep unconscious level. When the Council of Trent declared that we cannot know with absolute certitude of faith whether or not the Divine Persons abide within us by grace, perhaps there is an implicit reference to the deep unconscious.[186]

Is it possible that the kataphatic aspect of God's Being pertains to what can be reflected on the subconscious levels of the virtue of faith, because it can be brought to consciousness by acts of active and receptive attentions, and so become luminous to the believer? And does not the apophatic aspect of the Divine Being depend upon and derive from what always lies buried and hidden at the deep unconscious level of the believer's mind, so that the only thing praying Christians can do is to surrender themselves entirely to the hidden Mystery through ecstatic attention?

In conclusion, we began this chapter with a rather obvious statement: unless the mind of one who prays is attentive, his or her acts of prayer cannot be properly performed. Gradually we came to realize that the attention of the mind in prayer takes different forms. It can even be entirely absorbed into God in ecstasy or expanded beyond explicit awareness through unconscious awareness of his presence. And this is the awareness that can permeate a person's entire live.

We especially tried to describe as clearly as possible this latter deep-seated awareness with its constant, somewhat paradoxical and

---

[185] *Ibid.*, p. 60. Emphasis ours.

[186] "Cum nullus scire valeat certitudine fidei, cui no potest subesse falsum, se gratiam Dei esse consecutum." Sessio VI, *Decretum de Justificatione,* cap. 9.

uncanny unconscious form of attention to God. And we noted that this form of awareness has often been alluded to by various spiritual writers.

Doubtless it is more important to actually cultivate and maintain this experiential awareness of God's presence than to be able to express it in clear concepts and words. But clear explanations make a precious contribution to the realization and enrichment of such spiritual experience and should not be underestimated either. We hope that our attempt to clarify the issue of unconscious awareness of God's presence in prayer will help readers to become more profoundly and unceasingly self-aware and God-aware in their entire lives of prayer.

CHAPTER III

THE HEART OF PRAYER

i. The Differing Order between Attentions and Intentions

Knowledge and love intertwine so intimately in the life of prayer that one can never separate one from the other. When we say that theological faith is a knowledge born of love[187] we mean that the intellectual assent of faith to the Divine Truth is commanded by a voluntary love inclination toward the Divine Goodness.[188] So, when Christians seek in prayer for a better knowledge of God, they are motivated by their love toward him. And when they reach a better knowledge of him, their love toward him increases.

a. The interconnection between attentions and intentions

Some love toward God is already present in the first *active* attention of Christian prayer. The same love feeds the expectation of being granted union with him during the following practice of *receptive* attention. At the end, *ecstatic* attention offers the opportunity of reaching an intimate union of love with God.

Thus, while the mind's attentions to God's Truth in prayer take first an active then a receptive and finally an ecstatic form, the hearts intentions are more and more attracted by God's Goodness; until mind and heart join in surrendering the whole praying person to God's Truth and Goodness.

Given this continual interconnection of attentions and intentions throughout Christian prayerlife, should we not conclude that, as the mind successively exercises active, receptive and ecstatic attentions, so the heart too

---

[187] Cf. LONERGAN, pp. 115-117.

[188] "(Faith is) a disposition (habitus) of the mind that leads it to obey the will's orientation to the divine truth. For the mind does not assent to the truths of mysteries by being rationally convinced, but by being impelled to assent by the will. As Augustine puts it, *no one believes unless he wills to believe.*" (ST, I, q. 111, a. 1, ad 1um, BLACKFRIARS, vol. 15, p. 21). Cf. I-II, q. 56, a, 3, co.

follows the same order, producing first active then receptive and finally ecstatic intention?

Notwithstanding the apparent reasonableness of such a hypothesis, the Bible and Theology compel us to answer negatively to the foregoing question, and to assert that Christian life and prayer begin not with an active but with a receptive attitude of the heart.

b. Our primal need of being loved by God – Bible and Tradition

The Old Testament teaches that,

> "*The covenantal love of God is primary in the divine human relationship.* Man has to love God, but his love is derived from God's primal establishment of covenantal relationship. It is because Yahweh loves that the "faithful" are exhorted to "love Yahweh" (Ps 31:23)... Israel's covenantal love, therefore, is the response to the love Yahweh has first shown by his establishment of the covenant... *To love Yahweh is to know his primary love* and to live in responsible devotion to God. It is to 'hear the voice of Yahweh and to cleave to him' (Dt 30:20)."[189]

The New Testament proclaims,

> "By his (= Christ's) power, he has given us all the things that we need for life and devotion."[190]

This, of course, is true in a very special way of our charity towards God.

> "We were still helpless when at the appointed moment Christ died for sinful men... *What proves that God loves us is that Christ died for us while we were still sinners...* When we were reconciled to God by the death of his Son, we were still his enemies."[191]
>
> *"This is the charity I mean: not our love for God, but God's love for us, when he sent his Son to be the sacrifice that takes away our sins."* [192]

---

[189] GOOD, p. 167 b, 168 a and b passim. All emphasis ours.

[190] 2 Pt 1:3; cf. Jn 3:27; 1 Co 4:7.

[191] Rm 5:6-10.

[192] 1 Jn 4:10; cf. Jn 15:13-16.

> *"We have known and put our faith in God's love for us...* and live in faith in the Son of God who loved us and sacrificed himself for our sake."[193]
>
> So, *"nothing can come between us and the love of Christ...* Through all trials we triumph by *the power of Him who loved us.* For I am certain of this: neither death or live, no angel, no prince, nothing that exists, nothing still to come, not any power or height or depth, nor any created thing, can ever come between us and the love of God made visible in Christ Jesus our Lord."[194]

To this teaching of the Scripture the Fathers added their comments. St. Irenaeus, for one, reiterates the absolutely disinterested love that the Creator and Savior showed to human kind from the beginning.

> "In the beginning God created Adam, not because he needed man, but because he wanted to have someone on whom to bestow his blessing .... Nor did the Lord need our service. He commanded us to follow him, but his was the gift of Salvation: to follow the light is to enjoy the light ....
>
> The same is true of the service of God; it adds nothing to God, nor does God need the service of man. Rather he gives life and immortality and eternal glory to those who follow and serve him.... The reason why God requires service from man is this: because he is good and merciful he desires to confer benefits to those who persevere in his service.
>
> In proportion to God's need for nothing is man's need for communion with God."[195]

St. Augustine preaches that Christians cannot love God unless God first loves them and enables them to love him.

> "How can we choose (God as the object of our love) unless we are first chosen (by Him)? We cannot love unless someone has loved us first. Listen to the Apostle John: 'We love Him because He first loved us.,' *The source of man's love for God can only be found in the fact that God loved him first. He has given Himself as the object of our love, and He has also given us its source.*

---

[193] 1 Jn 4:16; Ga 2:20.

[194] Rm 8:35-39. Of course, all emphasis in the NT's texts is ours.

[195] *Adversus Haereses,* IV, 14, 1. English translation in LITURGY, vol. II, p. 77-78.

> What this source is you may learn more clearly from the Apostle Paul who tells us: 'The love of God has been poured into our hearts.' This love is not something we generate ourselves: it comes to us through the Holy Spirit who has been given to us."[196]

William of St. Thierry over and over again stresses the same teaching of Augustine.

> "O Lord, salvation is your gift...*what else is your salvation but receiving from you the gift of loving you or being loved by you?* ... By loving us and holding us dear, he (= Jesus, our Savior) *stirred us to love him who had first loved us to the end. And this is clearly the reason: you first loved us so that we might love you* – not because you needed our love, but because we could not be what you created us to be, except by loving you...
>
> Everything he did and everything he said on earth ... was actually you speaking to us in your Son, appealing to us by your love and stirring up our love for you...
>
> *You are the first to love all those who love you. Thus we hold you dear by the affection you have implanted in us...* Your love is your goodness, the Holy Spirit proceeding from the Father and the Son! ... By his inspiration and holy breath, he unites God to us and us to God."[197]

c. *Our primal need of being loved by God – Theology*

Aquinas acknowledges that the natural inclination common to all creatures to love the Creator above themselves (which is the only true way of loving God for God's sake) issues from the profound being of the human person.[198] But Aquinas is aware too that the moral consequences of original sin

---

[196] *Sermon* 34, 1-3. English translation in LITURGY, vol. II, p. 712. Emphasis ours.

[197] William of Sr. Thierry, *On the Contemplation of God,* nos. 9-11, passim. English translation in LITURGY, vol. I, pp. 271-272.

[198] "Since the good, taken quite universally, is God himself, and since all angels, all men and all other creatures exist as contained in that good – because every creature, precisely in respect of what it is by nature, belongs to God – it follows that the instinctive natural love of each angel and each man is for God first of all and for God more than for self." (ST, I, q. 60, a. 5, co., BLACKFRIARS, vol. 9, p. 201). Cf. II-II, q. 26, a. 3, co.

prevent the human person from loving God more than oneself. As a matter of moral experience, in our present condition whenever somebody brags about his obedience and love toward God, one can reasonably suspect that what he or she really seeks is his or her own sinful self-aggrandizement.[199]

Hence, unless God himself thoroughly heals and supernaturally elevates the human person's will by infusing it with the virtue of charity, he or she absolutely cannot love God for God's sake and as a Father.[200] This is what we mean when we say that the first contact of the human heart with God cannot be active but must be receptive.

The study of human psychology confirms that by its very nature love by and large is more receptive than knowledge. Doubtless the mind too must first receive the imprint of an object to know it. But knowledge is achieved through the mind's realization of the imprint received and the active casting of the results of that realization in the mould of a clear and distinct idea of the object.

On the contrary, when the heart loves, it not only receives an imprint of the object's goodness but is attracted by that goodness from the beginning to the end of its whole act of loving.[201]

That the human heart is more receptive than the human mind becomes particularly manifest before God. The human mind can by its own natural efforts reach a good deal of knowledge about God. In fact, the strengthening

---

[199] As the prayer of the proud Pharisee of the parable shows. Cf. Lk 18:11-12.

[200] "In the state of intact nature man...loved God more than himself and above all things. But in the state of spoiled nature man falls short of this in the desire of his rational will, which because of the spoiling of nature pursues a private good unless it is healed by God's grace." (ST, I-II, q. 109, a. 3, co., BLACKFRIARS, vol. 30, p. 79). "Charity attains God himself so as to rest in him without looking for any gain." (II-II, q. 23, a. 6, co., BLACKFRIARS, vol. 34, p. 25). Remember, though, that the natural inclination which the human person has to love God above oneself issues from his or her created being and its proper object is the Creator. So, besides receiving the healing of his or her natural inclination to love God for God's sake, the human person must be elevated by God's love to the condition of an adopted child, in order to become able to love God as Father.

[201] Aquinas insistently stresses the "passivity" of love: "This word (= love) indicates a living motion and impulse, as when somebody is said to be driven or impelled by his love to do something." (ST, I, q. 27, a. 4, co., BLACKFRIARS, vol. 6, p. 17).

given the human mind by supernatural faith is necessary only for the mind's knowledge of the inner Mystery of God.

But, the human heart has no way of loving God for God's sake by its own natural power. Because being, as we have said, sinfully bent back upon its own interests, it absolutely needs to receive supernatural charity to love God for God's sake.

A late Middle Ages English spiritual author gives the kernel of this theological teaching.

> "And that love (i.e., charity) is not the love that a soul has in itself for God; but the love that our Lord has for a sinful soul that knows nothing at all about knowing him is the cause why a soul comes to this knowledge, and to this love that comes out of it...
>
> Love uncreated, which is God himself is the cause of this knowledge ... Because he loves us so much he gives us his love, which is the Holy Spirit. He is both the giver and the gift, and by that gift he then makes us know and love him.[202]

Contemporary Christian theologians echo this traditional teaching when they emphasize the utter receptivity of the human will before the virtue of charity, which enables Christians to love God.

> "If this love (toward God) is a gift – *the unspeakable gift of God* – it should call the deepest passivity of the human will into play. Man can neither create it nor make it spring up in his own soul, *he can only open himself and receive it.*
>
> This is a metaphysical necessity, since love always presupposes at its source the transforming action of the being loved; it is also a necessity of the concrete case, since here we have to do with a love that introduces us to the intimacy of God, and wholly surpasses the powers of nature.
>
> *If then we are thus to love, God himself has to love us first, make good in man the power of loving, bestow the active capacity and efficacious power to love Him in return.*[203] Thus, by a purely gratuitous grace, He makes Himself the Act of this potency, and makes it divine by participation.

---

[202] HILTON, II, ch. 34, pp. 264.

[203] Emphasis ours.

And so there is a radical and substantial *pati divina* – a being acted upon by God – at the source of all supernatural love: in other words, to love is to be loved, to be known, chosen and called, to be created anew by God."[204]

"The intelligibility of divine charity is not to be found in any prior quality in ourselves which makes us 'worthy to be loved' (even though the love itself confers that). On the contrary it always depends totally and eternally on the freedom of God which is based on nothing else than God alone. In this radical sense *the love we are speaking of is, and remains eternally, 'grace' ... it is a pure act of reception.*"[205]

On this point a great Protestant theologian totally agrees with his Catholic colleagues:

"The revealed truth of the living God in his quickening Spirit has its content and force in the fact that it is He the first for man, and then and for that reason man is for Him. God precedes therefore, and sets man in the movement in which he follows.

He says Yes to him when man says No, and thus silences the No of man and lays a Yes in his heart and on his lips. *He loves man even though he is an enemy (Rm 5:10) and thus makes him the friend who loves him in return.*"[206]

Catholic authors, however, remind us that divine charity is not to be received in an absolutely passive manner, but the Christian has to strive for it; even though "wholeheartedly striving towards salvation consists solely of desiring and receiving it."[207]

More precisely, though somewhat paradoxically,

"We do whatever needs to be done in a spirit of receptivity, of passivity before God, so we are 'passively active or actively passive'."[208]

---

[204] MOUROUX [2], pp. 214-215.

[205] RAHNER [2], p. 255. Emphasis ours.

[206] BARTH, p. 48. Emphasis ours.

[207] DURRWELL, p. 24; cf. p. 174, 291.

[208] TUGWELL [3], p. 215.

The last words recall those written by a medieval English mystic about the right attitude the Christian should have in contemplation:

> "Almighty God himself, independently of all techniques, must always be the chief worker in contemplation. It is he who must always awaken this gift in you by grace. All that you (and others like you) must do is *make yourselves completely receptive,* consenting to and suffering his divine action in the depths of your spirit.
>
> *Yet the passive consent and endurance you bring to this work is really a distinctive active attitude:* for by the singleness of your desire ever reaching up to your Lord, you continually open yourself to his action...
>
> In many other good works man acts in partnership with God, but in this work God alone is the chief worker and he alone takes the initiative, while man consents and suffers his divine action."[209]

Vatican II recalled the traditional Catholic doctrine and drew from it important anthropological consequences.

> "'God is love, and he who abides in love abides in God, and God abides in him' (1 Jn 4:16). God has poured out his love in our hearts through the Holy Spirit who has been given to us (cf. Rm 5:5); therefore *the first and most necessary gift is charity, by which we love God above all things* and our neighbor because of him."[210]
>
> "The dignity of man rests above all on the fact that he is called to communion with God. The invitation to converse with God is addressed to man as soon as he comes into being. For if man exists it is because God has created him through love, and through love continues to hold him in existence. He cannot live fully according to truth unless he freely acknowledges that love and entrusts himself to his Creator."[211]

When this doctrine is applied to prayerlife it follows that,

> "Our existence as a whole is immersed in the bottomless ocean of love of the Father. This is something we must be aware of as we pray... Anyone who has ever sensed this fundamental mystery underlining our

---

[209] CLOUD, pp. 170-171 and 179-180. Emphasis ours.

[210] LG, n. 42. FLANNERY, p. 400.

[211] GS, n. 19, FLANNERY, p. 918.

existence will take the necessity of prayer for granted, particularly the prayer of listening and contemplation.

God himself, in establishing his relationship with his creature is shown to be the ultimate Lover, such that the creature's very existence seems to be a latent prayer – the creature only needs a certain awareness of what it really *is*, and it will break forth into prayer."[212]

Of the surprising phrase – "the creature's very existence seems to be a latent prayer" the following no less astonishing words could be an explanation:

"Even when we are unconscious of our message, or we try to cover it up, we always pray: everyone always prays. For our being always cries out something and God always hears us... When we look at it from God's point of view, our being always prays, because God always hears the 'cry' within us. Even when that cry comes out from the hearts of 'unbelievers' who have no desire or reason to pray to God"[213]

Some support for this theory can be found in the Scripture.

"The Lord hears even the weeping of a child (Gn 21:16-17) and responds to the condition of the slaves in Egypt (Ex 3:7-8), as later he treats the condition of the poor and the trials of Israel as a prayer (Is 41:17, 43:1-7: cf. Ps 79:10-11)....

In the NT it is the Spirit of God himself who prompts and gives meaning to prayer (e.g. Rm 15b-16:26-27). The Spirit interprets the mind of God who knows what we need before we ask (Mt 6:8)."[214]

In fact, though God sometimes seems to be absent, he is always available and caring, even when not called upon:

---

[212] VON BALTHASAR, pp. 43-44.

[213] WOLFF, pp. 17-18. Remember that PEĠUY, p. 51, wrote of certain obscure and secret desires which, although unconscious to those who have them, are known to God. Speaking of human unconscious desires known to God is perhaps putting in contemporary terms the natural inclination (acknowledged above by Aquinas) of all created beings to love the Creator more than themselves. As love toward God is the first source of all activity of prayer, such natural inclination to love God may be called prayer in a very broad sense.

[214] SMITH, p. 867 a.

> "I (= Yahweh) was ready to be approached by those who did not consult me, ready to be found by those who did not seek me. I said 'I am here, I am here', to a nation who did not invoke my name. Each day I stretched out my arms to a rebellious people who went their evil ways, following their whims."[215]

ii. The Major Kinds of Intention

Since it has been demonstrated that in prayerlife the arrangement of the heart's intentions cannot be the same as that of the mind's intentions, our analysis of the process of loving God in prayer must now start from receptive love-intention.

a. Receptive love-intention

At the beginning of Christian life and prayer receptive love-intention certainly includes the first acts of faith and conversion that Jesus demanded of those who were willing to welcome the coming of God's Kingdom.[216]

By faith one gives credit to God, trusting in his merciful love. By conversion one rejects and detaches oneself from whatever is opposed to or irreconcilable with God's will. Faith and conversion join to form the Christian's childlike openness to God's Kingdom.[217]

Such an openness certainly involves the receptive love-intention we are dealing with. Yet, it can be identified with the actual reception of the charity which is poured into our hearts by the Holy Spirit.[218] There are in the Scriptures beautiful descriptions of this receptive spiritual attitude.

> "Yahweh is good to those who trust in Him, to the soul who searches for Him. It is good to wait in silence for Yahweh to save."[219]

---

[215] Is 65:1-2.

[216] Cf. Mk 1:14-15.

[217] Cf. Mk 10:14-15; Mt 11:25, 18:3-4; Lk 10:21.

[218] Cf. Rm 5:5.

[219] Lm 3:26; cf. Is 8:17.

> "Enough for me to keep my soul tranquil and quiet like a child in its mother's arms, as content as a child that has been weaned. Israel rely on Yahweh, now and for always!"[220]

Ancient spiritual Masters recommend the practice of such an attitude in prayer.

> "By your prayer make yourself able and ready like a clean vessel to receive the grace that our Lord will freely give you, and this cannot be felt until you are purified by the fire of desire in devout prayer.[221]

Likewise a contemporary author claims that prayer without qualification is our conscious attention and free receptivity to God's action.

> "Prayer is the willingness to pay attention to God's action, or at least to experience which might be the actions of God, and to let our desire of God be aroused... For when I become conscious of God's action, no matter how dimly, then I am praying, even though I do not say a word."[222]

As it is God the Holy Spirit who directly acts on us in such a prayer, this form of prayer can be equated with "praying in the Spirit".

> "Praying in the Spirit is less an effort to love God and more a matter of letting Him love you. It is more a matter of receiving God's gift than strained effort on our part. Your poverty meets His giving in the silence of lovers. In your deep self - not the empirical self of daily affairs, but the ultimate truth of your being - you wait, trust and consent to be loved."[223]

Pope Paul VI once wrote of prayer in similar terms:

---

[220] Ps 131:2-3; cf. 33:9; 34:8, etc.

[221] HILTON, I, ch. 24, p. 97. In the note to this passage the editors of the book refer to a similar teaching of St. Augustine, St. Gregory the Great, and St. Thomas Aquinas.

[222] BARRY [1], p. 14. This author defines prayer as a "conscious relationship with God.": pp. 12-14, 59, 77.

[223] BOULDING, p. 33. Cf. pp. 83-84. Emphasis ours

"(Religious should dedicate) sufficiently long periods of prayer before the Lord to tell him their love and, *above all, to be loved by Him.*"[224]

The same idea is beautifully put in one of T.S. Eliot's most famous quatrains:

"I said to my soul, be still, and wait without hope,/ For hope would be hope for the wrong thing; wait without love./ For love would be love for the wrong thing; there is yet faith./ But the faith and the love and the hope are all in the waiting./
...So the stillness (shall be) the dancing."[225]

All this can be illustrated by a simile borrowed from Eastern Mysticism. The mother monkey transports her young from tree to tree on her chest or back: the baby must cling tightly to its mother's fur or suffer the worst. The tiger's cubs are carried instead in their mother's mouths, by which they are held safely and cannot fall. Likewise, to begin our loving union with God in prayer we must first let Him hold and carry us by his loving care as the mother tiger holds and carries her cubs.

b. Active love-intention

God'slove creates by infusing goodness into creatures. On his human creatures God showers his love and goodness because he especially wants to gain their hearts, as a lover desiring to be loved in return.
Actually,

"The First Sweet Truth shows that whatever he does to us is done with the love of his heart; and *you should respond with love.* He is our sweet God who wants nothing but love."[226]

---

[224] Paul VI, *L'Osservatore Romano,* March 8, 1980. Quoted in Sacred Congregation of Religious and Secular Institutes, *The Contemplative Dimension of Religious Life,* I, 2.

[225] *East Coker,* III.

[226] St. Catherine of Siena, *Le Lettere,* 72, vol. II, p. 5. Quoted by Gillett, p. 97.

When we consciously and willingly open our hearts to God's redeeming and sanctifying love we are gifted with the theological virtue of charity. This supernatural virtue enables us to love God in return for his own sake and above all else, as he deserves to be loved.

The Apostle John, who stresses that God loves us first, also reminds us that God expects us "to remain in his love by keeping his commandments"; especially the precept of "loving one another as Jesus has loved us", meaning that "as he gave up his life for us, we, too, ought to give our lives for our brothers."[227]

St. Augustine reminds us that the consequence of our being loved by God is that we ought to love him in return:

> "Since we have such assurance (of being loved by God) *let us love God with the love He has given us!*"[228]

For the love relationship between us and God, which is initiated through the love that God pours into our hearts, can only be maintained by the active return of our love to him.

> "We all keep falling back on self-love. But real love is always response to the love of another, a self-giving with no thought of return... Ultimately, it is always the love of God which is drawing us to give ourselves back in return for the love we have received."[229]

Accordingly, out active intention of charity toward God, far from contradicting the charity of God in loving us beforehand, is the natural result of the latter.

> "In giving itself with absolute generosity, (our) love simply prolongs the gift by which it is constituted – *it gives what it receives,* it can act because it is activated, and all the infinitude of its power comes from the adoring passivity in which it lies opened to God."[230]

---

[227] Cf. Jn 15:9-12 and 1 Jn 3:16.

[228] Cf. note 10 in this chapter.

[229] GRIFFITHS [2], p. 62.

[230] MOUROUX [1], p. 217.

Finally, both our receiving love, i.e., our receptive love-intention, and giving back love, i.e., our active love-intention, complete the exchange and circulation of love between us and God, which by continually spiralling upwards causes our ever growing union with him.[231]

Our love toward God, although it may at times be accompanied by feelings of devotion, is not only an emotion ut essentially consists in

> "Desiring with strong determination to please God in everything, in striving insofar as possible not to offend Him, and in asking Him for the advancement of the honor and glory of His son and the increase of the Catholic Church."[232]

These are all manifest signs of grateful active return of true charity towards God. In order to cultivate this love-intention in prayer there must first be a deliberate will to get rid of self-interest and attachment to self-gratification. Hence, one of the most ancient Masters of Christian prayer advised -

> "Go, sell all your possessions and give to the poor, and take up your cross so that you can pray without distraction... Do you long to pray? Renounce all things. First pray to be purified from all passions.[233] Secondly, pray to be delivered from ignorance. Thirdly, to be freed from all temptation and abandonment.
>
> Do you wish to pray? Then banish the things of this world. Have heaven for your homeland and live there constantly – not in mere words but in actions that imitate the angels and in more godlike knowledge...

---

[231] "All Christians will sanctify themselves more and more if they receive all things from the hands of the heavenly Father and cooperate with the divine will.": no. 41, FLANNERY, p. 400.

[232] ST. TERESA OF AVILA, *Interior Castle,* IV, 1, 7. This description is similar to Aquinas' definition of *devotio,* "Devotion is nothing other than the will to give oneself promptly to those things that pertain to the service of God" (ST, II-II, q. 82, a. 1, co., BLACKFRIARS, vol. 39, p. 37). Cf. The demands of the *Hesed,* which especially in Ho 2:21ff, stands for love intimacy between Israel and Yahweh within the context of their Covenant.

[233] About this requirement see what EVAGRIUS writes in chs. 50, 52, 53, 55, p. 63.

> To the extent you still give attention to the values of the body, and your mind concerns itself with the amenities of life, you have not yet seen the place of prayer. Rather the happiness of this way is still far off. When you give yourself to prayer, rise above every other joy – then you will find true prayer."[234]

This very demanding ancient advice has re-echoed throughout all the following centuries of Christian teaching on prayer. So, the genuine active love intention of the Christian heart involves something analogous to the purification of the mind as it frees itself of distraction in order to be actively attentive in prayer.

How praying Christians can reach such an active love intention of disinterestedly pleasing God in everything is suggested by another great master of prayer:

> "We should remember with what love Christ has bestowed all his favor upon us, and how great is the love that God has revealed to us in giving us such a pledge of the love which He bears for us; for love begets love. And though we may be only beginners and very wicked, let us strive ever to bear this in mind and awaken our own love in our hearts....
>
> He leaves nothing undone for those He loves, and when He sees that they accept His gifts, He gives and gives Himself. He loves everyone who loves Him, and how well loved is he who loves Him and how good a friend."[235]

It is through affective prayer that Christians experience how much God loves them and bestows upon them all his gifts in order to stir up their giving of themselves to him as a return of love. That is powerfully expressed by the famous "offering with deep affection" of St. Ignatius of Loyola, by which both receptive and active love-intentions are mentioned in the same breath –

> "Thou hast given all to me. To Thee, O Lord, I return it. All is Thine: dispose of it according to Thy will. Give me Thy love and Thy grace, for this is enough for me!"[236]

---

[234] EVAGRIUS, chs. 17, 36, 37, 142, 152, 153, pp. 58, 61, 78, 80.

[235] ST. TERESA OF AVILA, *Life,* XXII, 14-17; cf. *Way of Perfection,* XXVII, 12.

[236] SE, p. 104.

c. Ecstatic love-intention

At the highest stage of charity toward God the love-intention of Christians becomes ecstatic.

> "Divine love draws those whom it seizes beyond themselves; and this so greatly that they belong no longer to themselves but wholly to the object loved."[237]

The spirit of those who are perfect in charity

> "Is through ecstasis of love clothed entirely in God alone, and through mystical theology is brought altogether to rest in God."[238]

Becoming intoxicated by charity, they forget themselves and throw themselves into God, while their whole human affection in some ineffable manner melts and transfuses itself into the divine will.[239]

> "This is the way of all real love. The lover will utterly and completely despoil himself of everything, even his very self, because of the one he loves. He cannot bear to be clothed in anything save the thought of his beloved."[240]

---

[237] PSEUDO-DYONISIUS, *De Divinibus Nominibus,* IV, 13, col. 712.

[238] St. Maximus the Confessor, *Centuries on Theology and The Incarnation,* I, 39. Quoted by LOUTH [2], p. 193. In these words Maximus displays the influence on him of Pseudo-Dyonisius. Cf. "(The intellect) attains through unknowing the very principle of the divine unity." *Ib.,* II, 8.

[239] ST. BERNARD, *De Diligendo Deo,* 10, 28-29. PL 182, 990-991: "E divino inebriato amore animus oblitus sui totus pergit in Deum... Sic omnem tunc a sanctis humanam affectionem quodam ineffabili modo necesse erit a semetipsa liquescere atque in Dei penitus transfundi voluntatem." As this text makes clear, the love mentioned here "Is not merely an effusion of sentiment but an act of the will: an act often of so deep and comprehensive a kind as to involve the complete change of the outward no less than the inward life.": UNDERHILL [2], p. 197.

[240] CLOUD, p. 172. Aquinas acknowledges an essential ecstatic character in the love of friendship. "To 'suffer transport' *(ecstasim)* is to be carried outside of yourself... In love of friendship the ultimate term of the person's feeling is 'located outside of him' for he wants some good thing for his friend, and works for it, exercising

> "He who is in love is said to have his heart stolen and seized by the person whom he loves, for he has his heart out of himself and given to what he loves. So that he has no heart for himself, but for what he loves."[241]

A contemporary theologian attributes ecstatic love-intention to

> "Radical hope in God implied in perfect charity towards Him, which finds expression in allowing oneself to be grasped by the incontrollability of God and to be drawn out of oneself"[242]

These are just a few of the many Christian evidences about the ecstasis of charity, i.e., the experience had by those who love God so intensely that they feel forcefully drawn to surrender themselves entirely to their Divine Beloved and to be wholly transformed into him.

Such an ecstatic love-intention is the most perfect act of giving God the return of the charity first received from him. It is the only proportionate Christian response to the charity poured into our heart by the Holy Spirit. And such a return of love is so efficacious that it not only intimately unites, but makes Christians completely one with the Divine Persons. For the love which unites the Divine Persons with one another is shared by the same Persons with those in whom They come to make Their home on earth.

> "As the Father has loved me, so I have loved you. Remain in my love. If you keep my commandments you will remain in my love...
>
> I shall ask my Father and he will give you another Advocate to be with you forever, the Spirit of truth... You know him because he is with you, he is in you.
>
> If anyone loves me he will keep my word, and my Father will love him, and we shall come to him and make our home with him....
>
> Father, may they be one in us, as you are in me and I am in you... that they may be one as we are one. With me in them and you in me, may

---

thought and care about his friend's interest for his friend's sake" (ST, I-II, q. 28, a. 3, co., BLACKFRIARS, vol. 19, pp. 97-99).

241 CRUZ, *Cantico,* IX, 5, p. 948. Translation ours.

242 RAHNER [2], p. 255.

> they be so completely one that the world may realize that it was you who sent me and I have loved them as much as you loved me."[243]

Such a marvelous revelation has been interpreted in the sense that when we are loved by the Divine Persons, not only do we receive an infusion of the theological virtue of charity, but the Divine Persons Themselves come to dwell within us and give Themselves to us in such a way that by virtue of the charity we have received we can freely enjoy Them.[244]

Accordingly, the ecstatic love-intention of Christians, i.e., their "staying out" by charity towards the Divine Persons, is correlated and analogous to the "staying out" of the Divine Persons by their charity toward Christians. From all this it results that the Divine Persons and Christians mutually give, receive, give in return, and enjoy one another in the perfect oneness of divine charity.

In sum, in prayerlife active and receptive love-intentions converge and reach their climax in the ecstatic love-intention by which Christians reciprocate charity with the Divine Persons. Indeed, "we can only receive (God's charity) in so far as we are willing to give (him charity in return)".[245] The Christian self-surrendering ecstatic love-intention enhances the capacity of Christians to receive divine charity.

And John of the Cross explains:

> "If a soul is seeking God, its Beloved is seeking it much more; and, if it sends after Him its loving desires, He likewise sends after it the fragrance of His ointments, wherewith He attracts the soul and causes it to run after Him. These ointments are His Divine inspirations and touches, which, whenever they are His, are ordered and ruled with respect to the perfection of the love of God and of faith, in which perfection the soul must ever draw nearer and nearer to God... Until it reaches such a delicate and pure state of

---

[243] Jn 15:9-10; 14:15-17, 23; 17:21-23.

[244] "The meaning of possessing something is that it is in our power to use and to enjoy it at will" ... "The gift of grace empowers the intelligent being not only to have this created gift at his ready disposal, but also for loving union with the Divine Person." (ST, I, q. 43, a. 3, co.; *Ibid,* ad 1um; I, q. 38, a. 1. co., BLACKFRIARS, vol. 7, p. 247 and pp. 217-219).

[245] GRIFFITHS [2], p. 62.

preparation that it merits union with God and substantial transformation in all its faculties."[246]

Jesus gave the most perfect examples of ecstatic charity – toward the Father, when on the cross he prayed: "Into your hands, O Lord, I deliver myself!"[247] – and toward us, when instituting the Eucharist he said to the disciples:

> "Take and eat, this is my body... Drink all of you from this, for this is my blood, the blood of the covenant, which is to be poured out for many for the forgiveness of sins."[248]

Paul time and again vividly described how Christians surrender to ecstatic love-intention toward Christ, reciprocating Christ's love toward them:

> "The love of Christ overwhelms us, when we reflect that he died for us all so that living men should live no longer for themselves, but for him who died and was raised to life for them."
>
> I live not with my own life but with the life of Christ who lives in me. The life I now live in this body I live in faith: faith in the Son of God who loved me and sacrificed himself for me."[249]

St. Catherine of Siena specifies the consequences of this Christian ecstasis of charity:

> "The blood shed (by Christ for us) with the fire of divine charity heats Christians so much that they are thrown out of themselves. So that they cannot love themselves for their own sake, but for God's sake, and God for God's sake, and the neighbor for God's sake."[250]

---

[246] CROSS [3], III, 28, pp. 222-223.

[247] Lk 23:46; cf. Ps 31:5.

[248] Mt 26; 26-28.

[249] Ga 2:20; cf. 1 Co 6:19-20; 1 P 1:18.

[250] "El Sangue sparto col fuoco della divina caritá scalda tanto l'uomo che gitta sé fuori di sé, e quinci viene che non può volere sé per sé, ma sé per Dio, e Dio per Dio, e el prossimo per Dio." Quoted in SANTA CATERINA DA SIENA, p. 226. Translation ours.

Charles de Foucauld makes his own and elaborates on the dying Christ's prayer of ecstatic self-surrender to the Father:

> "Into your hands I commend my soul: I offer it to you with all the love of my heart, for I love you, Lord, and so I need to give myself into your hands, without reserve, and with boundless confidence, for you are my Father."[251]

d. A survey of all love-intentions

The love intentions described and explained so far follow one another and interact throughout the whole growth process of charity in Christian prayerlife.

In fact, this process:

— Begins with the grateful acceptance of God's beneficent love, i.e., with a receptive love-intention.
— Develops by loving God for God's sake, i.e., through an active love-intention.
— Reaches loving oneself for God's sake, i.e., entirely forgetting and surrendering oneself to God by an ecstatic love-intention.[252]

The entire process manifestly amounts to letting oneself be more and more enamoured with God through the ever growing practice of charity toward Him in prayer.[253]

The two first steps of the process fuse into the relationship of being loved and loving established between God and the Christian. As this exchange of charity intensifies, it leads to the perfect communion of the praying Christian with the Divine Persons which is caused by the ecstatic love-intention.

---

[251] Quoted by CARRETTO, p. 19.

[252] These three successive love-intentions correspond with the second, third, and fourth grade of love described by ST. BERNARD'S *De Diligendo Deo.*

[253] Cf. ST. TERESA OF AVILA, *Life,* XII, 2: "hacer muchos actos para determinarse a hacer mucho por Dios y despertar el amor... y acostumbrarse a enamorarse mucho."

During the long growth process of prayerlife this threefold pattern of receptive-active-ecstatic charity is time and again repeated at successively higher levels, so spiralling upwards through a more and more profound penetration of the praying Christian into the circulation of Eternal Love among the Divine Persons.

There is spiritual evidence that at the beginning of prayerlife Christians realize that they can only willingly and humbly open their hearts to receive the gift of charity that God graciously bestows upon them. As a necessary consequence of their being loved by God to the point of receiving from him the power of loving him in return there wells up and flows forth from their hearts an active grateful charity toward him.

At this stage Christians sense that when they pray their hearts are like mirrors reflecting back toward God the warmth of love that he first radiates upon them. And whenever this reflection is re-absorbed into the living flame of love which eternally burns within the Holy Trinity, the love-intention of the praying Christian becomes ecstatic; it is, as it were, staying out of itself and surrendering itself entirely to God.

iii. The Subliminally Deliberate Being-in-Love with God of Prayerlife

The three love-intentions which we have studied so far cover the growth process in Christian prayerlife of the deliberate activity of the will elevated by charity.

But the human psyche allows also for a lasting being-in-love, which lies beyond its deliberation. For want of a better word, we will qualify as "subliminally deliberate" the level of the psyche where such a habitual being-in-love with God is situated.

Undoubtedly, "love engages the whole person, drawing all the faculties, conscious and unconscious, to the one we love".[254] But we can hardly speak of an "unconscious love", since the distinction between conscious and unconscious properly pertains to the mind, and cannot be properly extended to the heart from which love is elicited. Therefore we have to look for a concept and term which can properly signify the love situated at that profound level of the human heart, one which analogously matches the unconscious level of the mind.

---

[254] JOHNSTON [2], p. 107.

Now, spiritual love is properly deliberate or indeliberate. But the kind of love we are talking about is not deliberate, as it remains in the depths of the human heart even when all deliberate acts of love are over. Neither is it indeliberate, because it is the outcome of deliberate acts of charity toward God elicited during the formal practice of prayer. Hence it can only be said to be subliminally deliberate, such being the best way of qualifying the level of the human heart which matches the subconscious level of the human mind.

a. The prayerful being-in-love with God

It is a matter of spiritual experience that, as long as praying Christians love God by deliberate acts of charity, their receptive, active, ecstatic love-intentions are bound to be limited and intermittent, just like the formal activity of prayer during which they are performed. But when praying Christians let the thrust of their love-intentions sink into and permeate the depths of their hearts, then a state of being-in-love with God beyond actual deliberation establishes itself there, as the result of their deliberate love-intentions.

Such an affective state has lost the deliberate character of the love-intentions that have preceded and caused it. But it compensates for that loss with its lasting all-pervasive influence on the whole lives of prayerful Christians, which follows from their previous deliberation.

Love is a certain psychic "touch" which attracts the loving subject towards the beloved object.[255] When this imprinted attraction permanently affects the lover, it brings about a state of being-in-love, characterized by the abiding love-presence of the beloved in the lover.[256]

A particular state of being-in-love with God is caused by the acts of charity in the prayerlife of Christians and makes them always steer their fundamental love-option towards God. It works both as an engine powered by charity always impelling them towards God, and as a compass built into their spiritual affectivity beyond the level of deliberate choices.

Christians who faithfully practice prayer sooner or later will be granted a subliminally deliberate state of being-in-love by charity with God. The following prayer written by a great Irish saint beautifully expresses this state:

---

[255] Cf. E.g., ST, I, q. 27, a. 4; q. 37, a. 1.

[256] Cf. HILL, p. 74. See also pp. 262-264.

> "Loving Lord, be pleased to show yourself to us who knock, so that in knowing you we may love only you, love you alone, desire you alone, contemplate only you day and night, and always be thinking of you.
>
> Inspire in us the depth of love that is fitting for you to receive as God. So *may your love pervade our own being, possess us completely, and fill all our senses, that we may know no other love but love for you who are everlasting.*
>
> May our love be so great that the many waters of sky, land and sea cannot extinguish it in us. Many waters could not extinguish love!"[257]

But how does this state of being in love with God by charity form in praying Christians?

b. The Formation of being-in-love with God

Aquinas thought that the best way to gain some understanding of the mystery of charity, poured into our hearts by the Holy Spirit, is to envisage it as a certain friendship between ourselves and God. Friendship - he explains - means here a love of mutual benevolence built on the analogical participation of Christians in the nature and life of God.[258]

An initial fundamental love-option of Christians for God is involved in their supernatural friendship with him. Such a fundamental love option is the essential dynamism of charity.

> "A man or a woman who is in grace and charity has always a good general will toward God in his soul - whether asleep or awake, eating or drinking or whatever good deed he is doing - by which will he desires and chooses God above everything. Although this will is only general."[259]

---

[257] St. Columba, *Instructio de Compunctione,* XII, 3 in LITURGY, vol. IV, p. 383. Emphasis ours. It is intriguing to notice that Columba's words perfectly match a contemporary psychological description of being-in-love with a human beloved: "The presence of the loved may engross the whole of his/her (i.e., the lover's) consciousness, blocking out any other object. All other people promptly disappear from his/her environment, he/she cannot ger her/him out of his/her mind. It is a sort of possession.": HARDING, pp. 29-30.

[258] ST, II-II, q. 23, a. 1.

[259] HILTON, I, ch. 72, p. 145.

This being in grace and charity can co-exist with venial sin, because the latter does not directly contradict grace and charity, although it is alien to them.[260]

Increasing their affective involvement with God, Christians produce more and more fervent acts of charity. These acts cause a more pervading and deeper friendship of Christians with God, which more and more shapes their horizon of interests and directs their activity.

Finally, praying Christians become really enamoured of or in-love with God; that is, they love him not just as a friend but as a beloved. Not in a sentimental manner, though; but in the sense of pressing towards perfect conformity of will and communion of love with the Divine Beloved.

Such a lasting affective state influences all the human activity of those who have reached it, in the sense that whatever they do proceeds from that state in a subliminally deliberate manner, as to enable them to avoid even venial sins most of the time.

Our contention is that the perfection of charity which is required by this state of being-in-love with God can be reached especially through the practice of prayer as communion in which charity towards God is cultivated in the form of intimacy with him.

Meister Eckhart uses two similes to clarify how a Christian "bears the imprint of his beloved, present God" so intensely that he is really enamoured or in love with him.

> "It is just like a man who is terribly thirsty; he can do other things besides drinking and can even turn his mind to other thoughts, but yet, whatever he does and in whatever company he is, he never loses the thought of drinking as long as the thirst lasts; and the greater the thirst, the greater and deeper and more present and persistent will be the thought of drink.
>
> Or if there is a man who is so passionately devoted to a thing that nothing else interests him or touches his heart, he is intent on that thing and nothing else; quite certainly, wherever or with whomever the man is, and whatever he takes or does, the image of what he loves never fades in him, and he finds its image in everything, and it is ever the more strongly present to

---

[260] "A venial sin is not imcompatible with charity that makes God one's fixed goal in life, it does not prevent God's glory from being the abiding end, but only from being the actually intended end of a particular action." (ST, I-II, q. 88, a. 1, ad 2um; BLACKFRIARS, vol. 27, p. 49).

him, the more the love for it increases. And that man will not seek rest, for no unrest disturbs him."[261]

Contemporary authors compare the affective state of Christians who are enamoured of God with that of a man and a woman who are in love with each other. Here is a description of what happens when one falls in love:

"A man or a woman who falls in love is engaged in loving not only when attending to the beloved, but at all times. Besides particular acts of loving, there is the prior state of being in love and that prior state is, as it were, the fount of all one's actions. It transforms an "I" and a "Thou" into a "We" so intimate, so secure, so permanent that each attends, imagines, thinks, plans, speaks, acts, in concert for both.[262]

The state of being-in-love which carries on the initial experience of falling in love continues to operate in the whole life of the lover, even when daily occupations and distractions prevent him or her from performing deliberate acts of love toward the beloved.

"A deep love for a friend or a spouse subsists and remains fully 'real' even though work, or some other matter demands our concentration and prevents our giving conscious attention to the beloved. Not only are such acts capable of subsisting on the superactual level, but by their very nature are not limited in existence to a full actual experience.

No love would be authentic if it were restricted to the fully actual experience, ceasing to be a reality in our soul as soon as we concentrated on something else. Such an experience subsists and colors every actual situation of our lives. A deep spousal love transforms and transfigures the work we may be engaged in, as well as our relationship with the people we must deal with."[263]

---

[261] ECKHART, p. 17.

[262] LONERGAN, pp. 32-33. Also St. Paul so much loved those for whose conversion he was instrumental that he kept them always present in his heart and was intimately united with them: "You arc in our hearts – together we live or together we die." 2 Co 7:3.

[263] VON HILDEBRAND, pp. 89-90. For these ideas she refers to the books of her husband, Dietrich von Hildebrand. She terms "superactual" what we term "subliminal", apparently in order to point out that, even when the love of the enamoured persons is not deliberately actuated, it still remains powerfully influential

An ancient authoritative spiritual writer assures that descriptions of falling-in-love and being-in-love with a human beloved fittingly serve to illustrate by analogy the being-in-love with the Divine Beloved caused by fervent charity in Christians.

> "There is nothing wrong about offering human analogies for longing and love of God. Happy the man who loves and longs for God as a smitten lover does for his beloved... Not even a mother clings to her nursing child as a son of love clings to the Lord at all times. Somebody truly in love keeps before his mind's eye the face of the beloved and embraces it there tenderly... A man wounded by love had this to say about himself – and it really amazes me – 'I sleep [because nature commands this] but my heart is awake [because of the abundance of my love]'."[264]

These analogies show also that Christian prayer can be continual by virtue of its always "working" effective component.

> "Once we have grasped the fact that prayer is simply an inward grace of knowledge and love turned towards God, we realize the possibility of continual prayer, for we can never, we must never, cease to love God and to make his love the motive of our actions. It is possible to remain in this attitude of loving attention to God even in the midst of the most absorbing occupations.
>
> This may become clearer if we compare it to living with someone we love. It is not necessary to speak to him or her the whole time, not even to be thinking of him or her explicitly, and yet one is always aware of his or her presence, continually delighting in it.
>
> We remain inwardly turned in mind and heart towards the beloved, whatever the occupation which engages the immediate attention. Application

---

upon his/her whole activity.

[264] CLIMACUS, [2], Step 30, p. 287. About the phrase of the Song of Songs (5:2) at the end of the text of Climacus, ARINTERO, vol. I, p. 123, goes so far as commenting: "Even when sleeping, the true servants of God can love and merit more than others who are praying and working for the good of souls, because even during their sleep their deified hearts keep vigil, praying and loving intensely, although the saints are not aware of it." At p. 124, Arintero refers to St. Francis de Sales, *Treatise of the Love of God,* VII, 3, as a confirmation of what he has written.

to the task is perfectly compatible with a permanent inward attitude of love for the beloved."[265]

Thus, we could apply to the subliminally deliberate being in love by charity with God a paraphrased version of Jesus' saying: "Where your beloved is, there will your heart be also!"[266]

c. *The joy of being-in-love with God*

In the light of the virtual identification of being-in-love with God with unceasing prayer made in the last quote, it is worth remembering that Paul inserted his words about unceasing prayer within a context of Christian gratitude and joy for the many gifts continually bestowed by God upon us.

> "Be happy at all times; pray constantly; and for all things give thanks to God, because this is what God expects you to do in Christ Jesus."[267]
>
> "I want you to be happy, always happy in the Lord: I repeat, what I want is your happiness... the Lord is very near. There is no need to worry. But if there is anything you need, pray for it, asking God for it with prayer and thanksgiving, and that peace of God, which is much greater than we can understand, will guard your hearts and your thoughts, in Christ Jesus."[268]

For sure, the diffuse happiness which animates those who are in love will also permeate the whole life of Christians who through their practice of prayer have become enamoured with God.

---

[265] DUJAT, pp. 116-117. See also VON BALTHASAR [1], p. 89: "'Unceasing prayer' is similar to the way a man is always and everywhere influenced by the image of the woman he loves." Other descriptions of unceasing prayer in HARDON, pp. 164-165, and CARTER, [2], p. 104. The whole question of unceasing prayer will be extensively studied in chapter 11 of this book.

[266] Cf. Mt 6:21; Lk 12:34. ST. TERESA OF AVILA, *Fundaciones,* V, 16, remarked: "El verdadero amante en todas parte ama y siempre se acuerda del amado. Recia cosa sería que solo en los rincones se pudiera traer oración." Teresa and John of the Cross call the two highest grades of being in love with God "spiritual betrothal" and "spiritual marriage".

[267] 1 Th 5:16-18.

[268] Ph 4:4-7.

"Just as you can really become happy with another person if you love this person for his or her sake alone and not for your own happiness, so there is a similar relationship between the human person and God.

We must love God for his own sake – love because He is eternal, holy, blessed, incomprehensible God. And if we have this relationship with him, only then is He also the God of our happiness, the God of loving, forgiving providence."[269]

But what kind of joy or happiness is meant for those whose prayerlife has grown to the point of rendering them enamoured with God? To this question St. Catherine of Siena, for one, answers as follows:

"Sometimes a soul may have gladness and rise from prayer still glad. But if such gladness is found to be void of any burning desire for virtue and is not anointed with humility and set ablaze in the furnace of divine charity, then the visitation and whatever consolation or vision the soul has received are from the devil and not from me (i.e., God), in spite of the sign of gladness that the soul feels."[270]

About the same subject the author of *The Cloud of Unknowing* advises his reader with great wisdom

"With all due reverence for God's gifts, it is my opinion that we should be quite careless of all delights and consolations of senses and spirit, regardless of how pleasurable and sublime they may be. If they come, welcome them,[271] but do not rest on them for fear of growing weak; believe me, you will expend a good deal of energy if you remain long in sweet feelings and tears. Possibly too, you may begin to love God on their account and not for himself.

You will know whether or not this is happening if you become upset and irritable when you do not experience them. Should you find this to be the

[269] RAHNER, [3], p. 108. Cf. Ps 48:2-3: "The righteous will be glad and rejoice in God's presence: they will be exceedingly happy."

[270] DIALOGUE, ch. 106, p. 199.

[271] Sound anthropological realism claims that: "It is better that man be bent on the good, not merely with his will, but also with his sensory *orexis* (= appetites). As the Psalmist says, *'My heart and my flesh cry out for the living God'* (Ps 83:3); the word 'heart'suggesting the intellectual orexis, and the word 'flesh' the sensible." (ST, I-II, q. 24, a. 3,; cf. q. 30, a. 1, ad 1um.; BLACKFRIARS, vol. 19, p. 41.)

case, then your love is not yet chaste and perfect. When love is chaste and perfect, it may allow the senses to be nourished and strengthened by sweet emotions and tears, but it is never troubled if God permits them to disappear. It continues to rejoice in God all the same."[272]

St. Francis de Sales thinks that imperfect devout Christians risk to

"Fall in love with the love they have for God, instead of being in love with Him they love. They love the love instead of loving the Beloved."[273]

Whereas the perfect devout Christian is

"content to have no further contentment but that of being without contentment out of love for the contentment and good pleasure of his God in whom he rests."[274]

So, Christians who love God by genuine charity do not expect as a reward to taste and feel the sweetness of their Beloved but they rather try

"To content themselves with merely a peaceful and loving attentiveness toward God, and to be without anxiety, without the effort, without the ability and without the desire to have experience of Him or to perceive Him. For all these yearnings disquiet and distract the soul from the peaceful quiet and sweet ease of contemplation which is here granted to it."[275]

At any rate, if we truly love God and practice virtuous indifference toward and detachment from emotive consolations, we still have

"A permanent happiness deep down, of which we are not always conscious as we go about our daily tasks. This basic contentment comes from a growing awareness of God: an awareness that the things which happen to us are indeed insignificant when measured by the greatness of our task in seeking God. Our search for God gives us a deep contentment of which, I

---

[272] CLOUD, ch. 50, p. 112.

[273] DE SALES, vol. II, IX, ch. 9, p. 120.

[274] DE SALES, vol. I, VI, ch 11, p. 299.

[275] CROSS [2], I, X, 4, p. 71.

> admit, we may not often get aware: it bestows serenity which must grow all the time."[276]

For, although it exists only in a subliminally deliberate condition, the permanent being in love with God has the effective power to draw the prayerful Christian towards an ever-growing intimacy with the Divine Beloved.

> "The human heart is drawn by love and with all its powers: memory, understanding and will. If these three powers are harmoniously united in my (= God's) name, everything else you do, in fact or in intention will be drawn to union with me, in peace through the movement of love. So my Truth (= Jesus Christ) indeed spoke truly when He said: 'For everything you do will be drawn to Him when He draws your heart and its powers'."[277]

In conclusion, praying Christians manifestly stop eliciting the receptive, active, ecstatic love-intentions, which were necessary to their practice of prayer, when their acts and exercises of prayer are over. But the virtue of charity, especially because one can hope that it has been increased by God on account of that practice, does not stop exerting its all-pervading influence upon their lives.

For the acts of charity produced during the activity of prayer have caused a state of being-in-love with God in the depths of the praying Christians' spiritual affectivity. Acting out of those depths charity can continue to drive and orient those Christians towards God, even though in a subliminally deliberate manner and no longer in that deliberate way which characterized the acts of charity, i.e., the actual love-intentions, during the formal acts of prayer.

Besides always exerting that distinctive subconscious influence, the subliminally being-in-love with God also emerges at times into the praying Christian's consciousness in the form of a "vague nostalgia" for the Divine Beloved. This is a particular bitter-sweet aftertaste of the gratifying intimacy with the Divine Persons relished in the practice of prayer and which, after sinking into the subconscious depths of the spiritual affectivity, time and again enkindles in Christians the yearning for a renewed conscious enjoyment of that intimacy.

Doubtless, there is some sadness in such a nostalgia, for the divine intimacy is not experienced as before. But there is also a profound joy caused

---

[276] HUME, p. 179.

[277] DIALOGUE, ch. 26, p. 65.

by the moving remembrance of the sweet encounter previously enjoyed with the Divine Beloved. This nostalgia is then like a life-buoy in the sea of non-experience in which one may feel adrift.

CHAPTER IV

KNOWING AND LOVING IN PRAYER

Knowing and loving intertwine so intimately in prayerlife that they can hardly ever be separated from one another. In the two preceding chapters we wanted to analyse the two most basic and essential component elements of prayerlife. So, we had to distinguish in it knowing and loving; acknowledging that such a distinction is real and verifiable.

Assuming the same distinction, in this chapter we will try to understand the reciprocal and complementary roles played by knowing and loving in prayerlife. We will first consider them in the practice of prayer.

i. *Knowing and Loving in the Activity of Prayer*

a. *Is prayer knowing or loving?*

Throughout history contrasting answers were given to this question. Here is a brief random selection of significant texts for each one of the two opposite opinions.

1. Evagrius Ponticus, a great Greek spiritual theologian (†399), is quite certain that,

> "*Undistracted prayer is the highest act of the intellect...* If you are a theologian you truly pray. If you truly pray you are a theologian... Prayer is activity which is appropriate to the dignity of the spirit *(nous);* or better it is appropriate for its nobler and adequate operation... Knowledge! The great possession of man. It is a fellow-worker with prayer, acting to awaken the power of thought to contemplate the divine knowledge... Just as bread is nourishment for the body and virtue for the soul, so *is spiritual prayer nourishment for the intelligence."*[278]

[278] EVAGRIUS, ch. 34, 60, 84, 86, 101, pp. 60, 65, 69, 72. Emphasis ours.

Evagrius manifestly knew the ancient Greek philosophers' maxim – "contemplation *(theoría)* is the end of human life,[279] and made it his own.

His statements are particularly significant because,

> "Whereas Paul had employed the word heart *(kardia:* 2 Co 3:3) Evagrius changes it (into *nous:* mind, spirit) to express the intellectual emphasis, and his bias toward contemplation, which is the proper activity of the *nous.* For Evagrius man is not, essentially, a creature composed of body and soul, but a *nous,* that is, an intelligence whose proper activity is religious contemplation."[280]

Chrysostom (†407) apparently follows Evagrius,

> "As the eyes of the body are enlightened when they see light, so our spirit, when it is intent [by praying] on God, is illumined by His infinite light. I do not mean the prayer of the outward observance, but prayer from the heart, not confined to fixed times but continuous throughout the day and night.... *Prayer is the light of the spirit (psyche), true knowledge (epignosis) of God.*"[281]

2. Richard Rolle (†1349) holds the very opposite opinion:

> *"We pray truly when we do not think about anything,* but our whole will is directed towards the highest things, and our soul is set ablaze with the fire of the Holy Spirit... And our whole prayer will be made with affection and effectiveness... for *the intention of our heart, by means of burning love, also sets our very prayer ablaze.*"[282]

Even though putting it more softly, *The Cloud of Unknowing* (latter half of the fourteenth century) holds the same opinion of Rolle:

---

[279] Apparently Anaxagoras was the first to use this maxim. Cf. CLEMENT OF ALEXANDRIA, *Stromata,* 2, 21.

[280] EVAGRIUS, p. 53, note 7 of J.E. Bamberger.

[281] CHRYSOSTOM, p. 461 and 464. The English translation is from LITURGY, vol. II, p. 68-69. Emphasis ours.

[282] ROLLE, p. 69. Emphasis ours.

> "A person who has long pondered these things [i.e., 'his sinfulness, the Passion of Christ, and the kindness, goodness, and dignity of God'] must eventually leave them behind beneath a *cloud of forgetting,* if he hopes to pierce the *cloud of unknowing* that lies between him and his God.
>
> So whenever you feel drawn by grace to the contemplative work and are determined to do it, *simply raise your heart to God with a gentle stirring of love.* Think only of God, the God who created you, redeemed you, and guided you to this work. Allow no other ideas to enter your mind. Yet even this is too much. *A naked intent toward God, the desire for him alone, is enough.*"[283]

Today, authors who claim that prayer is thinking do not neglect adding a mention of its affective character too.

> *"Prayer is a fundamental style of thinking, passionate and compassionate, responsible and thoughtful,* that is deeply rooted in our humanity... It is thinking in the presence of God and in the light of Christ."[284]

> "When we think about prayer, we are thinking about God, and about human consciousness of God... In prayer we are seeking to achieve a continuous state of recollection of and of wakefulness to the reality and presence of God. *Prayer then is closely linked with knowledge. But this knowledge is not a cold, intellectual knowledge...(it is instead) a passionate, contemplative insight, involving communion and sharing...* Prayer is closely allied with vision and insight."[285]

Indeed, Christian prayer, one way or another, always involves both knowing and loving. This is beautifully and simply stated by a great mystic of our time:

---

[283] CLOUD, ch. 7, p. 56. Emphasis ours. Both Rolle and *Cloud* work with the definition of prayer given by *Scala Claustralium,* PL 184, 475: "Oratio est *devota cordis intentio* in Deum." In the same vein, ST. TERESA OF AVILA (†1582) contends that "the soul progresses [in prayer] not thinking much but loving much.": *Fundaciones,* V,2: "El aprovechimiento del alma no está en pensar mucho, sino en amar mucho." A contention manifestly consistent with the Teresian definition of prayer as friendly sharing with God" cf. *Vida,* VIII, 5.

[284] MACQUARRIE, pp. 30 and 33. Emphasis ours.

[285] LEECH, pp. 7-10 passim. Emphasis ours.

> "To me prayer is an *élan of the heart, a simple look towards Heaven,* a cry of gratitude and love as well in joy as in sorrow."[286]

And precisely because prayer always involves knowing and loving, whoever critically reflects on it can hardly evade the question about which one of these two elements is primal and more important.

b. *Is praying mostly knowing or loving?*

There are authors who seem to overemphasize in prayerlife either knowing at loving's expense or loving at knowing's expense. But, in reality their contrasting opinions are not so irreconcilable with each other as they look at first sight. Here are two examples of what we mean.

Somebody insists on the necessity of "thinking of God" in prayer in order to point out not only that knowing God is absolutely prerequisite to loving him, but also that the spiritual advantage of knowing him by true faith is greater than the satisfaction that Christians who pray can draw from the "affective graces" of prayer.

> "We must know before we can love; to love God we must often think of Him; and when we come to love Him we shall also think of Him often, for our heart is where our treasure is....
>
> Let us devote ourselves entirely to knowing God; the more we know Him the more we want to know Him; knowledge is commonly the measure of love, the deeper and wider our knowledge, the greater will be our love, and if our love is great, we will love Him equally in sorrow and in joy.
>
> Let us not be satisfied with loving God, because of the graces He has given us or may give us, however great they may be; these favors, great though they are, will never bring us near to Him as does one simple act of faith; let us seek Him often by faith."[287]

Can we, therefore, say that the writer of the foregoing words thought that love is not necessary in prayer? Of course not.

On the other hand, there is enough evidence that even authors who emphasize loving to the point of apparently excluding knowing – as it appears

---

[286] St. Thérèse of the Infant Jesus, *Autobiographical Manuscripts,* C line 25, quoted by CCC, n. 2558.

[287] LAWRENCE, pp. 80 and 96.

from the above-quoted texts of Rolle and of *The Cloud of Unknowing* – do not really deny that knowing too has an essential role to play in prayerlife. They rather seem to be polemically over-reacting to other authors who would reduce the whole of prayerlife to thinking of God, understood as meditation in a strict sense.[288]

So, apparently opposite opinions may not be as irreconcilable as they seem. A contemporary author who often repeats that "our encounter with God in love is the very essence of prayer",[289] acknowledges that in prayerlife

> "The first stage is getting to know the Lord. We cannot really love what we do not know... True love is grounded on a real knowledge, gradually acquired, of him and of ourselves." (Only) "the second stage of prayer is the move from knowing to loving ... and praying becomes much more affective and much less reflective."[290]

So, at different stages of the growth process of prayerlife either knowing or loving may prevail. At any stage, however, neither loving nor knowing should ever be overemphasized to the point that either is excluded from prayerlife.

This is why to the question whether loving or knowing comes first in prayerlife one author responds as follows.

> "They are in constant interaction, no one really comes first."[291]

---

[288] E.g., ST. TERESA OF AVILA clearly acknowledges it: "Algunos he topado que le parece está todo el negocio (de la oración) en el pensamiento.": *Fundaciones,* V, 2. Also ROLLE, p. 69, concludes his above-quoted text: "Hence those certain people are to be rebuked who are pleased with meditation rather than with prayer." The above-quoted text of *The Cloud of Unknowing* is explicit about recommending pure affective prayer only after the practice of meditation, not against it, because "anyone who expects to advance without having meditated often...will most certainly go astray and fail in his purpose.": *Ibid.,* p. 56.

[289] Cf. GREEN [1], pp. 31-32, 65, 87, 96. Cf. GREEN [2], pp. 45-48: "real prayer is *being with* the Lord (author's emphasis)" which is identified with the Teresian affective "prayer of quiet".

[290] GREEN [2], pp. 19-20, passim.

[291] MACQUARRIE, p. 34, note 6. If "really" could be understood as "absolutely" we would be willing to make this statement on our own. In fact, not absolutely but from different points of view and at different stages of development either knowing or

Indeed, authors who place more emphasis on loving than on knowing are willing to acknowledge that God grants the light necessary to perceive something of his Mystery even in the most affective prayer.

The unknown author of *The Cloud of Unknowing* is one of those who emphasize the role of love in prayer when, after the period dedicated to meditation, the praying Christian is drawn to contemplation. But in that very dark contemplation there is an "awareness" of God, even though "blind".

> "In the higher degree of contemplation all is darkness and a *cloud of unknowing.* Here one turns to God with a burning desire for himself alone and rests in the *blind awareness* of his naked being."[292] For in contemplation one "seems to know nothing and to feel nothing except a naked intent toward God in the depths of your being... For if in this life you hope *to feel and see God as he is in himself* it must be within this darkness and this cloud."[293]

The claim of the *Cloud* is shared by John of the Cross according to whom praying Christians cannot use their natural knowledge as "a proximate means of union with God".

> "If we speak of the supernatural, the understanding in its bodily prison has no preparation or capacity for receiving the clear knowledge of God; for such knowledge belongs not to this state, and we must either die or remain without receiving it...
>
> No supernatural apprehension or knowledge in this mortal state can serve as a proximate means to the high union of love with God.[294]

And though,

---

loving comes first in prayerlife.

[292] CLOUD, ch. 8, p. 59. Emphasis ours. Cf. "the very heart of this work is nothing else but a naked intent toward God for his own sake.": ch. 24, p. 80.

[293] *Ibid.,* ch. 3, pp. 48-49.

[294] CROSS [1], II, ch. 8, nn. 4-5, pp. 197-198.

> "In this darkness (of all natural knowledge) we experience *an intuitive understanding of everything material and spiritual* without giving any special attention to anything in particular."[295]

It is worth remembering that, also according to Ruysbroeck, the union of love with God which occurs in the highest graces of contemplation excludes reflective knowledge, but it does include profound intellectual insights.[296]

Similarly, after having stressed many times that "love is the essence of prayer", a contemporary author acknowledges that in affective prayer,

> "Our primary need will be to be with the Lord, whom we have come *to know and love.*"[297]

After all, the same Holy Spirit who infuses our hearts with charity towards God gives us also the knowledge of the Divine Mysteries.[298]

In conclusion, loving and knowing are both equally essential to the life of prayer and always intertwined within it, although in different proportions and fashions. And it could not be otherwise, as the very first Christian approach to God made by Christian faith essentially is the human trustful acceptance of God's gift and truth.[299] Faith is indeed knowledge born of love,

---

[295] CLOUD, ch. 68, p. 137. Emphasis ours. Hence, William Johnston, who edited the *Cloud,* wrote that, even though "the activity (of contemplation) the author speaks of *is a blend of both (knowledge and love)...* he has no doubt that its predominant element is love and it is upon this that he puts all the emphasis.": p. 21. Emphasis ours.

[296] Cf. OECHSLIN, p. 1444.

[297] GREEN [1], p. 96. Emphasis ours. Cf. the same author says that "praying [which] is essentially not knowing but loving" is "essentially Paschal's *knowledge* of the heart". Emphasis ours.

[298] Cf. Rm 5:5; Jn 14:17-26; 16:13. "Our Lord says to his disciples: 'I will not now call you servants but friends; because all things whatsoever I have heard from my Father I have made known to you' (Jn 15:15). Therefore sinceby the Holy Spirit we are established as friends of God, fittingly enough it is by the Holy Spirit that we are said to receive the revelation of the divine mysteries" (SCG, 4, 21, p. 123).

[299] JOHN PAUL II [4], # 51, p. 871: "Fides, pro intima sua essentia, est animi apertio coram dono; coram dono illo, quo Deum seipsum communicat in Spiritu

i.e., reached through that discernment of values which is made by a person in love.[300]

Therefore the very first Christian effort to know God in prayer is motivated by love for him. And when the love of God increases, the knowledge of him does too.

c. A greater importance and priority in time of knowing or loving?

After the examination of the opinions about the relation between knowing and loving in prayerlife, we would like to suggest our own solution to the problem involved in that relation. Given the complexity of the interconnections between knowing and loving and the different approaches and criteria of evaluation used for them, the solution cannot be simple, but must be found through two different approaches to the problem.

Actually, two approaches can be used to examine the relations between knowing and loving in prayer.

— The former minds the different natures of these two spiritual activities.

— The latter attends to their intertwinement in the growth process of prayerlife.

Bearing in mind the distinctive nature of knowing and loving we claim that the activity or prayer is effected by the impetus of love, whereas the specificity of it is due to the enlightenment of knowing.

— This contention applies to prayerlife Aquinas' attribution of the force which originates human acts to the will, and of the distinctive determination which human acts receive from their proper objects to the intellect.[301]

Sancto." Cf. ST, I, q. 111, a. 1, ad 1um: "Fides est habitus intellectus, quo disponitur ad oboediendum voluntati tendenti in divinam veritatem; intellectus enim assentit veritati fidei, non quasi convictus ratione, sed quasi imperatus a voluntate." Cf. I-II, q. 56, a. 3.

[300] Cf. LONERGAN, pp. 115-117.

[301] "The will moves the mind with respect to the exercise of activity because a being true – the object of the mind – is contained within the universal good as a part of particular good. But with respect to the form and meaning of activity, which is defined by its object, the mind sets the will in motion, for a good is perceived as a special sample included within the general range of being true." (I-II, q. 9, a. 1, ad 3um;

Aquinas himself makes this application when he explains the reciprocating motion of loving and knowing in contemplative life.[302]

As far as the growth process of prayerlife is concerned, a distinction must be made between the early and the advanced grades of it. At the beginning knowing precedes loving, because praying Christians cannot love God as the goal and object of their prayer unless he is in some way known to them.[303]

But the praying person who really knows God cannot but love him, and from the growth of this love springs out an experiential and personal knowledge of him.

This is also the teaching of the *Catechism of the Catholic Church,* where it describes the passage from meditation to orison, i.e., of that kind of prayer which St. Teresa of Avila defined as friendly sharing with the Lord.

> "Meditation is above all a search. The spirit seeks to understand the why and how of Christian life... Meditation engages thinking, imagination, emotions and desire... This form of praying reflection has a great value; but Christian prayer must have a further aim - the love knowledge of the Lord Jesus, union with him...
>
> Oraciòn seeks 'the love of my soul' (Sg 1:7), that is Jesus and, in him, the Father. He is sought, for the desire is always the beginning of love, and he is sought in pure faith, that faith which makes us be born from him and live in him. One may meditate in orison too, but [in orison] the gaze is at the Lord.[304]

BLACKFRIARS, vol. 17, p. 67).

[302] "Although the contemplative life consists essentially in the intellect, it has its beginning in the will, since one is prompted by charity to the contemplation of God. And since end corresponds to beginning, the terminus and end of contemplative life will also be found in the will, because one delights in seeing the object loved, and the very delight in the beloved arouses an even greater love. Thus Gregory says that *when one sees the person he loves he is more inflamed with a more ardent love.* And this is the ultimate realization of contemplative life, namely that the divine truth should not only be seen but loved also." (II-II, q. 180, a. 7, ad 1um; BLACKFRIARS, vol. 49, p. 45.)

[303] "No one can in any way love a thing that is totally unknown" (ST. AUGUSTINE, *The Trinity,* X, i, 1, p. 291). "Good...can be loved only when one has knowledge of it" (ST, I-II, q. 27, a. 2, co.; BLACKFRIARS, vol. 19, p. 79).

[304] CCC, nn. 2705, 2708-2709 passim.

So, the growth process of prayerlife develops from knowing God in meditation to gaining a love-knowledge of him in orison. And the love-knowledge gained by practicing orison greatly increases the knowledge of him previously obtained through meditation.

> "The understanding is the most noble aspect of the soul. It is moved by affection, and it in turn nourishes affection... The more they [i.e., praying Christians] know, the more they love, and the more they love, the more they know. Thus each nourishes the other."[305]

Here is a clear summary of knowing coming before loving at the beginning, and of the later process of loving increasing knowing and more knowing increasing loving in prayerlife.

> "Love comes out of knowledge and not knowledge out of love: It is said that the glory of a soul consists in the first place in the knowledge and sight of God, with love: and the more he is known, the better he is loved.
>
> But as the soul cannot come to this knowledge - or to this love that comes from it - without love, I therefore said that you should desire only love, for love is the cause of the soul's coming to this sight and to this knowledge."[306]

In sum, granted that prayer essentially requires both knowing and loving, to the question whether some greater importance should be given to one or the other of its two essential components we can finally answer:

a) A different greater importance is due to each one of prayer's two essential components in consideration of their distinct natures. In prayer knowing has a greater importance as regards the orientation of prayer towards the true God, but loving has a greater importance as far as the motivation of prayer is concerned.

---

[305] DIALOGUE, chs. 50 and 85, pp. 103 and 157. This growth process verifies in prayerlife the mutual influences of intellect and will in human acts. "These powers (i.e., intellect and will) include each other within the scope of their acts. For the understanding knows that the will wills and the will wills the understanding to understand. And in the same way the idea of good falls within the idea of truth, in that it is a truth understood, while true is contained under good, in that it is a particular good to desire" (ST, I, q. 82, a. 4, ad 1um; BLACKFRIARS, vol. 11, p. 229-231).

[306] HILTON, II, ch. 34, pp. 263.

The special importance, and yet necessity of knowing in prayerlife derives from the fact that Christian prayer cannot be genuine, i.e., addressed to the true God, unless it is enlightened by the true knowledge of him who was revealed by Jesus Christ.[307]

> "True worshippers will worship the Father in spirit and in truth; that is the kind of worshipper the Father wants."[308]

Accordingly, one of the earliest theologians of Christian prayer contended that:

> "The person who does not think the truth about God or his Christ has fallen away from the true God and his only begotten Son. By supposing what his stupidity has fabricated to be the Father and the Son, he does not really worship."[309]

On the other hand, the particular importance and necessity of loving in prayerlife derives from the fact that prayer would not really unite the praying Christian with God, unless the knowledge of God attained by it impels the knower to love him.

> "Considerations and forms and manners of meditation are necessary to beginners, *in order that they may gradually feed and enkindle their souls with love.*"[310]

---

[307] As HAPPOLD, pp. 35-36, acknowledges, the experiences and conclusions of the mystics are deemed "of high relevance in the age-long effort of mankind to penetrate the ultimate secret of the universe, and of his own nature and destiny." And he adds that the term *theologia mystica* used by Christian medieval theologians "meant a particular type of insight and knowledge of God."

[308] Jn 4:23. About the meaning of "worship in spirit and in truth" JB comments: "The Spirit (14:26+), who makes a new creature of man (3:5), is also the inspiring principle of the new worship of God. *This worship is 'in truth' because it is the only worship that meets the conditions revealed by God through Jesus."* Emphasis ours.

[309] ORIGEN, *On Prayer,* XXIX, # 10, pp. 155-156. Also CDF: LETTER emphatically states – "Est praeponenda maximi momenti sententia, Christiana oratio semper Christianae fidei structurae innititur, in qua ipsa de Deo atque creatura veritas elucet.": n. 3.

[310] CROSS [1], II, XII, 5, p. 216. Emphasis ours.

> "Because in this life *only love can touch God as he is in himself, never knowledge.*"[311]

In summary: praying Christians must first confront the challenge of God'stranscendent Truth knowing him by sheer faith before they can be united to his infinite Goodness by charity.[312]

b) Knowing and loving alternate in the growth process of prayerlife. Christian prayer must be enlightened by Christian truth. So, knowing the truth about God must come first to authenticate Christian prayer.[313] However, in genuine prayer the knowledge of God leads to and feeds love toward him. Hence, when the growth process of prayerlife has gone beyond its first beginning, loving God takes precedence in Christian prayer.

The change from using mostly the mind at the beginning to using mostly the heart when one has progressed in prayerlife is clearly pointed out by the Medieval *Ladder of Monks:*

> "Reading is the *careful study* of the Scriptures, concentrating all one's powers in it. Meditation is the *busy application of the mind to seek with the help of one's own reason* for knowledge of hidden truth.

---

[311] CLOUD, ch. 8, pp. 39-40. Emphasis ours. Founded on the teaching of the New Testament. Aquinas often insists on the union with God caused by charity. "It is not knowledge alone, but charity, which does away with the estrangement from God caused by sin. Consequently *charity, loving God, knits the soul to him without any intermediary in a bond of spiritual union*" (II-II, q. 227, a. 4, ad 3um; BLACKFRIARS, vol. 34, p. 173). "A sympathy, or connaturality, with divine things, results from charity which unites us with God; *he who is joined to the Lord is one spirit with him'* (1 Cor 6:17)" (*Ibid.*, q. 45, a. 2, co.; BLACKFRIARS, vol. 35, p. 167). All emphases ours.

[312] This is apparently symbolized by the wrestling of Jacob with God throughout the whole night. At dawn Jacob begged God to tell his name: he was not told God's name, but was blessed by God. Cf. Gn 32:23-29.

[313] This claim is laid on praying Christians, who can know the truth about God by reading the Scripture and listening to the Magisterium. When they do not, so that the knowledge of God involved in their prayer counters scriptural and magisterial teaching, one can be sure that such prayer is not authentically Christian. But the same blame is not incurred by those faultless non-Christians, whose knowledge of God can hardly be without any error. The imperfect and blurred knowledge of God that in good faith they can afford may suffice to render their prayer as genuine as it can be.

> Prayer is the *heart's devoted turning* to God to drive away evil and obtain what is good. Contemplation is when the mind is in some sort lifted up to God and held above itself, so that it *tastes the joy* of everlasting sweetness.[314]
>
> "Reading is an exercise of the *outward senses;* meditation is concerned with *inward understanding;* prayer is concerned with *desire;* contemplation outstrips every faculty. The first degree is proper to beginners, the second to proficients, the third to devotees, the fourth to the blessed."[315]

And we said "mostly" and not "exclusively", for the heart's desire is active from the very first rung of *The Ladder,* as it manifestly appears from the following text:

> Reading *seeks for the sweetness of a blessed life,* meditation perceives it, prayer asks for it, contemplation tastes it.[316]

Indeed, it is the pursuit of "the sweetness of a blessed life" which renders both reading and meditation, which without this pursuit would be merely intellectual exercises, rungs of the ladder of prayer.

> "The good and the wicked alike can read and meditate; and even pagan philosophers by the use of reason discovered the highest and truest good. But they had not the grace to understand what they had the ability to see."[317]

So, all the rungs, even though "they differ in order and quality,"[318] make up only one "ladder of prayer" by which praying Christians "are lifted up from earth to heaven, for its lower end rests upon the earth, but its top pierces the clouds and touches heavenly secrets."[319]

In a word, all the rungs are four states of only one prayerlife.

---

[314] GUIGO II, II, p. 82. Emphasis ours.

[315] *Ibid.* XII, p. 93. Emphasis ours.

[316] *Ibid.,* III, p. 83. Emphasis ours.

[317] *Ibid.,* V, p. 85.

[318] *Ibid.,* II, p. 82.

[319] *Ibid.,* II, p. 82.

> "They are so linked together, each one working also for others, that the first degrees are of little or no use without the last, while the last can never, or hardly ever, be won without the first."[320]

Hence the following practical conclusion:

> "Let the soul rest now in one (degree), now in another, as the circumstances of time and place suggest to its free choice, even though, it seems to me, the soul is nearer to God the farther it climbs from the first degree."[321]

A contemporary author repeats that same older teaching:

> "The first stage of prayer is getting to know the Lord and ourselves, for true love is grounded on a real knowledge, gradually acquired, of the Lord and of ourselves...
>
> (But) it is not this knowledge which is the core of mature prayer's experience. More and more, knowledge becomes the handmaid of love, the intellect the handmaid of the heart. We begin to realize clearly that praying is essentially not knowing but loving the Lord – that knowing of Jn 17:3, which is equated with eternal life, is essentially Pascal's knowledge of the heart."[322]

At the latter stage of prayerlife mentioned by this author, the increased love of God grows to an affective knowledge of him, and, again, that knowledge increases the love of him...and so on. In short, the Christian life as such must begin with the practice of the virtue of faith, understood as the intellect's assent to the Divine Truth, so that a genuine charity can flow from that assent and bring it to completion. Likewise the Christian who begins a life of prayer must first practice meditation in order to increase his or her faith-knowledge of God, so that a genuine love of charity toward God may lead to contemplation, which is the completion of Christian prayerlife.

---

[320] *Ibid.*, XIII, p. 93.

[321] *Ibid.*, XIV, p. 96.

[322] GREEN [2], p. 19 and note 7.

ii. *Knowing and Loving in the Attitude of Prayerfulness*

In chapter two and three of this book different mind's attentions and heart's intentions of prayerlife were distinguished, described, and explained. The scope of our study encompassed even the subconscious or subliminal level of the human mind and heart.

Recalling what we wrote there, we now contend that the subconscious attention or being-aware-of and the subliminally deliberate intention or being-in-love-with God in prayerlife actually merge into a single permanent attitude of prayerfulness.

The distinction of the various mind's attentions and heart's intentions involved in the actual practice of prayer has clarifying value at the level of the human psyche, where explicit consciousness and deliberation occur. But that distinction makes little sense for the attitude of prayerfulness, which is situated in the depths of the soul where consciousness sinks into the unconscious and deliberate becomes subliminal.[323]

a. *A unified knowing and loving experience*

The description given by St. Thérèse of the Child Jesus can be taken as a confirmation that prayer in action is a unified prayerful attitude of mind and heart -

> "To me prayer is an *élan* of the heart, a simple *gaze* cast towards heaven.[324]

---

[323] In his Introduction to the CLOUD, Johnston, pp. 21-22, writes, "For the purpose of analysis it is possible to speak of knowledge and love in contemplation; but the activity the author speaks about is a blend of both, *a completely simple experience arising in the depth of the contemplative's heart: in the last analysis it is indescribable,* as the author declares when he says that 'Whatever we may say of it is not it, but only about it (p. 169)'." However, notwithstanding the indescribableness of such experience, Johnston goes on writing: "He (= the author of the Cloud) has no doubt, however, that its predominant element is love and it is upon this that he puts all the emphasis... *love which, however, is accompanied by a deep consciousness of God."* Emphasis ours.

[324] Quoted by CCC, n. 2558. Emphasis ours.

As a matter of spiritual fact, at the profound center of our being mind and heart melt[325] and produce

> "A knowledge of the heart, too deep not only for our words but for our own perceptions: although the mind is dark and blank, we do 'know' at another level 'the love of Christ which surpasses all knowledge'."[326]

The center referred to here is the innermost kernel and hotbed of spiritual life, from which our knowledge and love of God (i.e., the activity of theological faith, hope and charity and, according to Aquinas, of the seven gifts of the Holy Spirit) flow into one single prayerful response to him.

At the subconscious (or superconscious) level of the human spirit where such a prayerful attitude occurs our knowing and loving God merge and fuse into a single experience of him and can hardly be distinguished from each other. Here the distinctness of the human intellect and will cause by the differentiation of their proper objects, as it were, vanishes.

Such a unified spiritual response to God is the most appropriate we can give him, in whom transcendental truth and goodness are amalgamated into only one Godhead. Indeed, in the beatific vision we shall eternally give God this kind of perfectly unified knowing and loving response.

> "It would be possible to say that the (beatific) vision of God and the exchange of love with Him takes place *at the deepest level of the spirit where knowing and loving are not yet the separate faculties Aristotelian philosophy makes of them.*
>
> According to the Scripture, it is the heart which sees God. This is *the very center of man's being, where knowledge and love are one.* Paul says that love will endure forever, while knowledge disappears (1 Co 13:8-13). We must also remember that the Reality that is seen is Love itself, which allows itself to be seen only in an immediate exchange of love."[327]

The profound attitude of prayerfulness, which is imprinted in the subconscious center of our spirit by our knowing and loving God in our conscious acts of prayer, can, therefore, be considered as an anticipation of the

---

325 Cf. LOUF, p. 20.

326 BOULDING, p. 93.

327 SCHMAUS, p. 267. Emphasis ours. See also POZO, p. 211 ff.

"beatific vision", while we are walking on earth "by faith and not by sight, exiled from the Lord".[328]

b. Confirmation from Scripture and Tradition

The New Testament supports the contention that in the profound attitude of prayerfulness knowing and loving merge and are amalgamated.

> "We can be sure that we *know* God only by keeping his commandment... When anyone does obey what he has said, God's *love* comes to perfection in him... Everyone who *loves* is begotten by God and *knows* God. Anyone who fails to *love* can never have *known* God, because God is *love*... We ourselves have *known* and put our faith in God's *love* towards ourselves. God is *love* and anyone who *lives in love lives in God, and God lives in him.*"[329]
>
> "Christ may live in your hearts through faith, and then, *planted in love and built on love you will be knowing the love of Christ, which is beyond all knowledge,* and be filled with the utter fullness of God.[330]

The fusion of our knowing and loving God into only one response of prayer to him is a common tenet of the mystical theology of the Eastern Church.[331] In the Western Church such great Doctors as St. Augustine, St. Gregory the Great, and St. Bernard emphatically state that love itself is the cognizance that, by grace, we have of God.[332]

In the same vein, the late Abbé Monchanin incisively wrote.

---

[328] 2 Co 5:6.

[329] 1 Jn 2:3, 5; 4:7, 8, 16.

[330] Ep 3:17-19.

[331] Cf. LOSSKY.

[332] St. Augustine, *De Gratia Novi Testamenti,* Epist. CXL, c. 18. PL 33, 557: "Sapientia est caritas Dei." ST. GREGORY THE GREAT, *Homiliae in Evangelium,* 14, 3. PL 76, 1129: "Qui enim veritatem non diligit, adhuc minime cognovit." *Ibid.,* 24, 7. PL 76, 1207: "Amata jam novimus, quia amor ipse notitia est." ST. BERNARD, *Sermones de Diversis,* 29. PL 183, 620; *Sermones in Cantica,* 82, 8. PL 183, 181. Cf. LECLERCQ, especially p. 207 ff. Se also NARDINI, p. 215.

> "Let us keep alive the flame of thought and love: they are *one and the same flame.*"[333]

The author of *The Cloud of Unknowing* explains that God, who is infinite, and therefore cannot be fully comprehended by our knowledge, can be embraced and grasped by love. That is the "unending miracle of love"!

> "It is God, and God alone, who can fully satisfy the hunger and longing of our spirit, which transformed by his redeeming grace is enabled to embrace him by love.
>
> He whom neither men nor angels can grasp by knowledge can be embraced by love. For the intellect of both men and angels is too small to comprehend God as he is in himself... *Nobody can fully comprehend the uncreated God with his knowledge, but each one, in a different way can grasp it fully by love.*
>
> Truly this is the unending miracle of love: that one loving person, through his love, can embrace God, whose being fills and transcends the entire creation."[334]

A contemporary Catholic theologian entitled one of his many books on mysticism *The Inner Eye of Love.* And in it he claims that,

> All (mystics of the great religions of East and West) are aware that man has a third eye, an inner eye, *the eye of the heart, the eye of wisdom, the eye of love.* When this eye is awakened, man, blind from birth, sees the real glory and beauty and meaning of the universe."[335]

The inner eye of love can see the ultimate meaning of the universe because

---

[333] Quoted by MERTON, p. 47. See also DUNNE S. JOHN, especially pp. 46-54. Remember C.S. Eliot's words: "Lovers...think the same thought without the need of speech/ and babble the same speech without the need of meaning." Quoted in *LOVE,* p. 175.

[334] CLOUD, ch. 4, p. 50; cf. ch. 6, pp. 54-55; ch. 68, p. 136. Emphasis ours.

[335] JOHNSTON [1], p. 9. Emphasis ours. Bernard Lonergan called faith itself "the eye of love." Cf. DUNNE T., p. 118. Such a definition is not far from the concept of faith of Aquinas who writes: "To believe is an act of the mind assenting to the divine truth by virtue of the command of the will as this is moved by God through grace" (II-II, q. 2, a. 9, co.; BLACKFRIARS, vol. 31, p. 97).

> "The Ultimate Mystery of being, the Ultimate Truth is Love. Love is the essential structure of Reality."[336]

The late Catherine de Hueck Doherty identified prayer with the heart's watchfulness toward God:

> "Prayer is a man sleeping while his heart watches."[337]

In writing these words, she might have remembered the words of the bride in the Song of Songs:

> "I sleep but my heart is awake. I hear my beloved knocking."[338]

Perhaps the old Latin hymns at Compline in the Liturgy of the Hours resounded in her ears.[339] In any case, the point that she wants to make is quite clear - There is a prayer, which in her opinion is prayer par excellence, by which we "know" God by keeping a watchful heart, even when our intellectual conscious knowledge of him is, as it were, asleep.

This is traditional mystical theology in a nutshell.

> "This is the wakeful sleep of the spouse...the heart is awake, for it is keen and prompt to love Jesus and see him."[340]

> "The Bride declares in the Song that among the effects which that sleep and forgetfulness of herself produced was this unknowing... Although the soul in this state of knowledge believes itself to be doing nothing, and to be entirely unoccupied, because it is working neither with the senses nor with the faculties, it should realize that it is not wasting time. For, although the

---

[336] GRIFFITHS, [2], p. 60.

[337] Words printed on a prayer card. By prayer she manifestly means not a particular conscious act of prayer but the lasting subconscious attitude of prayerfulness.

[338] Sg 5:2.

[339] "Somno si dantur oculi/ cor ad Te semper vigilent... Te nostra corda somnient, te per soporem sentiant." LITURGIA, vol. I, p. 538.

[340] HILTON, II, ch. 40, p. 284.

> harmony of the faculties of the soul may cease, its intelligence is as we have said.[341]
>
> For this cause the Bride, who was wise, answered this question herself in the Song, saying: *Ego dormio et cor meum vigilat.* As though she were to say: Although I sleep with respect to my natural self, ceasing to labour, my heart waketh, being supernaturally lifted up in a supernatural knowledge."[342]

A contemporary theologian repeats this traditional teaching,

> "Mystical knowledge is not an intellectual knowledge, but one that comes to the soul pierced by the desire of beauty, goodness and union with God... it is a knowledge which is more the fruit of desire and love than intellectual study."[343]

But, as John of the Cross points out,[344] "putting to sleep" the intellect does not mean that the intellect is altogether excluded from contemplative, mystical prayer. After all, what is happening at this prayer grade is not only a perfect loving but also a real and very lofty knowing.

This is why Thomistic theologians have always maintained the essential involvement of the intellect in the love-knowledge of God reached through the Holy Spirit's gift of wisdom, from which, as they say, contemplative prayer is elicited.

> "The gift of wisdom was taken (by them) to be a knowing by connaturality, arising out of a love for God in which the very love acts as the formal medium for knowledge: it was a love-knowledge, akin to the sort of knowing at work in aesthetic experience but surpassing that in virtue of its being an awareness of a person.

---

[341] I.e., "...the soul has been united in pure intelligence, which belongs not to time... and it pierces the heavens, because the soul is united in heavenly intelligence; and when the soul awakens, this knowledge leaves in it the effects which it created in it without it being conscious of them, which effects are the lifting up of the spirit to the heavenly intelligence, and its withdrawal and abstraction from all things and forms and figures and memories thereof.": CROSS [1], II, ch. 14, pp. 230-231.

[342] *Ibid.*, pp. 231-232.

[343] FARRELLY, pp. 107-108.

[344] See note 71 of this chapter.

Aquinas calls it a 'quasi-experimental knowledge'[345] because it wells up from the very presentiality of the beloved: Bonaventure describes it with the illuminating word "cointuition".[346]

In fact, St. John of the Cross explicitly refers to this teaching of Aquinas when he describes the "dark contemplation and secret wisdom" infused into the soul by the Holy Spirit -

> "This dark contemplation ... is mystical theology, which theologians call secret wisdom, and which, as St. Thomas says, is communicated and infused into the soul through love."[347]

As it is manifest from this phrase, the mystical Doctor likes to use paradoxes. In fact, he says that "contemplation and wisdom" are knowledge, but, at the same time, are "dark and secret", as if there were no clear knowledge involved. How can such an apparent contradiction occur in contemplative prayer?

John responds to this question quite extensively. On the one hand, this contemplation is *dark and secret,* because it is infused into praying Christians.

> "So as to be hidden from the work of the understanding" and "the soul can neither speak of it and give it a name whereby it may be called, nor find any suitable manner or similitude by which it may be able to describe it", as "all the terms and words which are used in this life are base, defective and inapt to make us perceive it as it is".
>
> "The capacity of being described is not in the nature of pure contemplation, which is indescribable, for which reason it is called secret."

But on the other hand, this contemplation is *clear and lofty* wisdom.

> "[It is] an illumination of the soul, to whom this wisdom is communicated most clearly *(más a las claras se le comunica)."* "Such a lofty understanding *(inteligencia tan subida)* and such delicate spiritual feeling, inward and so simple, is so general and so spiritual that the soul is clearly

---

345 Cf. PATFOORT and note 79 below.

346 HILL, p. 304.

347 The editor of the book of St. John of the Cross adds the following note - "Propter hoc Gregorius (*Hom.,* 14, in Ezech.) constituit vitam contemplativam in caritate Dei." Cf. ST, II-II, q. 45, a. 2, co.

> aware that it is experiencing and partaking *(claramente ve y entiende y gusta)* in that same and delectable wisdom."
>
> "And so greatly does this abyss of wisdom raise up and exalt the soul, making it to penetrate the veins of the science of love *(metiéndola en las venas de la ciencia de amor)* as to give her a supreme knowledge and divine feeling by which Divine things and perfections are known and understood as they are."[348]

Nothing better affirms and explains the fusion of knowledge and love in contemplative prayer – and in the profound attitude of prayerfulness, which results from contemplative prayer – than these clarifications of the great mystical Doctor.

c. *Confirmations from modern psychology*

An important confirmation to this theory – not unknown to the above quoted theologians[349] – comes from contemporary psychologists, who teach that,

> "Love is active penetration of the other person. In the act of union I know you and I know nothing. I know in the only way knowledge of that which is alive is possible to man – by experiential union and not by the knowledge our thoughts can give...
>
> The only way to full knowledge lies in the act of love: this act transcends thought, it transcends words. It is the daring plunge into the experience of union. However, knowledge in thought, that is psychological knowledge, is a necessary condition for full knowledge in the act of love."[350]

---

[348] All the words quoted are a sort of mosaic of prayers drawn from CROSS [2], II, ch. 17, pp. 158-164.

[349] When JOHNSTON [1], p. 24, writes: "In human relations love can discover beauty and potentiality that reason alone cannot find," he shows himself aware of contemporary psychology's understanding of the special "knowing" role played by love in interpersonal relationships. Also Aquinas seems to imply that the understanding of natural interpersonal love can by analogy help us to catch a glimpse of how supernatural charity works, when he contends that charity is a certain friendship *(quaedam amicitia:* ST, II-II, q. 23, a. 1, co.) with him.

[350] FROMM, pp. 25-26.

> "Love is the only way to grasp another human being in the innermost core of his personality. Nobody can become fully aware of the very essence of another human being unless he loves him. By the spiritual act of love he is enabled to see the essential traits and features in the beloved person."[351]

Unassumingly the *Little Prince* clearly states the same psychological truth:

> "It is only with the heart that one can see rightly: what is essential is invisible to the eye."[352]

Why love is the only way to know another human being as a person, why it allows a penetration of the other person by experiential union, is clearly explained by a Thomist philosopher.

> "Union in love makes the being we love another ourself for us, another subjectivity that is ours. to the degree we truly love (which is to say, not for ourselves but for the beloved: and when – which is not always the case – the intellect within us becomes passive as regards love, and, allowing its concepts to slumber, thereby renders love a formal means of knowledge), to this degree we acquire an obscure knowledge of the being we love, similar to that which we possess of ourselves; we know that being in the very subjectivity (at least in a certain measure) by this experience of union."[353]

Thomas Merton summarizes this complex explanation with his usual clarity:

> "Love is only possible between persons as persons...and in that case my relationship to you is not merely the relationship of a subject to an object, but it is analogous to my relationship to myself."[354]

In other words, when I love you as I love myself, I "internalize" you into my very self, and my love for you in some way makes me know and love you as directly as I know and love myself. Did not Jesus himself hint at this

---

[351] FRANKL, pp. 176-177.

[352] DE SAINT-EXUPERY, p. 87.

[353] MARITAIN [3], p. 84.

[354] MERTON [2], p. 7.

kind of love-knowledge when he said of the Holy Spirit, "You know him, because he is with you, he is in you"[355]?

Conclusion

The whole question about the distinctive roles played by knowledge and love in the life of prayer concerns the acts produced during the practice of prayer, at the conscious and deliberate level of the human psyche by the mind and by the heart, by the intellect and by the will, understood as two faculties distinguished from one another.

But in the subconscious and subliminally deliberate center of the spirit, where the practice of prayer hands over the management of Christian life to the profound attitude of prayerfulness, mind and heart, intellect and will, knowledge and love, as it were, melt and are recast into only one mould, which is the profoundly personal and mysteriously immediate encounter of the prayerful Christian with God.

So, at this depth (one could equally well call it height) of the spirit the discussions, which have gone on for centuries, about whether knowledge should reign over love or love over knowledge appear useless, as they do not make much sense. Just as it wold not make much sense to ask whether one who is drinking a cup of coffee on a cold winter day savors first and most enjoys either the taste or the warmth of it.

Christian theologians since the early centuries have virtually taught the melting of knowing and loving God in prayer by means of their theory on the "spiritual senses", which Aquinas developed in his "experiential knowledge" of the Divine Persons.[356] Doubtless, when Aquinas focuses his attention on the conscious and deliberate level of the human psyche – which he does most of

---

[355] Jn 14:17.

[356] "(There is) affective and experimental knowledge of divine goodness and loving-kindness, whereby a person experiences within himself the taste of God's sweetness and the delight in his loving. Dyonisius says that *Hierotheus learnt divine things by sympathy* (*De Divinis Nominibus* 2, 9, PG 3, 648). It is in this way that we are told to prove God's will and to taste his sweetness." (ST, II-II, q. 97, a. 2, ad 2um; BLACKFRIARS, vol. 40, p. 93-95).

the time - he always makes a real distinction between intellect and will, attributing a certain supremacy to the former.[357]

But Christians who are animated by the profound attitude of prayerfulness respond to the Divine Persons at the subconscious (or superconscious) level of their psyche, and at that spiritual depth (or height) the Divine Persons cannot be met by distinct intellectual concepts and affections.

> "This dark contemplation is mystical theology, which theologians call secret wisdom, and which, as St. Thomas says, is communicated and infused into the soul through love. This happens secretly and in darkness, so as to be hidden from the work of the understanding and of the other faculties.
>
> Wherefore, inasmuch as the faculties aforementioned attain not to it, but the Holy Spirit infuses and orders it in the soul, as says the Bride in the Song, without either its knowledge or its understanding, it is called secret...
>
> The Master Who teaches the soul is within it in its substance, to which the devil may not attain, neither may the natural senses nor understanding."[358]

Indeed, the "secret wisdom" of "mystical theology" described by John of the Cross and the "experiential knowledge" taught by Aquinas try to explain the selfsame lofty prayer in which knowing and loving God melt into only one mystical experience.

---

[357] Eg., "Will and intellect mutually include one another; for intellect understands will, and will wills intellect to understand" (I, q. 16, a. 4, co.; BLACKFRIARS, vol. 4, p. 85-87.)

[358] CROSS [2], II, 17, no. 2, pp. 158-159.

CHAPTER V

PRAYER AS ASCENT

In the preceding chapters the many elements which make up Christian prayerlife, especially its *spiritual forces and powers,* were considered. This consideration, although fundamental, is insufficient. It does not directly and explicitly focus on Christian prayerlife as essentially referred to God.

In order to get a more adequate understanding of Christian prayerlife we must now follow two other avenues of research. One of them will lead us to consider the praying person's approaches to God, and the other to study the relationships with God, which can be established and cultivated by those approaches.

Christian spiritual masters have acknowledged that,

> "There are as many kinds of prayers as there are states of souls, as many kinds of prayers as there are souls."[359]
>
> "The attitude of prayer is the same for all, but there are many kinds of prayer and many different prayers."[360]
>
> "Doubtless, there are as many pathways of prayer as persons who pray, even though the same Spirit acts in and with all... The Lord leads each person in the roads and ways which He likes. And each of the faithful, on his or her part, responds to Him according to the resolutions of his or her heart and the personal expressions of his or her prayer...(e.g.) the methods of meditation are as many as the spiritual masters."[361]

Consequently, the term "prayer" can be taken in so many different senses that the various predicates and qualifications one attributes to it are not likely to be false, unless they are obviously mere nonsense. On the other hand, when one compares the statements spiritual authors make to describe and define prayer with the extremely rich, vast, and variegated prayerlife of Christians, one gets the impression that neither a single one of those statements nor many of them can suffice to express the whole truth about prayer.

---

[359] CASSIAN, IX, 8. CHADWICK, p. 218.

[360] CLIMACUS [2], 28, p. 273.

[361] CCC, 2672, 2699, 2707.

This is why an author warns against

> "Stifling the dynamism of the reality of prayer within the confines of a definition, for no one description can possibly capture the totality of the phenomenon.[362]

And another adds that

> "There is always a danger in overdefinition, because it tends to freeze what should be moving and often kills what has meaning only when it is alive. Even though this danger does not excuse us from the work of trying to think as clearly as possible and to construct some patterns which can be understood by others."[363]

And yet, anyone who sets out on a prayer journey does well to be equipped with a sound and clear understanding of prayer, because the meaning and value of one's experience of prayer could otherwise be missed or misconstrued. The lack of such sound and clear understanding of prayer caused much uncertainty and anxiety even to such a great and holy practitioner of prayer as Teresa of Avila, who confessed to suffering

> "Much unrest, afflictions, and terrible trials through lack of knowledge, for not understanding herself,"[364]

i.e., her own prayer experience.

Precisely in order to find a remedy for that lack of knowledge, we will try, to the best of our ability, to catch the whole of Christian prayerlife in a network woven out of its most relevant forms. We hope that such a network will give profound comprehension of the fabric of Christian prayerlife into which its fundamental components, studied in the foregoing chapters, are built. The result to be expected from this attempt is a clear understanding and a balanced evaluation of each and every major form of Christian prayerlife within a systematic theory of it.

---

[362] BERGANT, p. 8.

[363] SLADE, p. 26.

[364] *Interior Castle,* IV, 1.

There are two ways of looking at Christian prayerlife. It can be envisaged as coming down *from above,* from God to us, as his call, offer, gift.[365] Actually, in prayer, as well as in the whole Christian life,

> "God is the first to call the human person... The true and living God unceasingly calls each person to the mysterious encounter with Him in prayer. This step of God's faithful love always comes first: the human person's step is always a response. While God gradually reveals himself and reveals the human person to him or herself, prayer appears as a mutual appeal, an event of the Covenant. Through words and acts this event engages the heart. It manifests itself throughout all the history of salvation."[366]

However, neither can we have a prayerlife unless with determination *we* make time and learn to do it.[367]

And so Christian prayerlife can be considered as a human activity through which, both communally and privately,[368] one strives to get closer to God. Looking at prayerlife in this way, *from below upwards,* we see that it has two dimensions: the operational and the relational.

We call the former *operational,* insofar as prayerlife is acted out or performed by the praying Christian. We call the latter *relational,* insofar as prayerlife aims at establishing some relationship between the praying Christian and God.[369]

The operational dimension of Christian prayerlife produces two distinctive although complementary sequences of acts: Those performed in order to ascend towards God and those performed in order to address oneself to him. Hence one can further distinguish,

---

[365] Cf. CCC, nn. 2558-2564.

[366] CCC, n. 2567.

[367] Cf. *Ibid.,* nn. 2650 and 2710.

[368] "Communal prayer seems to have been customary in the primitive Church, both in public worship (1 Co 11:4 f; 14:13-16, 26) and in smaller gatherings (Mt 18:19), where Jesus attaches a special promise to communal prayer: (Ac 2:46 f; 12:12), though private prayer is the fountainhead of prayer in general (Mt 6:6); Jesus frequently prayed alone (Mt 14:23; Mk 1:35; Lk 5:16; 6:12; 9:18).": DNNT, vol. III, p. 869.

[369] BARILE, pp. 134-145, suggests a cataloging of all forms of prayer according to subjective, progressive, and objective criteria. The subjective criterion is similar to our operational dimension. The objective criterion resembles our relational dimension.

— in the operational dimension an *ascending* and an *addressing* form of praying.
— in the relational dimension a *worshipping* and a *communing* form of praying.

In the following chapters we will treat each one of these forms.

* * *

God is not easily attainable by human beings. He is not one of the innumerable objects of our direct knowledge and love. We call him the Supreme, the Transcendent, the Most High, etc. In a word, he is the Creator far above all creatures. Hence, praying Christians must reach beyond creatures for "heaven" where God is said to abide - "Our Father who art in heaven"! "Heaven", though, is a biblical figure of speech.

> "[It] does not mean a place ['the space'], but a mode of being: not the remoteness of God but his majesty... Our Father is not 'elsewhere': he is 'beyond'all we can conceive of his holiness.[370] But, precisely because he is the thrice Holy, he is quite near to the humble and contrite heart."[371]

Hence, in prayer we must start from the "depths" of our sins, crying for help to God with humility and contrition.[372]

We mean all this when we claim that Christian prayer is a spiritual ascent.

i. *The Bible's Descriptions of Prayer as Ascent*

a. The Old Testament's teaching

---

[370] Cf. CCC, n. 2809: "God's holiness is the inaccessible center of his eternal mystery."

[371] CCC, n. 2794.

[372] Cf. Ps 130: CCC, n. 2559: "Humility is the foundation of prayer... It is the necessary disposition to receive gratuitously the (divine) gift of prayer." See also the parable of the pharisee and tax collector (Lk 18:9-14) recalled *Ibid.*, n. 2613.

Yahweh, the God of Israel "lives above the circle of the earth" and "reigns transcendent in the heights".[373] But he is especially prayed to in the Temple built in Jerusalem on the summit of Mount Zion, the earthly dwelling place of God.

> "Yahweh is in his holy Temple, Yahweh whose throne is in heaven."[374]

1. Stretching out the hands and lifting up the eyes

Soul and body acted together when the Israelites prayed to their God. So, to mean "praying" the Bible can simply write "keeping one's arms raised".

> "As long as Moses kept his *arms raised,* Israel had the advantage [in the battle]; when he let his arms fall, the advantage went to Amalek. But Moses arms grew heavy...so Aaron and Hur supported his arms, one on one side, one on the other; and his arms remained firm until sunset."[375]

Often the phrases "stretching out or raising hands" are joined to words which explicitly signify prayer, with or without a reference to the Jerusalem Temple.

> "When you *stretch out your hands*...you may multiply your *prayers.*" "Loudly I cry to God, loudly to God who hears me. When in trouble I sought the Lord, all night long I *stretched out my hands."*
>
> "Yahweh, I am calling, hurry to me, listen to me, I am invoking you. My *prayers rise* like incense, my *hands* like the evening offering."
>
> "Solomon stood before the altar of Yahweh and *stretched out his hands...he stretched out his hands to heaven,* and said, 'Yahweh, God of Israel, etc."
>
> *"Stretch out your hands* towards the Sanctuary, bless Yahweh night and day." "Hear my voice, *raised in petition,* as I cry to you for help, as I *raise my hands,* Yahweh, towards your Holy of Holies."[376]

---

[373] Is 40:22; Ps 93:4.

[374] Ps 11:4.

[375] Ex 17:11-12; cf. Dt 32:40.

[376] Is 1:15; Ps 77:1-2; Ps 141:1-2; 2 Ch 6:12-13; Ps 134:2; Ps 28:2.

Indeed, Yahweh's throne is in heaven, but he

> "Has leaned down from the heights of the Sanctuary, has *looked down at earth* from heaven." "The *eyes of the Lord watch over those who love him,* he is their powerful protection and their strong support... He gives healing, life and blessing."
>
> "The *eye of Yahweh is on those who fear him, on those who rely on his love,* to rescue their souls from death and keep them alive in famine."[377]

Hence, lifting the eyes to heaven and fixing them on Yahweh, as if to meet his caring looking down at the earth at his people who pray to him, characterizes the Israelite's prayer.

> *"My eyes are always on Yahweh,* for he releases my feet from the net."
>
> *"I keep Yahweh before me always,* for with him at my right hand nothing can shake me."
>
> *"I lift my eyes to you,* to you who have your home in heaven; my eyes like the eyes of slaves fixed on their master's hands: like the eyes of a slave-girl fixed on the hand of her mistress, so *our eyes are fixed on Yahweh our God,* for him to take pity on us."
>
> *"You will lift your face to God.* You will pray, and he will hear."
>
> "Where could the Israelite go to escape from Yahweh's spirit? Where could he flee from Yahweh's presence?"[378]

2. Seeking and longing for God

The spiritual lifting up of the praying person to God, which his or her raising hands, eyes, face manifests and signifies, is often put as seeking Yahweh's face, longing, pining, thirsting, etc., for him.

> "One thing I ask of Yahweh, one thing I *seek:* to live in the house of Yahweh all the days of my life, to enjoy the sweetness of Yahweh and to consult in his Temple... Yahweh, hear my voice as I cry! Pity me! Answer me! My heart has said of you *'Seek his face'.* Yahweh, *I do seek your face:*

---

[377] Ps 102:19; Si 34:16-17; Ps 33:18-19.

[378] Ps 25:15; Ps 16:8; Ps 123:1-2; Jb 22:26-17; Ps 139:7.

> do not hide your face from me... Never leave me, never desert me, God my saviour! If my father and mother desert me, Yahweh will care for me still."
>
> *"Seek Yahweh* and his strength, *seek his face untiringly."* "Let us *stretch our hearts and hands* to God in heaven." "We hoped in you, Yahweh, your name, your memory are *all my soul desires.* At night my soul *longs for* you and my spirit in me *seeks for* you." "As a doe longs for running streams, so *longs* my soul for you, my God. Me soul *thirsts for* God, the God of my life; when shall I go to see the face of God?"
>
> "God, you are my God, I am *seeking* you, my soul is *thirsting for* you, my flesh is *longing for* you, a land parched, weary and waterless. I *long* to gaze on you in the Sanctuary, and to see your power and glory." "I look to no one else in heaven, I delight in nothing else on earth. *My flesh and my heart are pining with love,* my heart's Rock, my own God for ever!" "How my soul *yearns and pines for* Yahweh's courts!"[379]

3. Lifting up the soul

Since the deep source of all thirsting, longing, and seeking for God is the praying person's soul, Hebrew prayer is also described as "lifting up the soul" towards the Jerusalem Temple and towards Yahweh.

> "To you, Yahweh *I lift up my soul,* O my God... You are my God, take pity on me, Lord. I invoke you all the day long; give your servant reason to rejoice, for to you, Lord, *I lift my soul...* Let dawn bring proof of your love, for one who relies on you: let it show the right road, to one who *lifts up his soul to you.*"[380]

4. With all one's heart

Yahweh is a God who ought to be sought with all one's heart and soul, i.e., with fullness of love and faith, in order to be found.

---

[379] Ps 27:4, 8-10; Ps 105:4 = 1 Ch 16:11; Lm 3:41; Is 26:8-9; Ps 42:1-2; Ps 63:1-2; Ps 84:2.

[380] Ps 25:1-2; 86:3-4; 143:8.

"If you seek Yahweh your God *with all your heart and with all your soul,* you shall find him."[381]

"When you call to me, and come to plead with me, I will listen to you. When you seek me you shall find me, when you seek me *with all your heart;* I will let you find me - It is Yahweh who speaks."[382]

"Who has the right of climbing the mountain of Yahweh...and to stand in his holy place? He whose hands are clean, *whose heart is pure...* Such are the people who seek Yahweh, who seek your presence, God of Jacob!"[383]

And those who seek God with all their hearts and souls will be granted the joy of finding him.

"You are my God, take pity on me, Lord. I invoke you all day long: give your servant reason to *rejoice,* for to you, Lord, I lift up my soul; Lord, you are good and forgiving, most loving to all who invoke you."

"Let the hearts that seek Yahweh *rejoice!"* "How good Yahweh is - only taste and see! *Happy* the man who takes shelter in him."[384]

In conclusion, the bodily, psychic, and spiritual components of prayerlife (studied in the preceding chapters) are often mentioned in the Old Testament, where it describes the praying ascent to God.

The hands, face and eyes raised towards heaven by those who pray show that the whole body is involved in the activity of prayer. But the soul is lifted up toward God too, when one seeks and longs for him through prayer. Allusions to the spirit of prayer are made by the statements that God cannot be found in prayer unless one seeks for him with all one's heart.

A process of interiorization is pointed out when the descriptions of prayer pass from mentioning the raising of arms, hands, face and eyes to

---

[381] Dt 4:29; cf. 6:4-5. In the book of Deuteronomy this obligation first and foremost refers to the perfect observance of the whole Law. But worship and prayers offered to Yahweh are included as a very special part of such whole-hearted observance of the Law. Cf. Mt 22:37-40 = Mk 12:33-39 = Lk 10:27-28 - "This is far more important than any holocaust and sacrifice.": Mk 12:33; cf. 2 Ch 31:21; Am 5:21-24; 1 S 15:22; Ps 40:7-9.

[382] Jr 29:12-14; cf. Is 55:6; Dn 3:41.

[383] Ps 24:3-6; Ps 11:7.

[384] Ps 86:3-4; Ps 105:1-3; Ps 34:8; cf. 122:1; Jb 22:25-26.

speaking of the lifting up of the soul and heart toward God. This process is carried on into the New Testament.

b. The New Testament's teaching

Jesus Christ once made a general declaration which certainly includes the Old Testament's teaching and practice of prayer:

> "Do not imagine that I have come to abolish the Law or the Prophets. *I have not come to abolish but to complete* them. I tell you solemnly, till heaven and earth disappear, not one dot, not one little stroke, shall disappear from the Law until its purpose is achieved."[385]

Actually, Christian prayer, having its roots in Hebrew prayer, is also practiced by lifting up one's hands to God with a pure heart.[386]

But, when the Word, who is God, and the true light which enlightens all men, was made flesh and "pitched his tent among us", Jesus Christ replaced the Jerusalem Temple. Hence, the ascending aspect of Christian prayer can now be put in terms of an awaking to the light of Christ.[387]

1. Awakening to the light

Jesus Christ, "the rising Sun who comes from on high to visit us",[388] emphatically proclaims –

> "I am the light of the world; anyone who follows me will not be walking in the dark; he will have the light of life."[389]

---

[385] Mt 5:17-18 = Lk 16:17; cf. Rm 3:31; 10:4; 13:8-10.

[386] "Happy the *pure in heart:* they shall see God." Mt 5:8; cf. Hb 12:1; Mt 7:7; 21:22; Jm 1:5-8.

[387] From the very beginning of his book, LEECH speaks of Christian prayer as an "awakening, a heightening of consciousness and perception.": p. 3.

[388] Lk 1:78.

[389] Jn 8:12; cf. Mt 3:12-17 = Is 8:23-9:1: "God is light; there is no darkness in him at all.": 1 Jn 1:5.

Accordingly, those who are baptized in Christ Jesus are brought from darkness into the light, while they taste the gift from heaven, receive a share of the Holy Spirit, and the powers of the world to come.[390]

> "Darkness in the Bible is an image of terror, misfortune, corruption and death; it describes whatever is wretched...it is the kingdom of Satan and sin, as well as that of men, who are born there in darkness and produce wicked deeds... Out of darkness the Christian emerges triumphant in his following of Christ. This victory presupposes faith and brotherly love."
>
> "Light is a symbol of happiness, prosperity and joy, it comes from God, who is light... According to Paul, through the mediation of Christ, who was the reflection of God's glory, the light shines in our hearts... To believe is to become "a son of light". In John's writing Jesus Christ is the true light who transforms believers into sons of light, who have to believe in Jesus and love their brethren."[391]

Hence, Christian life is likened to awakening from sleep and night's darkness, putting on faith, hope, and love and so entering into the daylight.

> "You are all *sons of light and sons of day: we do not belong to the night or to darkness,* so we should not go on *sleeping,* as everyone else does, but *stay wide awake* and sober. Night is the time for sleepers to sleep and for drunkards to be drunk, but we *belong to the day* and we should be sober; let us put on *faith* and *love* for a breastplate, and the *hope* of salvation for a helmet."[392]

The life of Christians "as sons of light and day" involves their whole moral behavior.[393] But it certainly includes also their prayer, which greatly helps them "to stay wide awake" in faith, hope, and love.

---

[390] Heb. 6:4. Cf. CLEMENT OF ALEXANDRIA, 281-284. Cf. WALSH, p. 81.

[391] DNTT, pp. 156 and 269. Many biblical references are given.

[392] 1 Th 5:5-8.

[393] Rm 13:12-14.

2. Stay awake praying!

In the Bible by and large sleep is an image of bodily death.[394] Hence sleep in the darkness of the night symbolizes the spiritual death into which sinners have fallen.

> "(Christians) were darkness once, but now are light in the Lord, like children of light... The effects of the light are seen in complete goodness and right living and truth ... having nothing to do with the futile works of darkness, things done in secret that people are ashamed even to speak of; but anything exposed by the light will be illuminated and anything illuminated turns into light. That is why it is said: 'Wake up from sleep, rise from the dead, and Christ will shine on you'."[395]
>
> "This is what the Father has done; he has taken us out of the power of darkness and created a place for us in the kingdom of the Son that he loves, and in him we gain our freedom, the forgiveness of our sins."[396]
>
> So, Paul was sent by Christ "to open the eyes of the pagans, so that they may turn from darkness to light, from the dominion of Satan to God, and receive, through faith in Christ, forgiveness of their sins and a share in the inheritance of the sanctified."[397]

Because sleep and darkness symbolize virtually the same thing, Jesus warns his disciples:

> "Be on your guard, stay awake...because you do not know when the master of the house is coming, evening, midnight, cockcrow, dawn; if he comes unexpectedly, he must not find you asleep. And what I say to you I say to all: *Stay awake!*"[398]

Indeed, during his dreadful agony in the garden of Gethsemane, Jesus persistently asked of the apostles to stay awake and pray.

---

[394] Cf. Gn 47:30; 2 S 7:12; 1 Th 4:14; 5:10.

[395] Ep 5:8-14; cf. 1 Jn 2:8-11; Is 51:17-52; 26:19; Dn 12:2.

[396] Col 1:13-14.

[397] Ac 26:18. Many of these words are quotations from Jr 1; Is 9 and 42.

[398] Mk 13:33-37 = Mt 24:42-44; 25:13 = Lk 12:38-40.

> "He found them sleeping, and he said to Peter, 'Simon, are you asleep? Had you not the strength to keep awake one hour? *You should be awake, and praying not to be put to the test.* The spirit is willing, but the flesh is weak."[399]

"Praying at all times" is asked of all Christians, that they may be awake and ready to welcome their Master when he suddenly returns.

> "Watch yourselves, or your hearts will be coarsened with debauchery and drunkenness and the cares of life, and that day will be sprung on you suddenly, like a trap. For it will come down on every living man on the face of the earth. *Stay awake, praying at all times* for the strength to survive all that is going to happen, and to stand with confidence before the Son of Man."[400]
>
> "Everything will soon come to an end, so, *to pray better,* keep a calm and sober mind." *"Be persevering in prayer and be thankful as you stay awake to pray."*[401]

This "staying-always-awake" in watchful expectation of the Lord's return is the typical New Testament way of emphasizing Christians' need of unceasing prayer to overcome all the temptations and trials they will have to undergo before the parousia.[402]

3. Think of and look for heavenly things!

Since their Risen Lord ascended into heaven,[403] Christians yearn for "the glory, as yet unrevealed, which is waiting for them"[404] in heaven, where they will share in his glory. By baptism they

---

[399] Mk 14:37-38.

[400] Lk 21:29-31; cf. Mt 26:41 = Mk 14:38; Mt 24:42-44; Lk 12:35-40.

[401] 1 P 4:7 and Col 4:7.

[402] Cf. 1 Th 5:1-10 and 17 – *"pray constantly"* and Lk 21:36.

[403] Cf. Ac 1:9-11.

[404] Rm 8:18.

"Have been raised up with Christ through their belief in the power of God who *raised him from the dead* and brought them to life in him. They have been given a place with him in heaven, a homeland in heaven."[405]

(But as they still live and struggle on earth, they) "actually want to be exiled from the body and make their home with the Lord... They want to be gone and be with Christ, which would be very much better..."

(So, even though their spirits already) "possess the first-fruits of the Spirit, they groan inwardly as they wait for their bodies to be set free and must hope to be saved, since they are not saved yet, but must wait for it with patience...

They are in search of their homeland, longing for a better homeland, their heavenly homeland, [from where shall] come the Saviour they are waiting for, their Lord Jesus Christ, who will transfigure these wretched bodies of theirs into copies of his glorious body."[406]

This somewhat paradoxical "already-but-not-yet" situation, because of its "not-yet", instills into the prayerlife of the Christian a constant *yearning expectation and watchful waiting for* the return of the Risen Lord, who will bring them the glorious achievement of salvation:

"The Spirit and the Bride say, 'Come'. Let everyone who listens answer, 'Come'. ... I shall indeed be with you soon. Amen; come, Lord Jesus!"[407]

And because the "already" is still imperfect, it demands that Christians be ever thinking of and seeking for the perfect heavenly satisfaction of their heart's desire.

"Since you have been brought back to true life with Christ, *you must look for the things that are in heaven, where Christ is, sitting at God's right hand. Let your thought be on heavenly things, not on things that are on earth,* because you have died, and now the life you have is hidden with Christ in

---

[405] Col 2:12; Ep 2:6; Ph 3:20; cf. 2 Co 5:1.

[406] 2 Co 5:8; Ph 1:23; Rm 8:23-25 = 2 Co 5:1-5; Heb 11:13-16; Ph 3:20-21.

[407] Rv 22:17, 20; 1 Co 16:22. Cf. The acclamations in the Mass after the consecration of bread and wine: "Christ will come again! ...Lord Jesus, come in glory!"

> God. But when Christ is revealed - and he is your life - you too will be revealed in all your glory with him."[408]

The emphasized words of this passage incisively express the faith and hope in the resurrection that drive Christian prayerlife to "ascend" in spirit towards the heavenly kingdom where the risen Christ, "the first-fruits of all of us,"[409] sits at the right hand of the Father.

In conclusion, during the Old Covenant the ascending aspect of prayer was put as the soul's seeking in the Temple of Jerusalem for Yahweh who abides in heaven. But when the Old Covenant and Temple were radically renewed by the Word of God made flesh, the same ascending aspect of prayer was described in various ways as:

— getting up from sleep and the darkness of the night and staying awake and watchful in the daylight of Christ.

— eager expectation of his return as Risen Lord from heaven.

— lifting up of the mind to think of and the heart to yearn for heavenly things, which the Risen Lord already possesses and will share with us at the end of time.

ii. *The early Christian prayer as ascent*

Tertullian writes that in his time Christians were still following the old Hebrew custom of praying by

> "Lifting their eyes to the heavens with hands outstretched ... with their hands stretched out and up to God." Yet pagans also, in using the name of God in prayer "look to the heavens" and "lift suppliant hands to the heavens", for their soul - "by nature Christian" - knows that "there is the throne of the living God."[410]

Sulpicius Severus describes the dying St. Martin of Tour:

---

[408] Col 3:1-4.

[409] 1 Co 15:20.

[410] TERTULLIAN, *Apology,* ch xxx, p. 42 a and b; ch xvii, p. 32a and ch xxiv, p. 39a.

> "With eyes and hands always raised to heaven he never withdrew his unconquered spirit from prayer."[411]

For Evagrius Ponticus

> "To cease to pray" is "not to stand in the presence of the Lord our God, not to dare raise our hands in supplication to him."[412]

Evagrius himself, "the first to organize into a coherent system the teaching of the Desert Fathers on prayer",[413] defined prayer as follows:

> "Prayer is the ascent *(anabasis)* of the spirit *(nous)* towards *(pros)* God."[414]

J.E. Bamberger translates *nous* (which directly translates as mind) as "spirit", and explains:

> "For Evagrius man is not, essentially, a creature composed of body and soul, but a *nous*, that is, *an intelligence whose proper activity is religious contemplation.*"[415]

---

[411] LITURGY, vol. IV, p. 1553.

[412] EVAGRIUS, 46, p. 29.

[413] EVAGRIUS, Introduction of J.E. Bamberger, p. lxxxi.

[414] EVAGRIUS, ch. 35, p. 60. Cf. *Ibid.,* ch. 46, p. 62: "that excellent course pursued in prayer on the journey towards God." In PG the book of Evagrius is wrongly attributed to St. Nile: cf. Irenée Hausherr, *Les Leçons d'un Contemplative* (Paris: Beauchesne, 1960). The new CCC, n. 2559, quotes this definition of prayer, taken from St. John Damascene, *De fide orthodoxa,* 3, 24: PG 94, 1084D, and translates it: "Prayer is the rising of the soul to God."

[415] EVAGRIUS, p. 53, note 7. This concept of the human person follows the Platonizing presuppositions of Origen, for whom rational nature, mind, and soul are virtually synonyms, while the body is not integral to the definition of the human being, who is a soul or incorporeal nature making use of a body. Cf. Rowan A. Greer, *Introduction* to ORIGEN, pp. 11-12 and 15. Aquinas states more exactly: "Secundum veritatem *principalius* est in homine ipsa mens, unde secundum iudicium spiritualium hominum *mens dicitur homo interior.": Lectura in II Co,* c. IV, in ESP, vol. I, no. 146, p. 472. Emphasis ours.

This definition *literatim* is not in the Bible, even though, as we have seen, the Bible does in many ways speak of prayer as the "lifting up" of the human soul and heart to God. Evagrius drew his definition from the Hellenistic cultural milieu within which he developed his reflection on prayer. In doing that he have an early and significant example of the inculturation of which Vatican II wrote authoritatively -

> "The Church learned early in its history to express the Christian message in the concepts and language of different peoples and tried to clarify it in the light of the wisdom of their philosophers; it was an attempt to adapt the Gospel to the understanding of all men and to the requirements of the learned, insofar as that could be done. Indeed, this kind of adaptation and preaching of the revealed Word must ever be the law of all evangelization."[416]

a. Christian reinterpretation of the Platonic definition

Doubtless, the original sense of the Evagrian definition of prayer as ascent was Platonic. But the definition acquired a distinctive Christian meaning when it was used to signify Christian prayer.[417]

1. The *nous,* which Platonism thought capable of rising towards the higher spheres, where the deity was assumed to abide, was identified by Christians with the *human self,* on which the Creator stamps his own image and likeness, making him/her capable of directly knowing and loving him.[418] In fact, the sacred Scripture spoke of "spirit" or "heart" as the innermost source of the spiritual life which finds expression in prayer.

> "(In the OT) 'spirit' stands alongside 'heart' (e.g., Exod. 35:31-35), the idea behind the two words being very similar; the difference, however, is that the heart dwells within man, having indeed been created by God, but it is not a fleeting, oscillating gift, like the breath of a man's spirit.
>
> The heart may be said to denote a man's aims, his resolves, and his courage, while the spirit may be said to denote the direction in which a man's vitality flows, the self-expression involved in his behaviour - including

---

[416] GS, n. 44, FLANNERY, p. 946. Cf. LG, n. 13, FLANNERY, p. 364.

[417] Cf. ŠPIDLÍK, pp. 359-360.

[418] Cf. ŠPIDLÍK, pp. 180-181.

ecstatic behaviour... The spirit of man is essentially God's gift, spirit is essentially of God."[419]

The early Fathers explained that in and through the human spirit or heart the Holy Spirit himself "breathes" the prayer of God's adopted children to their heavenly Father.[420]

2. By focusing on the ascent "towards *(pros)* God" the definition emphasized the Godward dynamism which is the characteristic of prayer. According to Plotinus such a dynamism is fueled by *eros.*[421] Christian spiritual masters contended instead that the ascent of Christian prayer towards God is fueled by *agape.*[422]

Agape, i.e., charity, is a love that comes down from God the Father through his incarnate Son Jesus Christ and is poured by the Holy Spirit into the hearts of Christians.[423] Only this divine love can enable Christians to give their heavenly Father an adequate return of love, proved by effective conformity with his will and carried on as yearning for union with him.[424]

---

[419] DNTT, vol. 3, p. 691.

[420] ŠPIDLÍK, pp. 262-266. An echo of this teaching of the early Fathers is in CROSS [4], B, 38, 3.

[421] ŠPIDLÍK, pp. 262-266. It is worth noticing however that "Plotinus' confidence that the human mind has it in itself to rise to the highest heights was superceded by the later Platonist's belief that the mind is completely fallen and can only be united with God by the gracious act of his own condescension to us... Plotinus attributes the final self transcending move (by which one becomes united to God) to love (i.e., to *eros).* Proclus attributes it to faith and connects it with religious ritual (theurgy), in which God acts upon us to take us beyond the limits attainable by philosophy." TUGWELL [5], p. 41-42, where he refers to Steel. The theory of Proclus shows some similarity with Christian faith in salvation.

[422] *Agape* is the distinctive New Testament word for Christian love. It denotes a passionless love. On the contrary, *eros* denotes sexual desire, passionate aspiration, sensual longing. In Platonism *eros* was also used to mean the "upward longing to the eternal and divine". The New Testament writers avoided using the word *eros.* Cf. JOHNSTON G., p. 169 a.

[423] Cf. Rm 5:5.

[424] Cf. ŠPIDLÍK, pp. 192-194; 359-360. Aquinas clearly summarizes this Christian teaching: *"Prayer motivated by charity tends toward God...* and in this sense Damascene says, 'prayer is the lifting up of the mind to God'." (*De Fide Orthodoxa* III,

3. The *God* towards whom Christians rise through prayer is One in three Persons, the Holy Trinity, and not just *the* One of Neo-Platonism.[425]

In conclusion, each and every Greek substantive used to define prayer as ascent (namely: "mind", "ascent" and "God") was given a distinctive Christian meaning by Christian spiritual masters. So the originally Hellenistic definition became Christian through and through.

b. Developments of the definition

An "affective" version of the Evagrian definition can be found in the XIIth century:

> "Prayer is a devout *heart's intention* toward God."[426]

Several variations of this definition of prayer were given by the English mystics of the XIVth century:

> "Prayer is nothing but *desire of the heart* rising into God."[427]
> "Prayer is a *devout affection* of the spirit directed into God."[428]
> "Whenever you feel drawn by grace to the contemplative work and are determined to do it, simply raise your *heart* toward God with *a gentle stirring of love...* A naked intent toward God, the desire for him alone, is enough."[429]

24, PG 96, 1089): (II-II, q. 83, a. 1, ad 2um.; BLACKFRIARS, vol. 39, p. 49-51).

[425] ŠPIDLÍK, pp. 255-256, 281.

[426] "Oratio est devota cordis intentio in Deum": GUIGUES II, p. 84.

[427] HILTON, I, 25, p. 98.

[428] ROLLE, p. 85. Cf. this author's explanation, p. 69: "The intention of our heart, by means of burning love, sets our very prayer ablaze." For a definition of prayer very similar to that given by Rolle see in St. Bonaventure, *In III Sent.*, X, dist. 7, a. 2, q. 3.

[429] CLOUD, ch. 7, p. 56. This author also adds: "Think only of God, the God who created you, redeemed you, and guided you to this (contemplative) work. Allow no other ideas about God to enter your mind. Yet even this is too much." All emphasis in the last three quotes is ours.

Some contemporary spiritual authors maintain the same affective version of prayer as ascent:

> "Prayer is a devout *upsurge of love,* which draws us toward God."[430]
> "Prayer is a *desire and longing.*"[431]

Aquinas likes better the "intellectual" version of the Evagrian definition:

> "Prayer is the secret ascent of the *intellect* toward God."[432]

He stresses that prayer *(oratio)* first of all required the ascent of the mind towards God,[433] and explains that the ascent properly distinguishes this prayer from the various acts of entreaty, beseeching, thanksgiving, etc. [434]

Accordingly, a contemporary author rightly points out that prayer as ascent has a broader meaning than prayer of petition.

> "It is commonly held that we use prayer to communicate our mind and meaning to God... Prayer for many people seems to be little more than

---

[430] GUILLERAND, p. 124.

[431] MACQUARRIE [2], p. 585.

[432] ST, II-II, q. 83, a. 1, ad 2um. Aquinas received this definition from DAMASCENE, p. 1089.

[433] "Prayer tends towards God... because one ought to approach the person from whom he requests something...in mind when from God. Hence Dyonisius says, *when we call upon God in our prayer we unveil our mind in his presence* (*De Divinibus Nominibus,* 3, PG 3, 680)." (II-II, q, 83, a. 1, ad 2um; BLACKFRIARS, vol. 39, p. 50-51). "The first requirement for prayer (is that): the person praying *must approach God to whom he prays,* and this is signified in the very name of 'prayer', because prayer is a raising up of the mind to God...(Damascene, *De fide Orthodoxa,* II, 24).": II-II, q. 83, a. 117; BLACKFRIARS, vol. 33, p. 99). All emphasis ours.

[434] *"Prayer in a general sense* contains all the parts spoken of above (i.e., entreaty, thanksgiving, etc). But *in a special sense it means the ascent of the mind to God."* (II-II, q. 83, a. 17, ad 2um; BLACKFRIARS, vol. 33, p. 101). Emphasis ours.

petition; whereas we shall take the broader meaning, that is a lifting of the mind and heart to God."[435]

Seemingly, prayer as worship develops the "cognitive" understanding of prayer as ascent, whereas prayer as communion develops the "affective understanding of it.[436]

Definitions of prayer as ascent including both its intellectual and affective elements were popularized by Catechisms of Christian denominations:

> "Prayer is the raising up of *the mind and heart* to God."[437]
> "Adoration is the lifting up of *the heart and mind* to God."[438]

iii. *Spiritual and theological reflections on prayer as ascent*

a. The detachment and recollection necessary for prayer as ascent

By placing God, the object and goal of prayer, in the highest spheres of the cosmos, religious imagination implies that the ascent of prayer towards him demands an estrangement and detachment from creatures, in order to approach their Creator.

As their imagery was fed by sacred Scripture, early Christian theologians interpreted the migration of the people of Israel ("when they went out of the Land of Egypt with their power by the hand of Moses and Aaron"[439]),

---

[435] BUTLER, pp. 13, 125. GROESCHEL, p. 6, remarks that a quick comparison between our personal prayer experience with what prayer as ascent expects of us "can leave us feeling a little empty, since when we pray our resolution often wanes quickly and our heart and mind come crashing down to earth with a thud."

[436] See here below chs. VII and VIII.

[437] BC, p. 23. Emphasis ours.

[438] OF, p. 13. Emphasis ours.

[439] ORIGEN [2], *Homily XXVII on Numbers,* pp. 248 and 252.

the climbing of Moses to the summit of Mount Sinai[440] the ladder that Jacob saw in a dream[441] as allegories of the ascent of Christian prayer towards God.

As the people of Israel had to fight fierce battles against their enemies in order to reach the Promised Land, praying Christians must fight against the demons[442] in order to ascend towards God by prayer.

> "There is no effort comparable to prayer to God. In fact whenever you want to pray, hostile demons try to interrupt you. Of course they know that nothing but prayer to God entangles them. Certainly when you undertake any other work, and persevere in it, you obtain rest. But prayer is a battle all the way to the last breath."[443]

On the other hand, ascending towards God by prayer is no less toilsome to the spirit than climbing a mountain is to the body.

> "The knowledge of God[444] is a mountain steep indeed and difficult – the majority of people scarcely reach its base."[445]

In order to facilitate the ascent of the steep mountain of prayer Origen advises all to practice recollection:

> "It seems to me that the person who is about to come to prayer should withdraw for a little and prepare himself, and so become more attentive and active for the whole of his prayer. He should cast away all

---

440 Cf. GREGORY OF NYSSA'S *Life of Moses,* which was preceded by Philo of Alexandria's book with the same title.

441 Cf. ŠPIDLÍK, pp. 231-215. ORIGEN, *Commentary on the Song of Songs,* p. 235: "Jacob receives the object of contemplation of divine things and, since he saw the encampment of heaven and gazed at the house of God and the paths of the angels, the ladder that stretched from earth to heaven (cf. Gn 28:12, 17; 32:2)." Cf. CLIMACUS [2] and GUIGO II.

442 Among the ancient monks demons were often personifications of the distractions and temptations occurring during the exercises of prayer.

443 YUSHI, p. 103.

444 *Theologia,* i.e., the prayerful contemplation of the divine things.

445 GREGORY OF NYSSA, II, 57, p. 93. Cf. GREGORY NAZIANZUS, *Oratio,* 28, 2. PG 36, 28.

> temptations and troubling thoughts and remind himself so far as he is able of the Majesty whom he approaches, and that it is impious to approach Him carelessly, sluggishly, and disdainfully; and he should put away all extraneous things."[446]

Evagrius extensively develops this teaching of Origen by indicating both the most important purifications and contemplations demanded by the ascent of prayer towards God.

First of all, Christians who long to pray attentively should sell all possessions, i.e., practice detachment from this-worldly things, and take up the cross, as Jesus asked of his disciples –

> "Go, sell all your possessions and give to the poor, and take up your cross so that you can pray without distraction... Do you long to pray? Renounce all things. ...Do you wish to pray? Then banish the things of this world."[447]

The goal of such radical renunciation (remember that Evagrius writes for monks) is to forget about the pleasures of the body and neglect the amenities of life, because these hinder prayer.

> "To the extent that you give attention to the values of the body, and your mind concerns itself with the amenities of life, you have not yet seen the place of prayer. Rather the happiness of this way is still far off....
>
> When you give yourself to prayer, rise above every other joy – then you will find prayer."[448]

Since giving attention to and concerning oneself with the things of this world arouses passions which hamper prayer, those who want to pray must free themselves from passions, and from the lack of spiritual knowledge and temptations which follow them.

> "Do you long to pray? ... First of all pray to be purified from your passions. Secondly pray to be delivered from ignorance. Thirdly, to be freed from all temptations and abandonment,.. When man's irrational passions are thriving he is not free to pray and to seek the word of God.... The man who

---

[446] *On Prayer,* XXXI, 2, p. 164.

[447] EVAGRIUS, ch. 17, p. 58; ch. 36, p. 61; ch. 142, p. 78.

[448] *Ibid.,* ch. 152, p. 80; ch. 153, p. 80.

strives after true prayer must learn to master not only anger and his lust, but must free himself from every thought that is colored with passion."[449]

Therefore,

> "The state of prayer can aptly be described as an habitual state of imperturbable calm."[450]

However, being free from passions, even though it is necessary, does not suffice.

> "One who has become free from disturbing passions does not necessarily truly pray. It is quite possible for a man to have none but the purest thoughts and yet be so distracted mulling over them that he remains the while far removed from God."[451]

In a word, those who want to become "theologians" (that is, to reach the experiential knowledge of God which is attained by perfect prayer) must imitate the angels whose homeland is in heaven.

> "If you are a theologian you truly pray, if you truly pray you are a theologian....
>
> Keeping free from concepts ... you will receive the most precious gift of prayer.
>
> Do you wish to pray? ...Have heaven for your homeland and live there constantly. Not in mere words but in actions which imitate the angels and in more godlike knowledge."[452]

This Evagrian teaching became traditional in Christian spirituality. An echo of it can be found in Walter Hilton's claim that the Christian who is upward striving for God in prayer must free him/herself of all "passionate thoughts and distracting memories."

---

[449] *Ibid.,* ch. 37, p. 61; ch. 50, p. 63; ch. 53, p. 63.

[450] That is *Apatheia,* i.e., impassibility: ch. 52, p. 63.

[451] *Ibid.,* ch. 55, p. 63.

[452] *Ibid.,* passim.

> "In prayer he feels the thoughts of his heart drawn up from earthly things, streamed together with all his powers as it rises into our Lord by fervent desire and with spiritual delight."[453]

St. John of the Cross is the Doctor *par excellence* of the absolute need of turning away from all that is not God in order to ascent through prayer to the perfect union of love with him. His *Ascent of Mount Carmel* and *Dark Night of the Soul* are perhaps the most systematic development of the ancient teaching about the thorough purification both of the senses and of the spirit which are required to ascend towards God in prayer.

A contemporary author of the monastic tradition summarizes the same teaching.

> "A soul that prays has been caught up in an upward movement – a movement in God and toward God... The preparation for prayer is the movement of turning to God and *away from all that is not God.* That is why we are so right to define prayer as this movement. Prayer is essentially a "raising up", an elevation... Everything that raises us up *beyond and above created things, every moment of true and disinterested love* – all this is prayer and prepares us for a still more intimate prayer."[454]

CCC explains that prayer is defined as "the raising of the soul to God" because when we pray we must start not from the height of our arrogance but from the depth of a humble and contrite heart (cf. Ps 130:1). Actually, humility is the foundation of prayer and the human person is like a beggar before God.[455] CCC develops the long spiritual struggle needed to raise the soul to God by prayer is a section dedicated to *"The Combat of Prayer"*.[456]

---

[453] HILTON, I, 5, p. 8. Aquinas writes: "in quantum homo per divinam laudem ascendit in Deum, in tantum per hoc retrahitur ab his quae sunt contra Deum.": II-II, q. 91, a. 1, co.

[454] GUILLERAND, pp. 93, 113, 115. Emphasis ours.

[455] Cf. n. 2559.

[456] Cf. CCC, IV, ch. 3, art. 2, nn. 2725-2733.

b. Ascending towards the risen Christ and descending towards the Indwelling Trinity

Jesus Christ is the "Word made flesh who pitched his tent among us" and in whose "body lives the fullness of the divinity".[457] He replaces the Jerusalem Temple as the dwelling place of Yahweh among his people.[458] In him and through him all humans "have in the one Spirit their way to come to the Father."[459]

After his resurrection Jesus Christ "has been taken up into heaven".[460] Christians on earth are instead still "living in the body, exiled from the Lord"[461]; while they "believe in him whom they cannot see".[462]

So, even though Christians have already welcomed by faith and charity the Son of God who came from heaven to earth, they still ascend by prayer towards heaven, where the risen Christ is "seated at the right hand of the Father".

> "Since you have been brought back to true life with Christ, you must look for the things that are in heaven, where Christ is, sitting at God's right hand. Let your thoughts be on heavenly things, not on the things that are on the earth, because you have died, and now the life you have is hidden with Christ in God."[463]

True, the risen Christ shall visibly come back on earth at the end of human history. But before that final event, "the day and hour of which nobody knows but the Father only",[464] Christians can already attain a certain union

---

[457] Jn 1:14; Col 2:9; cf. 1:19.

[458] Cf. Mt 26:61; Jn 2:18-21.

[459] Ep 2:18

[460] Ac 1:11.

[461] 1 Co 5:6.

[462] Cf. 2 Co 5:7; 1 Co 13:12; Rm 8:24.

[463] Col 3:1-3

[464] Mt 24:36.

with him, spiritually ascending towards him by prayer in faith, especially when their minds and hearts are aglow with desire for him.[465]

Christ himself, when he was on earth, after many hours of ministering to the people by preaching and healing "would always go off to some place where he could be alone and pray".[466] During those periods of solitary prayer Jesus had an intimacy with God the Father such as no human being can ever reach.

Nevertheless, this prayer of Christ is a paramount example for all Christians, who by the adoptive divine sonship, granted to them through and in Christ, can reach an analogous intimacy with the Father. Such an intimacy is made possible by the ineffable grace of the indwelling presence of the Divine Persons within those Christians who show their love for Christ by keeping his word:

> "If anyone loves me he will keep my word, and my Father will love him, and we shall come to him and make our home with him".[467]

So, Christians can descend by their personal prayer into the depths of their spirit, where the Divine Persons dwell.

> "When you pray, go to your private room and, when you have shut your door, pray to your Father who is in that secret place, and your Father who sees all that is done in secret will reward you."[468]

These words of Jesus were interpreted by the early Fathers as a recommendation that praying Christians turn within their inner self, where they can encounter the Most Holy Trinity.

> "The person enters into his own "room" to the wealth treasured up there, since he has shut up for himself the treasures of wisdom and knowledge (cf. Mt 6:6; Col 2:3; 1 Tm 6:18-19). And without turning or gazing in any

---

[465] Cf. "Apud te mens nostra tuo desiderio fulgeat": LITURGIA, vol. II, p. 83. DO, vol. II, p. 43 translates: "may our hearts burn with love for you." CF. Lk 24:39: "Did not our hearts burn within us as he talked with us on the road and explained the Scripture to us?"

[466] Lk 5:16; cf. 9:28; Mt 14:23; Mk 1:35.

[467] Jn 14:23.

[468] Mt 6:6.

way toward what is outside, he shuts up every "door" of the senses that he may not be held by the senses, or his mind glutted by their impressions. And he prays to the Father, who does not shun or abandon such a hidden place, but dwells in it together with the presence of his Only Begotten Son. For he says, 'I and the Father will come and make my home with him (cf. Jn 14:23)'.[469]

Could one contend that, when extroverts pray, they are inclined to "ascend" towards God, whereas introverts feel more comfortable with "descending" towards him?

At any rate, both prayer approaches reach God, because (given his being both and at the same time transcendent and immanent) he can be visualized both as "above" and "below" our usual human experience.

Indeed, according to St. Augustine, God is at one and the same time "deeper than our innermost being and higher than the pinnacle of it."[470] Words that a modern author paraphrases as follows:

> "The reality of God is experienced in our *innermost* soul by the *loftiest heights* of our spirit and by all that is most pure in our being."[471]

This is why any approach of Christian prayer to God must be both "ascending and descending" or "descending and "ascending" towards the transcendent-immanent or immanent-transcendent God.[472] Practicing

---

[469] ORIGEN, *On Prayer,* XX, 2, pp. 121. See also St. Ambrose, who thinks that the private room of which the Gospel speaks is "quod in te est, in quo includuntur cogitationes tuas, in quo versantur sensus tui, ubique tecum est et ubique secretum est, cuius arbiter nullus est nisi solus Deus.": quoted in LITURGIA, vol. IV, p. 255-256. The translation given by LITURGY, p. 347, is rather free: "By 'room' you must understand not a room enclosed by walls that imprisons your body, but the room that is within you, wherever you are, and it is always a secret room, where ony God can see you." St. John of the Cross echoes this teaching in *Cantico B,* I, 9. See CRUZ, p. 914.

[470] "Interior intimo meo et superior summo meo": *Confessiones,* III, 6, 11, PL 32, 628. Karl Barth seems to be paraphrasing the words of St. Augustine when he writes: "For God it is just as natural to be lowly as it is to be high, to be near as it is to be far...to be abroad as to be at home." *Church Dogmatics,* vol. IV/I (Edinburg: T. and T. Clark, 1962.), p. 192.

[471] GUARDINI, p. 38. Emphasis ours.

[472] Jesus himself taught his disciples – "You should pray like this: *Our Father* [a God spiritually close, "immanent", as a loving father] *in heaven* [a God spiritually

exclusively an "ascending" or a "descending" approach in prayer would lead the praying Christian towards either an only transcendent or an only immanent deity, which is not the God of true faith and of sound Christian theology.

> "Here is a paradox: for Aquinas God's transcendence and immanence are never opposed but rather call for each other. As infinite self-subsisting act of existing (by which God *transcends* all), God is the only possible source of all created being and existing. But to be this source, God must be continually present and active in the deepest heart of creaturely being, must be most *immanent* in everything that is" (ST, I, q. 8, a. 1. See also *Ibid.* q. 103-105). For Aquinas this presence of God is *intensified* in human persons when the Father, Son, and Holy Spirit dwell in us as *friends* to be possessed and enjoyed through intimate, experiential knowing and loving. This happens when we are co-natured with the divine Persons through the gifts of wisdom and love (See *Ibid.* I, q. 43, aa. 3-5)."[473]

In short, since transcendence and immanence are both essential and inseparable "qualities" of God's Being, both "ascending prayer", which approaches God as transcendent, and "descending prayer", which approaches him as immanent, are necessary and complementary for Christian prayerlife.

In more concrete and scriptural terms, since the risen Christ is, with the Father, the sender of the Holy Spirit into the heart of the Christian, the "ascending" approach of Christian prayer towards the risen Christ is paralleled by a "descending" approaching towards the praying Christian's inner self, where the Holy Spirit, the Father and the Son dwell as in their temples.

A last but not least point. As Christ ascended into the glory of heaven with his risen body, "through him with him and in him" in some sense all material things have already entered the heavenly glory.

---

remote, "transcendent", as the Lord of heaven]."

[473] PRINCIPE, p. 18. Author's emphasis. In this way, Aquinas' theology rights the "unrestricted tendency of Origenist spirituality to strain 'upward', the interpretation of Christian life as an unequivocal 'ascent', with its inevitable effect on the evangelical theme of 'descent' - that of God into flesh ...(so that) what is implied by the *via crucis* is bound to be somehow neglected." (Hans Urs Von Balthasar, *Preface* to ORIGEN [2], p. 3). In fact, the "descent" through prayer towards the innermost depths of the Christian's spirit, where God the Holy Trinity dwells, is made possible by the "descent" of the Son of God into the flesh, his death and resurrection, and would be absolutely impossible without it.

> "Christ is the image of the unseen God and the first born of all creation, for in him were created all things in heaven and on earth; everything visible and everything invisible... As he is the Beginning, he was first to be born from the dead...because God wanted all things to be reconciled through him and for him, everything in heaven and everything on earth."[474]

Actually, everything in heaven and on earth shall be marvelously transfigured[475] in the "new heavens and new earth,"[476] which the risen Christ will forever establish at the end of time.[477]

Consequently, Christians who on earth strive to ascend by prayer towards the risen Christ do not need to reject earthly realities in order to reach "the things that are in heaven", but ought only to beware of whatever is sinful, i.e., opposed to Christ's salvation. All earthly things, material and spiritual, as they were redeemed by Christ, may instead be integrated in the ascent of Christian prayer towards the risen Christ.

---

[474] Col 1:15-20, passim.

[475] In a way analogous to the earthly transfiguration of the body of Jesus, whose "face shone like the sun and his clothes became as white as the light.": cf. Mt 17:1-9; Mk 9:2-10; Lk 9:28-36.

[476] Cf. Is 65:17; 2 P 3:13; Rv 21:1.

[477] These New Testament teachings are the foundations of Aquinas' principle: "Grace, far from supplanting nature, brings it to perfection." Cf. ST, I, q. 2, a. 2, ad 1um; II-II, q. 26, a. 13, sed contra; III, q. 71, ad 1um.

CHAPTER VI

PRAYER AS ADDRESS

Humans use gestural, vocal, and written language to address themselves to and communicate with one another. Wont as they are to employ language among themselves, religious people have always spontaneously used it to address themselves to and communicate with God in prayer, too.

Praying Christians ascend/descend towards God with the intention of reaching those spiritual heights/depths from which they can more effectively address themselves to him, who dwells in heaven and within the spirit of his adopted children.

In fact, referring to the "lifting up of the eyes and soul to God" described by the psalms (e.g., Ps 25:1; 123:1, etc.) Origen comments:

> "The *eyes of the mind are lifted up* from their preoccupation with earthly things and from their being filled with the impression of material things. And they are so exalted that they peer beyond the created order and arrive at the sheer contemplation of God and *conversing with him reverently and suitably as He listens.*"[478]

Guigo II explains:

> "Prayer *lifts itself up to God* with all its strength, *and begs for* the treasure it longs for, which is the sweetness of contemplation."[479]

i. *The Biblical Foundations of Prayer as Address*

a. The Judeo-Christian religion of the Word

---

[478] *On Prayer*, IX, 2, p. 99. Emphasis ours.

[479] GUIGO II, XII, p. 92.

The intrinsic efficacy of words is not obvious in our cultural milieu.[480] Hence, e.g., we are hardly surprised to read:

> "Abba James said: we do not want words alone, for there are too many words among people today. What we need is action, for that is what we are looking for, not words which do not bear fruit...
>
> If you have words, but not works, you are like a tree with leaves but no fruit. But just as a tree bearing fruits is also leafy, a person who has good works comes up with good words."[481]

In the same vein, the heavenly Father said to St. Catherine of Siena:

> "I am one who is pleased by few words and many works... I am not much pleased with one who simply shouts, 'Lord, Lord, I would like to do something for you!' ... What I want is many works of patient and courageous endurance and of the other virtues...interior virtues that are active in bearing the fruit of grace."[482]

On the contrary, the Hebrews thought that words have the power of bringing about what they mean.

> "[In the OT] word and reality are indissolubly united, such that *dabar* meant equally a word (account, commandment) and a thing (reality, affair) ... Word and action are bound together; to speak was to act, something true above all of the God who created by his word."[483]

Particularly the Word of Yahweh is said to have an irresistible efficacy:

> "Yes, as the rain and the snow come down from the heavens and do not return without watering the earth, making it yield and giving growth to provide seed for the sower and bread for the eating, so *the word that goes*

---

[480] Even though, e.g., nobody can deny the power of slogans used for propaganda and advertising.

[481] YUSHI, p. 106 and p. 40.

[482] DIALOGUE, ch. 11, p. 42.

[483] DNTT, p. 432. Cf. Ps 33:6; Gn 1:3.

from my (= Yahweh's) mouth does not return to me empty, without carrying out my will and succeeding in what it was sent to do."[484]

Seemingly, this belief in the absolute efficacy of the "Word of Yahweh" is the result of the inculturation of revealed religion - with all the purification and elevation that such a process requires - into an early superstitious mentality that attributed to words, especially to those of blessing and cursing, an innate power to bring about what they meant.

"Words still possess, in Hebrew thought, the quality of a magic spell. A word once uttered takes on a life of its own beyond the control of the speaker and achieves its effect by a kind of innate power....

Blessings, curses, and words of good and bad omen thus had a power which was something more than that of producing a psychological effect on those who heard them. They were believed to influence the course of events."[485]

Against the background of this belief

"The God of gods and Lord of lords, the great God, triumphant and terrible, the Most High to be dreaded, great and terrible to all around him."[486] has not spoken in secret, in a corner of a darkened land... I, Yahweh, speak with directness. I express myself with clarity... *Yahweh reveals his word to Jacob, his statutes and rulings to Israel.*"[487]

"This Law that I (= Yahweh) enjoin to you today is not beyond your strength or beyond your reach. It is not in heaven, so that you need to wonder: 'Who will go up to heaven for us and bring it down to us, so that we may hear it and keep it?' Nor is it beyond the seas, so that you need to wonder: 'Who will cross the seas for us and bring it back to us, so that we may hear and keep it?' *No, the Word is very near to you, it is in your mouth and in your heart for your observance.*"[488]

---

[484] Is 55:10-11.

[485] SANDERS, p. 869 b.

[486] Dt 10:17; Ps 47:2; 89:7-8.

[487] Is 45:15,19; Ps 147:19.

[488] Dt 30:11-14.

The open and direct address of his Word to the People demonstrates Yahweh's predilection towards them. It is out of a very special love that Yahweh communicates his powerful Word to them.

> "Was there ever a Word so majestic, from one end of heaven to the other? Was anything ever heard? Did ever a people hear the voice of the living God speaking from the heart of the fire, as you heard it, and remain alive?....
>
> He let you hear his voice out of heaven for your instruction.... *Because he loved your fathers and chose their descendants after them.*"[489]

The very efficacy of Yahweh's Word demands that it be not just listened to but assimilated, transformed, into flesh and blood by its hearers:

> "When your [i.e., Yahweh's] words came, I devoured them: your word was my delight and the joy of my heart, for I was called by your name, Yahweh, God of Sabaoth."[490]

And from this assimilation consequential action ought to follow. Hence the early Christian catechesis exhorted:

> "Accept and submit to the word which has been planted in you and can save your soul. But you must do what the word tells you, and not just listen to it and deceive yourselves. To listen to the word and not obey is like looking at your own features in a mirror and then, after a quick look, going off and immediately forgetting what you looked like."[491]

In conclusion, the whole Judeo-Christian religious history is characterized by the uninterrupted friendly communication in words and deeds between God and his chosen people. In the unfolding of this friendly dialogue, the inner efficacy of God's words is proved by the marvelous deeds that he accomplishes for the benefit of the people, while the sincerity of the people is proved by their heeding and obeying God's Word.

---

[489] Dt 4:32-40, passim.

[490] Jr 15:16.

[491] Jm 1:21-24; cf. Rm 2:13; Mt 7:24-27; Lk 8:21; 1 Jn 3:17 ff.

b. God's Word and the words of prayer

Given the paramount role played by God's word in the religion of Israel, hearing, not seeing, is primal in the communication which God establishes with his Chosen People.[492] Accordingly, the members of the Chosen People are characterized as *"hearers of the (divine) Word"*. In particular their communication with God in and through prayer consists in hearing, listening, and responding to God's Word.

Accordingly, their prayer naturally takes the form of address, of dialogue, of conversation with God.

> "In the OT prayer is all-important because of that which both characterizes and constitutes the nation of Israel, his relation to God. The whole history of Israel is therefore permeated with prayer. At all important points man is found in converse with God...
>
> The Israelite knows that God is a person. Therefore *he prays in a thoroughly personal and specific fashion, aware that he is actually speaking to God,* not merely invoking some dumb deity.
>
> In the NT [because of his resurrection] Jesus Christ is alive for evermore so that one can enter into living personal contact with him, *talking with him* just as one did when he was on earth (cf. Ac 9:10-16; 2 Co 12:8ff). It follows that *genuine prayer is not monologue but dialogue,* in which the person is often silent to listen to Jesus' word and command. As in the OT, therefore, *prayer is very personal and specific, a genuine conversation with God and Jesus.*" [493]

Since Hebrew prayer is carried on as a dialogue with Yahweh, Yahweh assures the people that, if they listen to and obey his Word, he, too, will hear and answer the words of prayer that they address to him.

> "Your integrity will go before you and the glory of Yahweh behind you. Cry and Yahweh will answer; call and he will say, 'I am here'." But if they do not listen to God's Word, "they will cry out to Yahweh, but he will not answer them. He will hide his face at that time because of the crimes they have committed."[494]

---

[492] SANDERS, p. 869.

[493] DNNT, vol. III, pp. 862-863, 867; cf. 873. Emphases ours.

[494] Is. 58:8-9; Mi 3:4.

Yahweh's Word usually reaches the People through the descending mediation of the prophets. Likewise, the words of prayer addressed by the people to God usually reach him through the ascending mediation of the prophets, the levites, the kings. The descending mediation of God's Word reaches its climax in the Son of God Jesus Christ:

> "At various times in the past and in various different ways, God spoke to our ancestors through the prophets; but in our own time, the last days, he has spoken to us through his Son, the Son he has appointed to inherit everything and through whom he made everything there is."[495]

Indeed, Jesus Christ, besides being "the only one mediator between God and mankind, himself a man"[496] is also the personified

> "Word of God, who was God, was made flesh, lived among us, and we saw his glory, the glory that is his as the only Son of the Father, full of grace and truth."[497]

Hence the famous statement of St. Jerome:

> "To be ignorant of the Scripture is to be ignorant of Christ."[498]

Actually, according to St. Augustine, Christ teaches us both externally, when he speaks through the Scripture and his preachers, and internally, insofar as he dwells within our very selves.[499]

This is also why most of the early ministry of Christ's disciples consisted in preaching the Word – i.e., the very Person of Jesus, Messiah and Saviour, and his Teaching – and presiding at the celebration of the Eucharist, during which the Faithful responded by active participation and prayers to Christ's Word and the sacramental reenactment of his Sacrifice.

---

[495] Heb 1:1-2.

[496] 1 Tm 2:5; cf. Heb 8:6; 9:15; 12:24.

[497] Jn 1:1 and 14.

[498] *Commentary on Isaiah,* prol. 1, PL 24; 17.

[499] *De Magistro,* XIV, 46.

"These (= early Christians) remained faithful to the *teaching of the apostles,* to the brotherhood, to *the breaking of the bread and to the prayers.*"[500]

"It would not be right for us [the Apostles] to neglect *the Word of God* to give out food... We will hand over this duty to them [the deacons], and continue to devote ourselves *to prayer* and to the *ministry of the Word!*"[501]

So,the Word of God preached and made sacramentally present by the Apostles' ministry became

"A power working within the believers...a word very near to them, in their mouths and in their hearts...the word of faith, which saves them."[502]

In fact, the early Christian liturgies were celebrations, whose participants, having welcomed Christ's Word into their lives, drew from it their inspired songs of praise.

"Let the message [i.e., the *Word*] of Christ, in all its richness, find a home with you... With gratitude in your hearts sing psalms and hymns and inspired songs to God."[503]

A spiritual theological reflection on God's word, quite significant for prayer as address as it originates from listening to and welcoming that Word into one's heart, is given by Baldwin of Canterbury in his comment upon a well-known text of Scripture:

"The word of God is something alive and active; it cuts as a double-edged sword but more finely; it can slip through the place where the soul is divided from the spirit, or joints from the marrow; it can judge the secret emotions and thoughts."[504]

Here is Baldwin's comment:

---

[500] Ac 2:42; cf. 1:14; 4:24-30.

[501] *Ibid.,* 6:2-5; cf. 12:5.

[502] 1 Th 2:13; Rm 10:8-10.

[503] Col 3:16.

[504] Heb 4:12.

"This Word, Christ, the power and the wisdom of God, was with the Father in the beginning, and in his own time was revealed to the apostles, then preached by them and humbly received in faith by believers. So, the word is in the Father, as well as on our lips and in our hearts.

This word of God not only is alive, but it is life.., is both life and life-giving... When this word is preached, in the very act of preaching it gives to its own voice which is heard outwardly a certain power which is perceived inwardly so much so that the dead are brought back to life and by these praises the sons of Abraham are raised from the dead.

This word then is alive in the heart of the Father, on the lips of the preacher, and in the hearts of those who believe and love him, since this word is so truly alive, undoubtedly it is full of power.

It is powerful in creation, powerful in the government of the universe, powerful in the redemption of the world... It is powerful in what it accomplished, powerful when preached. It does not come back empty: it bears fruit in all to whom it is sent.

It is powerful and 'more piercing than any two-edged sword' when it is believed and loved. For what is impossible to the believer? What is difficult to a lover? When this word is spoken, its message pierces the heart like the sharp arrows of a strong man, like nails driven deep; it enters so deeply that it penetrates to the innermost recess...it is stronger than any courage or power, sharper than any shrewdness of human ingenuity, keener than all human wisdom, or the subtlety of learned argument."[505]

c. *The biblical style of prayer as address*

In the Old Testament prayer as address is multifariously termed calling, crying, invoking, appealing, pleading, petitioning, entreating, thanking, praising, singing, etc., with great confidence that God will listen, hear, answer, grant, etc., his People's prayers.

The scriptural passages containing these verbs are extremely numerous. The Psalms teem with such expressions of prayer. The same terms are used also by the New Testament.

Both the Old and New Testament specifically recommend that those who address themselves to God in prayer should be reverent and brief, discarding all false confidence that pagans have in the efficacy of their mumbled, long, and monotonous repetitions of words.

---

[505] *Tract.,* 6, PL 204; 451-453. English translation in LITURGY, vol. IV, pp. 461-462. Emphasis ours.

> "Be in no hurry to speak; do not hastily declare yourself before God; for God is in heaven, you on earth. Be sparing, then, of speech." "Do not make long-winded speeches in the gathering of elders, and do not repeat yourself at your prayers."[506]
>
> "In your prayers do not babble as the pagans do, for they think that by using many words they will make themselves heard. Do not be like them. Your Father knows what you need before you ask him."[507]

A good commentary on these recommendations is given by John Climacus:

> "In your prayer there is no need for high-flown words, for it is the simple and unsophisticated babblings of children that have more often won the heart of the Father in heaven.
>
> Try not to talk excessively in your prayer, in case your mind is distracted by the search for words. One word from the publican sufficed to placate God and a simple utterance saved the thief.
>
> Talkative prayer *(polylogia)* distracts the mind and deludes it, whereas brevity *(monologia)* makes for concentration."[508]

Jesus himself taught his disciples the very meaningful but brief "Our Father" through which his disciples can most fittingly address their prayer to their heavenly Father.[509]

---

[506] Qo 5:1 and Si 7:14.

[507] Mt 6:7-8.

[508] CLIMACUS [2], p. 275. This passage is explained extensively in the *Intruduction* to the same book, pp. 44ff. Commenting on the same passage of the NT (Mt 6:5-9), ORIGEN, *On Prayer,* XXI, 1-2, p. 122, comes down strongly against those who "heap up empty phrases" of prayer.

[509] "Qui (= Christus) inter cetera salutaria sua monita et praecepta divina, quibus populo sui consulit ad salutem, etiam orandi ipse formam dedit, ipse quid precaremur monuit et instruxit. Qui fecit vivere docuit et orare, benignitate ea scilicet, qua et cetera dare et conferre dignatus est, ut dum prece et oratione quam filius docuit apud Patrem *loquimur, facilius audiamur...* Amica et familiaris oratio est Deum de suo rogare, *ad aures eius ascendere* Christi oratione. Agnoscat Pater *filii sui verba, cum precem facimus:* qui habitat intus in pectore, ipse et *in voce.*": ST. CYPRIAN, *De Dominica Oratione,* ch. 1-3. CSEL, 3, 267-268. Emphasis ours.

A good balance between the opposite extremes of uttering too many words when we pray or praying too little is struck by the following advice:

> "God urges you to pray earnestly and frequently, not offering long and wearisome prayers, but praying often and with perseverance. Lengthy prayers are usually filled with empty words, while neglect of prayer results in indifference to prayer."[510]

Christian teaching about God's Word and its relevance for Christian prayer is summarized by Vatican II.

> "By revelation the invisible God (cf. Col 1:15; 1 Tm 1:17), from the fullness of his love, *addresses men as his friends* (cf. Ex 33:11; Jn 15:14-15), and moves among them (cf. Ba 3:38), in order to invite them and to *receive them into his own company...*
>
> The Tradition that comes from the apostles makes progress in the Church, with the help of the Holy Spirit... This comes about in various ways. *It comes through the contemplation and study of believers who ponder these things in their hearts* (cf. Lk 2:19 and 51). It comes from the intimate sense of spiritual realities which they experience. Its riches are poured out in the practice and the life of the Church, *in her belief and prayer...* In the sacred books the Father who is in heaven *comes lovingly to meet his children, and talks with them.* And such is the force and power of the Word of God that it can serve the Church as its support and vigor, and the children of the Church as strength for their faith, food for the soul, and a pure and lasting fount of spiritual life....
>
> Let them (i.e., all the Christian faithful) remember that *prayer should accompany the reading of sacred Scripture, so that a dialogue takes place between God and man.*[511] For, 'we speak to him when we pray: we listen to

---

[510] St. Ambrose, *Treatise on Cain and Abel,* 1, 9, 34, quoted by LITURGY, vol. IV, p. 347.

[511] The paramount model for the use of Scripture in prayer is given by the celebration of the Liturgy. "For it is from sacred Scripture that lessons are read and explained in the homily, and psalms are sung. It is from the Scriptures that the prayers, collects, and hymns draw their inspiration and their force, and that actions and signs derive their meaning.": SC, no. 24. FLANNERY, p. 10. Hence, *in the liturgy God speaks* to his people, and Christ is still proclaiming his Gospel, and *the people reply* to God both by song and prayer." *Ibid.,* no. 33. FLANNERY, pp. 11-12. Emphasis ours.

him when we read the divine oracles.' (ST. AMBROSE, *De Officiis Ministrorum,* I, 20, 88; PL 16,50)."[512]

ii. *The Definition and Expressions of Prayer as Address*

a. *Prayer is speaking with God.*

Origen deems that those who pray are

> "Persuaded that they stand beside him (i.e., the Father of the universe), present and listening, and *are speaking with God.*"[513]

Likewise, Climacus speaks of prayer as

> "Standing before our King and God, and *speaking with him.*"[514]

When St. Isidore of Seville wrote: "Praying is equivalent to saying",[515] he was clearly referring to prayer as address.

> "St. Thomas Aquinas writes of prayer in *Summa Theologiae* II-II, 83. *Prayer, an act of the virtue of religion, is essentially a speaking* (*Ibid.* a. 1). Common prayer should be vocal for obvious reasons (*Ibid.* a. 12). Personal prayer, while it need not be vocal may be so, and for good reasons."[516]

While, in *sed contra* of the first article of his *quaestio* on prayer Aquinas of set purpose quotes St. Isidore's words, in the *corpus* of the same article he points out that he intends to deal here only with prayer of petition or entreaty.[517] So, Aquinas does not really say that prayer is "essentially a

---

[512] DV, nn. 3, 8, 21, 25: FLANNERY, pp. 751, 754, 762, 764. Emphasis ours.

[513] *On Prayer,* VII, 2, p. 98. Emphasis ours.

[514] CLIMACUS [2], Step 28, p. 274. Emphasis ours.

[515] "Orare idem est quod dicere": *Etymologiarum Libri,* X, PL 82, 388.

[516] BOLAND, p. 179.

[517] "In the present context we are considering prayer as a request or petition."

speaking", although he implies that the prayer he is talking about necessarily involves speaking.[518]

Cassiodore made a pun on *oris* (genitive of the Latin word *os,* the mouth by which words are uttered) and *oratio,* i.e., the uttered words of prayer,[519] certainly stress also that praying is speaking. But Aquinas was rather struck by the word *ratio* of this pun, which he understood as the practical reason from which the prayer of petition is elicited.[520]

John Henry Newman explains how we converse with God in prayer:

> "What, then, is prayer? It is (if it may be said reverently) *conversing with God.* We converse with our fellow-men, and then we use familiar language, because they are our fellows. We converse with God, and then we use the lowliest, awfullest, calmest, concisest language, because he is God. *Prayer, then, is divine converse,* differing from human as God differs from man....
>
> Not indeed meaning converse of words only, but intercourse and manner of living generally; yet still *in a special way converse of words or prayer*, because language is the special means of all intercourse."[521]

In line with this understanding of prayer a contemporary author reminds us that prayer "at its simplest is a straightforward talking to God",[522] and explains:

> "There is no need for elaborate theory here. For the medievals, as for the Christians of antiquity, praying was essentially a very straightforward thing; not a complicated and difficult exercise of the mind, as we moderns sometimes seem to suppose, but a simple talking to God. And that would mean talking aloud – real talking – though not necessarily talking loudly."[523]

---

518 Cf. ELDERS, pp. 15, 165.

519 "Oratio est quasi oris ratio": CASSIODORE, *Expositio in Psalterio,* Ps 38, PL 70, 285.

520 Cf. II-II, q. 83, a. 1.

521 NEWMAN [1], pp. 227-228.

522 TUGWELL [2], p. 129.

523 TUGWELL, [1], p. (7).

Other contemporary authors think, however, that the speaking of prayer is much more profound than simply talking to:

> "Prayer is above all conversation with God. It is the primary speech of the true self to the true God... We speak in prayer from our most hidden heart to the hiddenness of God, in whose astonishing image we were fashioned and find our true faces....
>
> The praying consciousness speaks out of what it knows of itself... We talk to ourselves and of ourselves and through ourselves to God in the heart of prayer.[524] *This is speech at its truest. This is primary speech, speech at its most elemental...meaning a speech that is of first importance and absolutely basic to our humanity...*
>
> Prayer consists of honest conversation that proceeds from true consciousness."[525]

b. Varieties of prayer as address

The different frames of mind, cultural background or milieu, situations and inspirations of the praying persons, etc., can lend a great deal of variety to prayers of address. Here are some of these varieties which today seem to be most common.

"Personal" is the prayer of address performed by the unique cognitive mind-set and affective make-up of each praying person. Personal prayer can be performed either in private or in community.

"Popular" is the prayer of address moulded by the folklore of people praying together; particularly during the celebration of certain traditional religious feasts. The Holy Rosary and the Way of the Cross are well-known forms of popular prayer as address.

"Liturgical" are well-structured, publicly recited or sung, prayers of address, whose major aim is to worship God on behalf of the whole ecclesial

---

524 That prayer is "speaking with oneself and God" is time and again stressed by St. Gregory Nazianzenus (Cf. EA, no. 295, p. 167; no. 307, p. 175; no. 310, p. 177).

525 ULANOV, pp. 24-28, passim. Emphasis ours. The article from which these passages are taken is a summary of ULANOV [2]. See also RINKER.

community. Liturgical prayers follow the succession of hours and sacred feastdays throughout the whole year.[526]

"Shared" are those prayers of address offered to God by a group of friends who get together to meditate and praise the Lord. One person of the group reads aloud a passage of the Sacred Scripture. After a period of reflective silence, those who feel like doing so may, one after the other, say something and prayerfully share the spiritual insights and devout aspirations that they have drawn from the Scripture reading. So, shared prayer is a publicly held meditative conversation with God.

A particular form of shared prayer is practiced by the prayer groups of the "charismatic renewal movement". Besides reading and meditating on the Scripture, the shared prayer of this movement involves giving testimony of how God has acted in one's life, praising him aloud, reciting prayers or singing popular religious hymns, "prophesying", "speaking in tongues", praying for healing over someone by laying hands on him or her, etc.

The "peak-experience" of the charismatic prayer meeting is the experience of a new "conversion", which is called by the participants "baptism in the Spirit", because it is believed to be effected by the Holy Spirit.[527]

These are a few types of the prayer as address which are practiced by contemporary Christians. But the ways of addressing oneself to God in prayer may be as many as human inventiveness can create by analogy with the innumerable ways that people have for friendly communication with one another.

c. Grades of prayer as address

Prayer as address not only has many different outward expressions but it grows through inner successive grades, too. The following ones are the most important in the growth process of prayer as address.

---

[526] To the question whether solitary or communal prayer is more profitable CLIMACUS [2], Step 28, p. 278, gives the following well-balanced answer: "One can be held back and distracted by the singing of psalms in a congregation. This does not happen when one is solitary. However, despondency can assail the latter, while in the former situation the brethren can give help by their zeal."

[527] Cf. CARTER, pp. 81-89; CHESTER-MORISSEY, p. 181.

1. This grade consists in speaking with God vocally, i.e., by uttering audible words. Several forms of vocal prayer have been mentioned above when the variations of prayer as address were described.

2. When prayer as address reaches the second grade,

> "The soul does not pray in the way it did before, or in the common manner of men - in a loud voice, or by speaking out fluently - but *in a very great stillness of voice and gentleness of heart...* The mind is wholly gathered together in itself, and the soul is set as in a spiritual presence of Jesus; and therefore every word and every syllable is pronounced with savor, sweetness and delight, and with heart and mouth in full accord.
>
> For the soul is then turned into a fire of love, and therefore *each word that it secretly prays* is like a spark springing out of a firebrand, warming all the powers of the soul, turning them into love, and filling them with light; so great is the comfort that the soul is pleased to pray all the time and do nothing else."[528]

At this second grade praying Christians address themselves to God with their minds and hearts along, without any audible words. Such a silent conversation is possible because

> "God does not need loquacious tongues as interpreters of human beings, but he directly knows the minds of all; and what the voice signifies to us is said to God by our very thinking... It is therefore allowable to perform a soundless prayer, provided that all the inner spirit which could be put into the sound of words is thought by the mind firmly turned to God."[529]
>
> "The Scripture teaches us that the voice which is melodious and ascends to God's hearing is not the cry made with the organs of speech, but the meditation sent up from a pure conscience (1 Tm 1:5)."[530]
>
> "To pray much is to knock for him to whom our prayer is addressed by the constant and devout fervor of the heart. Actually, this is more often a matter of groanings than of speeches, more weeping than words. In fact, God lets our tears come into his presence and our groanings are not hidden from

---

[528] HILTON, II, 42, pp. 289-290. Emphasis ours.

[529] CLEMENT OF ALEXANDRIA, *Stromata,* 7, 7, 43, 4-5. EA, n. 92, pp. 44-45. Translation ours. Cf. ORIGEN, *Selecta in Genesim,* 24, 21. EA, n. 111, pp. 57-58: "It is good to pray not by the voice that can be sensibly heard but in the heart to God who searches hearts". Translation ours.

[530] GREGORY OF NYSSA, II, 118, p. 82.

> him, who created everything by his Word and does not want for human words."[531]

This silent inner speaking with God became that prayerful thinking and loving him which was called meditation.[532]

3. Paradoxically the highest grade of speaking with God in prayer is reached when praying Christians are enabled by the Holy Spirit to address themselves to God in absolute outer and inner silence: *Silentium Tibi laus!* At this stage Christians address to God no inner words, but their whole self permeated by silent prayerfulness points to the God of infinite Majesty and ultimate Goodness. In a way it is analogous to the silence full of meaning through which lovers still communicate between themselves when everything else has been said and done:

> "This is what *the prayer of unknowing* is all about: we need to be with God without thinking about anything, or asking anything. We want to be in the presence of God as comfortably as we are with a person we love, with whom *silence itself is a kind of communication,* as delightful as we are with the person with whom we are in love."[533]

St. Isaac of Niniveh was singing the praises of this highly silent prayer when he wrote:

---

[531] ST. AUGUSTINE, *Epistulae,* CXXX, 10. 20. EA, no. 695, p. 355: "Multum precari est ad eum, quem precamur, diuturna et pia cordis excitatione pulsare. Nam plerumque *hoc negotium plus germitibus quam sermonibus agitur, plus fletu quam affatu.* Ponit autem lacrimas nostras in conspectu suo et gemitus noster non est absconditus ab eo, qui omnia per Verbum condidit et humana verba non quaerit." Translation and emphasis ours. Freely following St. Augustine, Aquinas similarly writes that the Holy Spirit makes us cry to God : "Non magnitudine vocis, sed magnitudine et fervore affectu. Tunc enim clamamus Abba-Pater quando per affectum accendimur calore Spiritu Sancti ad desiderium Dei.": ESP, vol. I, *Ad Galatas,* IV, Lect. 3, no. 215, pp. 613-614.

[532] During the Middle Ages *meditari* and *meditatio* meant to repeat time and again the words of a master or of a book in order to learn them by heart and grasp their profound meaning.

[533] BONDI, p. 99-100. The "prayer of unknowing" of which this author speaks seemingly refers to *The Cloud of Unknowing.*

> "Many are avidly seeking, but they alone find who remain in continual silence... Every man who delights in a multitude of words, even though he says admirable things, is empty within.
>
> If you love truth, be a lover of silence,.. *Silence will unite you to God himself...* More than all things love silence; it brings you a fruit that the tongue cannot describe.
>
> In the beginning we have to force ourselves to silence. But then there is born something that draws us to silence... After a while a certain sweetness is born in the heart of this exercise, and the body is drawn almost by force to remain in silence."[534]

Such wordless address to God in prayer creates in the Christian an expectant emptiness which is filled with the Father's and Holy Spirit's gift of the Eternal Word.

> "The Father utters only one Word in His eternal Silence, and this Word is His Son; a Word that the soul can listen to only in perfect silence!" (John of the Cross)

An author explains that this "silence" is,

> "A silence that the Spirit causes to ring with the echo of the eternal Word, a silence of expectation, a simple regard toward the One who is 'there', simple attention, simple awakening."[535]

iii. *Responses of Prayer to the Word of God*

a. *Responding to God's written Word*[536]

When Christians not only read the Scripture but also listen to God's inspired words with docility and gratitude they dispose themselves to pray. The *Imitation of Christ* gently exhorts its readers to do that:

---

[534] Quoted by LEECH, p. 58.

[535] Le Saux quoted by DUPUIS, p. 73.

[536] Cf. ROSAGE, ch. ii, Prayer is listening, pp. 21 ff; ch. iii, Praying scripturally, pp. 34 ff.

> "My son, says the Lord, listen to my words, the most delightful of all words, surpassing all the knowledge of the philosophers and wise men of this world. My words are *spirit and life* and cannot be comprehended by human sense alone. They are not to be interpreted according to the vain pleasure of the listener, but they must be listened to in silence and received with humility and great affection."[537]

Devout readers of the Scripture actually pray by getting in touch with God through his written words.

> "Prayer begins when we start to read our Bible listening primarily to God...to what God is saying to us at the present moment through our reading of a passage. 'One must read the Bible as a young man reads a letter from his beloved. It is written for me', declared Kierkegaard."[538]

God initiates his dialogue with us by speaking the words of the Scripture which we read. We respond to him by speaking the prayer that the Scripture which we have just read inspires us to say. The well-known parable of the sower illustrates very efficaciously such a listening-responding pattern of the hearers of the divine words so lavishly sown as seeds of life in the fields of human hearts.

Because they were aware of this dialogical character of Christian prayer as address, the Fathers deemed that:

> "When you pray, you address yourself to the Bridegroom (= Jesus Christ): when you read (the Bible) He speaks to you."[539]

---

[537] IC, III, 3, quoted in LITURGY, vol. III, p. 193.

[538] DALRYMPLE, p. 51. The simile of the love letter is used also by other spiritual writers. Cf. below, notes 72 and 73.

[539] JEROME, *Epistulae,* 22, 25. EA, no. 493, p. 278: "Oras, loqueris ad sponsum; legis, ille tibi loquitur." Throughout his Letters St. Jerome recommends the joining of the frequent reading of the Scripture with prayer. 107, 9. EA, no. 531, p. 289: "Orationi lectio, lectioni succedat oratio." 125, 11. EA, no. 546, p. 294: "Nusquam de manu et oculis tuis recedat liber: psalterium discatur ad verbum; oratio sine intermissione..." 148, 24. EA, no. 562, p. 300: "Tantum sit tibi divinae lectionis studium, tam crebrae orationum vices..." Cf. 54, 10; 60, 10; 70, 11. EA, no. 515, pp. 285-286; no. 519, p. 285; no. 528, p. 287, etc. He also adds 54, 10. EA, no. 515, p. 285: "Post Scripturas sanctas doctorum nominum tractatus lege, eorum dumtaxat, quorum fides nota est. Non necesse habes aurum in luto quaerere."

> "Your prayer is conversation with God: when you read [the Bible], God speaks to you; when you pray, you speak to God."[540]

In the same vein, some Catholic theologians today emphasize the responsive character of Christian prayer, pointing out that responding implies and presupposes listening:

> "Prayer is a conversation in which God's word has the initiative and we, for the moment, can be nothing more than listeners. The essential thing is for us to hear God's word and discover from it how to respond to him... This listening is the original wellspring of all Christian life and prayer."[541]
>
> "One way to understand prayer is simply receptivity to the Word. Prayer is not primarily an activity or a doing, but fundamentally a receptivity. Prayer is an opening of the heart to receive God's Word... Theologians such as Balthasar stress that all prayer has essentially this structure of receptivity to the Word...
>
> It is worth noticing Balthasar's insistence that the Christian's life with the Word is the decisive point which distinguishes Christian prayer from all other types of prayer. This point follows naturally from the unique foundation of Christian experience, namely that God has spoken."[542]

Vatican II authoritatively recalls this traditional teaching about listening by reading God's Word, and responding by speaking to God through prayer.

> "Remember that prayer should accompany the reading of sacred Scripture so that a dialogue takes place between God and man."[543]

---

[540] ST. AUGUSTINE, *Enarrationes in Psalmos,* 85, 5. PL 37, 1086. Of his mother, Monica, Augustine wrote: "Bis die, mane et vespere, ad ecclesiam tuam sine ulla intermissione venientis...ut te audiret in tuis sermonibus et tu illam in suis orationibus.": *Confessiones,* V, 10, 17. Before Augustine, ST. AMBROSE had written in *De Officiis Ministrorum,* I, 20, 88. PL 16, 50: "illum alloquimur, cum oramus: illum audimus, cum divina legimus oracula." After Augustine, ST. ISIDORE OF SEVILLE repeats in *Sententiae,* III, 8. PL 83, 679: "cum oramus cum Deo ipsi loquimur: cum vero legimus, Deus nobiscum loquitur."

[541] VON BALTHASAR [2], p. 15, 31.

[542] O'DONNELL, p. 148-149.

[543] DV, 25. FLANNERY, p. 764.

An Episcopalian Catechism stresses the essentially responsive character of our speaking with God to the point of defining Christian prayer simply as a response.

> "Prayer is *responding* to God, by thought and by deeds, with or without words... Christian prayer is a *response* to God the Father, through Jesus Christ, in the power of the Holy Spirit."[544]

After all, the medieval sequence of *lectio, meditatio, oratio, contemplatio,*[545] resulted from a development of the early Christian teaching on prayer as the response to God's word previously listened to by reading the Scriptures.

> "Reading is the careful study of the Scriptures. Meditation is the busy application of the mind to seek for the knowledge of hidden truth. Prayer *(oratio)* is the heart's devoted turning to God. Prayer lifts itself up to God with all its strength, and begs for the treasure it longs for, which is the sweetness of contemplation."[546]

So the Christian is exhorted to,

> "Seek in reading and you will find in meditation, knock in prayer and it will be opened to you in contemplation."[547]

And it is precisely in contemplation that one looks at God's Word as a significant sign of his presence, which eventually takes the personal features of the Word made flesh, Jesus Christ.

---

[544] OF, p. 12. Emphasis ours.

[545] Cf. GUIGO II. This book is quoted also by CCC, n. 2654.

[546] GUIGO II, II and III, pp. 82, 83, 92, passim.

[547] This maxim is attributed to St. John of the Cross. About the history of this sequence see TUGWELL [4], p. 43, note 112. Some medieval authors put the progression from *lectio* to *oratio* and from *oratio* to *meditatio: Ibid.,* note 113.

b. Responding to the Word made flesh

In the last analysis, the reading of Scripture demands of Christians a prayerful response to God, because Jesus Christ himself, the Only Begotten Son of God made man, is mysteriously but really present in the words of Scripture. And he is present, too, in the Christian community at prayer.

> "Christ is present in his word since it is he himself who speaks when the holy Scriptures are read in the Church. He is present when the Church prays and sings, for he has promised 'where two or three are gathered together in my name there I am in the midst of them'...
>
> It is from the Scriptures that the prayers, collects, and hymns (of the Liturgy) draw their inspiration and their force... In the liturgy God speaks to his people, and Christ is still proclaiming his Gospel. And the people reply to God both by song and prayer."[548]

Walter Hilton, for one, expounds at length on how the belief that Christ is present in the Scripture gives Christians the spiritual understanding of it and at the same time sharpens their contemplative loving insight into Christ. So that, having such a spiritual understanding of the Scripture, they can reach an intimate love relationship with Christ.

> "Jesus, who is all truth, is hidden and concealed in holy Scripture, wound in soft fine linen under fair words, so that he cannot be known and felt except by a pure heart because truth will not show itself to enemies, but to friends who love it and desire it with a humble heart...
>
> Truth and humility are faithful sisters, joined together in love and charity...inasmuch as a lover's soul is made humble through the inspiration of grace, by the opening of the spiritual eye and truly is desiring Jesus' presence: it therefore sees Jesus. For it sees the truth of the holy Scripture wonderfully shown and open, above study and toil and the reasoning of man's natural wit. For Jesus is the well of wisdom, and by the little pouring of his wisdom into a pure soul he makes the soul wise enough to understand all holy Scripture...
>
> The spiritual presence of Jesus opens the understanding of his lover who burns in desire for him, and by the ministry of angels brings to his mind the words and insights of holy Scripture, unsought and unconsidered, one after another, and readily expounds them, however hard and secret they may be. The harder they are and the farther from the natural understanding of man, the more delightful is the showing of it when Jesus is master...

---

[548] SC, 7, 24, 33: FLANNERY, pp. 5, 10, 11-12.

> You must know that such gracious intuitions in holy Scripture – or in any other book made through grace – are nothing else but sweet letters[549] sent between a loving soul and Jesus, the beloved; or else, if I am to speak more truthfully, between Jesus the true lover and the soul loved by him. He has love of very great tenderness for all his chosen children, and although he is absent from them – hidden high above in the bosom of the Father and filled with the delights of the blessed Deity – he thinks of them none the less and visits them very often through his gracious spiritual presence: he comforts them by his holy letters of holy Scripture... This is another work of contemplation: to see Jesus in the Scripture after the opening of the spiritual eye."[550]

The encounter between the Christian and God through Christ present in the Scripture is so realistically understood by St. Gregory the Great who claims that the reader of Scripture can see through it, as it were, the facial expression of God.

> "Truly thoughtful servants always pay attention to the facial expression of their masters so as to hear and follow their command with promptness. In the same way righteous Christians focus their minds on the presence of Almighty God and gaze upon his Scripture as upon his countenance."[551]

c. *Responding to God's word in the universe and history*

It is worth remembering, however, that it is not only the Scriptures that bring us into the presence of God and let us know his will. To those who were surprised that St. Anthony the Great had no book with him, not even the sacred Scripture, he explained:

> "My book is the nature of created things, and it is always at hand when I wish to read the words of God."[552]

---

[549] Cf. ST. AUGUSTINE, *Enarrationes in Psalmos,* 64, 2.

[550] HILTON, II, ch. 43, pp. 293-294, 296.

[551] GREGORY THE GREAT, *Moralia in Job,* 16, 35. PL 75, 1142. Translation ours.

[552] PL 73, 1018 c.

Indeed, a prayerful conversation with God can be begun also by seeing him reflected in the creatures of the universe no less than expressed in the words of the Scripture. However, as the Judeo-Christian religion is characterized more by the interventions of God in History than by his creative action in Nature, Vatican II especially exhorts Christians to read God's words in "the signs of the times".

So Christian prayer as address should also be a response of faith to the events of history in which God's words and messages are conveyed.

This is a consequence of the incarnation of the Word, after which Jesus Christ is mysteriously present and reveals himself in all historical events and human experience.

In conclusion, Christian prayer as address is the responding moment of a dialogue which God initiates with Christians in the Scripture, through and in Jesus, in and through all the creatures of the universe and events of history.

The phases of this divine-human conversation are: God addresses his Word to us; we listen to God's Word; we give our prayerful response to God's Word; God hears and answers our prayer.

* * *

Both prayer as ascent and prayer as address lead praying Christians to an interpersonal relationship with God. The ascent and address of prayer both support and are supported by this relationship.

Actually, sincere Christians practice prayer as ascent and as address with the intention of reaching such relationship with God. Hence it may happen that one and the same activity of prayer bears the character of both ascent and address (which belong to the *operative* dimension of prayerlife) and concomitantly builds or maintains an interpersonal relationship of the praying Christian with God (which belongs to the *relational* dimension of prayerlife).

CHAPTER VII

PRAYER AS WORSHIP

After the preceding analysis of the two major trends of the operative dimension of prayerlife we must now consider its relational dimension. For the operative dimension of prayer aims at and paves the way to its relational dimension.

The relational dimension of prayerlife differs according to the various relationships between God and the praying Christian, which it implies, builds, and develops.

> "We can know God - namely, reach out to him and have a personal contact with him - only in the way that we know other personal beings, that is to say, by *communion or communication at a personal level.* Indeed, we could say that we know God only to the extent that he knows us through his gracious self-communication and revelation.
>
> But what is this communion with God if it is not prayer and *worship?"* [553]

The recent *Catechism of the Catholic Church* puts it as follows

> "The *acts of faith, hope, and charity* prescribed by the first commandment are exercised in prayer. The lifting of the spirit towards God is expressed by our *adoration* of God." (n. 2098. Emphasis ours).

The two major relationships with God of the Christian who prays are:

—The relationship brought about by the offering of worship and reverence to him.

—The relationship established through an intimate living communion with him.

We will term *prayer as worship* the prayer practiced in the context of the former, and *prayer as communion* the prayer practiced in the context of the latter.

We will begin our research with prayer as worship because this kind of prayer is first and more commonly practiced by Christians.

---

[553] MACQUARRIE [2], p. 587. Emphasis ours.

i. *Prayer and Worship in the Bible*

a. Obedience and humility are more acceptable to Yahweh than sacrifices and words of prayer

Sacrifices and prayers are the two essential components of the worship due to Yahweh by the Chosen People.

> "All who observe the sabbath, not profaning it, and cling to my covenant – these I will bring to my holy mountain. I will make them joyful in *my house of prayer.* Their *holocausts* and their *sacrifices* will be accepted on my altar, for my house will be called a *house of prayer* for all peoples."[554]

Sacrifices and prayers are so tightly joined that some Hebrew verbs can be used to mean either prayer or sacrifice, or prayer and sacrifice. This is the case of the Hebrew verb "to seek (Yahweh)".

> "The sons of Israel will *seek Yahweh* their God... They will come trembling to Yahweh, come for his good things in those days to come...though they *go in search of Yahweh* with their sheep and oxen, they do not find him."[555]

The same is true of the Hebrew verb "to thank (Yahweh)".

> "They will come to offer holocaust and sacrifice, oblation, incense and *sacrifice of thanksgiving* in the Temple of Yahweh... From the tents of Jacob will come *thanksgiving and shouts of joy."*
>
> "Let men offer *thanksgiving sacrifices and proclaim with shouts of joy* what Yahweh has done." "I will offer you (Yahweh) the *thanksgiving sacrifice, invoking the name of Yahweh."*[556]

---

[554] Is 56:6-7

[555] Ho 3:5 and 5:6; cf. Zc 8:21-22; Ps 24:3,6; etc.

[556] Jr 17:26; 30:19; Ps 107:22; Ps 116:17.

The Prophets declare that worship is rejected by Yahweh when the offerers transgress his Law and do not do justice to the oppressed, the orphans and widows.[557]

> "Listen, my people, I (Yahweh) am speaking; Israel, I am giving evidence against you! I charge, I indict you to your face. I, God, your God, I am not finding fault with your sacrifices, those holocausts constantly before me....
>
> Do I eat the flesh of bulls, or drink goats' blood? *No, let thanksgiving be your sacrifice to God,* fulfill the vows you made to the Most High; then you can invoke me in your troubles and I will rescue you, and you will honor me... *Whoever makes thanksgiving his sacrifice honors me.*"[558]

The immorality of those who worship provokes their rejection

> "When you stretch out your hands I (= Yahweh) turn my eyes away. You may multiply your prayers, I shall not listen. Your hands are covered with blood, wash, make yourself clean."[559]

Above all Yahweh likes and accepts the broken spirit and crushed heart.

> "Sacrifice gives you (Yahweh) no pleasure, were I to offer holocaust, you would not have it. *My sacrifice is this broken spirit, you will not scorn this crushed and broken heart."* [560]
>
> "We have at this time...no holocaust, no sacrifice, no oblation, no incense... But *may the contrite soul, the humble spirit be as acceptable to you as holocausts* of rams and bullocks."[561]

---

[557] Cf. Is 1:11-31; Am 5:21-27.

[558] Ps 50:7, 14-15, 23.

[559] Is 1:15.

[560] Ps 51:16-17.

[561] Dn 3:38-39.

Yahweh is more present to the humble and contrite spirit than in the magnificent Temple of Jerusalem, where sacrifices of animals and words of prayer are solemnly offered.

> "Thus says Yahweh: 'With heaven my throne and earth my footstool, what house could you build me, what place could you make for my rest? All of this was made by my hand and all of this is mine' – it is Yahweh who speaks. But *my eyes are rather drawn to the man of humbled and contrite spirit, who trembles at my word." "Yahweh is near to the broken-hearted,* he helps those whose spirit is crushed."[562]
>
> "What I (Yahweh) want is love, not sacrifice; knowledge of God, not holocausts."[563]

In conclusion:

> "Contrary to the widespread impression that there was a fundamental antithesis between the religion of the law and that of the prophets, the truth is that the latter were not against sacrifice *per se*, but simply against the abuse of it; and as a matter of fact Isaiah (1:15) inveighed equally against hypocritical prayer.
>
> Their protest was directed primarily against the attribution to sacrifice of properties and virtues which in fact it did not, and could not possess; especially against the view that it expressed of itself the spiritual bond between the worshipper and God, and that a man could be spiritually shriven by being ritually cleansed."[564]

b. Christian prayers are spiritual sacrifices

The conviction that prayers elicited from a pure heart are "sacrifices of praise" carried over into the New Testament.

---

[562] Is 66:1-2; Ps 34:18.

[563] Ho 6:6; cf. 1 S 15:22-23.

[564] GASTER, p. 157 b.

> "Through him (Jesus Christ), *let us offer God an unending sacrifice of praise, a verbal sacrifice that is offered every time we acknowledge his name.*"[565]

The prayers of the saints are offered to God together with the incense of the heavenly sacrifice:

> "A large quantity of incense was given to the angel to offer with all the prayers of all the saints on the golden altar that stood in front of the throne; and so from the angel's hand the smoke of *the incense went up in the presence of God and with it the prayers of the saints.*"[566]

The identification of Christian prayer with spiritual sacrifice is made also by the early Fathers of the Church,

> "Prayer is a costly and noble sacrifice, dispatched from the chaste body, an unstained soul, a sanctified spirit."[567]
>
> "The Apostle Paul says that not only the tongues of those on earth and in the underworld but also of those in the heavens (Ph 2:10) render praise to the source of all things. This is the sacrifice pleasing God, a verbal sacrifice, as the Apostle says, the fragrance of prayer... In this tabernacle [of the human spirit] both the sacrifice of praise and the incense of prayer are seen offered continually at morning and evening."[568]

These spiritual sacrifices of Christian prayer ought to be offered with faith.

> *"In the NT true prayer is described as asking in faith* (Mt 21:22; Jm 1:5f; note the affinity between Jm and Mt). In prayer we are never to forget whom we are addressing: the living God, the almighty One with whom nothing is impossible, and from whom therefore all things may be expected...

---

[565] Heb 13:15; cf. Rm 1:9.

[566] Rv 8:3-4; cf. 5:8; Ps 141:1-2.

[567] TERTULLIAN, c. XXX, p. 42 a/b. Cf. Heb 10:22. See also the mention of "a sacrifice of praise" and of the "spirit of prayer" in the petitions at morning prayer of Monday of the Second Week of Lent: LITURGIA, vol. II, p. 127.

[568] GREGORY OF NYSSA, n. 182, p. 101.

> *True prayer is bound up with faith, i.e., with the certainty of being heard.* The NT encourages such a degree of certainty that the suppliant can believe he has actually received his request at the very moment of asking (Mk 11:24; 1 Jn 5:15).[569]
>
> *Also for Paul "prayer [of petition and intercession] is the most important evidence of true Christian faith* (1 Tm 2:11). It is the very mark of a Christian (1 Tm 5:5; cf. Ac 9:11). Ultimately the reason why a person who asks is certain of being heard is the certainty, given by Jesus to his own, of God's fatherly goodness and love (Mt 7:7-11)."[570]

Jesus often stresses that prayers ought to be made with a strong faith in order to be heeded and answered by God.[571] Several Gospel narratives highlight this truth.

> "To the centurion (who with an amazing faith had asked for the healing of one of his servants) Jesus said, 'Go back, then; *you have believed, so let this be done for you.'* And the servant was cured at that moment."
>
> The father of an epileptic demoniac besought Jesus saying: "'If you can do anything, have pity on us and help us'. 'If you can?' retorted Jesus, *'Everything is possible for anyone who has faith'.* Immediately the father of the boy cried out, 'I do have faith. Help the little faith I have!'" On another occasion "as Jesus went on his way two blind men followed him shouting, 'Take pity on us, Son of David'. And when Jesus reached the house the blind men came up with him and he said to them, *'Do you believe I can do this?'* They said, 'Sir, we do'. Then he touched their eyes saying *'Your faith deserves it.* So let this be done for you'. And their sight returned."
>
> Another "blind man said to him, 'Master, let me see again'. Jesus said to him, 'Go; *your faith has saved you'.* And immediately his sight returned."[572]

---

[569] Commenting on Mk 11:24, Cassian writes: "A man will deserve to be heard in proportion as he believes that God is looking upon him and that God can grant his prayer.": *Conferences,* IX, # 32. CHADWICK, p. 229.

[570] DNTT, vol. III, p. 857; cf. p. 868. Emphasis ours.

[571] This union between Christian prayer and faith leads Jm 5:15 to write – "the prayer of faith".

[572] Mt 8:13; Mk 9:23-25; Mt 9:27-29; Mk 10:51-52 = Lk 18:41-43; 17:19.

All these Gospel narratives clearly demonstrate that only prayer made with genuine *faith* deserves to be granted; whereas praying with little faith has very little effect. In a word, as Jesus himself tersely puts it:

> "Everything you ask and pray for, *believe that you have it already,* and it will be yours."[573]

The faith that gives efficacy to Christian prayer involves a deep sense of unworthiness before God and contrition for one's sins.

> "The tax collector stood some distance away, not even daring to raise his eyes to heaven; but he beat his breast and said, 'God, be merciful to me, a sinner'. This man, I tell you, went home again at rights with God."[574]

After all, these inner dispositions are essential components of the conversion required to receive God's Kingdom with faith.[575]

Love, too, must be joined to faith to give efficacy to Christian prayer, as is pointed out in the narrative of the woman of bad repute. Jesus emphasized that she had openly welcomed him not only with great faith but also with many gestures of tender love. Therefore,

> "'Her sins, her many sins, must have been forgiven her, or she would not have shown *such great love.*[576] It is the man who is forgiven little who shows little love'. Then he said to her, 'Your sins have been forgiven... *Your faith has saved you;* go in peace'."[577]

---

[573] Mk 11:24.

[574] Lk 18:13-14.

[575] Cf. Mk 1:15.

[576] The *New American Bible* in CSB translates: "her many sins have been forgiven: hence she has shown great love." and comments: "the whole episode is a powerful lesson on the relation between forgiveness and love."

[577] Lk 7:47-50.

St. Paul does not differ from the Gospels when he understands faith as an obedience through which Christians submit their whole minds and hearts and spirits to God.[578]

By emphasizing that only prayers which are expressions of faith and love are heard and answered by God, the synoptic Gospels implicitly teach that only these prayers are accepted by him as acts of genuine worship. In fact, the "faith" meant by the Gospels is a comprehensive, humble, confident, loving response of the whole human person to God worshipped as the Almighty and Merciful Father.

In conclusion, the Prophets of the Old Testament teach that of all the worship offered to him God really likes only a contrite and humble heart. And in the New Testament Christ confirms that God pays no heed to prayers not animated by faith, humility, contrition and love.

In both Testaments therefore only worship which does not limit itself to external gestures and lip-service but comes from the whole spirit, is accepted by God.

ii. *The Definition and Enumeration of the Acts of Prayer as Worship*

Since the Bible so often speaks of prayer as a spiritual worship agreeable to God, there was never any doubt among Christians that prayer is meant to offer God the worship due him. Hence, Aquinas claims that prayer is properly elicited from the virtue of religion, whose specific object is worship offered to God.[579]

So, instead of lingering over the definition of prayer as worship, we will muse upon its many expressions - petition, entreaty, confession, thanksgiving, praise, adoration, meditation, intercession, etc.[580]

The formulas of prayers available in the Old Testament, especially in the Psalms, contain all these expressions of prayer as

---

[578] Cf. Rm 1:5; 16:26; 2 Co 10:5-6.

[579] "Clearly prayer is an act of religion" (II-II, q. 83, a. 3, co.; BLACKFRIARS, vol. 39, p. 55). Cf. PINCKAERS, especially chs. ii-vi.

[580] Cf. SMITH, p. 858 a. Remember that, when these words are used in the Bible, they are not subject to exactness or equally distributed.

worship. And the New Testament shows that there is continuity between ancient Israel and the Christian Church in those expressions of prayer. The God of Israel and of Christians is worshipped in the same manner.[581]

a. Petition, intercession, penitence

1. The prayers of the poor, needy, and sick described by the Gospels are all prayers of petition, entreaty, beseeching, etc. Such prayers are the most fundamental and common acts of worship that Christians as well as all human beings offer to God.

There is a standard Christian definition of prayer of petition:

> "Prayer is asking fitting things of God."[582]

On the part of God, the efficacy of prayer of petition cannot be doubted.

> "Ask, and it will be given to you; search, and you will find; knock, and it will be open to you. For the one who asks always receives; the one who searches always finds; the one who knocks will always have the door opened to him.
>
> Is there a man among you who would hand his son a stone when he asked for bread? Or would hand him a snake when he asked for a fish? If you, then, who are evil, know how to give your children what is good, how much more will your Father in heaven give good things to those who ask him!"[583]

On the part of the praying Christian, faith is the decisive prerequisite for the efficacy of prayer of petition:

---

[581] BORTON, p. 52-53.

[582] Aquinas received this definition from John Damascene, III, 24, p. 1089. Cf. also Rabanus, Lib. VI, ch. 14, p. 136, which Aquinas thought to be a work of St. Augustine: ST, II-II, q. 83, a. 1, co.

[583] Mt 7:7-11 = Lk 11:9-13. Cf. Jn 14:13-14.

> "I tell you therefore: everything you ask and pray for, believe that you have it already, and it will be yours!"[584]

Petition is particularly efficacious when it is persevering.[585] But a too repetitious asking can degenerate into,

> "Magically attempting to subject the will of God to the will of man." Whereas, "religion is the attempt to subject the will of man to the will of God. And prayer is a religious activity."[586]

It is precisely in order to avoid any degeneration of prayer of petition into magic that an ancient Christian theologian advises:

> "Pray not to this end, that your own desires be fulfilled. You can be sure that they do not fully accord with the will of God. Once you have learned to accept this point, pray instead that 'thy will be done' in me. In every matter ask him in this way for what is good and for what confers profit on your soul, for you yourself do not seek this so completely as he does.
>
> Many times when I was at prayer, I kept asking what seemed good to me. I kept insisting on my own request, unreasonably putting pressure on the will of God. I simply would not leave it up to his Providence to arrange what he know would turn out for my profit. Finally, when I obtained my request I became greatly chagrined at having been so stubborn about getting my own way, for in the end the matter did not turn out to be what I had fancied it would...
>
> Therefore let us cast all our concerns upon him and it will be well with us... Persevere in your prayer with all sails unfurled, and do not set your heart on what seems good to you but rather what is pleasing to God when your pray."[587]

---

[584] Mk 11:24. Cf. Mt 18:19; Jm 1:5-8; 4:2-3; 5:16-17; 1 Jn 3:22; 5:14-15.

[585] Cf. Lk 11:5-8; 18:1-8.

[586] BUTLER, p. 60-61.

[587] EVAGRIUS, chs. 31, 32, 33, 88, 89, pp. 60, 70.

St. John of the Cross virtually gives the same advice[588] and severely blames Christians whose only aim in praying is having their petitions fulfilled.

> "What is indeed intolerable is that certain persons desire to feel some effect in themselves, or to have their petitions fulfilled, or to know that the purpose of the ceremonious prayers of theirs will be accomplished.
>
> This is nothing less than to tempt God and to anger Him greatly, so much so that He sometimes gives leave to the devil to deceive them, making them feel and understand things that are far removed from the benefit of their soul, which they deserve because of the attachment that they show in their prayers, not desiring God's will, rather than their own desires, to be done therein; and thus, because they place not their whole confidence in God, nothing else goes well with them."[589]

Consequently we pray as we ought when

> "In petition we present our needs, that God's will may be done."[590] For "most certainly it is right for us to ask in prayer and to put before God the problem of our burdensome existence. Yet it might profit us more if we direct our gaze away from ourselves towards Him."[591]

Humble and reverent petitions instill a sense of utter dependence on and confidence in God as they lead praying Christians to pay homage to his infinite majesty and rely on his infinite omnipotence.

> "To be man is to have one's being *from* and *in* God. Prayer, therefore, is not really a call for help but the acknowledgement of the fact that man receives substance and existence, life and meaning, et., through God's creative dispensation...
>
> All this may be called grace in a wider sense, because he receives as a free favor what he can neither claim nor enforce. Grace in the strict

---

[588] *Canticle A,* stanza II, n. 4 and 8.

[589] CROSS, [1], III, xliii, n. 3, p. 470.

[590] OF, p. 13.

[591] GUARDINI, p. 56.

> meaning of the term is everything that comes to us from God's redeeming love in the form of light, strength, guidance, spiritual comfort and liberation.
>
> Thus *all petition in prayer is ultimately petition for grace* in the wider as well as the more precise meaning of the term. This prayer for grace must be constantly renewed, since at every instant we have our being by the grace of God. *Prayer for grace is as essential to life as breath...* Our prayer should never cease to go out to God; not only as a call in distress, but as a *constant appeal to His creative might and sanctifying grace.*"[592]

Likewise, commenting on Jesus' words that the Father will not refuse the Holy Spirit to those who ask him (Lk 11:13), an author claims that:

> "All real prayer is implicitly and virtually a petition to God to take complete possession of our lives."[593]

There are authors who call *intercession* the petition to God for the praying person's needs.[594] But intercession is more commonly understood as the prayer of petition offered to God by asking favors for others.[595]

> "Intercession is customarily offered, in moments of fervor, for other men and women - our family, the peace of the world. To use St. Paul's words, we pray 'for all men, for kings, and all in authority' (Cf. 1 Tm 2:1-2)."[596]

Intercessors are inspired by their intimacy with God to pray for others. The hearts of intercessors are attuned with God's loving kindness

---

[592] GUARDINI, pp. 60 and 65. Emphasis ours.

[593] BUTLER, p. 115.

[594] Cf. CHESTER and MORRISEY, p. 182. Also BORTON, p. 50, seems to identify intercession with "prayer of asking" in general.

[595] Cf. CCC, nn. 2634-2635: "Intercession is a prayer of petition... asking in another's favor."

[596] Cassian, *Conferences,* IX, 13, CHADWICK, p. 220.

and merciful compassion toward all human beings, and especially his Chosen People.[597]

The rationale of prayer of intercession is explained by St. Augustine when he writes –

> "Paul knew that all things that he was doing in the way of planting and watering openly were of no avail, unless God who gives the increase in secret should give heed to his prayer on their behalf."[598]

A particular form of prayer of petition is *penitence.* In their present condition Christians offer their prayers of worship to God not only as creatures and adopted children but also as sinners. Christians are driven by their sinfulness to repent, confess their sins to the Most Holy, and ask for his forgiveness.

Cassian interprets the "supplications" mentioned by St. Paul, in 1 Tm 2:1, as "prayer of repentance,"[599] that is –

> "A beseeching or petition for sins. In it a person repentant for his present or past sins, asks for pardon... This 'seems particularly suitable for sinners, who are still smarting under the recollection of their sins'."[600]

When Christians petition their Creator for an increase of his natural gifts, they ask him to perfect his creation in them. When they beg of their Redeemer the forgiveness of their sins, they ask him to be saved from spiritual death and re-created, because their sins deprived them of divine life and presence:

> "Have mercy on me, O God, in your goodness, in your great tenderness wipe away my faults: wash me clean of my guilt, purify me from

---

[597] Abraham (cf. Gn 18:16-33), Moses (cf. Ex. 17:8-13; 9:32, 1-34, 9), and the Prophets often interceded for others (Am 7:1-6; Jr 7:16 and 15:1; etc.). Jesus "is living for ever to intercede for all who come to God through him." (Heb 7:25. Cf. Rm 8:34; 1 Jn 2:1).

[598] *De Correptione et Gratia,* II, 3.

[599] *Conferences,* IX, 11.

[600] *Ibid.* The translation is of CHADWICK, pp. 219-220 passim.

my sin. For I am aware of my fault, I have my sin constantly in mind, having sinned against none other than you, having done what you regard as wrong...

God, create a clean heart in me, put into me a new and constant spirit, do not banish me from your presence, do not deprive me of your holy spirit... Save me from death, God my saviour...my sacrifice is this broken spirit, you will not scorn this crushed and broken heart."[601]

The recent CCC terms this prayer "request for forgiveness" and emphasizes that it

"Incites to prayer of petition (cf. Lk 18:13). It is preliminary to a good and pure prayer... It is the preliminary act of eucharistic liturgy as well as of private prayer." (n. 2631)

This prayer is stirred up by the encounter with God's Holiness in prayer.

"As soon as man comes into proximity with God, he is confronted with His holiness. He becomes aware that he is sinful and guilty... Yet, at the same time, he knows that he stands in perpetual need of this holy prayer: for ultimately prayer is man's answer to God's Holiness.

It is God's holiness which makes prayer possible. It is only holiness which imbues God's omniscience, justice and reality and gives those powers of intimate contact which make prayer possible... Sin is ultimately resistance against the holiness of God. When resistance, open or otherwise, gains the upper hand, prayer becomes impossible."

"The holiness of God calls forth in us awareness of our own unworthiness, acknowledgement of guilt, repentance and new resolve. It also calls forth the awareness that God is the Saviour."[602]

"Because worship sets the awful Perfection of God over against the creature'simperfection, it becomes the most effective cause of 'conviction of sin', and hence the soul's penitence and purification; here disclosing its creative and transfiguring power."[603]

---

[601] Ps 51:1-4, 10-17 passim.

[602] GUARDINI, pp. 40-41 passim and 73.

[603] UNDERHILL, pp. 9-10.

To avoid the risk of limiting itself to wishful thinking prayer of penitence should be accompanied by all the penitent's acts: determination to amend one's life, satisfaction, resolution of avoiding the occasions of sin, etc., which are also required by a worthy and fruitful celebration of the sacrament of reconciliation.[604]

Humbly confessing their sins Hebrew penitents trusted in Yahweh's infinite forgiveness, thanked and praised him for his great mercy, and adored his infinite holiness.

> "If you never overlooked our sins, Yahweh, Lord, could anyone survive? But you do forgive us; and for that we revere you. I wait for Yahweh, my soul waits for him. I rely on his promise, my soul relies on the Lord more than a watchman on the coming of dawn ...For it is with Yahweh that mercy is to be found, and a generous redemption; it is he who redeems Israel from all their sins."[605]

The Gospels contain very moving prayers of penitence:

> "Father, I have sinned against heaven and you: I no longer deserve to be called your son; treat me as one of your paid servants."[606]
>
> "The tax collector stood some distance away, not daring even to raise his eyes to heaven, but he beat his breast and said, 'God, be merciful to me, a sinner'."[607]

An early Christian theologian of prayer thinks that

> "Kneeling is necessary when someone is going to speak against his own sins before God, since he is making supplication for their healing and

---

[604] Cf. OF, p. 13.

[605] Ps 130:3-8. Several psalms are called *laments.* "In some of the laments, Israel admits its guilt, pleads for forgiveness and an end to its suffering, and promises to amend its life." CSB, p. 247; cf. p. 254.

[606] Lk 15:18 and 21.

[607] Lk 18:13. Cf. Mt 6:12.

their forgiveness. We must understand that it symbolizes someone who has fallen down and become obedient."[608]

The early monks associated prayer of penitence with the "gift of tears".[609]

"Pray first for the gift of tears so that by means of sorrow you may soften your native rudeness. Then having confessed your sins to the Lord you will obtain pardon for them... Pray with tears and your request will find a hearing... When fountains of tears flow during your prayers your prayers have obtained the help you need to confess your sins with readiness and to conciliate the favor of the Lord...

The specific quality of (this) prayer is that it is respectful gravity which is colored with compunction. There is something of a deepfelt sorrow about it, the kind one feels when, amid silent groans, he really admits his sins."[610]

Early monks were moved to weep especially by meditating upon the infinite "distance and impurity" which separated them, "miserable wretches", from God.

"When you are of the mind that you do not stand in need of tears for your sins along with your prayer, then give some thought to the distance that separates you from God, whereas you ought to be in him constantly. Then you will shed more abundant tears than ever.

Surely when you take your own measure you will know a sweet sorrow and will call yourself, as Isaiah spoke of himself, a miserable wretch (6:5). For you yourself are impure, your very lips defiled and it is among such people as these rebels that you live and yet you dare to stand before the Lord of Armies."[611]

---

[608] ORIGEN [2], *On Prayer,* XXXI, 3, p. 165.

[609] Cf. HAUSHERR and ŠPIDLÍK [3], pp. 42-55.

[610] EVAGRIUS, chs. 5-7, 42; pp. 56, 61.

[611] EVAGRIUS, chs. 78, 79, p. 68.

The awareness of one's sinfulness can certainly turn one away from the infinitely Holy God.[612] But, Christians are assured that Jesus

> "Did not come to call the virtuous, but sinners", and he "has authority on earth to forgive sins." "For God sent his Son into the world not to condemn the world, but so that through him the world might be saved."[613]

So the fear of the Most Holy God's judgement can be overcome and replaced in the repentant sinner by a confidence in the Most Merciful God's forgiveness.

In other words,

> "The same holiness which turns man away also recalls him, for holiness is love. It rejects man so that he may find true humility and the new way. When it has done this - however insufficiently - it calls him back... God's holiness which makes us shrink back in the knowledge that we ourselves are unholy, at the same time makes us strive after him in the knowledge that in him lies our salvation."[614]

Jesus taught prayer of penitence in the very well-known petition of the "Lord's Prayer": "Forgive us our trespasses." But, in the same breath, he also added "as we forgive those who trespass against us." And this means that our request will be heard only on condition that we forgive those who have wronged us.[615]

Is it not frightful that God's mercy will not forgive us unless we do forgive others? If we have any doubt about that, here are the emphasized words of Jesus himself:

---

[612] Cf. Lk 5:8: "Simon Peter fell at the knees of Jesus saying, 'Leave me, Lord: I am a sinful man!'"

[613] Mt. 9:13 = Mk 2:17; cf. Mt 11:19 = Lk 7:34; 15:2, 7, 10; Lk 4:24; Jn 3:17; cf. Rm 5:8; 1 Tm 1:15.

[614] GUARDINI, p. 45 and 47. Guardini seems to apply to Christian prayer of penitence the theory of Otto, according to whom the Holy is experienced by human beings as a frightening and fascinating Mystery.

[615] For an extended and authoritative commentary see CCC, nn. 2838-2845.

> "Yes, if you forgive others their failings, your heavenly Father will forgive you yours; but if you do not forgive others, your Father will not forgive your failings either."[616]

Naturally, these words can hardly astonish whoever keeps in mind Jesus' commandment of loving one another as he has loved us, of loving even our enemies for we must be perfect just as our heavenly Father is perfect, as compassionate as our Father is compassionate.[617]

Paul faithfully echoes the Lord's teaching:

> "Be friends with one another, and kind, forgiving each other as readily as God forgave you in Christ. Try, then, to imitate God, as children of his that he loves, and follow Christ by loving as he loved you, giving himself up as a fragrant offering and a sacrifice to God."[618]

In conclusion, the prayer of petition which asks God to meet our own needs, if not selfish, is at least rather self-centered. Whereas the prayer of petition which intercedes for others seems to have overcome self-centeredness. But others can be members of our family or our friends, and so our prayer for them could be just an extension of our petitions for ourselves.

The ultimate overcoming of all self-centeredness in our petitions ought to occur in the prayer of penitence which asks God to forgive our sins. In fact, as Jesus strongly emphasized, this kind of prayer would be inefficacious[619] unless the Christians who practice it are willing to grant forgiveness to those by whom they have been wronged, in the first place. Since that prerequisite for the efficacy of prayer of penitence is virtually equivalent to love of one's neighbor, even of one's enemies as Jesus loves

---

[616] Mt 6:14-15. Cf. 5:23-24; Mk 11:25.

[617] Cf. Jn 13:34; Mt 5:43-44; Mt 5:48; Lk 6:36.

[618] Ep 4:32; 5:1-2.

[619] Not only prayer of penitence but also other kinds of prayer of petition may at times look as if they were inefficacious, i.e., unheard by God. For the problems caused and the questions raised by this trying Christian experience, with the solutions and answers to them suggested by Scripture and theology, see in CCC, nn. 2734-2741.

us, i.e., to perfect charity, an efficacious prayer of penitence dispels with respect to the neighbor self-centeredness from praying Christians.

The same happens with respect to God when they progress from prayer of petition to prayer of thanksgiving.

b. From petition to thanksgiving

We are showered with God's love and gifts before we even think of praying. Hence our first prayer should be a thanksgiving for God's innumerable gifts –

> "There are many kinds of prayer and many different prayers... But *heartfelt thanksgiving should have first place in our book of prayer*...this method of prayer is the best, as one brother was told by an angel of the Lord."[620]
>
> "The world has emerged out of the freedom of God, and His freedom is love; because it is love we can respond to it by *gratitude.* It is therefore meet and just and appropriate to *give thanks to God* for having created the world...
>
> It is proper that I should know and acknowledge in my heart that I constantly receive myself as a free gift from the hand of God... Nothing can be taken for granted: everything has the hallmark of the free gift and of grace: *one must give thanks for everything – one must give thanks for being able to give thanks."*[621]

On the contrary, being overconcerned with our needs and worried about their satisfaction, we usually address prayers of petition to God before any others.[622]

---

[620] CLIMACUS [2], p. 275. Emphasis ours. It is worth noticing that the only two explicit prayers uttered by Jesus during his ministry both begin with a thanksgiving to the Father (cf. Mt 11:25-27; Lk 10:21-22; Jn 11:41-42).

[621] GUARDINI, pp. 67-68. Emphasis ours.

[622] Our first concern about ourselves apparently "conditions" even God's revelation. "The primary concern [of sacred Scripture] is soteriological, only secondarily Christological, and even more remotely Trinitarian. To the extent a Trinitarian dimension appears at all, it does so in function of the other two concerns." HILL, p.

Christ, who encouraged his listeners to address such prayers to the Father with great confidence in his loving care,[623] complained when those who had received what they asked for did not give thanks and praise to God.[624] It seems, however, that any confident prayer of petition contains a sort of implicit thanksgiving. In fact, to be so trusted, the Father must have already proved on other occasions his thoughtfulness and care for his children.

So, although they may be first in time, prayers of petition are certainly not the most perfect of all prayers as worship. The realization of being desperately in need, joined to the experience that in certain situations human help is utterly powerless, forcefully spur praying Christians to ask for the intervention of Almighty God. And when God grants these petitions, those who have benefited from his loving care cannot but express their gratitude.

In this way, prayers of thanksgiving naturally follow upon prayers of petition and are their natural conclusion.

> "If you did not receive, ask in order to receive, when you have received, give thanks for what you did receive."[625]

Yet, petition and thanksgiving are so closely bound to each other in prayerlife that their interconnection initiates a spiral movement which develops through successive waves of asking, receiving, and thanking. As a matter of fact, the lists of prayer drawn up by St. Paul contain virtually only prayers of petition and thanksgiving.[626]

27, cf. p. 29.

[623] Cf. Mt 7:7-11 = Lk 11:9-13.

[624] Cf. Lk 17:11-19. Particularly v. 18: "It seems that no one has come back to give praise to God, except this foreigner."

[625] St. John Chrysostom quoted by EA, n. 362, p. 225. Translation ours.

[626] Cf. Ph 4:6; 1 Tm 2:1. See the articulate commentary on the latter text in ST, II-II, q. 83, a. 17. Also Origen, St. Augustine, Cassian had extensively commented upon the same Pauline text. Cf. BARILE, p. 116, note 21.

The Apostle especially exhorts to an all-pervasive thanksgiving as an essential element of the constant attitude of prayer, for there are no events or circumstances in which God does not deserve and expect to be thanked by us.

> "Pray constantly, and for all things give thanks to God, because his is what God expects you to do in Christ Jesus." "Be persevering in prayer and be thankful as you stay awake to pray."[627]

Christian prayer of thanksgiving reaches its summit in the celebration of the Eucharist,[628] through which the whole Church gives thanks; but expresses also all the other forms of prayer[629] to the Father for the salvation of humankind performed by Christ by His death and resurrection.[630]

c. *From thanksgiving to praise*

In the Deuteronomic school,

> "Prayer begins with recollection *(anamnesis),* proceeds to establish a ground for a request before making it, and states the end for which it is sought. Address and conclusion normally ascribe praise."[631]

The many eulogies and doxologies found in the Judeo-Christian liturgical traditions are expressions of the many ways the faithful used to

---

[627] 1 Th 5:18; Col 4:2. CCC, n. 2638, quotes these words of Paul to sustain that "all events and needs can become a motive of thanksgiving."

[628] Which in Greek means thanksgiving. Cf. CCC, n. 1328.

[629] Cf. CCC, n. 2643.

[630] CCC, n. 2636.

[631] SMITH, p. 867.

thank and praise their God by magnifying, blessing, glorifying, etc., him for his continual care and marvelous interventions in their history.[632]

In the heavenly liturgy Almighty God and the Lamb are worshipped in the following way:

> "All the angels who were standing in a circle round the throne (of God), surrounding the elders and the four animals, prostrated themselves before the throne, and touched the ground with their foreheads, worshiping God with these words, 'Amen. Praise and glory and wisdom and thanksgiving and honour and power and strength to our God for ever and ever. Amen'."[633]

A telling example of the manifold expressions of thanksgiving is the "Glory to God in the highest" recited or sung during the Mass –

> "Lord God ... we worship you, we give you thanks, we praise you for your glory."[634]

The beginning of St. Francis of Assisi's well-known *Canticum Fratris Solis vel Laudes Creaturarum* is virtually a free translation of these liturgical canticles into old Italian.[635] A beautiful example of

---

632 "A hymn is a song of praise to God ... *Thanksgivings* are similar to hymns in that they extol the marvellous works of God. What distinguishes the two is the sentiment that each elicits. Hymns call for *praise:* thanksgiving psalms are expressions of *gratitude...* They were probably part of the communal and personal liturgical life... There can be no thanksgiving until God has first been praised for the goodness that God has accomplished.": CSB, pp. 242-243, 248.

633 Rv 7:11-12.

634 The original Latin is even more redundant than the English translation. It multiplies synonyms – "Laudamus te, benedicimus te, adoramus te, glorificamus te, gratias agimus tibi propter magnam gloriam tuam, Domine Deus!"

635 "Altissimu onnipotenti bon signore, tue so le laude la gloria e l'honore et onne benedictione. A te solo, altissimo, se konfano.": FRANCIS, p. 88. See also his *Epistola ad fideles:* "Omnis creatura quae est in caelis, in terra, in mari et in abyssis (Ap. 5:13) reddat laudem Deo, gloriam, honorem et benedictionem, quia ipse est vita et fortitudo nostra, qui est solus bonus (Lc 18:19), solus altissimus, solus omnipotens, admirabilis, gloriosus et solus sanctus, laudabilis et benedictus per infinita saecula saeculorum. Amen.": *Ibid.,* p. 124, quoted by CDF, *Letter,* note 23.

praises offered to God as a thanksgiving leading into self-oblation is at the end of Morning Prayer on Saturday of the second week of ordinary time:

> "May our mouths, our soul, our life, praise you, Lord; and since what we are is your gift, all our living be yours!"[636]

Of course, God has no need of our thanksgivings, praises, oblations, etc., but we need them because through these prayers we dispose ourselves to welcome a fresh outpouring of God's grace.

> "You (God) have no need of our praise, yet our desire to thank you is itself your gift. Our prayer of thanksgiving adds nothing to your greatness, but makes us grow in your grace."[637]

During prayers of praise the goodness of God loved for its own sake attracts Christians more than their needs did when they were asking something of him.

> "We praise God, *not to obtain anything,* but because God's Being draws praise from us" and we offer "ourselves, our lives and labors, in union with Christ, *for the purpose of God.*"[638]
>
> "*Praise is the form of prayer which more directly recognizes that God is God!* It sings of him for his own sake, it gives glory to him for HE IS, apart from what he does... It completes the other forms of prayer and leads them towards him who is their source and end; the 'only one God, the Father from whom all things come and for whom we exist' (1 Co 8:6)."[639]

So, progressing from thanksgiving to praise, the focusing of prayer on God's goodness increases and becomes sharper.

---

[636] "Laudent te, Domine, ora nostra, laudet anima, laudet et vita, et quia tui muneris est quod sumus, tuum sit omne quod vivimus." LITURGIA, vol. III, p. 787. Translation ours.

[637] RM, Preface iv for Weekdays, p. 453.

[638] OF, p. 13. Emphasis ours.

[639] CCC, n. 2639. Emphasis ours. Cf. nn. 2640-2642, the many texts of the New Testament on prayer of praise.

> "When we praise God, we think above all of God himself and not so much of his gifts, as we may do in thanksgiving. Praise is more theocentric than thanksgiving. It is more absorbed in God and closer to adoration."[640]

But the borderline between thanking God and praising him appears rather fluid:

> "It is clear that giving thanks is very close indeed to praising, glorifying and exalting God... It is impossible for anyone to say with certainty were praise ends and thanksgiving begins."[641]

Also prayers to the saints should be more expressions of gratitude and praise toward God than petitions.

> "The prayers to the saints are an expression of gratitude and hope... Their object is not to arouse the attention or interest of the saints but rather to open the petitioner's heart to the praise of God and inspire thanksgiving to him... (These prayers) are a means of preparing the petitioner to share in the dialogue taking place between the saints and God through Christ."[642]

Prayer of thanksgiving is the human grateful response to God because he has actually bestowed his gifts and graces upon those who ask him. Prayer of praise directly and deeply looks into the loving kindness of God who unfailingly keeps his promises to care for and sustain those who by prayer show their trust in his almighty help.

> "Alleluia! Praise Yahweh, all nations, extol him, all you people! For his love is strong, his faithfulness eternal."[643]

---

[640] BOROS, p. 21.

[641] BOROS, p. 22. This is manifest in the following passage of ORIGEN [2] (*On Prayer,* XIII, 4, p. 106): "If one of us remembers with gratitude the benefits he has received and wishes to offer praises to God, how many of them would each of us recount in detail?"

[642] SCHMAUS, p. 176.

[643] Ps 117. Cf. Jn 1:14,17.

d. *From praise to adoration*

Prayer as worship progressing from petition through thanksgiving and praise reaches its summit in prayer of adoration. Christians usually begin prayer by asking something of God. They pray mostly in terms of "give me (or us[644])" and therefore show some kind of self-interest,[645] which is hardly the best way of worshiping God.

> "This is true (Christian) perfection; not to do good because we hope for reward, as if cashing in on the virtuous life by some business-like or contractual arrangement. On the contrary, disregarding all those things for which we hope and which have been reserved by promise ... we consider becoming God's friend the only thing worthy of honor and desire."[646]

Hence, by experiencing how good God is to us (as it happens when we humbly approach him through prayers of petition and thanksgiving) we come to realize that he is loving and faithful in himself (as in prayer of praise); and so we are led to worship him with adoration, which is the highest expression of disinterested worship.

> "Worship is essentially disinterested - it "means only God" - but prayer is only in some of its aspects disinterested. One offers, the other asks. It is true that throughout the history of religion there has always been a mingling of motives... But *as the genuine religious impulse becomes dominant, adoration more and more takes charge.*
>
> 'I come to seek God because I need him', may be an adequate formula for prayer. 'I come to adore his splendor, and fling myself and all that I have at his feet', is the only possible formula for worship... Thus worship will include all those dispositions and deeds which adoration wakes up in us,

---

[644] When we offer our petition to God interceding for others who are united with us by a bond of solidarity and charity, our self-centeredness is not individual, but communal.

[645] When self-interest becomes selfishness, then the person who prays looks at God only as a means to satisfy his or her own needs. This way of praying often ends up causing the pharisaic scandal of those who complain because their petitions are not heard by God (Cf. CCC, 2734-2737). But God's good children are not "more attached to the gifts than to the divine Benefactor." (Cf. *Ibid.*, n. 2740).

[646] GREGORY OF NYSSA, II, 320, p. 137.

all the responses of the soul to the uncreated, all Godwards activities of man."[647]

In short, prayer as worship reaches in adoration[648] its most perfect centering on God's infinite majesty, which compels praying Christians to surrender their whole selves to the Almighty.

> "To the majesty of God we respond through adoration: the act of homage signifying our complete yet voluntary surrender to God's almighty power. As we rejoice over the glory of God, adoration becomes praise."[649]
>
> "The act of pure adoration is the consummation of worship... Even the deep religious mood of dependence and of gratitude must give priority to the fundamental religious mood of adoration."[650]
>
> "Adoration is the fundamental disposition of the human person who acknowledges him or herself to be a creature before the Creator. It exalts the greatness of the Lord who created us and the almightiness of the Savior who delivers us from evil... The adoration of God thrice blessed and extremely lovable fills us with humility and gives confidence to our supplications."[651]

---

[647] UNDERHILL [2], p. 9, 17-18, etc. Emphasis ours.

[648] Remember that "Adoration" (from the Latin *ad-os/oris* = mouth) etymologically means lifting one's hand to the mouth in order to waft a kiss of loving reverence to the simulacrum of the divinity. The latin verb *adorare* translates the Greek *proskyneo.*

"The basic meaning of *proskyneo* (to worship, to do obeisance to, to prostrate oneself), in the opinion of most scholars, is to kiss. The prefix indicates the connection with cultic practices going back beyond Greek history. On Egyptian reliefs worshippers are represented with outstretched hands throwing a kiss (*kyneo,* from *kys* = kiss) to *(pros)* the deity. Among the Greeks the verb is a technical term for the adoration of the gods, meaning to fall down, prostrate oneself, adore on one's knees. Probably it came to have this meaning because in order to kiss the earth (i.e., the earthly deity) or the image of a God, one had to cast oneself to the ground...it can also denote the corresponding inward attitude of reverence and humility.": DNTT, vol. III, pp. 875-878, passim.

[649] GUARDINI, p. 73.

[650] UNDERHILL, pp. xii, 8; cf. p. 11.

[651] CCC, n. 2628.

So, prayer of adoration, which is both the fundamental disposition for and the consummation of worship, leads Christians into the mystery of God, Creator of the whole universe and Lord of salvation, making them catch a glimpse of his tremendous Majesty.[652]

The high achievement of prayer of petition in prayer of adoration is powerfully expressed in the following Pauline doxology:

> "Glory be to him whose power, working in us, can do infinitely more than we can ask or imagine; glory be to him from generation to generation in the Church and in Christ Jesus for ever and ever. Amen!"[653]

CCC rather extensively expounds on all the acts of prayer as worship we have treated so far.[654] They are qualified "normative for Christian prayerlife", since Christians hear and read them in the Scriptures and find them developed in the great liturgical and spiritual traditions of the Church.[655]

iii. *The Growth Process and Common Ground of Prayer as Worship*

a. *The growth process of prayer as worship*

The growth process of prayer as worship starts with the acts of prayer of petition and of penitence, and through the acts of prayer of thanksgiving passes to the acts of prayer of praise and of adoration. In petition and penitence God's Majesty is acknowledged as beneficent to the praying Christian; in praise and adoration the same God's Majesty is proclaimed magnificent in itself. Therefore prayer as worship progresses

---

[652] Cf. CCC, nn. 2096-2097, 2628, 2807.

[653] Ep 3:20-21.

[654] NN. 2628-2649. CCC, n. 2625, terms "forms of prayer" the various acts of prayer as worship. Really, they are *specific* "forms" of the *genus* of prayer as worship, to which we prefer to reserve the term "form of prayer". The terms *specific* and *genus* are taken here according to the meaning that Scholastic theology gave them.

[655] Cf. *Ibid.*, n. 2625,

from rather self-centered petition and penitence to God-centered praise and adoration.

Prayer of thanksgiving is, as it were, between petition, with its stress on the human need for God's help, and adoration, which proclaims God's infinite majesty. Prayer of thanksgiving has an eye for the human need met by God and an eye for God who met the need. Hence it mediates between the self-centered and the God-centered acts of prayer as worship.

The central position of prayer of thanksgiving in the whole growth process of prayer as worship might be one of the reasons why the Mass is fittingly called Eucharist, a Greek word which directly translates as thanksgiving.[656] Actually, in this sacramental sacrifice offered by Jesus Christ to the Father for our salvation the whole Christian prayer as worship with all its acts is summed up.[657]

In the progress of prayer as worship praying Christians experience a gradual increase of spiritual joy. As long as they cry out to God beseeching him to meet their needs, they are in the sad mood caused by the awareness that they lack many things. This sad mood can be soothed only by their hope that God will eventually hear and help them.

> "Listen to me, Yahweh, and answer me, poor and needy as I am... Lord, in trouble I invoke you, and you answer my prayer." "Hard-pressed, I invoked Yahweh, he heard and came to my relief." "Out of my distress I cried to Yahweh and he answered me: from the belly of Sheol I cried and you have heard my voice."[658]

But when they give thanks to the Lord because he has heard their prayer and bestowed his gifts upon them, they rejoice in his bountifulness. And their spiritual joy increases as they go on blessing, praising and glorifying him. When, in the end, God's majesty and glory

---

[656] Cf. "*We thank you* for counting us worthy to stand in your presence and serve you" (Eucharistic Prayer II). "We offer you in *thanksgiving* this holy and living sacrifice" (Eucharistic Prayer III).

[657] Cf. CCC, 2637 and 2643.

[658] Ps 86:1 and 7; 118:5; cf. 120:1; Jon 2:3, etc.

become the focus of their prayer of adoration, their worshiping prayer is performed with the greatest exultation.

> "Give thanks to Yahweh, for he is good, his love is everlasting!" "Bless Yahweh, my soul, bless his holy name, all that is in me! Bless Yahweh, my soul, and remember all his kindness... No less than the height of heaven over earth is the greatness of his love on those who fear him... As tenderly as a father treats his children, so Yahweh treats those who fear him."
>
> "Bless Yahweh, my soul. Yahweh, my God, how great you are! Clothed in majesty and glory, wrapped in a robe of light!... Glory for ever to Yahweh! May Yahweh find joy in what he creates... May these reflections of mine give him pleasure, as much as Yahweh gives me!"[659]

The Old Testament's cries of joy reach their climax in "the great joy, a joy to be shared by the whole people, that a savior has been born to us; he is Christ the Lord".[660] The same reason makes the Apostle exclaim:

> "I want you to be happy, always happy in the Lord; I repeat, what I want is your happiness... The Lord is very near. There is no need to worry; but if there is anything you need, pray for it, asking God for it with prayer and thanksgiving, and the peace of God, which is so much greater than we can understand, will guard your hearts and your thoughts, in Christ Jesus."[661]

After his description of the most important acts of prayer as worship, Origen, on his part, concludes by outlining not an ascending but a somewhat descending process of prayer as worship: from praise to thanksgiving, penitence and petition, ending with adoration.

> "It seems to me there are four topics that need to be sketched out and that I have found scattered in the Scripture. Each person should organize his prayer to these topics. This is what they are:
>
> In the beginning and the preface of the prayer something having the force of *praise* should be said of God through Christ, who is praised with him. After this each person should place general *thanksgiving*, bringing forward for

---

[659] Ps 118:1; Ps 103:1-2, 11, 13; Ps 104:1-2, 31, 34.

[660] Lk 2:10-11.

[661] Ph 4:4-7.

thanksgiving the benefits given many people and those he has himself received from God.

After thanksgiving it seems to me that he *ought to blame himself bitterly before God for his own sins,* and then ask, first for healing that he may be delivered from the habit that brings him to sin and, second, for forgiveness of the sins that have been committed.

And after confession, the fourth topic that seems to me must be added is the *request* for great and heavenly things both private and general, and concerning his household and his dearest.

And finally prayer should be concluded with a *doxology* to God through Christ in the Holy Spirit."[662]

b. The common grounds of all acts of prayer as worship

As prayer of petition acknowledges our total dependence on God and reverences him for his bountiful almighty power, it already contains what adoration will bring to highest expression.

Indeed, since adoration is expressed in the very first words of the "Our Father" - "hallowed by thy name!"[663] - all Christian childlike petitions already include some adoration.

> "In fact, the trustful childlike demand is itself an act of homage, insofar as it has the color of adoration."[664]
>
> "To remember that will prevent us from thinking that as we advance in prayer we will outgrow the prayer of petition. We never do, because we can always express our dependence on and union with God by petitioning his Father right up to the end of his life... When we move closer to God in prayer we make our recognition of this sovereignty no longer implicit but explicit."[665]

The distinctive components of prayer of petition (i.e., *reverence and request*) are, in different degrees, participated in by all

---

[662] ORIGEN, *On Prayer,* XXXIII, 1. Emphasis ours.

[663] CCC, nn. 2807 and 2097. See also nn. 2643 and 2637.

[664] UNDERHILL, p. 11.

[665] DALRYMPLE, p. 16.

forms of prayer. For all acts of worship include God, to whom they are addressed, and the human beings who offer them.[666] Through worship God is shown reverence, while human beings plead for his help.

Now, as petition and adoration are located at opposite extremes of a continuum that includes all forms of prayer as worship, one may conclude that the two essential components are also variously active in all other forms of prayer as worship practiced in between those extremes.

An author confirms this conclusion by pointing out that some kind of *request* is always implicit in all acts of prayer as worship.

> "The diversity of our *request* imparts to our prayer an infinite variety of shades... There is the prayer which consists solely of praise and adoration; *although in some cases we may not make our request explicitly,* it is none the less hidden under the words, and even in the intention... Often we collect together in one formula all the different kinds of prayer – we adore or thank, we ask for pardon and help."[667]

The existence of an essential component of *reverence* in all acts of prayer as worship, including prayers of petition which seem to be the least explicit about it, is sustained by the authority of Aquinas, who, referring to prayer of petition, writes:

> "By praying (i.e., by asking fitting things of God) we offer God *reverence,* in as much as we submit ourselves to him and profess that *we need him as the author of all that is good for us."*[668]

Contemporary authors similarly explain:

---

[666] "The worship of God regards both who is worshipped and men who perform the worship." (ST, I-II, q. 102, a. 4, ad 1um; Blackfriars, vol. 29, p. 157).

[667] GUILLERAND, p. 125. Emphasis ours.

[668] ST, II-II, q. 83, a. 3. Emphasis ours. This translation is ours. Cf. ST. AUGUSTINE, *De Civitate Dei,* X, 1, 3, p. 279.

"Prayer which is only religion in act is the movement of the soul recognizing that it is receiving something, and that it is only what it receives... *It restores us as creatures receiving all from the Creator."*[669]

"Prayer is the freely willed *response to the fact of our utter dependance on God*...our ultimate environment, in which we first exploit the deepest potentialities of our created, spiritual nature... Prayer is the acknowledgment of God and our relation to him, in adoration and thanksgiving, in penitence and petition."[670]

iv. *The Theological Substratum and Style of Prayer as Worship*

a. Foundation of prayer as worship

The first relation of human creatures to the Creator is founded in the created gifts which they unceasingly receive from him. The most fundamental of all these gifts is their very being as creatures. But the Creator is continually showering innumerable other benefactions upon his creatures. Prayer as worship aims precisely at expressing the human creatures' attitude to their Creator for his countless gifts, acknowledging that they utterly depend on him and can always trust in his infinite generosity.

The following psalm is a beautiful prayer of worship to Yahweh, who has crated and chosen his people.

"Know that he, *Yahweh, is God, he made us and we belong to him,* we are his people, the flock that he pastures. Walk through his porticos giving thanks, enter his courts *praising him; give thanks to him, bless his name!"* [671]

According to the Book of Revelation, the eternal God is solemnly worshiped as Creator in the heavenly liturgy:

---

[669] GUILLERAND, p. 125. Emphasis ours.

[670] BUTLER, p. 49. Emphasis ours.

[671] Ps 100:3-4. Cf. CCC, nn. 2096-2097.

> "Every time the *living creatures glorified and honored and gave thanks to the One sitting on the throne, who lives for ever and ever,* the twenty-four elders prostrated themselves before him to worship the One who lives for ever and ever, and threw down their crowns in front of the throne, saying:
>
> 'You are worthy, our Lord and God, to receive glory and honor and power, *for you have made the whole universe: by your will, when it did not exist, it was created!'"*[672]

The same God, Creator of heaven and earth, is also the Father of our Lord Jesus Christ, and as such bestows very special supernatural gifts upon Christians, for which, too, he deserved to be thanked and glorified.

> "Each one of us has received a special grace... If you are a speaker, speak in words which seem to come from God; if you are a helper, help as though every action was done at God's orders; so that *in everything God may receive the glory, through Jesus Christ, since to him alone belong all glory and power for ever and ever. Amen!"*[673]

So, Christian prayer as worship especially aims at expressing the gratitude of Christians toward God the Sanctifier by acknowledging that, as God's children, they utterly depend on him, even more than as creatures, and can always count on his special graces.

b. Prayer as worship and the divine attributes

Praying Christians use now one now another of the different acts of prayer as worship (petition, thanksgiving, praise, and so forth) according to the spiritual moods they are in at different moments of their prayerlife, e.g., when they have a need they naturally resort to prayer of petition, when their needs have been met by God's bounty they respond by prayer of thanksgiving, and so forth.

---

[672] Rv 4:9-11.

[673] 1 P 4:10-11.

To these various praying moods and acts correspond the many divine attributes which, as it were, make up the features of God, to whom the different acts of prayer as worship are offered.

> "The *holiness* of God calls forth in us awareness of our own unworthiness, acknowledgment of our guilt, *repentance* and new resolve... To the *majesty* of God we respond by *adoration* - the act of homage signifying our complete yet voluntary surrender to God's almighty power. As we rejoice over the *glory* of God, adoration becomes *praise...* To the *bountifulness* of God's ever-giving love we *appeal* in prayer for our many needs... By acknowledging as *God's gift* our entire existence, we *give thanks.*
>
> *Thus various facets of God's Being reveal themselves. We respond with various facets of our own being,* and in so doing we become ourselves - for only before God and in the measure we receive the truth from him and respond to it, do we become aware of our humanity."[674]

In other words, prayers of petition, thanksgiving, praise, adoration, etc., form a network of variegated responses inspired by faith in God's many attributes.

> "If I ask God for help, that presumes that I *believe* in his power to intervene in the affairs of this world. If I praise God, that means that I *believe* my homage reaches him in glory. If I stay in silence before him, plunged in adoration, it is because I *believe* he is my God."[675]

---

[674] GUARDINI, pp. 73-74. Emphases ours.

[675] RAGUIN, p. 29. Emphases ours.

Accordingly, the ancient[676] Christian tenet – *lex credendi legem statuat supplicandi*[677] (the law of faith ought to decide the law of praying) – should be applied to worshipping prayer in a special way.[678]

Jesus himself apparently enforced it when he "rebuked" James and John who were willing to "call down fire from heaven" to burn the Samaritan village whose inhabitants had not welcomed Jesus.[679] "Our Father in heaven" revealed by Jesus and to whom Christian prayer is addressed is quite different from Yahweh of whom Elijah asked that "fire come down from heaven to destroy" his enemies![680]

Evelyn Underhill specifies that,

---

[676] Mind that: "Today we tend to distinguish between explicit theological statements on the one hand and prayer on the other. In many ways this is a false distinction. Statements of faith may well be the reflection on or the development of theological thought, but *prayer is theology as it is experienced.* It is quite clear that the early Christians seldom made such distinctions. For them the psalms were not only vehicles of prayer, but they also contained important statements of faith, statements that found their fulfilment in the person and mission of Jesus (cf. Lk 24:44).": CSB, p. 251. Emphasis ours.

[677] Cf. PIUS XII, p. 54; JOHN XXIII, p. 546. The tenet was also implicitly recalled by Vatican II: "The Church in her doctrine, life and *worship,* perpetuates and transmits in every generation all that she herself is, *all that she believes...* its (of *this Tradition*) *riches* are poured out in the practice and life of the Church, *in her belief and her prayer* (credentis et orantis Ecclesiae).": DV, n. 8, FLANNERY, p. 754. Emphasis ours.

[678] Cf. ST, II-II, q. 44, a. 1, co.: "Illa quae pertinent ad divinum cultum ordinantur ad habendam rectam fidem." In fact, the ancient maxim, "the law of faith ought to establish the law of praying," regulates the whole Liturgy of the Church, and especially its center and core, i.e., the Eucharist (cf. SC, no. 10, FLANNERY, p. 6), which is "the summit toward which the activity of the Church is directed...thc fount from which all her power flows," and whose celebration involves all the most important acts of prayer as worship. Cf. AUMANN, pp. 208-226.

[679] Cf. Lk 9:53-55.

[680] 2 K 1:10-12.

> "The character of worship is always decided by the worshipper's conception of God and his relation to God: it always has a theological basis... Christian worship is always conditioned by Christian belief."[681]

Actually, faith is one of the best means praying Christians have of knowing God, to whom they offer their worship. And the faith knowledge infused with charity into their hearts by the Holy Spirit becomes experiential and savoury in the practice of prayer.

> "The (prayerful and faithful) soul does not see him (= God) as he is, for the sight is only in the glory of heaven. But he sees that He is[682] an unchangeable being: *a supreme power, supreme truth, supreme goodness, a blessed life, an endless beatitude.* This the soul sees, not blindly, nakedly and without savor, as with a scholar who sees him by his learning only, through the power of his naked reason; but *it sees him through an understanding which is strengthened and illuminated by the gift of the Holy Spirit, with a wonderful reverence and a secret burning love, and with spiritual savor and heavenly delight – more clearly and more fully than it may be written or thought*...and from this kind of seeing and knowing the soul grounds all its inward practice in all the affections, for then *it fears God in man as truth, wonders at him as power, and loves him as goodness.*[683]

At any rate, as adoration is the highest expression of worship, this perfect act of worship apparently gathers into itself the many different worshipful responses given to God's many attributes by the other acts of prayer. This is what actually happens in the various hymns of adoration addressed to God himself or to Jesus Christ throughout the Book of Revelation.

> "(Those hymns) make use of ever-varied language and ideas, constantly finding new titles of dignity with which to praise God, and *ascribing to him the most excellent merits (eternity, omnipotence, honour, wisdom, holiness, power, etc.), in a faltering attempt to confess his name.* In

---

[681] UNDERHILL [2], p. 60.

[682] Cf. St. Thomas Aquinas, *In Boethium de Trinitate,* q. 1, a. 2, ad 1um.

[683] HILTON, II, ch. 32, p. 259. Emphasis ours.

the face of adoration such as this, human petitions and thanksgivings fade away into silence."[684]

c. *The mediation of Christ in prayer as worship*

The redemptive incarnation of the only begotten Son of God, Jesus Christ, radically transformed God's transcendence and immanence. In virtue of this saving event, which is the very center of the whole History of Salvation, and was accomplished by our Risen Lord Jesus Christ, who is now "living forever to intercede for all tho come to God through him",[685] all Christian prayers of petition ought to be offered to the Father in the name of Jesus.

> "*Whatever you ask for in my name* I will do, so that the Father may be glorified in the Son... The Father will give you *whatever you ask him in my name...* Until now you have not *asked for anything in my name.* Ask and you will receive, and so your joy will be complete... You will *ask in my name* and I do not say that I shall pray to the Father for you, because the Father himself loves you for loving me and believing that I came from God."[686]

Likewise, St. Paul exhorts Christians to give thanks to God "in the name of Jesus".

> "Sing the words and tunes of the psalms and hymns when you are together, and go on singing and chanting to the Lord in your hearts, so that always and everywhere you are *giving thanks to God who is the Father in the name of our Lord Jesus Christ...* With gratitude in your hearts sing psalms and hymns and inspired songs to God, and never say or do anything except *in the name of the Lord Jesus, giving thanks to God the Father through him.*"[687]

---

[684] DNTT, p. 878. Emphasis ours.

[685] Heb 7:25. Cf. Rm 8:34.

[686] Jn 14:11-13; 15:16; 16:24, 26.

[687] Ep 5:19-20; cf. Col 3:16-17.

Tertullian writes that praying Christians in the second century followed this norm of prayer even under tortures.

> "We say, and before all men we say, and torn and bleeding under your tortures, we cry out - *'We worship God through Christ!'* Count Christ a man, if you please; by Him and in Him God would be known and be adored."[688]

But, Christians address their prayers also to Jesus Christ himself. For, although he truly is a man and as such he plays the role of mediator of our prayer to the Father, he is also the only begotten Son of God, "our Lord and our God".[689] So, the worship of the Godhead is practiced by Christians when they pray to Jesus Christ as Son of God.

Accordingly, genuine Christian worship has always both a christo- logical and trinitarian character, which inspires Christians to pray

> "Through Christ our Lord, who is God and lives and reigns with the Father in the unity of the Holy Spirit for ever and ever."

In sum, Christians who owe religious worship to God Creator, can be sure that he will accept their worship; because through and in Jesus Christ he has become their Father and they are his adopted children. But even though the Christian relates to God in prayer and worship both as his creature and as his children, God himself is only one; so also their prayer as worship is only one.

v. *From Prayer as Worship to Prayer as Communion*

Prayer as worship is expressed and carried on by a sort of give-and-take transaction. Christians deal with God as creatures, asking for his gifts and gratefully responding when they receive them. This "transaction" does not seem to require any intimate kind of encounter through which the partners share their very persons with each other.

---

[688] TERTULLIAN, ch. XXI, p. 36 a.

[689] Jn 20:28.

Because in worship what is exchanged between human creatures and their Creator is simply the human requests or thanksgivings and the divine gifts.

The object of prayer of adoration is God's absolute lordship and supreme majesty. This prayer is the summit of all prayer as worship. Christians, as it were, fly beyond that summit when they relate to God as to a Personal Presence.[690] By this flight Christians enter into another form of prayer, whose distinctiveness is the communion with God attained by charity "poured into our hearts by the Holy Spirit" (Rm 5:5).

A hint about the passage from prayer as worship to prayer as communion can be found in St. Luke: "The heavenly Father will give the Holy Spirit to those who ask him" (11:13). As a matter of fact, asking belongs to prayer as worship, while the Holy Spirit pours into our hearts the divine charity which enables us to commune intimately with God in prayer.

Such a transition from prayer as worship to prayer as communion represents a qualitative leap in Christian prayerlife. But, although prayer as communion may "outdo" prayer as worship, the transition occurs by way of a fulfillment, which does not discard any of the spiritual riches involved in prayer as worship.

> "Petition, Thanksgiving, Sorrow, Praise...later tend to coalesce into the general one of *communion with God,* when there is no longer some business between us and God and we dwell on him without further ado: we are just content to stay with God. Prayer simplifies life towards silence, wordless silence and *shared intimacy with the Lord in prayer.*"[691]

Even those acts of prayer as worship which make us realize our profound unworthiness in the face of the Holy One and shrink back from him, under the impetus of longing for God caused by charity, can eventually lead us into communion with him.

---

[690] According to OF, p. 13, "adoration is the lifting up of the mind and heart to God, asking nothing but to enjoy God's presence."

[691] DALRYMPLE, pp. 16-19. Emphasis ours.

> "The turning away from God, conscious that we are unworthy of him, and the striving after him in the longing for union – are to some degree present in every prayer which deserves the name. By these two contradictory trends we testify to God's holiness; for it is God's holiness which makes us shrink back in the knowledge that we ourselves are unholy, but which at the same time makes us strive after him in the knowledge that in him lies our salvation."[692]

These descriptions of prayer as worship leading into prayer as communion can hardly be reconciled with the claim that even if Christians were guided towards prayer as communion, they would still be "deflected by the demands of apparently more elevated notions of prayer.[693]

Doubtless, there are good enough reasons for contending that "the ordinary Christians[694] have the right to go on saying their prayers in a perfectly ordinary way".[695] But these reasons are taken too far if they are used to qualify "vague" prayer as communion, and to deem it caught up into the "clutches of the affective understanding of prayer".[696]

---

[692] GUARDINI, p. 47.

[693] TUGWELL [5], p. 278.

[694] But, of course, at least by state of life, not all Christians are "ordinary". Actually, according to can. 663, § 1, Religious are expected to strive for prayer as communion: "The first and principal duty *(Officium)* of all religious is to be contemplation of things divine and constant union with God in prayer.": CCL, p. 120.

[695] Perhhaps what Tugwell wants to say is the same which we read in the following observation: "Not infrequently the rhetoric of the believing community creates the impression that all the faithful should be experiencing such a relationship (that is, a close personal relationship with God) and that they are in some way at fault if they do not. Clearly, countless thousands of devout people travel in the dark as did Qoheleth, and they can find dignity in the believing community because Qoheleth was deemed worthy to have a place among the biblical writings." At any rate this author also acknowledges that: "Surely, the book of Qoheleth needs to be complemented by the other voices of Scripture, but his voice is of considerable importance.": WRIGHT ADDISON, pp. 490-491.

[696] TUGWELL [5] recognizes that since the time of St. Clement of Alexandria, Christian prayer was "pushed" in the direction of "communing with God": *Ibid.*, p. 274. But aparently all he has to say about it is that such a "push" involves the risk of

Christians who are personally inclined to and like better to practice prayer as worship may tend to overevaluate it. This can be easily understood. But if they contend that *their own* favoured kind of prayer is the most if not the only secure one, they manifestly fall into the fallacy of deeming one kind of prayer better than another, just because they are more used to it and feel more comfortable with it.

We think instead that what Meister Eckhart claims to be "the cornerstone" of his teaching should be applied to different forms of prayer:

> "We should just follow what God points out for us, that is, what we are inclined to and to which we are most often directed, and where our bent is... People often wonder whether their inclinations come from God or not, and this is how to find out: if a man finds it within himself to be willing above all things to obey God's will in all things, provided he knew and recognized it, then he may know that whatever he is inclined to, or is most frequently directed to, is indeed from God...
>
> *If you get more of God in one way than the other, that is fine, but it is not the best. God is in all ways and equal in all ways, for anyone who can take him so."*[697]

The lecture given by St. John of the Cross to the spiritual directors who would make their directees stick to the practice of meditation even when they are manifestly called to contemplation, can be extended to all those who seem to have misgivings about prayer as communion.

> "Since such persons have no understanding of the degrees of prayer or of the ways of the Spirit... Let them not merely aim at guiding a soul according to their own way and the manners suitable to themselves, but let

---

falling into "the clutches of the affective understanding of prayer": *Ibid.*, p. 277.

[697] WALSHE, vol. III, pp. 147-148; HILTON, II, ch. 19, p. 223, thinks that beginners should keep using their spiritual practices as "convenient means till better come." But "in using them they should long for something better."

> them see if they know the way by which God is leading the soul, and, if they know it not, let them leave the soul in peace and not disturb it."[698]
>
> "Many spiritual masters do much harm to many souls, for, not themselves understanding the ways and properties of the spirit, they commonly cause souls to lose the unction of these delicate ointments, wherewith the Holy Spirit gradually anoints and prepares them for Himself, and instructs them by other and lower means which they have used and of which they have read here and there, and which are unsuitable save for beginners.
>
> They themselves know no more than how to deal with these - please God they may know even so much! - and refuse to allow souls to go beyond these rudimentary acts of meditation and imagination, even though God is seeking to lead them farther, so that they may never exceed or depart from their natural capacity, whereby a soul can achieve very little."[699]

In conclusion, it is never right either to regard prayer as communion as supererogatory, or to depreciate prayer as worship. Both prayer trends are needed and important to Christian prayerlife at different stages of its development.

In comparing prayer as worship with prayer as communion the following wise advice should be kept in mind:

> "Our Lord gives diverse gifts wherever he wills - not all to one or one to everybody - apart from charity, which is common to all. Therefore if a man or a woman has received a gift from our Lord, such as devotion in prayer or in the passion of Christ, or any other, be it never so small, let him not leave it too soon for anything else, unless he truly feels a better one.
>
> Nevertheless, if later it is partly withdrawn and he should see something better toward which he feels his heart stirred, then it seems a call from our Lord to the better, and that is the time to follow it and get it."[700]
>
> "(Beginners have) to use their gifts as convenient means till better comes; so if a better (gift) should come, more spiritual and stronger in drawing the thought from fleshiness and from the sensuality and vain

---

[698] CROSS [3], A, III, 39-40, p. 110-111; see also 43-52, pp. 116-121.

[699] *Ibid.*, B, III, 31, p. 224. A contemporary spiritual writer agrees with the Mystical Doctor: "Spiritual direction over the years has repeatedly impressed upon me how extensive is the damage done in well-meaning souls who do not understand what is happening in their communion with the Lord." DUBAY, p. 74.

[700] HILTON, I, ch. 41, p. 111; cf. all ch. 42.

imagination – and if that should be hindered through their usual practice, then let them leave it, provided it can be left without scandal or distress to others, and follow what they feel. But if neither hinders the other, then let them use both if they can. I do not mean practices that are obligatory through bonds of law or rule, or penance, but others taken by choice."[701]

[701] *Ibid.,* II, ch. 19, p. 223. Hilton takes as an example "saying many prayers, which hinders a better work" (ch. 21, p. 230), and recognizes that for "those who are neither subtle by nature nor made spiritual through grace, it is good to keep on with their own practice – in imagination with human affection – until more grace comes to them freely. It is not safe for anyone to abandon one good before he sees and feels better.": ch. 29, p. 256.

CHAPTER VIII

PRAYER AS COMMUNION

The form of prayer we are going to consider in this chapter is termed "prayer as communion" for two reasons.

1. The term communion has a definite interpersonal intimate overtone which suits the spiritual union with God cultivated by this form of prayer.

2. The intimacy of Christians with God achieved in this form of prayer essentially results from charity poured out into their hearts by the Holy Spirit, whom theologians describe

> "As the mutual personal love between the Father and the Son, as their *personal communion.*"[702]

And it expresses the divine adoptive sonship of Christians, which

> "Takes upon itself a specifically trinitarian mode: *it is communion* with the Father, through the Son, and in the Holy Spirit. *It is communion* of adoptive sons with the Father, accomplished historically through the temporal mission of the natural Son, and transhistorically in the temporal mission of the Pneuma."[703]

The same idea is put by John Paul II in slightly different terms:

> "Salvation in Christ, as witnessed to and proclaimed by the Church, is *God's self-communication:* 'It is love which not only creates the good, but also grants *participation* in the very life of God: Father, Son and Holy Spirit. For he who loves desires to give himself'."[704]

In Christian spirituality there has always been more agreement about the terms used for acts of prayer as worship than about the terms used for acts

---

[702] HILL, p. 271. Emphasis ours.

[703] *Ibid.,* p. 290. Emphasis ours.

[704] JOHN PAUL II [2], n. 7, p. 17.

of prayer as communion. Because the former derive from Scripture and Liturgy, whereas the latter have been thought out and coined by Christian spiritual masters, who do not have an authority in the Church as firmly fixed as do the Scripture and the Liturgy.[705]

Besides, descriptions and interpretations of the various acts and grades of prayer as communion given by Christian spiritual masters are quite diverse. Such differences seem to stem from the fact that the documents which report those acts and grades of prayer refer, for the most part, to the personal prayer experiences of the writers themselves and/or of others. And praying Christians hardly, if ever, go through the very same experiences of prayer as communion.

> "God leads each soul along a different road and there shall hardly be found a single spirit who can walk even half the way which is suitable for another."[706]

A Letter of the Congregation for the Doctrine of Faith acknowledges that in the end the experience of Christian prayer is "something personal". The first cause of that is God himself, who lavishes particular yet unique "graces of prayer" on each one of his children.[707]

Besides,

> "Since *no two souls possess an identical equipment* (i.e., education, capacities, and temperament), this is the general reason for the various kinds

---

[705] The Faithful read the Scripture and listen to prayers of worship during the celebration of the liturgy. As these prayers are expressed in apostolic and canonical writings, they are normative for Christian prayerlife (cf. CCC, n. 2625). Liturgical prayers can continue in the hearts of those who pray, who assimilate (cf. *Ibid.*, n. 2655) and transform them into prayer as communion.

[706] CROSS [3], B, III, 59, pp. 243-244.

[707] "Non desunt certae gratiae mysticae...quae denotant eorum (quibus ditantur) peculiarem orationis experientiam, et eas Christifideles nequeunt, qua tales, imitari neque postulare... Ceterum *orationis experientiam (...) semper, ad summam, manet quiddam personale,* cum Deus personis ipsis gratias suas largiatur in ordinem ad orationem.": *CDF: Letter,* nn. 24-25. Emphasis ours. But, of course, the unique "graces of prayer" granted by God to each and every one of his children cannot run against the common grace of faith, offered to all. Cf. ST. TERESA OF AVILA, *Vida,* XXII, 8.

and degrees of prayer described by different teachers and the confusing and even contradictory directions which are often given with respect to them.

Yet all these kinds and degrees of prayer, from the most formal to the most formless, are the sacramental expression of *one simple but absolute act...* This act, or total theocentric disposition of the self, is a habitude of *charity, implanted by the Eternal Charity...* All great masters of prayer witness to the reality of this transcendental life in man."[708]

i. *Prayer as Communion in the Bible*

When praying Christians lovingly welcome the presence of God into their spiritual lives, there comes about an intimate "communion" between them and God. So, prayer as communion essentially involves the interlacing of the spiritual activities of two partners: the divine activity by which God offers his loving presence, and the human activity of praying Christians who lovingly respond to it.

Perhaps nowhere in the Bible is this point made so clearly and powerfully as in the following passage of St. John:

> "We ourselves saw and testify that the Father sent his Son as saviour of the world. If anyone acknowledges that Jesus is the Son of God, *God lives in him, and he in God.* We ourselves have known and put our faith in God's love towards ourselves. *God is love and anyone who lives in love lives in God, and God lives in him.*"[709]

We will briefly indicate how the Bible describes the divine and human loving relationship and presence involved in prayer as communion.

a. God's love and presence in the Old Testament

Here are some conclusions of Old Testament scholarship which show how the love which bound Yahweh to his People led the ancient Hebrews to practice prayer as communion with their God.

> "Love is a pervasive quality in human relationship for the OT. From the higher pitch of sexual communion to the calmest and most detached

---

[708] UNDERHILL [2], p. 171. Emphasis ours.

[709] 1 Jn 4:14-16.

> kindness, the rightly ordered human relationship is one of mutuality in love. *Human covenants are always reciprocal, and love is the characteristic of the relationship.*
>
> The whole range of human relationships is therefore viewed in the OT as directed and determined by love. This love is, however, no abstract emotion, but the concrete acts of love and loyalty which go to the maintenance of human society.
>
> Consonant with the personal and active character of human love is the view of divine love in the OT. God's love is his redeeming activity in human history. To call it love is to recognize that this activity produces the relationship of persons between man and God. The love of God manifests itself most strongly in Israel's history.
>
> Election love and covenantal love (of Yahweh for his people) are closely related, since the act of Yahweh's choice of Israel and the covenant between Yahweh and Israel are two aspects of the same relationship. *Covenantal love is the love which maintains a relationship already established. It is a love which presupposes the mutuality of relationship.* It is a faithful love, a steadfast, unshakable maintenance of the covenantal relationship: 'For his steadfast love endures forever' (Ps 136)."
>
> "The love which Yahweh has shown is a love which initiates and sustains the covenant, and Israel's life in the covenant can properly be only a life of love for Yahweh. *Israel's worship is thus undertaken in love toward Yahweh. The combination of the two ideas is not often found, but worship is sometimes the expression of the love of the chosen people. The pious love Yahweh because he answers prayer* (Ps. 116:1). Those who love his name participate in ritual exaltation of him (Ps 5:11)."[710]

The mutual love relationship between Yahweh and his People is first described in terms of friendship when the Old Testament narrates the religious experiences of Abraham and Moses. But later on the same friendship is extended also to all pious Jews.

> "In calling Abraham, a pagan like the others (Gn 24:2f), to become His friend (Is 41:8), *God expresses his love in the form of friendship: Abraham becomes the confidant of His secrets* (Gn 18:17). If such is the case,

[710] GOOD E.M., vol. III, pp. 165a-168a passim. Emphasis ours. Cf. CCC, n. 2658: "The prayer which is shaped by the liturgical life draws all from the love of Christ toward us and enables us to respond to his love with the same love. Love is the fountain-head of prayer: who draws from love, reaches the climax of prayer."

it is so because Abraham responded to the demands of divine love: he left his country at the request of God (12:1).

Moses from his calling (Ex 3:4) to his death did not cease to advance in *intimacy with God, dealing with Him as with a neighbor* (33:11): he had had the revelation of the tremendous tenderness of God, of a love which without sacrificing anything of its holiness is mercy (34:6f).

After the exile, Israel, purified by the trial, discovers that *God is addressing Himself to the heart of each man.* Formerly one used to speak of love of Yahweh for the group (Dt 4:7) or for his leaders (2 S 12:24): now it is known that each Jew is loved, especially the just (Ps 37:15-19; 146:8), the poor, and the lowly (Ps 113:55-9).

At the approach of Christ's coming, *the pious Jew (Ps 4:4; 132:9,16) knows himself loved by God whose merciful fidelity to the covenant (Ps 136; Jl 2:13), whose goodness (Ps 34:9; 100:5) and grace (Gn 6:8; Is 30:18) he sings. In return, he repeats unceasingly his love for God* (Ps 31:24; 73:25; 116:1) and for all that belongs to Him: His name, His law, His wisdom (Ps 34:13; 119:127; Is 56:6; Si 1:10; 4:14)."[711]

Now, the friendly relationship that God's covenantal love maintains with his chosen People establishes a very special Divine Presence in the pious Jews. A biblical scholar who has thoroughly researched the reality of this Presence writes:

"The reality of the presence of God stands at the center of biblical faith. This presence, however, is always elusive... The Hebrews developed a unique theology of presence. They worshipped a God whose disclosure or proximity always had a certain quality of elusiveness.

It is the distinctiveness of the Hebraic theology of presence rather than the ideology of the covenant which provides a key to understanding the Bible. It is the peculiarly Hebraic theology of presence which explains the importance of the covenant in Israel's religion, and not the converse. The motive of presence is primary, and the covenant is secondary."[712]

Particularly,

"The religion of the psalmist seems to hinge on the notion of God's presence with his people. Hymns are sung and prayers offered 'before

---

[711] DBT, p. 284-285, passim. Emphasis ours.

[712] TERRIEN, pp. xxvii-xxviii. For a biblico-theological summary of the Judeo-Christian doctrine of God's presence see GIARDINI [1], pp. 15-83.

Yahweh', a metaphor drawn perhaps from the language of the royal court...

The idea that to live in the presence of God is better than literally any kind of earthly prosperity undoubtedly tends in a 'spiritual' direction, and has been fruitful theme not only for Christian but also of Jewish mysticism.

Even without such development, however, we can say that the presence of God is one of the central themes of the Old Testament."[713]

Ancient Jews were deeply convinced and justly proud that Yahweh was especially present to them:

"Indeed, what great nation is there that has its gods so near as Yahweh our God is to us whenever we call to him?"[714]

Naturally this was believed to occur especially during the prayers made in the Jerusalem temple.

"Yahweh my God, listen to the cry and to the prayer your servant makes to you today. *Day and night let your eyes watch over this house, over this place of which you have said, 'My name shall be there'.* Listen to the prayer that your servant will offer in this place. Hear the entreaty of your servant and of Israel your people as they pray in this place... And the foreigner, too, not belonging to your people Israel (...), if he comes and prays in this Temple, hear from heaven where your home is, and grant all the foreigner asks."[715]

The same faith in Yahweh's very special presence in the Temple of Jerusalem is expressed by the psalms that biblical scholars put into the category of "songs of Zion", in which Yahweh is depicted

"Not distant from the people, but living in their midst, allowing them to approach the divine presence which is somehow mysteriously dwelling in

---

713 BORTON, pp. 55-56.

714 Dt 4:7.

715 1 K 8:29-30; 41-42.

the Temple... Thus God is perceived as near and accessible and Zion and the Temple command veneration."[716]

This presence of Yahweh in Zion and particularly in the Temple of Jerusalem is a privileged application of the typically Hebrew *Shekinah* concept.

"Forming the backdrop of the whole biblical revelation is a pronounced sense of God, which to the semitic mind means an *invisible God dwelling with his people in some domain of visibility...* In the *Targumin* this was thematized in the image of *Shekinah Yahweh,* the 'dwelling place' of God in some perceptible manner... The *Shekinah* concept is applicable wherever visible. Earthly realities are involved, behind which or in which God comes to appearance, so that he can be said to dwell therein."[717]

Yahweh is present to the praying Hebrews who are faithful to him..

"Righteous in all that he does, Yahweh acts only out of love, *standing close to all who invoke him, close to those who invoke Yahweh faithfully.* Those who fear him need only to ask to be answered; he hears their cries for help and saves them."[718]

But if "the people approaches Yahweh only in words, honours Yahweh only with lip-service while its heart is far from him',[719] Yahweh is hardly present and listening to its prayers. Therefore, the prophets remind the people –

"Seek good and not evil so that you may live, and that Yahweh, God of Sabaoth, may really be with you as you claim he is." "I live in a high and holy place – it is Yahweh who speaks – but I am also with the contrite and

---

[716] CSB, p. 246. Cf. "The key characterization of the Lord [in the psalms] is 'covenant partner'.... Everything that isimportant to Israel flows from this perception of God.": p. 249.

[717] HILL, p. 23.

[718] Ps 145:17-19.

[719] Is 29:13; cf. Jr 12:2.

humbled spirit, to give the humbled spirit new life, to revive contrite hearts."[720]

Indeed, only those

> "Whose hands are clean, whose heart is pure, whose soul does not pay homage to worthless things and who never swears to a lie, have the right to climb the mountain of Yahweh, to stand in his holy place."
>
> Only they can "keep Yahweh before them always", and be sure that their "cry (of prayer) may approach Yahweh's presence."[721]

In other words, only observant Israelites could expect that the advances they make to Yahweh in prayer will lead them to his presence, and allow them to commune with him.

b. Christ the perfect model of prayer as communion

In the New Testament the love relationship between God and Christians, God's presence to them and their communion with God, which is especially brought about in prayer, has its perfect model in Jesus Christ, the Son of God made man.

> "By His very existence, Jesus is the concrete revelation of (God's) love: *Jesus is the man who fulfills the filial dialogue with God and bears witness of it to men.* Jesus is God who comes to live out His love in the fullness of humanity and who came to make us understand the ardent appeal of love. In His very person man loves God and is loved by Him.
>
> The entire life of Jesus witnesses to the twofold dialogue. Given over to the Father from the very beginning (Lk 2:49: cf. Heb 10:5ff), *living in prayer and thanksgiving* (cf. Mk 1:35; Mt 11:25), and above all in perfect conformity to the divine will (Jn 4:34; 6:38). *He is untiring in listening to God (5:30; 8:26,40), which assures Him of being heard by God (11:41f: cf 9:31).*"[722]

---

[720] Am 5:14; Is 57:15. Cf. the usual phrase "to walk in God's presence" in Gn 5:22; 6:9; 17:1, etc.

[721] Ps 24:3-4; Ps 16:8; cf. 25:14-15; Ps 119:168-170.

[722] DBT, p. 285 b. Emphasis ours.

Christians are given the grace necessary to imitate their Master's prayer to the Father. In fact, according to Jesus (cf. Jn 17), Christians not only share in a love relationship with God, analogous to that which the Son has with the Father, but are actually "incorporated in a unity with the Divine Persons".[723] This is the foundation of all Christian communing with the Divine Persons in prayer.

This revelation of the unheard-of unity and communion of Christians with God implies an entirely "new theology of divine presence".

> "It was *a new theology of presence, drawn from the Hebraic complex of cultus and faith, which presided over the emergence of Christianity from Judaism....* For Christians of the first generation, divine reality was mediated no longer through the temple of Jerusalem but through a living reality - the person of the risen Lord... The temple ideology was applied to the spiritual body of the risen Jesus and thus, to the Church."[724]

Jesus Christ, named "god-with-us" *(Emmanuel)* by Isaiah and the Angel who announced his birth to Mary, is the "temple not made by human hands, in whose body lives the fullness of the Divinity".[725]

> So, "since 'the word of God became flesh and dwelt among us' (Jn 1:14) the body of Christ is the *Shekinah Yahweh,* the locus of God's dwelling among his people."[726]

But, by virtue of faith and baptism, Christ lives in Christians, who are sacramentally crucified and risen with him, so that they no longer live their own lives but the life of Jesus who lives in them.[727] Hence, through Christ and in the Holy Spirit sent to them, Christians too, both as individuals and as a community, are made "temples of God".

> "Didn't you realize that you were God's temple and that the Spirit of God was living among you? ...The temple of God is sacred; and you are that

---

723 DBT, p. 286 a.

724 TERRIEN, p. 5. Emphasis ours.

725 Is 7:14; cf. Mt 1:22-23; Mk 14:58; cf. Mt 26:61; 27:40; Jn 2:19; Col 2:9.

726 HILL, p. 23.

727 Cf. Ep 3:17; Ga 2:20; Rm 6:3-4.

temple... Your body, you know, is the temple of the Holy Spirit, who is in you since you received it from God."[728]

"You are part of a building that has the apostles and the prophets for its foundation, and Christ Jesus for its cornerstone. As every structure is aligned on him, all grow into one holy temple in the Lord: and you too, in him, are being built into a house where God lives, in the Spirit."[729]

In other words,

"[From the time when] the death of Christ marks his disappearance beyond the horizon of historical and visible existence with men, the disciples of Christ [insofar as they receive the Spirit of Jesus] become the visible dwelling place of God... The body which is the Church becomes the surrogate, as it were, for the natural body of Christ."[730]

Now, the Holy Spirit renders Christians temples of God by "pouring out the love of God into their hearts". Such love ought to be concretely proved by keeping God's commandments, particularly the commandment of loving one another as Jesus loves us. All other commandments are summed up in this first commandment.[731] By its observance the love of God infused into Christians reaches its completion, and God himself, who is love, lives in them.

"As long as we love one another God will live in us and his love will be complete in us... God is love and anyone who lives in love lives in God and God lives in him. Love will come to perfection in us."[732]

In this love coming to perfection in us the Divine Persons come to us and make their home within us.

"If you love me you will keep my commandments. I shall ask the Father, and he will give you another Advocate to be with you for ever, that Spirit of truth whom the world can never receive since it neither sees nor knows him: but you know him, because he is with you, he is in you... If

---

[728] 1 Co 3:16-17; 6:19; cf. 2 Co 6:16; Jn 14:23.

[729] Ep 2:20-22.

[730] HILL, p. 24.

[731] Cf. Rm 5:5; Jn 13:34 = 1 Jn 3:11; cf. Rm 13:8-10.

[732] 1 Jn 4:12, 17.

anyone loves me he will keep my word, and my Father will love him, and we shall come to him and make our home with him."[733]

In the history of Christian spirituality Origen was the first to use this teaching of St. John[734] to interpret the OT's *Song of Songs* as an allegory,

> "In which (the author) urges upon the soul the love of the heavenly and the divine under the figure of the bride and the bridegroom, teaching us that we must attain fellowship with God by the path of loving affection *(caritas)* and love *(amor)*."[735]

In this way, the union of love of Christians with the Divine Persons, taught by the NT, became the foundation on which Christian prayer as communion stands.

c. Prayer in the Spirit and Prayer as communion

More precisely, the Christian practice of prayer as communion is made possible by the descent on Christians of the Holy Spirit, who pours charity into their hearts. Jesus is the perfect model of prayer in the Holy Spirit. St. Luke, who more than the other evangelists reports Jesus' solitary prayer,[736] remarks –

> "While Jesus after his own baptism was at prayer, heaven opened and the Holy Spirit descended on him in bodily shape, like a dove, and a voice came from heaven, 'You are my Son, the Beloved: my favor rests on you."[737]

---

[733] Jn 14:15, 23.

[734] Cf. "If loving affection remains in us, God remains in us (cf. 1 John 4:12). And God, that is the Father and the Son, come to him who is perfect in loving affection according to the words of our Lord and Savior, who says, 'I and my Father will come to him and make our home with him' (cf. 1 John 4:18; John 14:23).": ORIGEN [2], p. 226.

[735] *Ibid.*, p. 232.

[736] Cf. Lk 5:16; 6:12; 9:18, 28-29; 22:41.

[737] Lk 3:21-22.

Jesus himself "speaks to his disciples of the Holy Spirit with regard to prayer". (CCC no. 728; cf. Lk 11:13)

St. Paul ascribes an experience of prayer in the Holy Spirit to Christians -

> "Everyone moved by the Spirit is a son of God. The spirit you received is not the spirit of slaves bringing fear into your lives again: it is the spirit of sons, and it makes us cry out, 'Abba, Father!' The Spirit itself and our spirit bear united witness that we are children of God."[738]

Some biblical scholars think that in this passage "Paul has in view the situation of worship, not a process in the soul." Hence they also judge "a mistake" the interpretation of the term "to cry out" *(krazein),* used by Paul, if it were "referring evidently and primarily to (personal) prayer." According to them, it is instead "to be recognized as a technical term of acclamation by which the congregation is uttering an ecstatic cry in response to the message of salvation."[739]

But intellectual integrity compels one of these scholars to acknowledge that many other exegetes interpret this passage as if Paul had in mind the personal prayer of Christians. Do the two interpretations need to be mutually exclusive? Cannot they be taken as complementary? Of course,

> "The Spirit who speaks in worship bears witness to what the Spirit who dwells within us must acknowledge."[740]

In the same way as Jesus in the garden of Gethsemane cried out *Abba!* to the Father,[741] so the Holy Spirit enables Christians to express a filial, yet

---

[738] Rm 8:14-16.

[739] KÄSEMANN, pp. 228 and 240-243.

[740] KÄSEMANN, pp. 228-229. Aquinas comments that the Holy Spirit makes us cry to God in prayer "non magnitudine vocis, sed magnitudine et fervore affectu. Tunc enim clamamus Abba-Pater quando per affectum accendimur calore Spiritus Sancti ad desiderium Dei.": *In Epist. ad Galatas,* IV, Lect. 3.

[741] Cf. Mk 14:32-42.

childlike calling upon God in prayer. For by the gift of the Spirit, Christians become one with Jesus even as he and the Father are one.[742]

The fact that Jesus taught his disciples to address God as Father is interpreted by John Paul II as meaning that

> "The Kingdom (of God) will grow insofar as every person learns to *turn to God in the intimacy of prayer as to a Father...*(as) the Kingdom's nature is one of communion of human beings with one another and with God."[743]

Such a communion and intimacy of prayer with God is not at all natural for us, but the Holy Spirit reproduces in us those attitudes and dispositions which characterize Christ, the Son of God. That is why when we pray in this manner,

> "The Holy Spirit comes to help us in our weakness. For when we cannot choose words in order to pray properly, the Spirit himself expresses our plea in a way that could never be put into words, and God who knows everything in our hearts knows perfectly well what he means, and that the pleas of the saints expressed by the Spirit are according to the mind of God."[744]

---

[742] Cf. Jn 17:20-26; Heb 2:10 13.

[743] JOHN PAUL II [2], n. 14, p. 25. Because the Pope writes these words within the context of the Christian Mission *ad gentes,* he also adds: "The ultimate purpose of mission is to enable people *to share in the communion which exists between the Father and the Son":* # 15, p. 26; virtually stating that the intimacy of prayer with God as Father is the ultimate purpose of the Missions. Love is not mentioned in the Lord's prayer, but it is surely implied in the opening words: *'Abba, Father'* (Lk 11:2). Secret prayer is a means to real fellowship with God, who is to be loved for himself alone (Mt 6:1-6, 16-18).

[744] Rm 8:26-27. "The Greek verse 26 literally says that the Spirit 'intercedes over and above' our own intercession 'with ineffable groanings'. It is possible that these groanings refer to the 'words that cannot be uttered' heard by Paul in the third heaven (1 Co 12:4).": PILCH, p. 1089 a.

Christians may pray in the spirit uttering only sighs and groanings.[745] These groanings express the human spirit's yearning for the eternal glorification of the children of God, as well as the troubled expectation of the Lord's return at the end of time.

> "The Apostle passionately longs for the liberation of existence from temptation and decay in favor of a mode of being in a world that belongs to God alone. This is the object of the groaning of the Christians as they wait for the parousia."[746]

Paul sensed this same yearning and expectation diffused throughout "all creation including mankind with no sharp line of differentiation"[747], as in a "great act of giving birth" to a "new creation."

> "From the beginning till now the entire creation, as we know, has been groaning[748] in one great act of giving birth: and not only creation, but all of us who possess the first-fruits of the Spirit, we too groan inwardly as we wait for our bodies to be set free."[749]

The Apostle acknowledged that there are moments in Christian prayerlife when we do not know what to say to God. We feel mute, for the words that we once addressed to him do not seem to make sense any more. In those moments the Holy Spirit, who abides in our hearts, comes to our help by praying in us, not by teaching us better words of prayer, but by prompting "undecipherable aspirations (quite beyond the articulate *Abba)* that are discernible to the searcher of hearts".[750]

---

[745] This is the literal meaning of the Greek word *stenagmòs,* which the Jerusalem Bible translates "our plea."

[746] KÄSEMANN, p. 237.

[747] KÄSEMANN, p. 233.

[748] The Greek word *sustenazein* used here has the same root sense of *stenagmòs.*

[749] Rm 8:22-23.

[750] JONES C.P.M., in SS, p. 81. According to Käsemann's interpretative slant, "what is at issue here is the praying in tongues of 1 Co 14:15, which finally expresses itself in ecstatic practices of worship, in such a way that not even the community itself knows its true meaning and is represented by the Spirit.": KÄSEMANN, p. 242.

Through these aspirations prompted by the Holy Spirit we already share in the life of the Holy Trinity and intimately commune with the Divine Persons, though still imperfectly.

In conclusion, according to St. Paul the Holy Spirit animates Christian prayer, by pouring charity into the hearts of Christians and drawing them into communion with the Divine Persons.

> "The Spirit bears witness with the spirit of man (Rom. 8:16,27) and causes him to set his mind on the things of the Spirit (vs. 5). Since the Spirit alone knows the mind of God (1 Cor 2:10-12; cf. Rom 8:27), he can intercede for men, and he actually teaches them to pray (Rom 8:26-27), interpreting to God their inarticulate sighs according to God's will. Only the Spirit can teach man to say 'Lord' (1 Cor 12:3), and it is he who cries in us: 'Abba".[751]

St. John joins the teaching of St. Paul on prayer in the Holy Spirit when he reports the words addressed by Jesus to the Samaritan woman,

> "The hour is coming when you will worship the Father neither on this mountain nor in Jerusalem... The hour will come – in fact it is here already – when true worshippers will worship the Father in spirit and in truth. This is the kind of worshipper the Father wants. God is spirit and those who worship must worship in spirit and in truth."[752]

For "the Most High God does not live in houses built by men". To maintain that he does is "to resist the Holy "Spirit" and forget that all human beings are his children who "in him live and move and are."[753] Yahweh set his benevolent eyes more on the Israelite of humble and contrite heart than on the magnificent temple of Jerusalem.

Continuing with and re-enforcing this truth by what he says to the Samaritan woman, Jesus

> "Shifts from the place of worship to the manner of worship", even though "in proclaiming worship in Spirit and in truth, Jesus is not contrasting external worship with internal worship. An ideal of purely internal worship

---

[751] SMITH C.W.F., vol. III, p. 864 a.

[752] Jn 4:21, 23-24; Cf. Is 66:1-2.

[753] Cf. Ac 7:48-51; 17:24-29.

ill fits the NT scene with its eucharistic gatherings, hymn singing, baptism in water, etc..

Here it is the Spirit given by Jesus that is to animate the worship that replaces worship in the Temple... For God can be worshipped as Father only by those who possess the Spirit that makes them God's children, the Spirit by which God begets them from above (Jn 3:5). This Spirit raises them above the earthly level, the level of the flesh, and enables them to worship God properly."[754]

So, St. Augustine, for one, thinks that those who are reborn in the Spirit ought to pray "spiritually". They would pray "illicitly" if they prayed "carnally".

When Jesus taught his disciples the "Our Father", he included all the petitions that God's children ought to offer to God in the Holy Spirit. So, in Augustine's view, any prayer which cannot be included in or derived from the "Our Father" is "carnal".[755]

This prayer "in the Spirit" demanded of Christians leads them into intimate communion with God"

"In John *pneuma* (Spirit) means all that belongs to God and the heavenly world, in contrast to all that is earthly and human; by speaking of worship in Spirit and in Truth Jesus is inviting men *to seek God, to an unheard-of intimacy with the Father."*[756]

Prayer in spirit and in truth, i.e., by the Holy Spirit, is an earthly anticipation of the heavenly liturgy - which has no need of a temple:

"I saw that there was no temple in the city (the heavenly Jerusalem) since the Lord God Almighty and the Lamb were themselves the temple, and the city did not need the sun or the moon for light, since it was lit by the radiant glory of God and the Lamb was a lighted torch for it... His servants

---

[754] BROWN [1], p. 180. Emphasis ours.

[755] Cf. *Epistula CXXX,* 12, 22.

[756] SCHNACKENBURG, vol. I, pp. 437-439. Emphasis ours. See at p. 438 a development of the profoundly trinitarian spiritual doctrine contained in the dialogue between Christ and the Samaritan woman reported by St. John.

will worship him, they will see him face to face, and his name will be written on their foreheads."[757]

To be sure, the human nature of Christ immolated on the cross and risen to heavenly glory is now the heavenly temple wherein true worship is offered to God in the Spirit.[758] But Christians, grafted by faith and through baptism onto the death and resurrection of their Lord, are made themselves temples of the Holy Spirit.[759]

So, they too ought to be

> "Worshipping God in a way that is worthy of thinking beings, by offering their living bodies as a holy sacrifice, truly pleasing to God."[760]

In conclusion, the Old and New Testaments put at the center of the History of Salvation the covenant offered by God and accepted by his people. Such a covenant establishes a relationship of faithful love between God and the people. The unitive force of that love creates a stable presence and enduring communion between the two parties of the covenant. So that God makes a covenant with his people for no other reason than to draw them into intimate communion with himself.

The Old Covenant reaches its perfection in Jesus Christ. By baptism Christians are "grafted onto" the death and resurrection of the Lord and receive from the Father and the Son an outpouring of the Holy Spirit that transforms them into dwelling places of the Divine Persons.

So, a profound interiorization of the Divine Presence is brought about in Christians and enables them to join their prayers to Christ's, to address themselves to God as *Abba,* to pray in the Spirit; in short, to have an intimate prayerful communion with the three Divine Persons.

Accordingly, a scholar can briefly describe biblical prayer in terms of

> "Heights of *spiritual communion and identification of will and activity with God...* In general terms, prayer is *attempted intercourse with*

---

757 Rv 21:22-23; 22:3-4.

758 Cf. Jn 2:19-22.

759 Cf. Rm 6:4-11; 1 Co 3:16-17; 6:19; 2 Co 6:16; Ep 2:21.

760 Rm 12:1; cf. 14:17.

> *God*....designed by means of the creation of *personal contact* to affect the nature and course of the relationship....
>
> A lifelong and whole-person response to the divine reality, a posture of the will oriented towards the divine majesty is the essence of prayer."[761]

ii. *The Christian Tradition of Prayer as Communion*

The communion of Christians with the Divine Persons taught by the New Testament is especially expressed and cultivated in the life of prayer. This is pinpointed by the following ancient definitions.[762]

> "Prayer is continual intercourse of the spirit with God... What greater thing is there than to converse intimately with God and to be preoccupied with his company?"[763]
>
> "Prayer and converse *(homilia)* with God is a supreme good: it is a partnership *(koinōnia)* and union *(enōsis)* with God."[764]
>
> "Prayer is the human person's being-with *(synousia)* and union *(enōsis)* with God."[765]

---

[761] SMITH C.W.F, p. 857a - 867b. The section of the study on biblical prayer which this author dedicates to the Fourth Gospel is significantly entitled "prayer as communion". Here are the conclusive words of this section: "The essence of Jesus' prayer is that the oneness between himself and God may be shared by the disciples with him and with one another (Jn 17:11b, 21). *In this prayer, rooted in communion, seeking communion, biblical prayer reaches its climax.* It is summed up in 1 John 5:13-15 in the belief, knowledge, and confidence the believer has in Christ, assuring him that in whatever he asks according to the will of the Son of God, he is heard and answered.": p. 865 b. Emphasis ours.

[762] Was WILLIAM JAMES referring to the following early Christian definitions of prayer when he wrote that the "essence of religion" and "religion in act" is "any kind of actual communion and conversation or interchange with God"?: p. 361.

[763] EVAGRIUS, ch. 3, p. 56 and ch. 34. Cf. p. 60: "What state of the soul then is required that the spirit might thus strain after his Master without wavering, living constantly with him without intermediary?"

[764] CHRYSOSTOM, p. 461. The English translation is from LITURGY, vol. II, p. 68.

[765] CLIMACUS, ch. 28, p. 1129a. Translation ours. It is worth remembering that "with the exception of the Bible and the service books, there is no book in Eastern

a. Hellenistic and Christian meanings

As the Greek Fathers used the terms *homilia*[766] (= company, intercourse, converse[767]), *koinōnia* (= communion, fellowship, sharing[768]), *synousia* (= being with, shared possession, dialogue), *enōsis* (= union, unity[769]) etc., to define Christian prayer as communion, one may surmise that they were influenced by the cultural milieu of their time.

In fact, somebody thinks that the very early Christian definition of prayer given by St. Clement of Alexandria: "prayer is keeping company with God"[770]

> "is derived from the popularized Platonist, Maximus of Tyre, 5, 8, ed. H. Holbein (Leipzig, 1910)."[771]

But, also the Cynics described their relationship with God as a

> "*Pros theous homilia (Epict. Diss.,* III 22,22); the worshipper is not so much the *doulos* [= slave] as the *philos* [=friend] of God."[772]

At any rate, whatever might have been the literary origin of the definition of prayer as communion adopted by the early Fathers, such

---

Christendom that has been studied, copied and translated more often than *The Ladder of Divine Ascent* by St. John Climacus... Its popularity equals that of *The Imitation of Christ* in the West.": CLIMACUS [2], pp. 1, 27, translates the quoted definition of prayer: "Prayer is by nature a dialogue and union with God... It achieves a reconciliation with God."

766 Besides the quoted Chrysostom, see also the earlier CLEMENT OF ALEXANDRIA, VII, 7, 456.

767 Cf. GELNT, p. 565.

768 Cf. *Ib.*, p. 438.

769 Cf. *Ib.*, p. 271.

770 TUGWELL [6], p. vii.

771 TUGWELL, [5], p. 346, note 9.

772 TDNT, vol. II, p. 265.

definition became definitely Christian when its hellenistic contents were entirely replaced by the intimacy which praying Christians can have with God by virtue of charity,[773] for they are adopted by the heavenly Father as children through his only begotten Son Jesus Christ, in the Holy Spirit.

Such intimacy is confirmed by the amazing "out-spokenness" *(parrhesía)* of the praying Christian with God. Within the Greek city-states the word *parrhesía* meant "freedom of speech". In the New Testament it often means the attitude of Christian missionaries, who have the courage of openly preaching the Gospel,[774]. But it also means the extremely confident familiarity, casting out all fear,[775] with which Christians can pray to their heavenly Father.

The late Thomas Merton wrote that,

> "*Parrhesía* symbolizes the perfect communication of man's intelligence with God by knowledge *(gnosis)* and contemplation *(theoria)*. It symbolizes also the perfect communion of the will with God by charity."[776]

The substiantial change in meaning that the Greek definition of prayer as communion underwent when Christian spiritual masters appropriated it to signify Christian prayer, demonstrates that the decisive factor in their understanding of prayer was not the popularized Greek philosophy of the time, but their living out of the New Testament's teaching about intimacy with God in prayer. What the early Fathers really did was to use the Greek wording as a blank mould into which they cast their distinctively Christian experience of prayer.

---

[773] CHRYSOSTOM, for One, in the already quoted homily on prayer (p. 465) said that "prayer is longing (pothos) for God and charity (agape) towards God".

[774] Cf. JOHN PAUL II [2], ch. 5, n. 45, p. 60.

[775] According to CCC, n. 2778, the "typically Christian" meanings of the *parrhesía,* which inspire us to pray the "Our Father" are: "candid simplicity, filial confidence, joyful assurance, humble audacity, certitude of being loved." The biblical references for all these shades of meaning are: Ep 3:12; Heb 3:6; 4:16: 10:19; 1 Jn 2:28; 3:21; 5:14.

[776] MERTON [3], p. 75. Cf. 1 Jn 2:28; 4:18. See Zorell, p. 1012: "Nobis, a Christo redemptis Deoque reconciliatis atque a Deo adoptatis et pollicitationem exaudiendarum precum nostrarum nactis, oritur novum genus *parresías,* quo erga Deum utimur: *fiducia filialis laeta qua ad Deum accedere eumque precari audemus."* Emphasis ours.

After all, being with God and communing with him in and through prayer is the most appropriate faith and love response of praying Christians to God revealed in Jesus Christ as the "Immanuel, a name which means 'God-is-with-us'."[777] Actually, prayer as communion is the prayerful response of Christians to the Divine Persons, receiving them into participation in Their divine trinitarian communion, through Jesus Christ.

Such a sublime communion of Christians with God was explicitly asked for by Jesus:

> "May they all be one. Father, may they be one in us, as you are in me and I am in you, so that the world may believe it was you who sent me. I have given them the glory you gave me, that they may be one as we are one. With me in them and you in me, may they be so completely one that the world will realize that it was you who sent me and that I have loved them as much as you loved me."[778]

John Cassian played the role of mediator between the early Greek Fathers and the Medieval Latin spiritual Masters by describing the highest form of Christian prayer as follows:

> *"The mind throws itself into love for God and converses familiarly with him as with his own Father.* The first words of the Lord's prayer 'Our Father' teach us to strive for this state. When we confess the God and Lord of all creation to be our Father, we confess that we have been called from the state of slavery to the state of adopted sons."[779] This is "the loftier state of prayer,[780] formed by the contemplation of God alone and by a charity that burns like fire."[781] "No mortal can understand and describe [it] ... It is an ineffable prayer which very few men know by experience."[782]

---

[777] Mt 1:23. Cf. Is 7:14.

[778] Jn 17:21-23. By these words Jesus explained the profound meaning of the name *Immanuel* given Him by the Prophet and the Angel. Cf. the preceding note.

[779] CASSIAN, *Conferences,* IX, 18. CHADWICK, p. 222. Emphasis ours.

[780] Cassian repeats this evaluation several times. Cf. *Ibid.,* IX, 18:25; 28: "There is no loftier state of prayer than this.": X, 11 etc.

[781] *Ibid.,* IX, 18, CHADWICK, p. 222.

[782] *Ibid.,* IX, 15; 25. CHADWICK, pp. 221, 226.

He terms this prayer "the leaping of a flame", a "spark-like prayer",[783] and explains that it is "prayer in the Spirit".

> "Recollecting the generosity and the mercy of the Lord, past or present or future, (those who pray) are rapt into that spark-like prayer... It consists of a powerful and wordless pouring forth of prayer to God, which *the spirit, with groanings which cannot be uttered, sends up* though not conscious of its content. In that moment it conceives and puts forth what no one can describe, and which the mind apart from that moment cannot remember....
>
> The mind illuminated by an outflowing of light from heaven, does not define it in the narrow limit of human language... Sometimes the mind withdraws into a kind of secret abyss of silence, sudden illumination leaves it speechless, the awestruck spirit locks his feeling within or loses feelings altogether and *pours itself out into longings for God, in groanings that cannot be uttered.*"[784]

The repetitions of "groanings which cannot be uttered"[785] manifest that Cassian identifies his "spark-like prayer" with the prayer in which the Spirit makes us cry out, "Abba, Father!"[786], namely with the prayer as communion taught by the New Testament.

b. Modern and contemporary testimonies

When St. Teresa of Avila wrote:

> "In my opinion, prayer is nothing else than a frequent solitary *sharing with a friend* of whose love we are certain,"[787]

---

[783] *Ibid.,* IX, 15, 25; X, 11. CHADWICK, pp. 221, 226, 244.

[784] *Ibid.,* IX, 15, 25; 27. CHADWICK, pp. 221, 226, 227.

[785] It is a literal quotation of Rm 8:26-27. The same Pauline passage is used to describe the spark-like prayer. *Ibid.,* X, 11. CHADWICK, p. 244.

[786] Cf. Rm 8:14-17.

[787] "Que no es otra cosa oración mental, a mi parecer, sino *tratar de amistad,* estando muchas veces tratando a solas con quien sabemos nos ama": *Vida,* ch. 8, n. 5. Emphasis and translation ours. These well known words of St. Teresa are quoted by CCC, n. 2709, as a description of the contemplative prayer which follows meditation.

she described her own experience of prayer as communion. St. John of the Cross, who worked with virtually the same concept of prayer,[788] claimed that the whole purpose of Christian prayerlife is to

> "Attain to the divine light of *the perfect union of love of God,* as far as possible in this life....when *the transformation of the soul is wrought through its perfect love.*"[789]

It is likely that the many contemporary authors who emphatically write that prayer is love are "variously quoting" St. Teresa's definition, even though they do not explicitly mention her.[790] Indeed, such seems to be the case with the following definitions:

> "Prayer is our life of personal intercourse and communion with God, who loves us, and whom we love or want to love."[791]
> "(When we pray) God is with us and we are his, and in this peace our hearts learn to commune silently with God in loving union with him."[792]
> "Prayer is union with God."[793]

---

[788] Cf. E.g., "Toma a Dios por esposo y amigo con quien te andes de continuo.": *Dichos de Luz y de Amor,* 65. "Olvido de lo criado,/ memoria del Criador,/ atención a lo interior/ y estarse amando el Amado.": *Poesias,* XXII, CRUZ, pp. 1269, 1330.

[789] CROSS [1], prologue, 1, p. 94 and I, iv, 3, p. 112. Words like these are repeated very often, as a sort of refrain, by the Mystical Doctor. Do these words define "mystical" prayer? Yes, especially if we take mysticism in the sense HENRI BERGSON understood it: "God is love, and the object of love: herein lies the whole contribution of mysticism... What the mystic does state clearly is that divine love is not a thing of God: it is God himself.": p. 240.

[790] This, at least, is the opinion of KAVANAUGH, p. 13.

[791] BUTLER, p. 51.

[792] RAHNER [4], p. 15.

[793] MOTHER TERESA of CALCUTTA.

It is worth noticing that these authors are not speaking of any particular act of prayer, but of the practice of prayer by and large, i.e., of the life of prayer.[794]

Of the same kind are the general descriptions of prayer which we find in the new CCC:

> "The (Christian) Mystery demands that the faithful believe in it, celebrate it, and live it out in a *living and personal relationship with the living and true God. Such a relationship is prayer.*"[795]
>
> "As the grace of the Kingdom is 'the union of the whole Holy Trinity with the whole human spirit,[796] *the life of prayer consists in habitually being in the presence of God, three times Holy, and in communion with Him.*"[797]

Many authors today stress that prayer is love. And by the word "love" they mean the communion or friendly sharing that Christians have with God, when love inspires their prayer. This point is clearly made by Guillerand –

> "God is love. We enter into communication with him when we love, and in the measure of our love the soul that loves and that has been introduced by love into that dwelling place where love abides, can speak to him."[798]

One of these authors over-emphasizes prayer as love.

> "Christian prayer is love: it is communication in love... It is a communion and union in love, and besides this, everything else is secondary and inconsequential."[799]

---

[794] This is manifest in BERGANT, p. 9: *"Praying or the practice of prayer* are more like acts of love or making love." Emphasis ours.

[795] No. 2558. Emphasis ours. Cf. n. 2564: "Christian prayer is a relationship of Covenant between God and the human person." 2567: "[Prayer] is a mysterious encounter.... an event of Covenant (with God)...revealed throughout the whole history of salvation."

[796] ST. GREGORY OF NAZIANZEN, *Orationes,* 16, 9: PG 35; 954 c.

[797] No. 2565. Emphasis ours.

[798] GUILLERAND, p. 126.

[799] PENNINGTON [3], pp. 387 and 389.

Several other authors express the same conviction, but in a way that makes the reader surmise that in Christian prayerlife, besides that form of prayer which can be identified with love, there are other forms of prayer.

> "Prayer is an adventure into the unplumbed depths of the love of God, the depths of God who is love... Prayer, *as in these pages we have come to understand,* is the response of our love to God's love for us."[800]
>
> *"When God moves the Christian to seek him in prayer, prayer is interchangeable with love.* For now prayer is no longer simply an act of communication with God, but is rather one's yielding to the solitary recognition of being at one with God in his love. This communion is not of this earth. It is of God in his will for us to be one with him."[801]

An author makes very clear what he means writing time and again – "prayer is love".

> "If Jesus has told us that the Christian life is centered in love, then prayer, a very important exercise of the Christian life, must also be rooted in love. Prayer in various ways helps us to love, and to love more perfectly. *Prayer is many things, but primarily it is love.*"[802]

Hence, the same author always takes care to qualify exactly his frequent statement – "prayer is love", by adding – "primarily, basically, fundamentally," etc.[803]

Likewise other authors write:

> "Our encounter with God in love is *the very essence* of prayer."[804]
>
> "True prayer is *ultimately* love. To the degree that you surrender yourself to the leadership of the Indwelling in each moment, to that degree

---

[800] BUTLER, pp. 58 and 74. Emphasis ours.

[801] FINLEY, p. 8. Emphasis ours.

[802] CARTER [1], Preface. Emphasis ours. STEINGRAEBER is an exposition of St. Alphonsus de Liguori's teaching on prayer.

[803] CARTER [1], pp. 1-8 passim.

[804] GREEN [1], pp. 31-32. Cf. pp. 65, 87, 96. Emphasis ours.

> you can consider yourself as a person of *authentic* prayer and a true Christian."[805]

Unfortunately, all these emphatic qualifications may give readers the impression that prayer in which love is not "primarily, essentially, ultimately", etc., involved is not true prayer. But,

> "As often happens, with the emphasis of one truth, there comes about a de-emphasis of the truth at the other end of the continuum!"[806]

So, when we say – "prayer is love", we should mean that

> "This love cuts across all methods of prayer, all possible stages... Whether my prayer is predominantly discursive, containing many thoughts and images, or whether it has become deeply contemplative, leaving behind the multitude of concepts and images, this prayer of mine still depends mainly upon my love."[807]

Accordingly, what here is called prayer is not different from the love which pervades the whole Christian life, so that prayer and Christian life are inseparable.[808]

The CCC quotes the description of prayer as communion of St. Teresa of Avila (which we have given above) and calls it "oraciòn" and "mental orison".[809] This prayer is said to be seeking and desiring the beloved through the recollection of the heart, by abiding within oneself, which is the abode where the Lord is waiting for us.

> It is "receiving and responding to the gift of God's love",[810] "The most simple expression of the mystery of prayer...a gift of grace...the relationship of the covenant concluded by God at the depth of our being, the

---

[805] MALONEY [2], p. 89. Emphasis ours.

[806] CARTER [1], p. 2.

[807] CARTER [1], pp. 4-5.

[808] Cf. CCC, n. 2745.

[809] CCC, nn. 2709 and 2724.

[810] *Ibid.*, nn. 2711-2712.

communion in which the Most Holy Trinity makes the human person, who is God's image, resemblant to It...

It is contemplation, a look of faith focusing on Jesus... The listening to God's word with the obedience of faith, the unconditional acceptance of the servant, and the perfect love agreement of the son or daughter... It is the silence of love, in which the Father speaks to us his incarnate Son, suffering, dead and risen, and the filial Spirit makes us participants of the prayer of Jesus... *It is a communion of love* which brings life to the multitude."[811]

This complex description of the practice of this form of prayer clearly says that its most characteristic aspect is the communion of the praying Christian with Christ and the Divine Persons.

iii. *Style and Grades of Prayer as Communion*

Undoubtedly, prayer as communion has a distinctive style and goes through many graces of growth.

a. Style of prayer as communion

Prayer as communion approaches God as a partner who is close and intimate to praying Christians. The old Testament expresses this closeness of God, saying that in prayer the Israelites could "stand before God", "pour out their soul before him", "contemplate his face", etc.[812]

Their prayerful thinking of and experiencing God as intimately close brings to the fore his loving kindness and care, his very real even though mysterious "Divine Presence". This term "Divine Presence" covers the whole mystery of God: Father, Son, and Holy Spirit, with all his divine attributes.

"It must be known that *God, in His own and simple Being, is all the virtues and grandeurs of His attributes:* for He is omnipotent, wise, good, merciful, just, strong and loving, and has other infinite attributes and virtues whereof we have no knowledge here below; and, as *He is all these things*

---

[811] *Ibid.*, nn. 2714-2718 passim.

[812] Cf. 1 S 1:9-15 passim; Ps 11:7; 15:1; 16:18; 17:15, etc. See also Mt 26:38-39 and parallels. "Standing before God is common to all those who pray.": CLIMACUS, 28, p. 1129.

> *when He is united with the soul,* at the time when He is pleased to reveal His knowledge to it, it is able to see in Him all these virtues and grandeurs, clearly and distinctly – namely, omnipotence, goodness, wisdom, justice, mercy and so forth, all in one simple being.
>
> And, as *each of these things is the very Being of God in one sole reality, which is the Father or the Son or the Holy Spirit,* each attribute being God Himself and God being infinite light and infinite Divine fire, as we have said above, it follows from this that in each of these attributes, which, as we say, are innumerable, and are his virtues, He gives light and burns as God."[813]

Since it responds to "the very Being of God in one sole reality, which is the Father or the Son or the Holy Spirit, and in his own simple Being is all the virtues and grandeurs of his attributes", prayer as communion is more unified than prayer as worship, which, as we said in the preceding chapter, expresses a variety of different prayerful responses to the many attributes of God.

Prayer as worship approaches God as ultimate goal, who appears to praying Christians variously qualified by his many attributes. Prayer as communion encounters the very Persons of the Holy Trinity, who sum up all divine attributes and are willing to bestow a participation in them to praying Christians who commune with Them through the intimacy of love.

So, prayer as communion consists in simply receiving and enjoying with gratitude the intimate presence of the triune God with all his attributes.

> *"He that loves another and does him good loves him and does him good according to his attributes and properties.* And thus since the Spouse within thee is omnipotent...wise...good...holy...just ...merciful ...compassionate and clement...strong and sublime and delicate...clean and pure...true...liberal...of greatest humility..., He is joyfully revealing to thee, in these ways, His countenance, full of graces, and saying to thee: *'I am thine and for thee, and I delight to be such as I am that I may give Myself to thee and be thine'.*"[814]

The ancient spiritual masters compared the growth process of the Christian prayerlife to climbing a mountain at whose summit Christians are admitted to God's presence and can commune with him and enjoy with him all the riches of his Divinity. The prayer practiced on the summit of the mountain

---

813 CROSS [3], III, n. 2, pp. 82-83. Emphasis ours.

814 CROSS [3], III. n. 6, pp. 86-87. Emphasis ours.

could therefore be imaginatively described as basking in the glow and warmth of the Divine Presence.[815]

This style of prayer pervades the many grades of communion with God. For the summit of the mountain of prayer is not a pointed peak, where climbers must come to a full stop, lest they lose the heights laboriously gained. It is, rather, a large plateau on which praying Christians walk growing into an ever closer intimacy with God.

Indeed, St. John of the Cross, writing his *Living Flame of Love* – after having already dealt in his preceding books with "the most perfect degree of perfection to which man may attain in this life, which is transformation in God" – still can

> "Treat of a love which is even more completed and perfected within this same state of transformation. For, although it is true that one can speak of a state of transformation beyond which, as such, a soul cannot pass, yet none the less, with time and practice, as I say, the soul may become more completely perfected and grounded in love.
>
> Even so, when a log of wood has been set upon fire, it is transformed into fire and united with it; yet, as the fire grows hotter and the wood remains upon it for a longer time, it glows much more and becomes more completely enkindled, until it gives sparks of fire and flame."[816]

b. Teresian grades of prayer as communion

St. Teresa of Avila is undoubtedly one of the greatest experts and promoters of prayer as communion. Teresa experienced that Christians who often engage in friendly converse with the Lord in prayer are gradually led by him to make their Beloved Lord the only center of their thoughts and affections.

Actually, after many years of struggle with the usual difficulties of beginners, she was enabled to have continual "communication" and "conversation" with the Lord.[817] And by virtue of such communion she made

---

[815] In the passage quoted above, note 113, John of the Cross writes that "God being infinite light and infinite Divine fire... gives light and burns as God."

[816] CROSS [3], B, prologue, 3, p. 150.

[817] "Con el Señor tenía conversación continua": *Vida,* ch. 38, n. 5: "Deudo y amistad se pierden con la falta de comunicación": *Camino de Perfección,* ch. 26, n. 9.

a marvelous spiritual journey which extended to the highest grades of intimacy with him.

Teresa also had, time and again, opportunities to write fine descriptions of the many "mansions" she passed through on that journey, always adding new details and clarifications to her subject. The route of prayer she described is not the only one that leads Christians to the most intimate union with God in prayer. But, it was tested and found sound by the supreme Catholic doctrinal authority, who proclaimed Teresa a Doctor of the Church.

The abundant literature which is available on the grades of prayer described by Teresa dispenses us from the task of giving more than a brief interpretative synopsis of them.[818]

The whole prayer-journey of Teresa includes two fundamental stretches. The first covers the grades of prayer mostly produced or *acquired* by human effort, while the second comprises the grades of prayer God graciously *infuses* into praying Christians.

Human activity predominates throughout the former stretch, although praying Christians draw the spiritual force they need to act efficaciously from the common divine grace available to all God's children. During this stretch prayer develops from a *vocal* form, i.e., composed mostly of words of prayer addressed to God, into a mental form, consisting in the discursive use of phantasy and reason which Teresa calls *meditation.*

Teresa's greater contribution to the understanding of the growth-process of prayer as communion is her subtle psychological description of the infused grades this kind of prayer goes through.[819] Experience taught Teresa that, after the grade of meditation, those who persevere in prayer as communion receive the infusion of many "graces of prayer" which gradually lead them into a more and more intimate union with the Lord. The whole "infused" stretch of the prayer-journey is covered by what Teresa terms the two moments of "quiet" and "union".

Recollection – a simplified loving prayerful centering on God's presence – is the beginning of that calm intuitive inner attitude which

---

[818] The major passages concerning these grades are in her *Vida,* ch. 14-21; *Camino de Perfección,* ch. 29-32; *Relación,* V; *Moradas,* IV-VII. A systematic and brief presentation of all grades can be found in AUMANN, pp. 316-357.

[819] Before St. Teresa spiritual writers had distinguished various grades of contemplative prayer. See, e.g., HILTON, I, chs. 4-9, pp. 79-83; chs. 26-32, pp. 98-103.

characterizes the prayer of quiet. This is already prayer of "quiet" because it comes after the spiritual labour needed for discursive meditation.

Prayer of quiet, properly so called, is a very peaceful and deeply silent prayer.[820] In this grade the heart is not only centered on God in intimate awareness of his presence, but the whole person is powerfully drawn to remain still with the Lord.

> "There is a new-found joy simply in being still in the presence of the Lord, just as good friends find joy in being together.... They just *are,* and are happy to be together.... Real prayer is *being with* the Lord...the joy of 'being with'."[821]

With *prayer of union* a new mode of approaching God begins. God – as Teresa puts it – now enters into the spirit of the praying Christian without going through the doors of the imagination, intellect and will. Two complementary aspects can be distinguished in this prayer: a tending towards total self-surrender to God in order to achieve the most perfect union with him, and an ever-growing detachment from the self-serving joys of prayer. The progressive actualization of these two complementary aspects leads praying Christians through three major grades.

— The grade called *simple union* is the first and the least perfect. Here praying Christians reach quiet, intimate union with God, but they are still attached to the joys of prayer.

— The prayer called *spiritual betrothal* is the grade in which attachment to the joys of prayer is gradually severed. The thorough spiritual purification occurring here is caused especially by the distressing realization of the praying Christians' incapacity to understand and accept God's way of dealing with them, accompanied by their yearning for perfect self-surrender to him.

This painful spiritual experience deeply detaches one not only from the joys of prayer, but even from one's very self, to the point of causing a spiritual death – which Teresa describes by the picturesque image of the silkworm

---

820 "Quiet" is *hesychía* in Greek. The Greek term had several meanings in Byzantine spirituality. "But more commonly it is employed in an interior sense, to indicate one who practices inner prayer and seeks silence in the heart.": WARE, p. 243. Aquinas writes: "Quiet of the soul is especially necessary for one who contemplates.": (II-II, q. 186, a. 3, ad 4um; BLACKFRIARS, vol. 47, p. 111).

821 GREEN [2], pp. 45-46. Author's emphasis.

which must undergo death to become a butterfly. In this grade, praying Christians are called upon to practice "conforming union" with the Lord.

— The prayer called *spiritual marriage* is the pinnacle of union with God reached "in the extreme interior of the soul". It is called "marriage" because the union of praying Christians with God achieved here is effected by an all-encompassing and indissoluble bond of spiritual love analogous to the union of the bride and the bridegroom in Christian marriage.

Those who attain this summit of prayer as communion have achieved a permanent "transforming union" with their Beloved Lord. They are inflamed with great missionary zeal, reach a perfect unity of contemplative prayer and apostolic activity in their lives, and willingly rejoice in the trials and persecutions that they endure for the sake of their "Divine Bridegroom".

c. *John of the Cross' theological explanations*

The "mansions" or grades of prayer as communion accurately described by St. Teresa of Avila are acknowledged[822] and theologically expounded by St. John of the Cross. We think that his explanations can be briefly summarized as follows.

On the one hand, John takes with utter seriousness the fact that God himself absolutely transcends all divine truth and goodness Christians can know and love on earth. Hence, in striving for intimate communion with God, praying Christians must gradually discard all the knowledge and love of him that are capable of attaining by prayer. They must go through an all-pervading and thoroughgoing spiritual purgation of senses and of spirit, which John poetically put as "the darkness and emptiness of the night."[823]

---

[822] Cf. CROSS [1], II, ch. 11, n. 9, p. 211: "If the soul conquers the devil upon the first step, it will pass to the second; and if upon the second likewise, it will pass to the third; and so onward, through the seven mansions (the phrase is suggestive of St. Teresa, though the Spanish word used by St. John of the Cross is not *moradas,* but *mansiones),* which are the seven steps of love, until the Spouse shall bring it to the cellar of wine of his perfect charity."

[823] A "mysticism of the divine darkness" in which the soul is united in love with the unknowable God was already taught by the Cappadocian Fathers. Such mysticism is "an obscure sense of presence, of possession, or rather of being possessed. It is most adequately understood as the soul's awareness of her being the object of God's love, a love which awakens within herself a passionate response of love as she senses the

On the other hand, the dwelling and abiding presence of the Holy Trinity in Christians sanctified by grace allows them to reach a very intimate communion with the Divine Persons through the activity of theological faith, hope, and charity, especially through the living flame of charity enkindled in the praying Christians by the Holy Spirit.

On balance, Christians who yearn and strive through prayer for the most perfect union with God possible in this life, must first respond to his absolute *transcendence* by receiving a complete purgation of their soul, in order to dispose themselves to reach that perfection of pure and ardent charity which enables them to enjoy his *immanence,* i.e., the intimate presence of the Divine Persons.[824]

iv. *The Necessary Mediation of Christ*

Christians believe that Jesus Christ,

> "In whose body lives the fullness of divinity" and "from whose fullness we have, all of us, received", "is *the only one mediator between God and mankind.*"[825]

Theologizing about this Christian tenet, St. Augustine writes:

> "The Son of God became 'the mediator of God and man' (1 Tm 2:5) in that the Word of God, God with God, both laid aside His majesty down even to the level of the human and raised human lowliness up even to the height of the divine, that He might be the mediator of God and men, and man through God transcend man."[826]
>
> "Lo, thou art far from God, O man, and God is far above man. Between them the God-man placed Himself. Acknowledge Christ, and through Him as Man ascend to God."[827]

---

beauty of God which transcends any apprehension.": LOUTH, pp. 167-168.

[824] For further details, quotes, and references see: GIARDINI [2].

[825] Col 2:9; Jn 1:16; 1 Tm 2:5.

[826] PRZYWARA, n. 319, p. 195-196.

[827] *Ibid.*, n. 302, p. 187.

Aquinas does not differ from Augustine:

> "We are in continual contact with the ever-present humanity of Christ as well as with the divinity of Father, Son, and Holy Spirit (see *De Veritate*, q.29, a.5)... For us, in *our* human history of salvation, there is only one Way to the Father, and that is Christ and His life, death, resurrection, and continuing presence to give us the Spirit."[828]

This tenet of faith is of great consequence for prayer by and large, especially for prayer as communion. We can think of God as the First Cause of all creatures without supernatural revelation. But the Mystery of God, Father, Son and Holy Spirit, would be entirely unknown, unless Jesus Christ had revealed it to us.

> "No one has ever seen God: it is the only Son, who is nearest to the Father's heart, who has made him known.'[829]

Hence, Jesus Christ, the Son of God made man, is the fountain-head of Christian religion.

A contemporary theologian reminds us that:

> "The sole approach to the Trinity is by way of Christology. It cannot be the other way around at the very beginning of theological exploration, for then there is no way of grounding the knowledge of the Trinity in human experience... It is Christology that provides the way to a confession of the Trinity...
>
> It is solely the Christ-event that leads the believing intelligence into the mystery of God's three-personhood. The christological confession – namely, that in Jesus we have to do with God himself, who, as very God, became flesh and dwelt among us – signals the awareness that God's uncreated and eternal being is itself primordially a mystery of inner-communication."[830]

---

[828] PRINCIPE, p. 19 and 25. Author's emphasis.

[829] Jn 1:18.

[830] HILL, pp. XII, 26, 284. This author, however, adds: "But an 'ascending' (from below) Christology, if it be true to itself, must eventually rejoin a 'descending' Christology... for the faith in Christ as the Christ of God is operative in this so-called Christology 'from below' all along...

In short, the mediation of the Incarnate Son of God, Jesus Christ, is absolutely necessary for the whole of humankind to enter into communion with the Divine Persons. This faith conviction has been recently reaffirmed by John Paul II:

> "Christ is the one mediator between God and humankind. 'For there is one God, and there is one mediator between God and men, the man Christ Jesus, who gave himself as a ransom for all.' (1 Tm 2:5-7; cf. Heb 4:14-16). No one, therefore, can enter into communion with God except through Christ, by the working of the Holy Spirit. Christ's one, universal mediation, far from being an obstacle on the journey towards God, is the way established by God himself, a fact of which Christ is fully aware."[831]

Hence, Christ's mediation is also absolutely necessary for reaching communion with the Divine Persons in prayer. When Christians begin to practice prayer as communion they usually image the human nature of Jesus Christ and use such imagery as a lens helping their minds and hearts to focus on his Divinity.

Here is, e.g., how St. Teresa of Avila describes the beginnings of her prayer as communion:

> "I used to try to think of Jesus, our God and Lord, as present within me, and it was in this way that I prayed...
>
> The soul can picture herself in the presence of Christ and accustoms itself to become enkindled with great love for His sacred humanity and to have Him ever with it and speak with Him.... This is an excellent way of making progress, and making it very quickly...
>
> Although we are always in the presence of God, it seems to me that those who practice prayer are especially so, because they can see all the time that He is looking at them, whereas others may be in God's presence for several days without ever remembering that He can see...

Similarly, man first encounters the Trinity within the economy of Salvation, but is spontaneously brought to where he is enabled to speak, however haltingly, of the 'immanent' God... of God's very being ultimately. Then, theology is about God in himself, even though that question cannot be separated from the question concerning God's meaning to us." p. 27.

[831] JOHN PAUL II [2], n. 5, p. 15. Not only the Pope's first phrase but also the last one is supported by the New Testament's explicit teaching: "The Father has sent his Son as saviour of the world. *If anyone acknowledges that Jesus is the Son of God, God lives in him, and he in God."* (1 Jn 4:14-15).

> We must not always tire ourselves by going in search of ideas; we must sometimes remain by His side with our mind hushed in silence. If we can, we should occupy ourselves in looking upon Him who is looking at us; keep Him company; talk with Him. Anyone who can do this, though he may be a beginner in prayer, will derive great benefit from it."[832]

But St. Augustine explained the words of Jesus. "It is for your own sake that I am going,[833] as if the withdrawal of his humanity from the disciples were expedient to increase their love of his Divinity.[834]

Following St. Augustine, St. Bernard advised his monks to strive to progress in prayer from "carnal" love toward Christ's humanity to 'spiritual' love toward his divinity. But he also exhorted them not to presume to outgrow devotion to the humanity of Christ, for on earth Christ's humanity plays for us the role of shadow under which we can approach his dazzling Divinity.[835]

Walter Hilton develops St. Bernard's teaching:

> "It is expedient for some that our Lord should withdraw the bodily and carnal likeness from the eye of their soul, so that the heart might be set and fixed more attentively on the spiritual desire and feeling of the divinity...
>
> Beginners and proficients do not know...how to love Jesus spiritually, but all humanly and carnally... That is good and comes from grace, but it is much less and much lower than...when the soul by grace beholds God in man.
>
> I do not say that we should separate God from man, but we are to love Jesus, both God and man; God in man, and man in God; spiritual and not carnal...

---

[832] TERESA, vol. I, *Life,* pp. 23, 71, 49 and 89.

[833] Jn 16:7.

[834] ST. AUGUSTINE, *Sermo* CXLIII, 4, PL 38, 786. Aquinas repeats the Augustinian interpretation of Jn 16:7 – "Discipuli quodam carnali amore afficiebantur ad Christi humanitatem, necdum erant elevati amore spirituali ad eius divinitatem." He confirms his interpretation with the words of St. Paul – "From now onward (i.e., after Christ's death and resurrection) we do not judge anyone by the standard of the flesh. Even if we did once know Christ in the flesh, that is not how we now him now." (1 Co 5:16): ESI, cap. XVI, lect. ii, no. 2088, p. 394 b.

[835] BERNARD ST., *Sermones in Cantica*, XX, 2-9; vol. I, pp. 132-133.

> The purer and the more subtle the soul is made and the further it is parted from carnality, the sharper the sight it has and the stronger its love for the divinity of Jesus."[836]

In any case, as the Son of God assumed forever a real human nature in the unity of his Divine Person, Christian prayer of communion ought never to forget or discard the mediation of the human nature of Jesus Christ with the specious motive of contacting God in a supposedly more direct and spiritual manner.[837]

This is the firm belief that St. Teresa of Avila drew from her prayer-experience.

> "I clearly see that ...God desires that these graces (of prayer) must come to us from the hands of Christ, through His most sacred humanity, in which God takes delight. *Many, many times I have perceived this through experience. The Lord has told it to me. I have definitely seen* that we must enter by this gate if we wish His Sovereign Majesty to reveal to us great and hidden mysteries. A person should desire no other path, even if he is at the summit of contemplation; on this road he walks safely. All blessings come to us through our Lord."[838]

Teresa's experience perfectly harmonizes with Catholic doctrine.

> "For Christian prayer there is no other way than Christ. Our prayer, communal or personal, vocal or internal, reaches the Father only if we pray

---

836 HILTON, I, ch. 36, p. 107; II, ch. 30, pp. 153-155; ch. 32, p. 260.

837 Historians of Christian Spirituality trace back to Origen and Evagrius Ponticus the viewpoint, derived from Neoplatonic philosophy, that Christians can unite directly to the Holy Trinity without the mediation of the Incarnate Son of God, Jesus Christ.

838 *Vida,* XXII, 6-7. Emphasis ours. Cf. *Ibid.,* XII, 5; *Moradas*, VI, 7, especially no. 5 and ff. Teresa's major passages on this point are collected and commented upon by DUBAY, pp. 217-220. By emphasizing her point Teresa is tacitly carrying on a controversy against her contemporary Bernardin of Laredo, who in his *Ascent to Mount Sion,* III, 4, deemed that "the perfection of love does not consist in the mediation of the sacred humanity (of Christ) but in the perfect and calm contemplation of the unapproachable Deity."

'inthe Name' of Jesus. Hence the holy Humanity of Jesus is the way through which the Holy Spirit teaches us to pray to God our Father."[839]

The spiritual expediency of this teaching is explained by a contemporary author:

> "It may be tempting to abandon oneself to the 'divine in itself' or to seek God as He is 'beyond all words and ways', but there is great danger in this. At all times must we put the person of Christ into the centre, refer to Him, think of Him and commit everything into His hand"[840]

In reality, only our Lord Jesus Christ can lead us into that intimacy with the Divine Persons which we yearn for through prayer as communion. By Christ Christians are grafted onto his saving mystery of death and resurrection and transformed into adopted children of God the Father. As Risen Lord, in union with God the Father, he sends the Holy Spirit, who infuses sanctifying grace and divine charity into our hearts.

So, the profound transformation of Christians caused by the Holy Spirit renders all their prayer a "prayer *in Christ"*:

> "Prayer in Christ is a sharing in the mystery of the Cross and Resurrection: we pray as limbs and organs in his crucified and risen Body. The whole activity of prayer takes place within the context of the life, death and resurrection of Jesus, within the context of a life outpoured and renewed."[841]

Since Christians are united with the Divine Persons through Christ, they also commune in prayer with the Divine Persons through Christ. Namely, as a contemporary author - who terms "prayer of presence" what we call "prayer as communion" - puts it:

---

[839] CCC, n. 2664; cf. 2574.

[840] GUARDINI, p. 110.

[841] LEECH, p. 15. As we are first joined to Christ by baptism, "all Christian prayer is a manifestation of Christian baptism, or baptismal": pp. 27 and 29.

"The Christian prayer of presence is *a prayerful presence in Christ to the Divine Persons of the Holy Trinity.*"[842]

This is why St. Paul can describe the prayer addressed by Christians to God the Father in the same way the Evangelists described the prayer that Christ himself addressed to his Father in the Holy Spirit:

> "Everyone moved by the Spirit is a son of God. The spirit you received is not the spirit of slaves bringing fear into your lives again; it is the spirit of sons, and it makes us cry, 'Abba, Father!' The Spirit himself and our spirit bear united witness that we are children of God...
>
> The Spirit too comes to help us in our weakness. For when we cannot choose words in order to pray properly, the Spirit himself expresses our plea in a way that could never be put into words, and God who knows everything in our hearts knows perfectly well what he means, and that the pleas of the saints expressed by the Spirit are according to the mind of God."[843]

Theological reflection distinguishes in Christ's mediation a "descending" and "ascending" aspect. By means of the former, in a certain way, the Father generates us as adopted children uniting us with his natural Son, Jesus Christ, so that in his loving look toward Jesus the Father loves us, too, with his divine love which is the Holy Spirit.

By means of the latter, receiving the gift of the Father's and Son's Spirit, we can breathe back to the Father, in union with Jesus, the love of the Holy Spirit. So Jesus is our only way from and to the Trinity; and only in and through him are we "touched" by and are enabled "to touch" the Divine Persons by communing with them.

But besides being a child-father encounter as regards God the Father, the prayerful communion with the Divine Persons can also be experienced as

---

[842] VAN KAAM AND MUTO, p. 12. The subtitle of this book is *"our awareness of God's presence."*

[843] Rm 8:14-15; 26-27.

a brother-brother, friend-friend, bride-groom relation-ship[844] as regards God the Son and God the Holy Spirit.

In any case, all these modes of communing with God in prayer imply a person-to-person relationship[845] which can be established between praying Christians and the Divine Persons only through the mediation of Christ. This is why the mediation of Christ is absolutely necessary for all communion of Christians with the Divine Persons in prayer.

A consequential conclusion of this necessary mediation of Christ is that Christian mystics are witnesses not only of God eternal, as all authentic mystics are, but also, at one and the same time, of Christ as Risen Lord, ascended with his very human nature into God's eternal glory.

This conclusion manifests what an essential value and role by virtue of Christ is granted to human nature in Christian mysticism, and clearly distinguishes the latter from the mysticisms of all other religions.

---

[844] Cf. ST. TERESA OF AVILA, *Camino de Perfección,* ch. 28, n. 3: "Tratad con El como con padre, y como con hermano, y como con señor, y como con esposo; a veces de una manera, a veces de otra, que el os enseñara lo que habéis de hacer para contentarle."

[845] HANEMANN rightly observes that Teresa of Avila's whole teaching on prayer as communion is "a reminder of what is truly essential in prayer, especially that it is a person-to-person contact between intimate, loving friends.": p. 36.

CHAPTER IX

DYNAMIC INTEGRATION OF ALL FORMS OF PRAYER

The foregoing chapters offered an analytical survey of the major forms of Christian prayerlife. But, as Christian prayerlife is one, those forms could be misunderstood if held in isolation from one another, as if they were a muddle of separate fragments. It is expedient therefore to show that all the forms of prayerlife can be integrated into a dynamic whole.

We will first show how the integration of particular prayer forms happens. Christians may prefer now one then another of the various prayer forms, but eventually all prayer forms tend to coalesce and amalgamate in the practice of prayerlife.

i. *Integration of Ascent and Address into Worship and Communion*

a. *The merging of ascent and address*

Prayer as ascent and prayer as address are both different and closely linked to one another. The causes of this linking are psychological and theological. It is a matter of psychological fact that whenever people want to address themselves to someone who is "higher" than they are they first try to approach that person by "ascending" towards him or her. Such an ascending clearly aims at getting a chance to address that person, when they will eventually be close to him or her.

Analogously, praying Christians strive to "ascend" towards God, "the Most High", in order to find the opportunity of addressing themselves to him. This is why prayer as ascent and prayer as address are closely linked to one another. Consequently the distinction between prayer as ascent and prayer as address should never be taken as an insuperable line of separation in the actual unfolding of prayerlife. They rather are to be conceived as two complementary aspects naturally bound to merge into only one stream of prayerlife flowing towards God.

This merging can explain why spiritual authors sometimes make no distinction between prayer as ascent and prayer as address and speak of both forms of prayerlife in the same breath.

In the ongoing process of prayerlife acts of prayer as ascent and as address joined together also serve as a preparation for and converge into prayer as worship and as communion.

b. Ascent and address merge into worship

When we ascend toward and address ourselves to God by prayer in order to beseech, thank, praise, and adore him, our ascent and address lead us into prayer as worship.

Here is a scriptural text which clearly describes this process. First the ascent and address of prayer is mentioned:

> "Solomon stood before the altar of Yahweh and, stretching out his hands towards heaven, said, 'Yahweh, the God of Israel, not in heaven above nor on earth beneath is there such a God as you, true to your covenant and your kindness towards your servants when they walk wholeheartedly in your way... Yet will God really live with men on the earth? Why, the heavens and their own heavens cannot contain you. How much less this house which I have built!"

Then, a worshipping prayer of petition is expressed:

> "Listen to the prayer and entreaty of your servant, Yahweh my God; listen to the cry and to the prayer that your servant makes to you today. Day and night let your eyes watch over this place of which you have said, 'My name shall be here'... Hear the entreaty of your servant and of Israel your people as they pray in this place. From heaven where your dwelling place is, hear; and, as you hear, forgive...hear from heaven, and act."[846]

Accordingly, a *Catholic Catechism* published in England some time ago gives a comprehensive description of prayerlife which includes prayer as ascent, address, and worship in only one phrase.

"(In prayer) we raise our mind and heart to God (= ascent) by thinking of God; and by begging of him (= address) all blessings for soul and body."[847]

---

[846] 1 K 8:22-32.

[847] Revised Edition (London: Catholic Book Society, 1971), p. 23.

Similarly a theologian, who wrote a Manual of Spiritual Theology very much in use in Catholic seminaries before Vatican II, gave a general definition of prayer which is a combination of ascent and worship:

> "Prayer is an elevation of our soul to God (= ascent), to offer Him our homage and ask His favors (= worship), in order to grow in holiness for His glory."[848]

c. Ascent and address merge into communion

When we ascent toward and address ourselves to God in order to attain a love relationship with him, both our ascent and address lead us into prayer as communion.

Indeed, in prayer a very high ascent is necessary to reach communion with God:

> "Who is going to associate intimately with God must go beyond all that is visible – lifting up his own mind, as to a mountain top, to the invisible and incomprehensible – and believe that the divine is there where the understanding does not reach."[849]

On the other hand, whoever lives in union of love with God constantly speaks with him in prayer:

> "The man who loves God constantly lives and speaks with him as a Father."[850]

---

[848] TANQUEREY, p. 243. It seems that in the last words of this definition there is an implicit allusion to prayer as communion, too.

[849] GREGORY OF NYSSA, II, n. 46, p. 43.

[850] EVAGRIUS, ch. 54, p. 63. Cf. "Summum bonum est precatio et colloquium cum Deo; nam est consociatio et unio cum Deo.": St. John Chrysostom, Homily 6, *De Precatione,* PG 64, 462, quoted in LITURGIA, vol. II, p. 54. Cf. also JOHN PAUL II, *Pastores Vobis Dabo,* n. 72, in *L'Osservatore Romano,* April 8, 1992, p. 14: "Sacerdos quotidie...omnino personaliter Jesu conveniatur, fidens cum Patre colloquium instituatur, Spiritus alta experientia agatur."

So, prayer as ascent, prayer as address, and prayer as communion can be cast into a single mould.

> "There is *only one essential prayer* – it is the movement *drawing the soul upwards to God* (= ascent), *and the relationship that follows* (= communion). As soon as the soul turns from the dark valley to the heights where there is light and gladness, it prays. It meets him who has never been absent and who is always turned toward the soul, his hands full of blessings, his heart overflowing with eternal love, and the relationship which is love and life begins...
>
> Prayer *raises us up* (= ascent) to his (=God's) level, to his presence *and* is the prelude to many *colloquies of the highest form of prayer* (= address and communion)... The soul that prays raises itself up to God (= ascent), stands in his presence and speaks to him (= address) – *a raising up and a holy converse* (= ascent and communion): otherwise it is not prayer.
>
> The important thing is to realize the *definition of prayer* – the soul, freed from what is transitory, turns and tends to our heavenly Father by whatever ways and means it can. As soon as the contact is made, the soul prays; when that contact is fervent, the prayer is excellent... Prayer is a *raising* of the mind to God *and living in his presence,* on his heights (= ascent and communion)."[851]

The merging of prayer as ascent into prayer as communion can occur so naturally that somebody considers these two forms of prayer to be virtually identical.

> "A conscious relationship (= communion) in prayer is another way of saying that prayer is the raising of the mind and heart to God (= ascent)."[852]

d. Merging is not confusing

Undoubtedly, praying Christians hope that communion with God results from their practice of prayer as ascent and address. But such a hope should not overlook the specific differences of those forms of prayer. For this

---

[851] GUILLERAND, pp. 42, 63, 65, 101. Emphasis ours.

[852] BARRY, p. 13. Charles de Foucauld wrote a similar definition of prayer: "Prayer is raising heart and mind to God in continually renewed acts of love." Cf. CONGAR, p. 12.

confusion would cause unbecoming and misleading cognitive and practical consequences. Here are the consequences we mean.

> "From the very first week of his *Spiritual Exercises,* St. Ignatius of Loyola exhorts the retreatant to conclude the "meditations" with a "colloquy" *(coloquio).*
>
> The colloquy is made properly speaking as one friend speaks to another, or as a servant speaks to his master, now asking some favor, now accusing oneself for some wrong deed, or again, making known his affairs to him and seeking his advice concerning them."[853]

In a similar vein, Butler describes passing from

> "Pondering prayerfully about God" to "direct 'speaking' with him, whether in words spoken, or thought, or in wordless interior acts" so that "pondering melts into prayer and heart speaks to heart."[854]

St. Ignatius does not suggest any specific difference between the way a friend speaks to a friend, and a servant to his master. Seemingly because during the first week of the *Spiritual Exercises* prayer is still petition and confession of sin. Only in the fourth week does prayer become communion. In fact, the fourth week's description contains a paragraph entitled: "contemplation to attain divine love". St. Ignatius explains that the love he means,

> "Consists in a mutual interchange *(comunicación)* by the two parties, that is to say, that the lover gives to and shares with the beloved all that he has or can attain, and that the beloved acts toward the lover in like manner. Thus if he has knowledge, he shares it with the other who does not have it. In like manner they share honors, riches, and all things...
>
> (Such love is practiced) "Standing in the presence of God our Lord asking for a deep knowledge of the many blessings I have received, that I may be filled with gratitude for them, reflecting within myself and considering that I, for my part, with great reason and justice, should offer and give to his Divine Majesty all that I possess and myself with it, as one who makes an offering with deep affection, saying 'Take, O Lord, all that I have and possess. Thou hast given all to me; to Thee, O Lord, I return it. All is Thine, dispose

---

[853] SE, p. 56.

[854] BUTLER, pp. 52-55.

of it according to Thy will. Give me Thy love and Thy grace, for this is enough for me."[855]

This "contemplation" to attain divine love can be emphasized to such an extent that the effort to raise the mind and heart to God to perform discursive meditation involves the risk of a semi-pelagian confidence in human effort.

> "Today we have realized that our effort is utterly secondary to the work of God in our encounter with him in love – which is properly prayer. The idea of raising our minds and hearts to God still seems to imply that prayer is largely a matter of our own effort – that God is simply there while we in prayer find ways and means to pull ourselves up to him. Such a view would obviously be semi-pelagian, and hence unacceptable to the Christian."[856]

It is quite possible that some past schools of Christian meditation did at times overstress the active spiritual exercises required to raise one's mind and heart to God. If they did, they may be rightly blamed for fostering at least a certain semi-pelagianism in their pupils.[857]

But presuming to enter into contemplation, before training one's mind and heart in the exercises of active meditation, is to expose oneself to the

---

[855] SE, p. 103-104.

[856] GREEN [1], p. 30. According to this author, "being with the Lord whom we have come to know and to love" is "the substance of our prayer, the essence of prayer," p. 96. Mind that also Butler does not call prayer "pondering prayerfully about God" (i.e., meditation), but reserves this term to "speaking heart to heart" with God.

[857] The last quoted passage must be understood as an overreaction to the exaggerated activism in the practice of prayer to which, according to his personal character and spirituality, this author yielded at the beginning of his prayer life: "I am a planner, an organizer, not one to leave things to chance... Since I am also a spiritual son of a man, Ignatius of Loyola, who must rank as one of the most active and organized of saints – it is not surprising that I find myself a take-charge sort of person." Of course, persons like these might be "tempted" by Pelagianism. But their efforts to overcome such a "temptation" may drive them into the opposite extreme.

As a matter of fact, this author goes on writing about a "remarkable change he has seen in himself over the years, as he discovered that he had to listen (in prayer)." (So that) "somehow I feel sure this is the right way for me... Moreover, I am becoming convinced that it is really the only way.": GREEN [2], p. 161. See also p. 162.

hazard of falling into the quietistic error: that is, into the error of those who do not make the spiritual effort that is normally required to dispose oneself to be granted communion with God in contemplation.

Not without reason Screwtape advises a tempter devil to persuade a praying Christian to aim in prayer at

> "Something entirely spontaneous, inward, informal, and unregularised; and what this actually means to a beginner will be an effort to produce in himself a vaguely devotional *mood* in which real concentration of will and intelligence have no part. Coleridge has recorded that he did not pray 'with moving lips and bended knees' but merely 'composed his spirit to love' and indulged 'a sense of supplication'.
>
> That is exactly the sort of prayer we (= the devils!) want; and since it bears a superficial resemblance to the prayer of silence as practiced by those who are very far advanced in the Enemy's (= God's) service, clever and lazy patients (= Christians) can be taken by it for quite a long time."[858]

All this has to be kept in mind because

> "Christians cannot begin immediately with the simple, negative (lacking distinct concepts and discursiveness) gaze of contemplation and pass over the myriad of reasonings, ideas, and conceptualizations of meditation. Merton points out the possible danger in such an approach: 'There is a temptation to a kind of pseudo-quietism which afflicts those who have read books about mysticism without quite understanding them.
>
> And this leads them to a deliberately negative spiritual life which is nothing but a cessation of prayer, for no other reason than that one imagines that by ceasing to be active one automatically enters into contemplation.' In this statement, Merton is in accord with what Catholic spiritual writers and theologians have traditionally maintained."[859]

St. Catherine of Siena shows herself to be very wise when she says:

> "A person has to walk step by step. I – it is God who speaks – know well that, because the soul is imperfect before being perfect, her prayer is imperfect as well. She should certainly, while she is imperfect, stay with vocal prayer so as not to fall into laziness, but she should not omit mental prayer. In other words, while she says the words she should make an effort

---

[858] LEWIS, p. 24-25.

[859] CARTER [1], p. 33.

> to concentrate on my love, pondering at the same time her own sins and the blood of my only-begotten Son."[860]

Granting that "the ordinary modern man (if also a Christian) is not very likely to fall by accident into quietism: the temptation is rather to be too activist"[861] the above-quoted words of Green about the risk of semi-pelagianism may be interpreted as an over-reaction against the activism that might hinder contemplative prayer, which, "insofar as it is distinguished from simple prayer - is union with God."[862]

However, in order to avoid both Pelagianism and Quietism - two opposite but equally blamable extremes on the same continuum - it is wise to maintain that, although in different ways, both the raising of mind and heart to God (necessary to meditation) and prayer as communion with God (i.e., contemplation) have their momentous roles to play in the harmonious and steady growth of Christian prayerlife. Referring to his experience, Butler contends that

> "Many people will in practice find that it is easy, and more satisfactory, to interweave their prayer (and he means - speaking heart to heart with God, i.e., communion with him) with their 'pondering' (i.e., meditation) and *vice versa.*"[863]

The following well-balanced words show pretty well how to avoid both Pelagianism and Quietism in prayer.

> "We make the effort to be friendly or to love, but ultimately friendship and love come to us in grace and we receive them as a gift. A Christian lives in this tension of prayer, which is acquired by his effort and yet accepted as a gift."[864]

---

[860] DIALOGUE, p. 126.

[861] BUTLER, p. 56.

[862] NICOLAS, p. 257.

[863] BUTLER, p. 56.

[864] BOROS, p. 2.

ii. *Integration of Worship and Communion*

a. The many differences between prayer as communion and prayer as worship

An attentive comparison between prayer as worship and prayer as communion manifests that they differ in many ways.

Prayer as worship proclaims that God alone ultimately deserves reverence. All other beings, real or imaginary, which humans are tempted to worship, are idols. Whoever worships the only one and true God destroys all idols.

Prayer as communion proclaims that only God can fill the radical need for intimacy of the human heart. God is the Supreme Other whom the human heart yearns and seeks for in all companionships. Only the Divine Persons, in whose image and likeness we are created and restored, ultimately can meet all human desires for friendship and company.

Prayer as worship and prayer as communion are animated by different spiritual forces and led by different motivations. Prayer as worship is inspired by the "holy fear of God", which induces the worshipping Christians to reverence him. Prayer as communion is all-pervaded by the "holy love of God", which draws praying Christians towards an ever closer union with him.

Prayer as worship and as communion are elicited from different human powers and virtues. The theological virtues of faith and hope elevate the intellect and will of Christians so as to make them realize and experience how entirely they depend on God and desperately need his care and help. And so these virtues enable Christians to practice prayer as worship; whose perfection is attained when one submits one's will to God's will. The theological virtue of charity, by moving Christians to love Jesus Christ as Brother and God as Father, is conducive to prayer as communion.

Christians by prayer as worship behave as servants, who offer their homage and services to their Divine Lord in exchange for his help and gifts. Whereas, Christians by prayer as communion act as friends of Christ and adopted children of God the Father, and, in the highest grade of this prayer, are so closely united with the Divine Persons that the substance of the Deity "touches" the innermost substance of the praying person.[865]

---

[865] According to St. John of the Cross, at the highest grades of prayer as communion "the substance of God touches the substance of the soul": CROSS [1], II, 24, 4, pp. 306-307; CROSS [3], A, II, 16-19, pp. 67-70 passim.

Individual propensities or preferences either for prayer as worship or for prayer as communion seemingly depend on the intellectual and emotional makeup of the praying person.

> "There are extroverts with a strong artistic sense and a need for ritual, whose prayer life will value material objects such as crucifixes and rosaries, and who will derive great strength from corporate *worship.* There are thoughtful introverts for whom the way forward is through inner absorption of doctrine, as it becomes integrated into *prayer and reflection.*"[866]

But, after all, given the common ground of prayer as worship and prayer as communion all their differences cannot ever separate them in the actual flow of Christian prayerlife.

b. Dogmatic and spiritual grounds for integration of worship and communion

The integration of prayer as worship and prayer as communion is first of all founded on the very Mystery of God, which is also the common ultimate goal and object of these two forms of prayer.

Julian of Norwich imaginatively describes what John of the Cross calls "the substance of the soul" - "The Lord opened my spiritual eyes and showed me *the soul in the middle of my heart.* The soul was large as if it were an eternal world... In the midst of it sat our Lord Jesus, God and Man, beautiful in person, most majestic of kings, and most worshipful Lord.": quoted by LEECH, p. 4. Emphasis ours.

[866] LEECH, p. 27. Emphases ours. According to WARE [3], p. 198, "within the tradition of Eastern Christendom there are two ways of praying, the one iconic, symbolic, 'cataphatic', the other non-iconic, hesichastic, 'apophatic'. These two ways are not alternatives, still less are they mutually exclusive, but each deepens and completes the other." Leech adds the following comment to his declarations: "There is no standard, or correct, way to pray. But prayer should aid the maturing of the personality, the union of conscious and unconscious in a process of transcendence, a discovery of the true self which is wholeness."

An attempt - in our opinion, scarcely satisfying - to find affinities and connections between the various forms of prayer and the many temperaments was made by CHESTER AND MORRISEY. Temperament is understood by these authors as "the characteristic or habitual inclination of a person to choose one attitude or one function rather than another as their customary behavior.": *Ibid.*, p. 184.

The *first* dogmatic ground for the integration of prayer as worship and as communion is the unity, even the identity in God of transcendence and immanence.

The OT proclaims such identity by mentioning transcendence and immanence within the same context.

> "Thus speaks the Most High, whose name is eternity, whose name is holy: *'I live in a high and holy place, but I am also with the contrite and humbled spirit,* to give the humbled spirit a new life, to revive contrite hearts... *With heaven my throne* and earth my footstool, what house could you build me, what place could you make for my rest? All of this was made by my hand and all of this is mine - it is Yahweh who speaks. But *my eyes are drawn to the man of humbled and contrite spirit, who trembles at my words.*"[867]

This passage is commented on by an exegete as follows:

> "The God of the OT is a hidden God not through any weakness or inadequacy, but because of his very glory and the unworthiness of human creatures. Yet the God who is hidden from sight in the cloud of his own glory can be known by the person who does not seek to see him, but rather to obey him."[868]

Jesus uttered words which contain virtually the same teaching:

> "I bless you, Father, *Lord of heaven and earth,* for hiding these things from the learned and the clever, and *revealing them to mere children.* Yes, Father, for that is what it pleased you to do."[869]

And when he taught his disciples the "Our Father" Jesus significantly juxtaposed and united in the first two clauses of this prayer *('Our Father who art in heaven')* the Christian intimacy and awe before God, the affinity with and distance from him.[870]

---

[867] Is 57:14-15; 66:1-2.

[868] BORTON, p. 57.

[869] Mt. 11:25-26.

[870] Mt. 6:9. Cf. EVANS, p. 29.

He meant that the selfsame God who is in heaven, remote or "transcendent", is very close or "immanent" to those who by his grace can dare to address themselves to him as their Father.

In Christian literature the theme that God's transcendence implies his immanence seemingly occurs for the first time in *The Shepherd of Hermas* (around the middle of the second century) where God is said to be

> "One who made everything from nothing, and who is uncontained while containing everything."[871]

A strong statement of the divine transcendence-immanence can be found in Pseudo-Dyonisius (sixth century):

> "God is known in all things and apart from all things... Therefore everything can be ascribed to him at one and the same time, and yet he is none of these things."[872]

Now, our dissimilarity from God, which explains his "remoteness" or transcendence, demands our prayer as worship; while our likeness with God, which results in his "closeness" and immanence, makes possible our prayer as communion.

The *second* dogmatic ground for the integration of prayer as worship and prayer as communion is the unity in the Mystery of the Holy Trinity of "Theology", or the *ad intra* (= inner) relations uniting the Divine Persons to one another, and the "Economy" or the *ad extra* (= outer) saving activity of the Divine Persons, within the history of Salvation.[873]

Now, prayer as worship ascends through the "outer" saving activity of Christ towards the Divine Persons.

> "Through Christ, with Christ, in Christ, in the unity of the Holy Spirit, all glory and honor is yours, almighty Father, forever and ever."[874]

---

[871] Cf. ORIGEN [2], Introduction, p. 7-8.

[872] *De Divinibus Nominibus,* VIII, 3, 872 a; V, 8, 824 b.

[873] This distinction was made by the early Eastern Fathers and became traditional in the whole Church.

[874] This is the concluding doxology of all Eucharistic Prayers of the Roman Missal.

Prayer as communion is linked instead with the "inner" triune unity of the Divine Persons, who make their home within Christians, who, by their sharing in the divine charity are taken into the mutual exchange of love which intimately joins the Divine Persons with one another.[875]

And as the "inner" and "outer" Deity is only one Mystery, so also prayer as worship and prayer as communion are to be ultimately only one prayerlife.[876]

The spiritual grounds for the unification of prayer as worship and prayer as communion are also twofold.

The first ground is psychological.

One and the same freewill elevated to obey and love God is the source both of prayer as worship and of prayer as communion. In other words, Christian prayer as worship and prayer as communion sprout from a common natural root and a common infused supernatural virtue of charity.

Some confirmation for this assertion can be found in the words of Jesus, "the heavenly Father will give the Holy Spirit to those who ask him".[877] These words seemingly suggest that prayer as worship, to which belong our petitions to God, will eventually bring forth prayer as communion, which is practiced by virtue of charity poured into our hearts by the Holy Spirit given to us.

In fact, St. Paul implies that Christians are filled with the Holy Spirit who is the divine source of charity and of prayer as communion inherent to charity, even when they celebrate the liturgy, which is a public, solemn form of prayer as worship –

---

[875] Cf. BARILE, pp. 97-98. Cf. CCC. n. 2655: "Even when it is lived 'in secret' (Mt 6:6), prayer is always a prayer of the Church, is communion with the Holy Trinity." See n. 2098 too.

[876] Perhaps it is not far-fetched to read in the words of Jesus in St. John's Gospel some allusion to prayer as worship leading into prayer as communion. "If anyone loves me he will keep my word (as the first word-commandment to be kept is 'I am Yahweh your God... You shall have no gods except me... For I, Yahweh your God, am a jealous God.' [Dt 5:6-9]. Jesus' 'word' first of all certainly demands prayer as worship), and my Father will love him, and we shall come to him and make our home with him (which enables Christians to practice prayer as communion with the Divine Persons) (Jn 14:23)." Later on Jesus asks of the Father that all his disciples "may be one as we (= Jesus and the Father) are one. With me in them and you in me, may they be so completely one." (*Ibid.,* 18:22-23).

[877] Lk 11:13.

> "Be filled with the Spirit. Sing the words and tunes of the psalms and hymns when you are together, and go on singing and chanting to the Lord in your hearts, so that always and everywhere you are giving thanks to God who is our Father in the name of our Lord Jesus Christ."[878]

The second ground for the integration of prayer as worship and prayer as communion is sacramental.

Through the reception of the sacrament of baptism the Christian participates in both the priesthood and the divine sonship of Christ.[879] The participation in the priesthood of Christ enables the praying Christian to offer prayer as worship in union with Christ, the High Priest, as a sacrifice of praise pleasing to God.[880] Participation in the divine sonship of Christ enables the praying Christian to relate to God as *Abba* and so to enjoy a filial communion with him in prayer.[881]

But as these two participations originate from the same sacrament of baptism, so also the effects which they have on Christian prayer cannot but tend to be integrated in action by their common sacramental root.

c. Communion and worship are actually united in Christian prayerlife

Evagrius stressed that praising God in himself (i.e., perfect prayer as worship) and praying to him with perfect charity (i.e., perfect prayer as communion) are possible because both Christ and the Holy Spirit are given to praying Christians.

> "God gives prayer to the man who prays. On that account call upon him saying: 'Hallowed be thy Name, thy Kingdom come', that is, the Holy

---

[878] Ep 5:18-20.

[879] Cf. LG, n. 11. FLANNERY, p. 361: "Incorporated into the Church by Baptism, the faithful are appointed by their baptismal character to Christian religious worship, reborn as sons of God."

[880] Cf. Second petition of Morning Prayer, first week, Tuesday, in LITURGIA, vol. IV, p. 540: "O Rex omnipotens, qui, per baptismum, regale nobis sacerdotium contulisti, fac ut laudis tibi semper sacrificium offeramus."

[881] Ga 4:4-6: "God sent his Son, born of a woman...to enable us to be his adopted sons. The proof that you are sons is that God has sent the Spirit of his Son into our hearts: the Spirit that cries, 'Abba, Father'."

Spirit and your only Begotten Son. This is what the Lord taught when he said: 'The Father is adored in Spirit and in Truth' (Jn 4:24)....

A man who worships God in Spirit and in Truth no longer honors the Creator of his work, but praises him because of himself... It is perfect and spiritual charity in which prayer is offered in Spirit and in Truth."[882]

The actual union of worship and communion is described by the following words,

"Stillness *(hesychia)* is *worshipping* God and *waiting on* him. Let the remembrance of Jesus be present with your every breath. Then indeed you will appreciate the value of stillness."[883]

And since perfect prayer as worship and perfect prayer as communion are both granted by God to praying Christians, both are to be offered together to him with gratitude -

"I would wish your purpose and your will always be whole to work in the spirit and at no time be idle, but always *lifting up your heart by desire and for the glory of heaven,* whether you are eating or drinking or engaged in any other bodily work, as far as you can, do not leave it."[884]

This is also why several contemporary authors can mention prayer as worship and prayer as communion in the same breath:

"In prayer the human being talks with God and surrenders to the Lord in the depth of his spirit, by *love* and *adoration.*"[885]

"Love and prayer (...) deepen a relationship of *reverence* and *intimacy.*"[886]

---

[882] EVAGRIUS, chs. 58, 59, 77, pp. 64, 68.

[883] CLIMACUS [2], p. 269-270. Emphasis ours.

[884] HILTON, I, ch. 22, p. 96. Emphasis ours. In the emphasized words Hilton seemingly refers both to the Augustinian prayer of desire, which belongs to prayer as communion, and to the Pauline doing everything for the glory of God, which belongs to prayer as worship.

[885] MOUROUX, p. 101. Translation and emphasis ours.

[886] BERGANT, p. 9. Emphasis ours.

> "The life of prayer is a developing relationship of *loving worship* between the one who prays and God."[887]

These authors could find support in Vatican II which says that religious institutes of contemplative life, by establishing their houses in missionary territories,

> "Bear an outstanding witness among non-Christians to the *majesty* and *love (majestatis et caritatis)* of God, and to union in Christ."[888]

Of course, nothing prevents praying Christians from practicing prayer as communion during their prayer as worship, and from practicing prayer as worship, during their prayer as communion.

This intermingling of those two forms of prayer actually occurred in Western medieval monasticism, which gradually turned from mostly being a "school of God's service", according to St. Benedict's *Rule of the Monks,* to emphasizing its being a "school of charity", according to St. Bernard. This development was promoted by recommending, besides the liturgical prayer as worship, the personal prayer as communion.

> "Bernard gave the Cistercians as a central theme their specific concern with the analysis of the soul in its relationship with God... He proposed, with fervor and charity, a mystical theology of love and knowledge... He makes the pursuit of love the sole aim of the monk: 'Remain alone, in order to preserve yourself for him who alone of all things you have chosen to yourself among all'."[889]

In any case, since the union of praying Christians with God is the end of prayerlife, and this union is above all caused by charity which animates

---

[887] BUTLER, p. 121. Emphasis ours.

[888] AG n. 40, FLANNERY, p. 854. Emphasis ours.

[889] WARD, pp. 287-288. SOMMERFELDT, p. 47 quotes St. Bernard saying: "Above all, our place (= the Cistercian monastery) is to keep the more excellent way (cf. 1 Co 12:31), which is the way of love." Cistercian monastic theologians "have in common the fact that they were monks, that is to say, essentially religious men *preoccupied with union with God.* LECLERCQ, p. 227. Emphasis ours.

prayer as communion, prayer as worship which rather serves right faith is related to prayer as communion as to its end.[890]

To us God's transcendence and God's immanence, the "inner" and the "outer" Holy Trinity appear as opposite concepts which seem to exclude one another, because our intellect cannot hold both of them in focus at the same time. But they really coincide in God's Being. Hence, we cannot catch a glimpse of the Divine Being unless at the same time we acknowledge God as transcendent and immanent, and the activity of the Holy Trinity as "inner" and "outer", never capitulating to either of these divine antitheses, but keeping them instead in tension within our intellect.

The will and behavior must, however, follow the lead of the intellect, which cannot help making those conceptual distinctions. So, we find it difficult to respond to God's transcendence and immanence, to the "inner" and "outer" Trinity by the same form of prayer.

But, since our intellect must always keep in tension within itself the two distinct and opposite concepts of the divine antitheses in order to reach a true glimpse of the Divine Mystery, so our prayerful response to God must include both prayer as worship and prayer as communion. This is why both prayers must always ultimately converge on the only one God in the flow of Christian prayerlife.

In the end, no one of these two forms of prayer alone can encompass the whole Christian prayerlife, no more than transcendence and immanence, "inner" and "outer" Trinity taken alone can adequately cover the whole Mystery of God.

The spiritual experience of God's transcendence is founded on the mystery of Creation and causes that reverence toward the Creator's power and majesty which drives the praying Christian to worship him. The spiritual experience of God's immanence, or better still, presence, feeds on the mystery of Sanctification, which draws the praying Christian so close to the Divine Persons as to enable him to commune intimately with them.

---

[890] "The aim and end of spiritual life is that man be united to God, which union is achieved in charity. Everything else in the spiritual life is subordinated to that... Now all the virtues whose acts are commanded (...) for keeping a right faith are those having to do with the divine worship." (II-II, q. 44, a. 1, co.; BLACKFRIARS, vol. 35, p. 141). Remember that, according to Aquinas, prayer as worship is elicited from the virtue of religion, whose object is divine worship: *Ibid.,* q. 83, a. 3.

> "It is not that God demands honor, when he says, 'If I am a father, where is my *honor?'* (Mi 1:6). Truly he says that as a father.[891] But if he shows himself as a bridegroom, I think he will change his voice and will say, 'If I am a bridegroom, where is my *love?*'"[892]

St. John of the Cross, too, distinguishes between "the *service* of his/her whole life", which the Christian owes to God as creator, and "all the rest and the reciprocation of his/her *will's love",* which the Christian owes to God as Redeemer and Sanctifier.[893]

Now, to God as Creator, i.e., first effective cause and ultimate end of all his created natural gifts, praying persons are naturally proportioned as creatures, so that prayer as worship is commanded to them by their very nature. But human beings are not proportioned to God Redeemer and Sanctifier by their nature. Hence Christian prayer as communion is made possible only by virtue of sanctifying grace and charity.[894]

So, first of all, praying Christians ought to honor their transcendent Creator by worshipping him as creatures. But when they become aware of enjoying with him as Father the intimacy of adopted children, they also can dare to commune with him.

Therefore, Christian prayerlife develops through an alternation of acts of prayer as worship and acts of prayer as communion. Indeed, on the one

---

[891] The author means "God, the Father, the Almighty, Creator of heaven and earth, of all that is seen and unseen," as the Creed recites.

[892] BERNARD ST., *Sermones in Cantica,* II, 4; vol. I, p. 83. The honor, i.e., obedience and worship, due to God is commanded. But can love be commanded? St. Basil the Great responds to this question: "Love of God does not consist in the imposition of an external command but it is infused into our hearts as a seed, which contains in itself the power and the necessary impetus of love... Even though the precept of loving can bring it to perfection.": BASIL THE GREAT, *Regulae Fusius Tractatae,* Resp. 2, 1 PG 31, 908-910. Translation ours.

[893] "Servicio de toda su vida... todo el resto y correspondencia del amor de su voluntad." *Canticle,* Anotación, pp. 909-910.

[894] "Our reason and will by nature go out to God in that he is the cause and the end of nature, and this is the measure of their innate capacity. Yet this is not enough for them to reach out to him as the object of supernatural happiness." (ST, I-II, q. 62, a. 1, ad 3um; BLACKFRIARS, vol. 23, p. 139). Cf. I, q. 1, a. 8, ad 2um.

hand, there could be no acts of prayer as communion unless acts of prayer as worship had paved the way for them. On the other hand, in offering to God prayer as worship, praying Christians yearn for prayer as communion to crown it all.

This point is clearly made when one writes that adoration, i.e., the most perfect act of prayer as worship, is asking to enjoy God's presence, which is distinctive from prayer as communion. Such ordering of prayer of petition, which is the first and most common act of prayer as worship, to prayer as communion is explained by Aquinas as happening under the impulse of charity, which animates and makes possible that communion.[895]

Christians who especially practice prayer as communion have an intense experience of God's transcendence during the grades of this form of prayer which go through the "nights" of the senses and of the spirit.[896] But, of course, they could not experience God's transcendence in their prayer if he were not present to them in the first place. Therefore in the growth process of prayer as communion the distinction between striving for a transcendent God and reaching out to a present God cannot ever be taken as a strict separation. It has rather to be taken as the distinction of two facets of a unified prayer experience.

In the concrete unfolding of Christian prayerlife the merging of prayer as worship and prayer as communion occurs especially in prayer of thanksgiving. Prayer of thanksgiving is central in the growth process of prayer as worship. In that process thanksgiving is the first response of reverence to God almighty which leads one to center on his prevenient generosity. And the whole growth process of prayer as communion is an ever more grateful response to God who first loves us.

Prayer of thanksgiving is, therefore, the crossroad where prayer as worship and prayer as communion meet and coalesce into one both reverent and grateful prayerful response to God almighty and bountiful.

---

[895] Referring to a description of prayer as self-surrender to and union with God given by PSEUDO-DYONISIUS (*De Divinibus Nominibus,* I, PG 3, 680), Aquinas grants that "The will moves the reason to its goal; hence an act of reason can be directed by the will to union with God which is the goal of charity. Prayer motivated by charity tends toward God first, in so far as the thing requested is concerned, because when we pray we should ask principally to be united to God." (II-II, q. 83, a. 1, ad 2um; BLACKFRIARS, vol. 39, p. 49).

[896] CROSS [2], II, chs. 5-8, pp. 100-119.

Eventually, at the summit of Christian perfection, the most perfect act of prayer as worship, viz., the sacrificial self-offering to God, can hardly be distinguished from communion with him.

> "Every act performed in order to cling to God, *remaining in communion with him* and so be in his joy, is a *true sacrifice.*"[897]
>
> "In the state of union the soul becomes naught else than *an altar whereon God is adored in praise and love, and God alone is upon it* .... an altar worthy of the presence of His Majesty.... *The love of God must never fail in the soul, so that the soul may be a worthy altar.*"[898]

In conclusion, prayer as worship and prayer as communion converge because the ultimate purpose which is common to both is letting the transcendent and immanent God be, at one and the same time, the reverenced and beloved Lord of the praying Christian. In fact, God is perfectly reverenced by adoration and perfectly loved in intimate union with him.

The relationship of Christians with the Divine Persons, and especially with God-Father, brings to perfection on earth the immanence-presence of God-Creator to human beings. A certain divine immanence-presence is implied also by prayer as worship. It is the immanence-presence founded on the natural gifts that God-Creator never stops bestowing on human creatures. But, as it was pointed out above, the prayer relationship between human creatures and God-Creator that follows from the latter divine immanence-presence is mediated by divine gifts to our nature and is not a direct person-to-person relationship.

A great enhancement of God's immanence-presence in Christians occurs when in an entirely gratuitous manner they are granted

> "Entry into God's being *as it is proper to Him,* i.e., entrance into the uncreated divine life of Father, Son, and Spirit – possible to the creature only as the term of its intentionality of knowledge and love."[899]

---

[897] ST. AUGUSTINE, *De Civitate Dei,* X, 6.

[898] CROSS [1], I, V, 7, pp. 121-122. Emphasis ours. The same fusion of worship and love can be found in ST. AUGUSTINE. "Cultus Dei [est] ...amor eius, quo nunc desideramus eum videre, credimusque et speramus nos esse visuros.": *De Trinitate,* XXI, 14, 22; PL 42, 1009.

[899] HILL, p. 276.

There is a profound continuity between the immanence-presence of *causality* established by God-Creator in his human creatures and the immanence-presence of *intimacy* established by God-Father in his adopted children, while, at the same time, the latter infinitely perfects and surpasses the former.

Hence prayer as reverent worship toward God-Creator is more fundamental than prayer as loving communion with God-Father and precedes and prepares for prayer as communion. But prayer as communion, being the expression of that pure charity toward God which crowns all Christian life, perfects and surpasses prayer as worship.

Christians who live in prayerful communion with God, even though they are not all the time explicitly thinking of offering their worship to him, are actually doing that by loving him as the ultimate infinite Divine Goodness, which is virtually equivalent to adoration, the most perfect prayer as worship.

All this is distinctive of Christian prayerlife. But we cannot deny that followers of other religions may also yearn for a union with God implicitly similar to the communion with him brought about by Christian prayer. "Indeed, authentic prayer is prompted by the Holy Spirit, who is mysteriously present in every human heart".[900]

In fact, a description of prayer that seems to include not only worship of God but also communion with him is given by an author who does not seem to be Christian –

> "Prayers are *confessions of our unworthiness or our weakness ... prayer is a yearning of the heart to be one with the Maker,* an invocation for his blessing."[901]

iii. *The Fusion of all Forms of Prayer*

We can conclude the study of the major forms of prayer made so far by viewing the whole Christian prayerlife as a vast organic net of relationships in which each major form of prayer is harmoniously bound and linked with each other. To illustrate this intertwining and weaving the analogy of building

---

[900] JOHN PAUL II [3], p. 1089. These words of John Paul II apply to prayerlife the statement of Vatican II, GS, n. 22, FLANNERY, p. 924: "...All men of good will in whose hearts grace is active invisibly." Cf. LG n. 16, FLANNERY, pp. 367-368.

[901] GANDHI, p. 492. Emphasis ours.

up an interpersonal relationship may serve better than the ancient imagery of climbing a mountain to meet God at its summit.

Actually, people who have achieved an interpersonal relationship first got acquainted with one another. To meet a few times may be enough to get acquainted. But some deep personal involvement is necessary to build a lasting friendship.

Prayer as ascent and as address offer praying Christians the first opportunity of getting acquainted with God. Prayer as worship and as communion bring about and develop an interpersonal relationship characterized by reverence and intimacy of praying Christians with God.[902]

So, making the first acquaintance with God and then building up an interpersonal relationship of reverence and intimacy with him precipitates the dynamic fusion of all forms of prayer into only one comprehensive ongoing process of Christian prayerlife.

However, even when all the major forms of Christian prayerlife merge like streams mixing their waters in the same river, a clear knowledge of their specific differences, as the one we have tried to achieve in the foregoing chapters, does not become irrelevant or useless. At least it helps the reader to realize how rich and variegated Christian prayerlife can be.

* * *

Here our research into the many elements and forms of Christian prayer comes to an end. What we have tried to do can be fittingly summarized. At the beginning we were confronted with the problem of the "jumble" of Christian prayerlife. Starting from there we developed an analytical description and explanation of the most essential elements and forms of prayer that we were able to depurate from the ally of that "jumble". At the end we forged them into Christian prayerlife in action. What we really did was to use the sound analytico-synthetic method to study Christian prayerlife, in order to gain a profound organic understanding of it.

With all our analyses and classifications we hope to have offered an outlook on the whole Christian prayerlife, which can dissolve the confusion and disorientation that its natural complexity provokes in those who are confronted with it without a clear frame of reference and keynote concepts.

In fact, we have so far

— offered an articulate description of every major prayer form,

---

[902] Cf. DALRYMPLE, pp. 20-24.

— pointed out which position each one of them holds and the role it plays in the growth process of Christian prayerlife,
— charted the pathways that lead through the development of all prayer forms towards the attainment of perfect prayer.

Of course, to get a comprehensive outlook of Christian prayerlife, one does not need to emphasize the distinctions, as it is not necessary to focus on the details when one wants to look at a picture in its entirety. That is precisely what an author is doing when he writes:

> "When we pray, we raise our hearts and minds to God in movements of adoration, thanksgiving, petition, and pure presence."[903]

"Raising hearts and minds to God" describes prayer as ascent. "Adoration, thanksgiving, petition" are acts of prayer as worship. "Pure presence" hints at prayer as communion. So, these words virtually mean that, when we actually pray, all forms of prayer may join and merge into only one spiritual activity.

Even such a lover of distinctions as Aquinas, when he approaches Christian prayerlife in its dynamic wholeness, gives a description which mentions in the same breath all the major prayer trends.

> "The very prayer which we utter toward God (= address) makes us God's familiar friends, while our spirit rises towards him (= ascent) and with spiritual affection converses with him (= communion), adoring him in spirit and in truth (= worship)."[904]

Indeed, all prayer forms which we distinguished above ultimately converge in God, who is their common object and ultimate goal. Ultimately, this single divine object and goal causes also the unification of all prayer's habitual dispositions which accrue to praying Christians as they persevere in all these prayer forms.

---

[903] VAN KAAM AND MUTO, p. 61.

[904] CT, II, 2, vol. 1, n. 548, p. 127: "Ipsa oratio quae ad Deum emittitur, familiares nos Deo facit dum mens nostra elevatur ad ipsum, et quodam spirituali affectu Deo colloquitur, in spiritu et veritate ipsum adorans." Translation ours.

CHAPTER X

THE GROWTH PROCESS OF CHRISTIAN PRAYERLIFE

Looking at Christian prayerlife as a process we can image it as a tree with an interlacement of roots, a trunk, and many fruits.

"Roots" are the powers or faculties from which the different forms of prayer rise up, and "fruits" are the habitual active dispositions that the repeated acts of prayer cause in the faculties from which they are elicited. Between the roots and the fruits, between the faculties and the habitual active dispositions falls the practice of prayer. This practice first brings the faculties to bloom in distinct prayer-acts and then to yield fruits of various habitual dispositions.

The life that thrives within the roots has a rather mysterious way of flowing into the fruits of the tree, so that the likeness between roots and fruits is far from evident. And yet both belong to the same tree. Fruits are fed by the roots while roots reach their fulfillment in fruits. Analogously, the human faculties from which the activity of prayer is elicited and the habitual dispositions caused in them by the practice of prayer are closely linked with one another, even though they may not look alike.

Actual prayer meets the urge to pray by engaging the faculties and producing habitual dispositions of prayer. And thus the growth process of one's prayerlife continues and tends towards its climax. We will consider the major roots or faculties and fruits or habitual dispositions of Christian prayerlife, hoping that the description of the passage from the former to the latter will also show the principle pathways through which the growth process of Christian prayerlife develops.

1. THE SOURCES OF CHRISTIAN PRAYERLIFE

Various urges to pray are at the origin of the practice of prayer. Those urges emerge from different spiritual powers or faculties with which praying Christians are endowed. We term "sources of prayerlife" the human faculties and their urges to pray taken together. We will try to describe each one of these complex sources with full particulars.

i. *The Source of Prayer as Ascent*

a. *The natural desire to know God*

It is a matter of experience that humans are naturally inclined to know and honor God.

> "Ever since God created the world his everlasting power and deity – however invisible – have been there for the mind to see in the things he has made" so as to "honor him as God or thank him".[905]

Aquinas explained

> "It belongs to human nature to look for the causes of things; that is how intellectual problems arise."[906]

He admittedly drew such an idea from Aristotle and traced it back to the rational nature of human beings.[907]

A thomist scholar thinks accordingly that

> "the spirit of science is driven by an eagerness which, through definite methods, regards an unlimited universe of truth and establishes in spite of all valid boundaries, a sort of continuity between positive sciences and the philosophy of human action, metaphysics and *theology*.[908]

Naturally, this desiring wonder mostly aims at reaching some knowledge of God as the First Supreme Cause of all things.[909]

Vatican II confirmed Aquinas' teaching by stating that

---

[905] Rm 1:20-21. Cf. Ws 13:1-9; Ac 17:24 ff.

[906] ST, I, q. 12, a. 1, co.; cf. I-II, q. 3, a. 8, co.; BLACKFRIARS, vol. 3, p. 5.

[907] ST, III, q. 5, a. 4, co. Cf. *Metaphysics*, I, ii, 982b12 - 983a12.

[908] SIMON, p. 54. Emphasis ours.

[909] "There is naturally present in all men the desire to know the cause of whatever things are observed... Man naturally desires, as ultimate end, to know the first cause. But the first cause of all things is God. Therefore the ultimate end of man is to know God." SCG, 3, 25, p. 101).

> "The intellectual nature of man finds at last its perfection, as it should, in wisdom, which gently draws the human mind to look for and to love what is true and good. Filled with wisdom man is led through visible realities to those which cannot be seen."[910]

St. Augustine dramatized his spiritual ascent towards God by asking all visible creatures to tell him something about God and they cried out at the top of their voices: "He made us!"[911]

St. John of the Cross explicitly refers to this Augustinian passage when he writes that on the spiritual journey towards knowing and loving God the consideration of creatures is the first prayer exercise to be practiced after the one of self-knowledge. The creatures – he writes – are like a divine footprint *(como un rastro del paso di Dios)* by which one can trace the greatness, power, wisdom, etc., of God.[912]

Christians who are particularly keen on sensing, honoring, and praising the Creator by ascending to him from creatures are living models of this teaching. The well-known "Canticle of Creatures" shows that St. Francis of Assisi was a holy Christian who perfectly developed in his prayerlife the habitual disposition to ascend towards God from creatures.[913]

b. The supernatural yearning for the vision of God

Christians share in divine nature and life by virtue of sanctifying grace. The divine gift of grace adds to their natural desire a fresh supernatural urge to ascent towards God. This supernatural urge is first of all linked with the theological virtue of faith.

Driven by the natural desire to know the Supreme Being who is the first cause and ultimate goal of the whole created universe and whom we call God, human beings can attain the knowledge of the divine existence and

---

910 *GS* n. 15, FLANNERY, p. 916.

911 "Et dixi omnibus his quae circumstant fores carnis meae: dicite mihi da Deo meo, quod vos non estis, dicite mihi de illo aliquid. Et exclamaverunt voce magna: 'Ipse fecit nos!' Interrogatio mea intentio mea et responsio eorum species eorum.": *Confessiones,* X, 6, 9; cf. IX, 10, 25.

912 *Cántico Espiritual,* Canción iv, 1; Canción v. 3. CRUZ, pp. 932-936.

913 FRANCIS, pp. 83 ff.

attributes. But, unless strengthened with the supernatural virtue of faith they will catch not even a glimpse of the innermost mystery of God.[914]

In some sense those who are gifted with supernatural faith have their natural desire of knowing God met beyond their expectations, because faith enables them to receive the revelation of the innermost mystery of God. But at the same time, their desire of knowing God is greatly enhanced by the paradoxical obscurity of the "light" that faith sheds on their spirit precisely as regards God's innermost mystery.

> "Now we are seeing a dim reflection in a mirror... The knowledge that I have now is imperfect."[915] "To live in the body means to be exiled from the Lord, going as we do by faith and not by sight."[916]

And yet, the imperfect knowledge that faith brings is an anticipation and a foretaste of the heavenly full knowledge of God.

> "Then we shall be seeing (God) face to face... Then I shall know as fully as I am known."[917] "We are already the children of God but what we are to be in the future has not yet been revealed; all we know is, that when it is revealed we shall be like him because we shall see him as he really is."[918]

Living immersed in the twilight of faith, Christian believers cannot but feel a profound yearning for the "face-to-face" vision of God. Hence, the prayer inspired by Christian faith is continuously pining away with yearning for the vision of God.[919] As grace presupposes and elevates nature, so the faith-inspired yearning for the vision of God takes up the natural human desire of knowing him as the Supreme Being. Accordingly, the natural desire for

---

[914] Cf. "It is by the gift of the Holy Spirit that man, through faith, comes to contemplate and savor the mystery of God's design.": GS, n. 15, FLANNERY, p. 916.

[915] 1 Co 13:12.

[916] 2 Co 5:7; Cf. 1 P 1:8; 1 Jn 4:20.

[917] 1 Co 13:12.

[918] 1 Jn 3:2.

[919] See the commentary of St. John of the Cross to his – "¿Adonde te ascondiste, Amado y, me dejaste con gemido? como ciervo huiste, habiéndome herido; salí tras tí clamando ¡eras ido!": *Cántico Espiritual,* I, 2-22. CRUZ, pp. 910-921.

knowing the Creator and the faith-yearning for the ultimate vision of "the Father's face" are joined in the praying Christian to form only one comprehensive inner source of prayer as ascent.

ii. *The Source of Prayer as Address*

It is manifest that all acts and exercises of prayer as address aim at and strive to attain communication with God. By analogy with the interpersonal communication which we can have with one another, Christian communication with God by means of prayer cannot happen without our addressing ourselves to him.

Naturally, nobody would make the effort or dare to address himself or herself to God, unless he or she trusted in God's benevolent willingness to turn a loving and caring ear to human prayer. Such trustful confidence is fundamentally grounded in the human creatures' conviction of utterly depending on the Creator and needing therefore to rely heavily upon his providential care. But it receives a supernatural unshakable assurance from the infusion into Christians of the theological virtue of hope.

a. The natural need to address oneself to the Creator

Human persons in many ways are not self-sufficient and desperately need one another. Accordingly, the human spirit is by nature naturally inclined to give affirmation to and take it from others, which can also be put this way: human persons are naturally open to and communicative with one another.

Such natural profound human need of communication urges religious persons to address themselves to the "Wholly Other" Creator in order to communicate with him and receive from him affirmation, help, consolation etc., which as human creatures they most desperately need. From such a need derives prayer as address.

b. The supernatural urge to address oneself to the Father

Christians are elevated to the supernatural status of God's adopted children. As children they strongly need to address themselves to their Father in heaven and communicate with him to be reassured about his merciful forgiveness and loving care. In fact, they are enabled to address their appeals to him with great confidence in all the circumstances of their lives by the supernatural virtue of hope poured out into their hearts by the Holy Spirit.

Actually, within God's adopted children the theological virtue of hope is the main source from which their prayer as address gushes forth and appeals to their Father in heaven.

Human creatures naturally yearn to address themselves to God; to communicate with him. But they also know that the transcendent Creator is absolutely beyond their reach unless he benevolently leans down to listen to their requests. So, the theological virtue of hope comes to help human weakness by infusing in us not only greater courage in addressing our demands to God but also and especially giving the firm assurance of being heard and answered, because now they can ask the Father in Jesus' name.

> "I tell you most solemnly, anything you ask for from the Father he will grant in my name. Until now you have not asked anything in my name. Ask and you will receive, and so your joy will be complete... When that day comes you will ask in my name; and I do not say that I shall pray to the Father for you, because the Father himself loves you for loving me and believing that I came from God."[920]

iii. *Source of Prayer as Worship*

a. The natural religious instinct

Within the context of worship offered to God and termed the "religious act", a theologian writes of a "religious instinct", which is its source and "becomes articulate in prayer as the free response to the essential claim made upon man by God".[921] Apparently, such a "religious instinct" can be equated with "a deep religious sense" which is the result of the natural human perception of the Supreme Deity's mysterious power and wisdom diffused and reflected in the course of Nature and in the events of History.

> "Throughout history even to the present day, there is found among different peoples *a certain awareness of a hidden power (agnitio illius arcanae virtutis),* which lies behind the course of nature and the events of human life. At times there is even *a recognition of a Supreme Being, or still more of a Father (agnitio Summi Numinis et etiam Patris).* This awareness

---

[920] Jn 16:23-27.

[921] METZ, pp. 288-289.

and recognition results in a way of life that is imbued with *a deep religious sense (intimo sensu religioso).*"[922]

The following psalms are beautiful prayer expressions of the "religious instinct" or "deep religious sense".

> "Yahweh is king, robed in majesty, Yahweh is robed in power, he wears it like a belt. You have made the world firm, unshakable; your throne has stood since then, you existed from the first, Yahweh..."[923]
>
> "Let them (creatures) praise the name of Yahweh, at whose command they were created."[924] "All things the Lord has made, bless the Lord: give glory and eternal praise to him."[925]

The existence within human beings of a religious instinct or sense can be drawn from the life sciences.

> "Humanistic and humane studies disclose the restless heart described by St. Augustine. Exploration into the heart of man often leads to the discovery of God via the infinity of human desire."[926]

Such an "instinct" is properly qualified "religious" for it is the inner source from which gushes forth religious life and prayer as worship.

b. The supernatural virtue of religion

The natural religious instinct does not suffice to produce the worship and prayer that Christians are supposed to offer to the Father of our Lord Jesus Christ. Aquinas claims that certain moral virtues, which are gratuitously infused into Christians by God himself[927] and are specifically different from the

---

[922] NA, n. 2, FLANNERY, pp. 738-739. Emphases ours. About "religious instinct" see: GIARDINI [3], pp. 78-83.

[923] Ps 93:1-2 etc. Cf. Ps 100:3.

[924] Ps 148:5 etc.

[925] Dn 3:57 etc.

[926] SIMON, p. 53-54.

[927] "(Virtus) infusa causatur ab ipso Deo per eius gratiam.": ST, I-II, q. 100, a. 12, co.

acquired moral virtue of the same name,[928] are the only proportionate instruments of the supernatural leading influence that sanctifying grace through the theological virtues brings to bear on Christian life.[929]

Likewise, a virtue of religion directly infused by God must be postulated so that Christians can perform acts of prayer which are suitable expressions of their life elevated by God's grace and animated by the theological virtues. Hence, acts of Christian prayer as worship must be directly elicited from an infused virtue of religion and only remotely derived from the natural religious instinct which is elevated by that virtue to supernatural Christian prayerlife.

iv. *The Source of Prayer as Communion*

a. Called to communion with God

Vatican II claims that humans are called to communion with God as soon as they come into being.

> "The dignity of man rests above all on the fact that he is called to communion with God. The invitation to converse *(ad colloquium)* with God is addressed to man as soon as he comes into being. For if man exists it is because God has created him through love, and through love continues to hold him in existence. He cannot live fully according to truth unless he freely acknowledges that love and entrusts himself to his Creator."[930]

To this primordial invitation Christians respond adequately when their prayer

> "Properly takes the form of a personal, intimate and very profound dialogue between the human person and God and expresses the communion of the redeemed creatures with the innermost life of the Persons of the Trinity,

---

[928] ST, I-II, q. 63, a. 4.

[929] Cf. ST, I-II, q. 51, a. 4; q. 63, a. 3; q. 110, a. 3; etc.

[930] GS, n. 19, FLANNERY, p. 918.

bringing about an encounter between the infinite freedom of God and the finite freedom of the human being."[931]

Not even the secularism which today is so widespread in the Northwestern hemisphere can extinguish the profound human longing for conversing with God from which prayer as communion bursts forth.

> "When persons in conscience have the courage to face the most serious questions of human existence – particularly questions related to the purpose of life, to suffering and to dying – they are unable to avoid making their own the words of truth uttered by Saint Augustine: 'You have made us for yourself, O Lord, and our hearts are restless until they rest in you...' (*Confessiones,* I, 1: CCL 27, 1). In the same manner the present-day world bears witness to this as well, in ever-increasing and impressive ways, through an openness to a spiritual and transcendent outlook towards life, the renewed interest in religious research, *the return to a sense of the sacred and to prayer,* and to demand for freedom to *call upon the name of the Lord.*"[932]

On the part of God the reason of our *inquietum cor* is that

> "God did not create because he wanted toys to play with. It would be unworthy of him to create except for the sake of entering into a relationship of mutual love with his *personal* creatures who are capable of loving."[933]

The explanation of our *inquietum cor* given by Aquinas adds another reason on our part.

> "While some goods attract the will to a certain degree, nothing moves it adequately except the universal good that God is."[934]

---

[931] "(Oratio Christiana) formam habet, ut proprie loquamur, personalis *colloqui,* intimi scilicet et altissimi, inter hominem et Deum. Ea igitur exprimit creaturarum redemptarum *communionem* cum intima Trinitatis Personarum vita... Vere Christianam orationem duabus esse componendam inter se occurentibus libertatibus, infinita scilicet Dei cum hominis finita libertate.": *CDF Letter,* n. 3. Translation and emphasis ours.

[932] JOHN PAUL II [1], n. 4, pp. 13-14. Emphasis ours

[933] SS, "The Theology of Christian Spirituality," p. 11. Author's emphasis.

[934] I-II, q. 106, a. 2, co.; BLACKFRIARS, vol. 14, p. 97; cf. *Ibid.,* q. 105, a. 4, co.

All this implies that in every person there is a longing for union with God which sums up all human aspirations and from which prayer as communion springs forth.

> "The deepest core, the highest aspirations, the whole essence and purpose of man's striving can be summed up in the proposition: *man's soul longs for union with God.* This is not the expression of a pious sentiment; it is precise truth... This finds expression in the prayer in which we strive for God; strive to partake of his plenitude, *strive to be at one with him. In this striving, prayer becomes love,* for love means seeking to be completely at one with another autonomous being... We must therefore beseech God for the grace of his love and for grace to respond to it, striving after him in the longing for union (...) in the knowledge that in him lies our salvation."[935]

Doubtless, the natural resources of human beings are utterly insufficient to start a love-relationship with God, namely to accept his invitation to friendly converse with him. To think otherwise would bring God down to our level and deny the necessity of divine grace. Human beings commune with God in love when, through Jesus Christ, they are made able to share in the divine nature.

> "By his divine power, he (Jesus Christ) has given us all the things that we need for life and for true devotion, bringing us to know God himself, who has called us by his own glory and goodness... Through these gifts you will be able to share the divine nature."[936]

b. Charity as friendship with God

Theologians contend that the virtue of charity is the most essential component of that Christian sharing in the divine nature which they call sanctifying grace. And the virtue of charity is within Christians the direct source of their communion with God.

Jesus himself told the disciples that they were his friends, for he loved them with self-sacrificing love and communicated to them his own divine knowledge and nature.

---

[935] GUARDINI, p. 46-47. Emphasis ours.

[936] 2 P 1:3-4.

> "A man can have no greater love than to lay down his life for his friends. You are my friends... I call you friends because I have made known to you everything I have learned from my Father."[937]

Aquinas uses the Aristotelian concept of friendship to theologically demonstrate that our charity toward God is a sort of friendship with him. Friendship, he explains, is a mutual benevolence founded on communication between the partners. God out of pure love grants us a real participation in his nature, life, and beatitude (imperfectly on earth, but perfectly in heaven). Hence our return of love founded on that communication is a certain friendship with him.[938]

The friendship that charity establishes between us and God is the good soil in which prayer as communion can thrive. In our opinion that is what contemporary authors virtually say by claiming that prayer is a love relationship between Christians and God.

Some authors write about this relationship with God during the activity of prayer, without mentioning that the fundamental friendship established between Christians and God by charity is essentially presupposed to that activity as the source is to the river.

> "'Prayer',according to one ancient definition, 'is keeping company with God' (Clement of Alexandria, *Strom.* VII 7,39,6; Evagrius Ponticus, *De Or.* 3.). And that really throws us right at the deep end. Prayer is not another part for us to act, another skill for us to master, another subject for an examination: *it is a relationship, and a relationship with God...* Any relationship except the most superficial affects and changes us; it challenges us to respect the freedom, the mystery, the otherness of the other... how we respond to such a challenge will in very large measure decide whether we grow and mature in life, or whether we shrivel up."[939]

Other authors explicitly refer to the interpersonal relationship of the Christian with God which preexists its expression in prayer.

---

[937] Jn 15:13-15.

[938] Aquinas concludes his reasoning with the words: "Accordingly it is manifest that charity is a friendship of man and God." (II-II, q. 23, a. 1; BLACKFRIARS, vol. 34, p. 7). Evidently, the term *amicitia* (friendship) must be taken here in a real analogical sense.

[939] TUGWELL [6], p. vii. Emphasis ours. Recently William A. Barry has insisted on "prayer as personal relationship" with God. See BARRY [1] and [2].

> "Seeking God's holy face the worshipper tries to establish, *or rather give expression and effect to, the 'I-thou' relationship with God which is man's birthright...* Though I may be as nothing in his sight, yet it has pleased God to call me to establish a relationship in which I am alone with him. *Into this mystery of love one enters through prayer.*"[940]
>
> "Both love and prayer *first presume and then deepen* a relationship of reverence and of intimacy."[941]

v. *A Comprehensive View of All Prayer Sources*

A conclusive statement can sum up the whole content of this chapter – all sources of Christian prayerlife together make up the typically Christian "capacity for God."

According to St. Augustine, to say that the human "soul or mind" is "capable of God" *(capax Dei),* i.e., capable of remembering, knowing, loving God, is the best way of explaining the Bible's teaching that "God created man in the image of himself."[942]

In the wake of St. Augustine Vatican II states:

> "Sacred Scripture teaches that man was created 'to the image of God', as able to know and to love his creator."[943]

Aquinas developed the Augustinian insight by explaining that the human spirit, insofar as it is the image of God, is naturally capable of "seeing him", in which consists our perfect beatitude.[944] But the human creature is so ontologically remote from God's infinite perfection that it could hardly have any effective capacity to see him, unless it were supernaturally elevated by sanctifying grace, through which it is granted a participation in the divine

---

[940] GUARDINI, pp. 26-27. Emphasis ours.

[941] BERGANT, p. 9. Emphasis ours.

[942] Gn 1:27. Cf. *De Trinitate,* XIV, ch. 8, PL 42, 1044: "Eo ipso imago eius (Dei) est (anima), quo eius capax est, eiusque particeps esse potest." *Ibid.,* ch. 12, PL 42, 1048: "Trinitas mentis propterea est Dei imago... quia potest meminisse, et intelligere, et amare a quo facta est."

[943] *GS,* n. 12, FLANNERY, p. 913.

[944] ST, III, q. 9, a. 2, co.; I-II, q. 5, a. 1, co.; III, q. 6, a. 2, co.

nature. In fact, only sanctifying grace enables Christians to reach and adhere to God without the mediation of creatures.

Hence, as well as being capable of God the human spirit must be also "naturally capable of grace" *(capax gratiae),*[945] for only sanctifying grace is the necessary and sufficient means through which humans can attain eternal life and "glory".[946]

Now, sanctifying grace plays in the human spirit the role of inner wellspring of all virtues granted to Christians by the Holy Spirit[947] and especially of the theological virtues[948] by which Christians are predisposed to obtain without medium supernatural beatitude in God.[949] So the extensive concept of sanctifying grace encompasses the theological virtues.

This is why we said that we could sum up the teaching of this chapter by contending that all sources of Christian prayerlife - which comprise the human soul, its spiritual faculties, and the infused theological virtues added to them - make up the naturally created and supernaturally elevated Christian "capacity for God".

It is in order now to go on researching how that "capacity" can be enhanced by the outflow of the spiritual powers inherent in those sources into the actual practice of Christian prayerlife.

2. THE HABITUAL DISPOSITIONS OF CHRISTIAN PRAYERLIFE

In actually adhering to God the prayer sources have a double effect. They flow ahead to produce acts of prayer and rebound to cause intensifications of their powers. For want of an exact single word we will term those powers' various intensifications – habitual active dispositions to praying.

i. *The Habitual Disposition of Prayer as Ascent*

The repeated actualizations of the natural desire to know God and of the supernatural yearning to see his face carried out in acts of prayer as ascent

---

945 *Ibid.*, I-II, q. 113, a. 10, co.

946 *Ibid.*, I-II, q. 98, a. 1, co.

947 *Ibid.*, III, q. 89, a. 1, co.

948 *Ibid.*, I-II, q. 79, a. 3, co.; q. 110, a. 4, co.

949 *Ibid.*, I-II, q. 63, a. 3, ad 2um.

create in praying Christians a permanent readiness (called *habitus* by the Scholastics)[950] to promptly and easily burst again into similar prayer acts.

As the Bible recommends the heart's continual readiness to observe God's commandments[951] and to welcome always his "coming",[952] so it also describes the heart's readiness to ascend towards him in prayer –

> "My heart is ready, God, my heart is ready; I mean to sing and play for you; awake, my muse, awake, lyre and harp, I mean to awake the dawn!"[953]

Through the repetition of its specific acts this readiness grows into a kind of *habitus,* viz. a permanent active disposition to prayer as ascent.

In Christians such an habitual disposition can hardly be distinguished from the *theological virtue of faith.* Indeed, it seems to be nothing else than a certain permanent promptitude for praying in which Christians channel their impetus of faith into their acts of prayer as ascent. This promptitude is particularly manifested by the quick and frequent raising of the mind and heart to God beyond and above this-worldly appearances, with which the praying Christian's daily living is studded.

Naturally, such promptitude increases or diminishes according to the ebb and flow of the actual practice of those raisings and other expressions of prayer as ascent.

ii. *The Habitual Disposition of Prayer as Address*

The habitual disposition of prayer as address is formed in the spirit of the Christian by the repetition of the appeals to God that this kind of prayer brings forth. Those repetitions gradually lead praying Christians to address themselves more and more trustfully and frequently to God, and end up by stamping in them an habitual active disposition to appeal to him with the greatest confidence on any occasion.

---

[950] *Ibid.*, I-II, q. 51, a. 2, co.

[951] Ps 119:60; 112:7-8; Tt 3:1.

[952] Is 40:3 = Mt 3:3 = Mk 1:3 = Lk 3:4; Mt 24:44: "You must stand ready...": cf. Mt 5:10; Lk 12:20.

[953] Ps 57:7-8 = 108:1-2.

Such an habitual active disposition does not seem substantially different from the *theological virtue of hope.* It rather appears as a high grade of this virtue, in which long practice of prayer as address has created a special readiness to channel its impetus into the appeals that this kind of prayer makes to God. Since such readiness was created by the practice of prayer as address, it also grows and diminishes according to the increasing or decreasing practice of this kind of prayer.

iii. *The Habitual Disposition of Prayer as Worship*

According to the already-mentioned law of the formation of *habitus,* we can assume that the oft-repeated practice of prayer as worship creates in praying Christians an habitual active disposition for promptly, easily and pleasantly bursting again into prayers of the same kind. What is the nature of this disposition?

According to the teaching of Aquinas such an habitual disposition accrues to the *infused virtue of religion,* since it is directly caused by prayers that are properly acts of that virtue of religion.

> "It is distinctive of (the virtue of) religion to offer honor and reverence to God... Through prayer human persons offer reverence to God, insofar as they subject themselves to God and profess by praying that they need God as the producer (*auctore* = giver and increaser) of all their goods. Hence it is manifest that prayer properly is an act of the virtue of religion."[954]

To clearly understand this way of thinking it is worth remembering that according to Aquinas

> "Religion offers fitting worship to God. Worship is the matter or object of religion. Acts of worship do not contact God directly. Hence it is

[954] *Ibid.*, II-II, q. 83, a. 3, co. Translation ours. The last phrase of Aquinas clearly shows that the prayer of which he is speaking in this question is properly prayer as worship. So, without explaining what kind of prayer Aquinas is here talking about, it does not seem exact to state that this "is surely far and away the clearest and most coherent treatise on prayer since Origen" (TUGWELL [5], p. 275), unless one is determined to restrict all the riches of Christian prayerlife to prayer as worship.

> clear that God is related to the virtue of religion not as its object or matter but as its end."[955]

Not even the act through which praying Christians submit and in a certain sense offer their spirit to God through reverence "achieves direct union with him, because that is not different from offering the bodily members and exterior things to his service."[956]

In short, prayer as worship consists of acts of the virtue of religion, insofar as they give God the worship due to him, which is the specific object of the virtue of religion. But the acts and the habitual active disposition caused in the acting subject by their repetition belong to the same virtue. Hence, the habitual active disposition of prayer as worship belongs to the virtue of religion.

In spite of the clearness of this conclusion, a question may be raised about the place reserved to the habitual disposition of prayer as worship within the virtue of religion.

Acts of sacrifice and of prayer can aim equally at giving God the worship due to him. Hence they are all included by Aquinas in the selfsame virtue of religion. Therefore, the whole virtue of religion is broader than the habitual active disposition of prayer as worship. In other words, even though the virtue of religion certainly includes the habitual disposition of prayer as worship, there can be in it also other habitual active dispositions, for instance, one related to acts of sacrifice.

Are the habitual disposition to offer sacrifices and the habitual disposition to burst into acts of prayer as worship two different *habits?* Or are they just two incomplete habitual active dispositions both belonging to the one virtue of religion, accruing to it by the practice of distinct acts of prayer and of sacrifice? This is a question which would have delighted the intellectual curiosity of the Scholastics.

It suffices to claim that an habitual operative disposition of prayer as worship is caused within the virtue of religion by oft-repeated acts of this kind of prayer.[957]

---

[955] *Ibid.,* q. 81, a. 5, co.

[956] *Ibid.,* ad 3um. For a recent systematic presentation of Aquinas' teaching about prayer see: PINCKAERS, especially chs. ii-vi.

[957] Cf. PINCKAERS, pp.224,226: *la vertu de la prière,* where a translation into French of a sermon of J.H. Newman is quoted as saying "le pouvoir de prier étant une habitude (exactement an habitus, une disposition stable acquise par l'exercise)", p. 225.

Christians whose virtue of religion is advanced by that habitual active disposition to prayer as worship are always ready and prompt to ask, thank, praise, adore God, whose providence they see at work in all great events as well as in the apparently most insignificant daily occurrences. They really believe that he can "write straight with crooked lines". To these Christians God's providential care is more real than any of the apparent facts of life and history.

Job, "the sound and honest man who feared God and shunned evil", who in the midst of all his dreadful troubles kept on praying–

> Yahweh gave, Yahweh has taken back. *Blessed be the name of Yahweh!...* If we take happiness from Yahweh's hand, must we not take sorrow too?"[958]

– is portrayed as an Israelite who deserves the name, having attained an extremely perfect habitual active disposition to prayer as worship.

The whole spirituality and prayerlife of St. Catherine of Siena is grounded on the knowledge of self and of God's goodness within the self. When Catherine speaks of prayer against the background of this fundamental experiential knowledge of hers, she rejoins St. Thomas' teaching on prayer as worship and vividly illustrates it.

> "You will find humility in the knowledge of yourself when you will see that even your own existence comes not from yourself but from me (God), for I loved you before you came into being... For I (God) am who I am (Ex 3:14), whereas you have no being at all of yourself. What being you have is my doing; I am the Creator of everything which has any share in being. But sin is not my making, for sin is nonbeing... *the knowledge of yourself, and of me within yourself,* is grounded in the soil of true humility. If your knowledge of yourself were isolated from me there would be a beginning in self-knowledge, but apart from me it would end in confusion...
>
> Indeed, this soul (Catherine) remembered well what Truth had taught her; that *she should always know herself and God's goodness at work in her,* and that the medicine by which he willed to heal the whole world and to soothe his wrath and divine justice was humble, constant, holy prayer... Oh, *how delightful to the soul and pleasing to me (God) is holy prayer made in the house of self-knowledge and knowledge of me!...* The soul should season her self-knowledge with knowledge of my goodness, and her knowledge of me with self-knowledge. In this way vocal prayer will profit the soul who

---

[958] Jb 1:21; 2:10.

> practices it and it will please me. And if she perseveres in its practice, she will advance from imperfect vocal prayer to perfect mental prayer."[959]

iv. *The Habitual Disposition of Prayer as Communion*

Acts of prayer as communion not only express, as is obvious, but also deepen the praying Christian's fundamental friendship with God and make the virtue of charity grow. How can this happen granted that charity is God's gift and Christians cannot cause or increase their charity through human effort? The most they can do is to dispose themselves to receive an increase of charity from God.

All acts of charity, be they of prayer, of devotion, of sacrifice, etc., and more generally of obedience to God's commandments, suffice to predispose Christians for that increase. However, acts of prayer as communion have their own distinctive contribution to make.

Certain human faculties must be activated to maintain and develop a friendship. That activation occurs also in the expression and cultivation of the special friendship established by charity between Christians and God. In fact, such an activation always occurs when praying Christians bring into action the virtue of charity that is involved in the acts of prayer as communion. In the long run, this activation causes in the human faculties which are involved a certain habitual active disposition to easily, promptly, and enjoyably burst into more acts of friendship and communion with God in prayer.

This habitual active disposition is natural, as well as the human effort which caused it. Therefore it differs essentially from the supernatural virtue of charity. But it is as closely interlaced with charity as nature is to grace, for the supernatural virtue of charity needs the opening of this natural disposition to penetrate into the human psyche and elevate it to perform acts of communion with God in prayer.

We are convinced that Aquinas' theory about the increase of charity supports our explanation. In fact, according to him,

> "Every act of charity disposes to the increase of charity insofar as it renders the person more prompt to act again according to charity. That promptness gradually builds up within the person an ability to continue to do so. The growth of that ability eventually makes the person burst into a more

---

[959] DIALOGUE, chs. 4, 18, 19, 10, 66, pp. 29, 56-57, 41-42, 123, 125.

fervent act of spiritual love by which he strives for the attainment of more charity. At that moment charity is actually increased."[960]

The "ability" Aquinas is referring to in this passage is manifestly a natural, habitual, active disposition of the human faculties activated through the performance of acts of charity. It is an ability formed in these faculties by the repetition of acts of charity to which the faculties essentially contribute. It is an ability which grows through repeated acts to the point of rendering these faculties actively disposed to be easily, promptly, and pleasantly employed again by the virtue of charity for the performance of its acts.

This growing disposition concerns only the human faculties for Aquinas clearly distinguishes it from the increase of the virtue of charity. It is the necessary human preparation for receiving an increase of charity, not the efficient cause of it. The increase of charity actually takes place when God judges that natural disposition sufficient to receive it.[961]

So, we can assume that a natural disposition to receive an increase of charity normally results from the repeated acts of prayer as communion. When the increase of charity is actually given, such a disposition and charity itself melt into one alloy of intimacy with God in prayer. But in that single response, the habitual active disposition of prayer as communion is essentially distinct from, even though actually joined with, the virtue of charity.

The notion of devotion put forward by St. Francis de Sales, which apparently is a development of Aquinas' notion of devotion[962], looks very similar to this habitual active disposition of prayer as worship.

> "Inasmuch as divine love strengthens us to do good, it is called charity. When it has reached a degree of perfection at which it not only makes us to do good but also to do this carefully, frequently, and promptly, it is called devotion... In short, *devotion is simply that spiritual agility and vivacity by which charity works in us or by aid of which we work quickly and*

---

[960] This is our translation of: "quilibet actus (caritatis) disponit ad caritatis augmentum, in quantum ex uno actu caritatis homo redditur promptior ad agendum iterum secundum caritatem, et habilitate crescente, homo prorumpit in actum ferventiorem dilectionis, quo conetur ad caritatis profectum; et tunc caritas augetur in actu": ST, II-II, q. 24, a. 6, co.

[961] St. Augustine had written that charity merits to grow and be perfected: "Caritas inchoata meretur augeri, ut aucta mereatur perfici". *Epistula 186: ad Paulinum,* ch. 3, PL 33, 819. Quoted by Aquinas in ST, I-II, q. 113, a. 10, co.

[962] Cf. ST, II-II, q. 82, a. 1, co.; a. 2, co.

> *lovingly...* To be good a man must have charity, and to be devout, in addition to charity he must have *great ardor and readiness in performing charitable actions...* devotion consists in a certain degree of eminent charity...
>
> To conclude, charity and devotion differ no more from one another than does flame from the fire. Hence devotion adds nothing to the fire of charity except *the flame that makes charity prompt, active and diligent* not only to observe God's commandments but also to fulfill his heavenly counsels and inspirations."[963]

True, St. Francis de Sales calls devotion charity's great ardor and readiness in performing charitable actions, and he specifies that these actions are the observance of God's commandments and the fulfillment of heavenly counsels and inspirations. He does not mention prayer and the life of prayer. However, as there is an "obedient" devotion, there can be a "prayerful" devotion too. The definition of devotion given by St. Francis fits both: "that spiritual agility and vivacity by which charity works in us and by aid of which we work quickly and lovingly." What obedient devotion represents in the domain of active Christian life, prayerful devotion represents in the domain of contemplative Christian prayer. More accurately expressed, prayerful devotion is that habitual active disposition which is incorporated in the virtue of charity so that they can - together - quickly and lovingly elicit acts of prayer as communion, i.e., fervent expressions of that intimate friendship between Christians and God fundamentally established by the virtue of charity.

v. *The Results of Christian Prayerlife's Growth*

It is time to end this chapter by making a list of the most relevant results yielded by the growth process of Christian prayerlife.

First of all, the growth of Christian prayerlife increases the perfection of Christian life by and large. By imprinting habitual active dispositions to pray in the infused virtues of religion, faith, hope, and charity, Christian prayerlife's growth increases the perfection of those virtues. But those virtues constitute the core of Christian life. Consequently, progress in Christian prayer and in Christian life keep pace with each other.

---

[963] SALES FRANCIS OF [2], pp. 40-41. Emphasis ours. Elisabeth Stopp pointedly explains Salesian "devotion" as follows - "you don't only *do* the right and so often hard thing, but *you jump to it"*: STOPP, p. 383. Latter emphasis ours.

Secondly, as we wrote above, the four prayer sources and their inherent spiritual powers are essential components of the radically human and specifically Christian "capacity for God". Now, since the practice of the major forms of Christian prayerlife increases the infused virtues of religion, faith, hope, and charity, which are also the principal components of the Christian capacity for God, it follows that the growing practice of the major forms of Christian prayerlife eventually brings about an intensification and enhancement of the Christian capacity for God.

Thirdly, besides causing an increase in the perfection of Christian life and an enhancement of the Christian capacity for God, the growth of Christian prayerlife also brings forth a specific outcome in the field of prayer. That is the praying Christian's comprehensive readiness to respond promptly, easily and pleasantly to God. In fact, when the qualities expressed by the adverbs of the preceding phrase are present in the prayerlife of a Christian, they clearly manifest that an overall active attitude of prayer has been stamped upon his/her spiritual personality, a permanent attitude which renders him/her habitually prayerful, i.e., continually ready to pray. Given an opportunity, such a person bursts out into and performs the various forms of prayer described above.

Naturally, however, the specific acts of prayer which are elicited by the praying Christian in a particular moment will depend on the prompting of the Holy Spirit and on the spiritual moods and circumstances in which he/she finds him/herself at that moment.

3. CHRISTIAN PRAYERLIFE'S PATHWAYS OF GROWTH

All the preceding analyses give a comprehensive view of Christian prayerlife and disclose the main pathways taken by Christians toward growth in prayer.

i. *A Spiralling Approach to God Transcendent and Immanent*

The God of Christians is paradoxically the nearest and the farthest, the most transcendent and the most immanent of all partners humans can have. Hence the Christian capacity for God increases by enabling praying Christians to come closer and closer to the transcendent/immanent Godhead.

The first spiritual growth of praying Christians is attained by the practice of the two fundamental forms of prayer which belong to the operative dimension of prayerlife, namely prayer as ascent and prayer as address. Apparently, prayer as ascent approaches God as transcendent; while prayer as address approaches him as immanent. These two forms of prayer are the first necessary steps on the prayer journey, but they do not reach God as perfectly as possible. Therefore the forms of prayer which belong to the relational dimension of Christian prayerlife must be added to them.

When the latter forms of prayer are practiced the approach to God goes on at a higher level in the upward spiral towards him, but follows the same pattern of the former prayer forms. In fact, prayer as worship is the praying Christian'sresponse to the transcendent frightening Majesty of God, according to a pattern of servant-master relationship with him; while prayer as communion makes praying Christians enjoy intimacy with God experienced as a fascinating immanent Presence, according to a pattern of lover-beloved relationship with him.

So, the whole journey or growth process of Christian prayerlife progresses through a rhythmic repetition of experiences of God's transcendence and immanence at different levels of an upward spiralling approach to him.

ii. *Towards a Personal God*

The first ascending stretch of the growth process of Christian prayerlife leads us to seek God as the supreme and somewhat impersonal cause of all creatures. But soon another pathway branches out from this first stretch of the prayer journey. By running along the latter, praying Christians start addressing themselves to God, while he gradually takes on in their eyes certain personal features.

The first ascent towards God in prayer is prompted by imagining him as a distant addressee. But then we realize that in spite of his tremendous majesty and utter transcendence he wishes to show us a welcoming face. And so we dare to address ourselves to him hoping that he will lend a listening ear to our pleas. When we can trust him enough to practice prayer as address, then the Supreme Being begins to take for us the shape of an approachable Person.

This prayer evolution seems to parallel the progress from deism to theism in religious philosophy. In fact,

> "The deist admits that we can cognize by pure reason alone the existence of a Supreme Being, but at the same time maintains that *our conception of this being is purely transcendental,* and that it possess all reality, without being able to define it more closely. The theist asserts that reason is capable of presenting us, from the analogy with nature, with a more

> definite conception of this being, and that *its operations, as the cause of all things, are the result of intelligence and free will.*"[964]

Indeed, prayers of natural religion can scarcely reach a "personal God". But Christian prayer is animated by faith, hope, and charity, which impel those who pray towards the heavenly Father revealed by our Lord Jesus Christ.

Undoubtedly, there are Christian sinners who pray supported solely by theological faith and to whom God hardly appears as a friend. Only when theological hope adds its distinctive confidence in God to the assent of theological faith, do praying Christians approach him as the Providence on which they can rely. But unless Christian life is crowned with theological charity praying Christians cannot experience God as a caring and loving friend.

So, only when faith, hope, and charity act harmoniously together do Christians approach God in prayer as a "Person" with whom they can establish interpersonal relationships of submission and of communion.

This consideration leads us into the following pathway in the growth process of Christian prayerlife.

iii. *Towards a Relationship of Quasi-Equality*

Both prayer as worship and prayer as communion are practiced within a certain interpersonal relationship between Christians and God. And yet the relationship of prayer as worship is manifestly less intimate than the relationship which characterizes prayer as communion. We said above that the former is analogous to the relation which exists between servants and their masters. The latter resembles instead the relationship which exists between children and parents or bride and bridegroom.

God's creatures and servants ought to offer the worship of prayer to their Creator and Lord on the basis of their utter inequality, i.e., "distance or extraneity", with respect to him. Whereas God's adopted children and brides can practice prayer as communion with their heavenly Father and Bridegroom on a footing of "closeness or intimacy" with him that appears as if it were of quasi-equality.

By virtue of his ongoing act of creation God unceasingly gives human beings a certain participation in his infinite Being, yet leaving their creatureliness at an insurmountable ontological distance from him. Set in that

---

[964] KANT, II, iii, 7, p. 190 a. Emphasis ours. Mind that "person" is usually defined as "an intelligent and free being".

"remoteness" from God human beings ought to acknowledge their utter dependance on him and offer him their religious worship, accepting and manifesting in this way a relationship with him which not only does not bridge but rather affirms the ontological gap which separates them from him.

Christians, of course, are and remain God's creatures no less than other humans. And yet God's love grants those of them, who freely and gratefully receive it, a very special sharing in his own divine life. That is sanctifying or better still "deifying" *grace,* by which human created nature is neither destroyed nor superseded but enhanced and elevated to a mysterious supernatural condition described by the Holy Scripture as the status of God's children and brides. In the context of the very special closeness and intimacy with God granted by such status, we can speak of a quasi-equality of Christians with God. This ineffable quasi-equality finds on earth its most perfect expression in prayer as communion. But, even in the case of prayer as communion we cannot properly speak of an experience of unqualified equality between Christians and God, because Christians always remain creatures and as such absolutely cannot equal God: not even by virtue of their real sharing in the divine life and their being forcefully driven by charity, so to speak, to melt into the divine truth, goodness and beauty in the highest grades of prayer as communion.

On the contrary, the most authentic experiences of Christian prayerlife show that the closer praying Christians approach God as friends, children, brides, the greater grows their reverence as servants towards the Most Holy.[965]

At any rate, having been granted the status of God's adopted children, Christians can really call God *Abba!* in a manner analogous to the way the Incarnate Son of God used to address his Father in prayer. This bears evidence

---

[965] The *CDF Letter* emphatically states: "Numquam, nullo modo, conandum est nos aequare obiecto contemplationis, libero amori scilicet Dei, ne tunc quidem cum, ex misericordia Dei Patris, per Spiritum Sanctum, qui missus est in corda nostra, nobis gratuito donetur in Christo, sensibilis repercussus huius divini amoris et sentiamus nos esse quasi attractos veritate ac bonitate et pulchritudine Domini. *Quod magis datur cuidam creaturae, ut ad Deum propinquet, eo magis crescit in ea reverentia ante Deum ter Sanctum.* Intelligitur tum verbum S. Augustini, 'Tu licet dicas amicum, ego confiteor servum' (*Enarrationes in Psalmos* CXLII, 6, PL 37, 1849; cfr. etiam *Tract. in Iob,* IV, 9, PL 35, 1410: 'Quando autem nec ad hoc dignum se dicit, vere plenus Spiritu Sancto erat, qui servus Dominum agnovit, et ex servo amicus fieri meruit'), vel illud familiarius verbum quod prompsit ex ore mulieris quam gratificatus est ipse Deus summa sua ac intima familiaritate: 'Respexit humilitatem ancillae suae' (Lc 1,48)". Emphasis ours.

that by joining their prayers with the prayer of Christ, Christians are somehow allowed into the intimate communication eternally engaged in by the Divine Persons with one another in the unity of the Holy Trinity. Consequently, we can say that the christocentric dimension of Christian prayer extends into a trinitarian dimension which makes us pray to the Father through Christ in the Holy Spirit.

As John Paul II recently wrote

> "The communion of Christians with Jesus has the communion of God as Trinity, namely, the unity of the Son to the Father in the gift of the Holy Spirit, as its *model and source,* and it is itself *the means to achieve this communion:* united to the Son in the Spirit's bond of love, Christians are united to the Father."[966]

So the profound meaning of our being created in the image of God is manifested in this marvelous union of ours with the Holy Trinity. Prayer as communion, in which such union is especially cultivated, is therefore, at one and the same time, the most specific form and the highest peak-experience of Christian prayerlife. It is the most specific form because prayer as ascent, as address, and as worship can be also variously found both in primitive and developed natural religions. It is the highest peak-experience because prayer as communion assumes and brings to their achievement all the spiritual bearings and reaches of prayer as ascent, as address, and as worship, which in the growth process of Christian prayerlife precede and prepare it.

iv. *From Possessing God to Being Possessed by Him*

Another pathway of Christian prayerlife is opened by the praying person's perception of a rather distant and somewhat indifferent God and the consequent aspiration to have some contact with him. In the initial stretch of this pathway praying Christians are mostly driven by their need of obtaining something from God, but in the final stretch they delight in surrendering themselves entirely to his overwhelming love.

In the initial stretch, in which prayer as ascent and as address mostly resolve into prayer of petition, praying Christians call for God's attention and ask for his help and gifts, with a mostly self-centered attitude.

---

[966] JOHN PAUL II, [1], p. 46. Emphasis Ours.

In the final stretch praying Christians practice prayers of thanksgiving, praise, adoration, and all the forms of prayer as communion, which overturn the self-centeredness of the preceding stretch and transform it into a more and more yielding self-surrender to God by submission and love.

It seems that in the initial stretch of this pathway, praying Christians are mostly striving to gain Christ and through him to "possess" God, as if they were somehow able to do it through their spiritual efforts. This approach might find some justification in Jesus' rather enigmatic words:

> "Up to this present time, *the kingdom of heaven has been subjected to violence and the violent are taking it by storm...* The kingdom of God has been preached, and *by violence everyone is getting in.*"[967]

Which could be explained by two of Jesus parables:

> "The kingdom of heaven is like treasure hidden in a field which someone has found: he hides it again, goes off happy, *sells everything he owns and buys the field.* Again, the kingdom of heaven is like a merchant looking for fine pearls; when he finds one of great value he goes and *sells everything he owns and buys it.*"[968]

The same idea is put more clearly in Paul's declarations:

> "Because of Christ I have come to consider all the advantages (of the Law) that I had as disadvantages... *For him I have accepted the loss of everything, and I look on everything as so much rubbish if only I can have* (the Greek verb *kerdaino* used here means to earn, to gain) *Christ* and be given a place in him. I am no longer trying for perfection by my own efforts, the perfection that comes from the Law, but I want only the perfection that comes through faith in Christ, and is from God and based on faith."[969]

It seems that when the indwelling presence of the Holy Trinity (which becomes at the end the main focus of Christian prayer) is theologically interpreted as if praying Christians were "possessing" the Divine Persons, this implicitly happens in reference to all that they strive for during the initial stretch of Christian prayerlife. But in the final stretch of the same pathway the

---

[967] Mt 13:12 and Lk 16:16.

[968] Mt 13:44-46.

[969] Ph 3:7-9.

divine indwelling is clearly experienced as "being possessed" by the Divine Persons.[970]

This may explain why, according to Aquinas who summarizes an older tradition, the Divine Persons are said to be both "present in" and "possessed by" praying Christians by virtue of God-given faith and charity.

> "The verb 'sent' rightly applies to a divine person in that he is newly *present (novo modo existit)* in someone; the verb 'given' in that he is *possessed (habetur)* by someone. Neither occurs except by reason of sanctifying grace...
>
> There is a special presence consonant with the nature of an intelligent being in whom *God is said to be present (in qua Deus dicitur inesse)* as the known in the knower and the loved in the lover. And because *by these acts of knowing and loving the intelligent being touches* (*attingit:* this verb may mean both reaches and touches by a direct union with God, i.e., without the medium of some created good) *God himself,* by reason of this special way of being present we have the teaching that God is not merely in the intelligent creature, but *dwells there* as in his temple.
>
> Likewise the meaning of possessing something is that it is in our power to use and enjoy it at our will. To have *the power to rest joyfully (fruendi) in a divine person* is ours by reason of grace alone. Still, *as grace is given (in ipso dono gratiae gratum facientis) the Holy Spirit himself is possessed (habetur)* and dwells in a person and so it is he himself who is given and sent."[971]

Praying Christians are "possessed" by the Divine Persons insofar as the latter attract and, as it were, absorb (of course, psychologically not ontologically) the former into the circulation of knowledge and love eternally going on within the Holy Trinity, the ultimate goal of Christian life. What the Son of God said of himself can, in fact, be said also of the Father and of the Holy Spirit, to whom the Son is indissolubly united.

> "I am the bread of life... that comes down from heaven, so that a man may eat it and not die. I am the living bread which has come down from heaven. Anyone who eats this bread will live for ever... Who eats my flesh and drinks by blood *lives in me and I live in him. As I, who am sent by the*

[970] The active and receptive explanations are both hinted at by the above quoted words of Paul: "If only I can *have* Christ and *be given* a place in him."

[971] ST, I, q. 43, a. 3, co.; BLACKFRIARS, vol. 7, pp. 217-218. Emphasis ours.

> *living Father, myself draw life from the Father, so whoever eats me will draw life from me.*"[972]

Commenting on this relation of inner mutual presence between Christians and Christ, which is over and over again emphasized by St. John, Aquinas writes:

> "Whoever is *incorporated into the mystical body through the union of faith and charity* is the one who eats (Christ) spiritually. As a matter of fact, charity makes God be present in the human person and vice versa: 'Anyone who abides in charity abides in God and God abides in him' (1 Jn 4:16). And this is what the Holy Spirit performs: 'Wecan know that we are abiding in God and God is abiding in us because he gave us his Spirit' (Ibid. 13)."[973]

So, we can say that we possess God insofar as we can reach him through the free exercise of the theological virtues with which we are endowed by God. But God himself takes an extremely profound possession of our being from his very first pouring into us of sanctifying grace. At this moment the Divine Persons come to abide as in their own temple in the deepest recesses of our hearts. And their abiding within us and possessing us is always necessarily prerequisite to our holding and possessing them by virtue of our faith, hope, and charity.

Therefore, praying Christians are first and much more possessed by the Divine Persons than they can possess them, even though beginners and proficients do not always realize it as is the case of the perfects. In fact, when these latter attain the highest grade of prayer as communion they vividly experience that they are profoundly possessed by God's indwelling Presence.[974]

---

[972] Jn 6:48-51, 56-57.

[973] "Ille manducat spiritualiter qui *corpori mystico incorporatur per unionem fidei et caritatis:* caritas autem facit Deum esse in homine, et e converso; I Io, iv, 16: *Qui manet in caritate, in Deo manet, et Deus in eo.* Et hoc est quod facit Spiritus Sanctus; unde ibid 13: *In hoc cognoscimus quod in Deo manemus, et Deus in nobis, quia de Spiritu suo dedit nobis":* ESI, no. 976, p. 184 b. Emphasis ours except for the scriptural passages.

[974] Cf. ST. TERESA OF AVILA, *Moradas,* VII, 1, 7; 2, 10.

CHAPTER XI

UNCEASING PRAYER

The process whereby Christian prayerlife grows will gradually render praying Christians true "persons of prayer". This happens through two complementary and progressive simplifications of their prayerlife. The first simplification proceeds from a prayer which was an occasional and discontinuous activity, to a prayer which has become a continual and unceasing state. The latter unites the many habitual forms into a single comprehensive attitude of prayerfulness.

Such a growth process brings about a spiritual progress in prayerlife both in extension and in intention. Its extension reaches the maximum when prayer permeates the entire Christian existence. The state of prayer is most intensive when it penetrates the core of the Christian person.

In this chapter we will explore the extension of Christian prayerlife achieved by unceasing prayer.

i. *Unceasing Prayer in the Bible*

a. *Unceasing prayer in the Old Testament*

A psalm describes with elation the response of unceasing prayerful attention to Yahweh's caring presence:

> "*I keep Yahweh before me always,* for with him at my right hand nothing can shake me. So my heart exults, my very soul rejoices, my body, too, will rest securely, for you will not abandon my soul to Sheol, nor will allow the one you love to see the Pit: you will reveal the paths of life to me, give me unbounded joy in your presence, and at your right hand everlasting pleasures" (Ps 16:8-11).

Apparently, "keeping Yahweh before oneself always" is equivalent to "bearing oneself blameless in God's presence" (Gn 17:1). It was essential to the faith that Abraham "put in Yahweh, who counted this as making him justified" (Gn 15:6):

"Abraham took Yahweh at his word. He believed the truth of the promise made to him. He placed his entire trust in the epiphanic speech. He *responded with the entirety of his being to the articulate thrust of the divine presence...* This is not an intellectual assent to a propositional truth. It is *the insertion of the wholeness of one's personality into a relation of total openness toward the reality of God...*

The *attitude* so described is precisely akin to that of 'righteousness', in the Hebrew sense ... which indicates a *dynamic and harmonious relationship* between two human beings, between social groups, or again between God and man... The text points to the *inwardness of Abraham's attitude and to the totality of his devotion...* This Hebraic notion is *intrinsic part of the theology of presence...* It is a way of describing man's living under God, or, in a favorite metaphor of the Hebrew religious semantics, man's 'walking under God'."[975]

According to the eschatological discourse which concludes the book of Isaiah, such prayerful keeping Yahweh before oneself always will reach its climax in

"The new heaven and new earth that Yahweh shall make... (wherein) from New Moon to New Moon, from sabbath to sabbath, all human kind will come to bow down in my presence, says Yahweh" (Is. 66:23).

These prophetic words point to the unceasing prayer of Christians.

b. Unceasing prayer in the New Testament

The reader of the New Testament cannot but be impressed by its many passages which recommend unceasing prayer. So, according to a contemporary author, if somebody asks,

"To what extent is man, in the dark depths of his existence, capable of prayer? Jesus' answer to this man - and to no other - was: 'You ought always to pray and not lose heart'. Paul's 'pray constantly' reinforces the Lord's words."[976]

---

[975] TERRIEN, pp. 77-78. Emphasis ours.

[976] BOROS, p. 3.

In fact, Jesus often exhorts his disciples to pray at all times, to be always watching for his return, to be ready to welcome him at once when he will come.[977] Jesus used a very evocative imagery to illustrate this teaching of his.

> "See that you are dressed for action and have your lamps lit. Be like men waiting for their master to return from the wedding feast, ready to open the door as soon as he comes and knocks. Happy those servants whom the master finds awake when he comes. I tell you solemnly, he will put on an apron, sit them down at table and wait on them.
>
> It may be in the second watch he comes, or in the third, but happy those servants if he finds them ready. You may be quite sure of this, that if the householder had known at what hour the burglar would come, he would not have let anyone break through the wall of his house. *You too must stand ready, because the Son of Man is coming at an hour you do not expect"* (Lk 12:35-40; cf. Mt 25:1-13).

This constant readiness in waiting for the Master to return is an alert hopeful expectation motivated by eschatological hope.[978] Such an attitude joined with faith and charity, ought to animate the entire life of Christians.

Meister Eckhert gives an insightful spiritual exegesis of the passage last quoted

> "A man should be as our Lord said, 'Like people on the watch, always expecting their Lord' (Lk 12:36).
>
> For, indeed, people who are expectant like that are watchful, they look around them to see where he whom they expect is coming from, and they look out for him in whatever comes along, however strange it may be, just in case he should be in it. *In this way we should consciously discover our Lord in all things.*
>
> This requires much diligence, demanding a total effort of our senses and powers of mind; then those who manage this are in a right state: *taking God equally in all things, they find God in equal measure in all...* He to whom is God thus present in all things has heaven indeed."[979]

---

[977] Cf. Lk 21:36; 12:35-38; Mt 24:42; Mk 14:38.

[978] Cf. WRIGHT, p. 163.

[979] ECKHART, vol. III, pp. 20. Emphasis ours.

It would be wrong, however, to think that this spiritual attitude fosters escapism from daily duties and tasks (cf. 2 Th 3:7-13). The parables of the ten bridesmaids, the talents, and the final judgment, gathered by St. Matthew at the end of his section about the teaching ministry of Jesus, clearly contradict any such escapism. These parables clearly make the point that the Christian attitude of praying in continuous expectation for the final return of the Lord ought to be accompanied by a very active commitment to use the talents received in order to double them and do works of mercy to the least of Christ's brothers, as if they were done to Christ himself (Mt 25).

When the Apostles asked Jesus: "Master, teach us to pray, just as John taught his disciples", Jesus answered by teaching them the "Our Father".[980] This prayer could hardly ring true unless it were uttered "in the Holy Spirit", who alone, by abiding within the hearts of praying Christians into whom he pours charity, can enable them to call God their Father.[981] And the objects of petition made by this prayer have a marked eschatological character while the petitions are an expression of nostalgia for paradise; particularly when the "Our Father" is recited or sung during the eucharistic celebration.

> "The Lord's Prayer manifests the *eschatological* character of its own petitions. It is the typical prayer of the 'last times', the times of salvation which started with the effusion of the Holy Spirit and shall be accomplished with the Lord's Return."[982]

Hence the frequent recitation of the Lord's prayer should enkindle that continual expectation of God's Kingdom, which is so distinctive of the unceasing prayer of Christians. Such an expectation constitutes the broader context of Paul's frequent exhortations to pray without ceasing.

> "*Pray constantly;* and *for all things* give thanks to God, because this is what God expects you to do in Christ Jesus." "So that *always and everywhere you are giving thanks to God* who is our Father in the name of our Lord Jesus Christ." "Do not give up if trial comes; and *keep on praying.*"

---

[980] Cf. Lk 11:1ff.

[981] Cf. Rm 5:5; Ga 4:6; Lk 11:13.

[982] CCC, n. 2771, cf. 2770 and 2772. Today's exegetes recognize that the Our Father is teeming with eschatological overtones. "The *Our Father* places the one praying on the brink of eternity: for it is a prayer of 'the last days'": JONES, p. 72. Cf. BROWN [2].

Pray all the time, asking for what you need, praying in the Spirit on every possible occasion. *Never get tired of staying awake to pray* for all the saints."

"The Lord is very near. There is no need to worry; but *if there is anything you need, pray for it, asking God for it with prayer and thanksgiving,* and the peace of God which is so much greater than we can understand will guard your hearts and your thoughts, in Christ Jesus."

"Be persevering in your prayers and be thankful as you stay awake to pray." "In every place I want the men to lift their hands up reverently in prayer... A woman who is really widowed and left without anybody can give herself up to God and *consecrate all her days and nights to petitions and prayer."*[983]

These Pauline passages, joined to the words of Jesus quoted above,[984] demonstrate that,

"The New Testament requires and indeed assumes that Christians will pray without ceasing."[985]

"The Christian ought always to live in the presence of his Lord and converse with him, and constantly be looking to him."[986]

Accordingly, a contemporary master of prayer can write:

"It is our conviction that the *central message of the New Testament* is that there is only one prayer, the prayer of Christ. It is *a prayer which continues in our hearts day and night.* I can describe it only as a stream of love that flows constantly between Jesus and the Father. *This stream of love is the Holy Spirit...*

The most important task for any fully human life is to become as open as possible to this stream, this cosmic river of love. *We have to allow this prayer to become our prayer...* We have to create a space within ourselves that will allow the higher consciousness of the prayer of Christ to envelop us in his powerful mystery."[987]

---

[983] 1 Th 5:17; Rm 12:12; Ep 5:20; 6:18; Ph 4:5-7; Col 4:2; 1 Tm 2:8; 5:5.

[984] "The injunction to 'pray constantly' [1 Thess. 5:17] which Paul gives in accordance with the exhortation of Jesus." (ORIGEN [2], XII, 1, p. 104)

[985] RICHARDSON, p. 457b.

[986] DNTT, pp. 869-870.

[987] MAIN [2], p. ix. Emphasis ours.

A theologian summarizes the result of his research about unceasing prayer in the New Testament as follows:

> "The expression 'unceasing prayer' has two meanings in Scripture: 1) frequently repeated acts of prayer, returning again and again to praise, thank, and petition God. It is clearly supposed that this kind of unceasing prayer is an integral part of Christian life.
>
> 2) An ongoing quality of life, even outside times of formal prayer. The express activity of formal prayer overflows to communicate a quality of prayer to the whole of one's life. Both kinds of unceasing prayer are rooted in the presence of the Holy Spirit."[988]

ii. *Tradition and Interpretation of Unceasing Prayer*

a. The tradition of unceasing prayer

A few quotes suffice to show that a tradition of unceasing prayer developed during the early centuries of the Christian era.

St. Ignatius of Antioch exhorts Polycarp,

> "To prayer give yourself unceasingly... watch without letting your spirit flag" (*Letter to Polycarp,* I, 3).

According to Clement of Alexandria,

> "God continually hears all the inward converse of the (Christian) gnostic, who prays all through his life, and having reached this, he leaves behind all that is of no service...
>
> In every place but not ostensibly and visibly to the multitude, he (the gnostic) will pray."[989]

---

[988] WRIGHT, p. 165.

[989] *Stromateis,* VII, 7, 40.3, quoted by MEREDITH [2], pp. 113. Meredith, however, claims that Clement's rarefied conception of the gnostic's prayer has little obvious similarity with the New Testament's unceasing prayer. It rather resembles the private intellectual contemplation outlined in Plato's and Aristotle's writings.

St. Athanasius writes about St. Anthony, the great father of the early Egyptian monks,

> "He prayed constantly, since he learned that it is necessary to praying unceasingly in private."[990]

Evagrius Ponticus likewise maintains that monks have the obligation to pray unceasingly.

> "We do have the obligation to pray without ceasing... By its very nature the spirit is made to pray."[991]

Cassian emphasizes and explains:

> "*Every monk aims at uninterrupted prayer.* As far as it is possible to a frail man, he struggles for imperturbable peace and purity of mind. This is the reason why we try so unwearyingly to practice the different disciplines of the body and of the spirit. The discipline of the body and the spirit on the one side, and *unceasing prayerfulness* on the other, cannot help having a mutual effect upon each other. The keystone in the arch of all virtues is *perfect prayer,* and without this keystone the archway becomes rickety and insecure."[992]
>
> "The unity which is now between Father and Son shall be poured into our feelings and our mind: and as he loves us with a pure, sincere, unbreakable charity we on our side shall be linked to him by *lasting affection that nothing can spoil. In that union whatever we breathe or think or speak is God.* So the end of his (= Jesus') prayer is attained in us: 'that they be one as we are one' (Jn 17:21,26; 1 Jn 4:10)...
>
> *This should be the aim and purpose of the solitary:* to seek to possess in some measure, even while mortal man, the first bridal gifts from the heavenly country and glory. I repeat: this is the end of all true goodness, that the mind may every day be lifted beyond the material sphere to the realm of the spirit, *until the whole life and every little stirring of the heart becomes one continuous prayer...*

---

990 ATHANASIUS, p. 32, n. 3.

991 EVAGRIUS, ch. 49, p. 29. Quoted also by CCC, n. 2742.

992 CASSIAN, IX, 2. CHADWICK, p. 214. Emphasis ours.

> By meditation God can be grasped and conceived... and (we) preserve this thought, whatever it is, *uninterruptedly...* the conception of God is retained *permanently*"[993]

Many centuries later, Meister Eckhart teaches even beginners in spiritual life how they can fulfill the obligation of unceasing prayer.

> "Since a man cannot in this life refrain from activities, which are human and manifold, so *a man should learn to have his God in all things* and remain unhindered in all acts and places. And so, when a beginner has to deal with people, he should *first arm himself strongly with God and fix Him firmly in his heart, uniting all his intentions, thoughts, will and strength with Him,* so that nothing else can arise in that man's mind."[994]

b. Interpretations of unceasing prayer

No less than we, the early Church wondered about the meaning of "unceasing prayer" commanded by the New Testament.[995] The assumption that this demanding obligation had to be feasible in order to be really binding led to various interpretations of unceasing prayer. In the fifth century,

> "The problem of how to pray without ceasing was resolved (by the Fathers) in four different ways: by the observance of set hours during the day; by considering all good actions as prayer, as Origen and other suggested; by the practice of the prayer of the heart, which was especially the method of the Desert Fathers; and by the equation of desire with prayer, as Augustine says."[996]

These interpretations manifestly depend on and result from different ideas of prayer.

---

[993] *Ibid.,* X. 7-8. CHADWICK, pp. 237-238 passim. Emphasis ours.

[994] MEISTER ECKHART, vol III, p. 21. Emphasis ours.

[995] Cassian himself, before giving his own interpretation of unceasing prayer, had asked: "What sort of prayer it is that ought always to be offered?" *Conference,* IX, 7, CHADWICK, p. 218. Cf. also PL 73, 941-943. RAMSEY, ch. IX; ŠPIDLÍK, pp. 348-349, 360-361.

[996] RAMSEY, p. 172.

1. The fulfillment of the obligation of praying unceasingly through *the observance of set hours* by day and night was a very ancient Christian practice,[997] which was received and institutionalized by the early monks. It is still obligatory for the religious and clerics of our time.

> "The divine office, in keeping with ancient Christian tradition, is so devised that the whole course of the day and night is made holy by the praise of God... Priests who are engaged in the sacred pastoral ministry will pray the divine office the more fervently, the more alive they are to the need to heed St. Paul's exhortation, 'Pray without ceasing' (1 Th 5:17).[998]

This practice assumes that the unceasing prayer commanded by the New Testament is to be mostly understood as prayer of worship. This form of prayer can hardly be unceasing in a strict sense. Therefore, practicing it in order to fulfil the obligation of praying unceasingly implies that one interprets "unceasingly" in the broad sense of "as often as possible".

St. Cyprian, however, maintaining that prayer ought to be practiced day and night, reminds Christians that Christ is the never setting Sun of their spirit.

> "There should be no hour in which Christians do not frequently and always worship God, to that we who are in Christ – that is in the Sun and the true Day – ought to be constant throughout the day in petitions and prayer.
>
> And when by the law of nature the night comes around again, those who are praying cannot be harmed by the nocturnal darkness because, for the children of light, day exists even during the night. For when is he without light who has the light in his heart? And when is he without the sun and the day whose sun and day is Christ?
>
> We who are in Christ – that is, always in the light – ought never to cease from prayer during the night... Let us, dearest brethren, who are always in the light, who remember and keep hold of what we have begun to be by grace, consider the night as day... Let there be no lack of prayers during the

[997] As a matter of fact, it is already described in Hippolytus' *Apostolic Tradition,* 41 (quoted in RAMSEY, pp. 165-166), in which the exhortation to pray at nine, twelve, three o'clock, before going to bed, midnight, and at cockcrow is supported by various reasons referring to the events of the life of Christ.

[998] SC, 84, 86; FLANNERY, p. 24-25.

hours of the night, let there be no idle and shameful waste of the times of prayer."[999]

It seems that, by tracing unceasing prayer back to the constant presence of Christ in the heart of the Christian, Cyprian prepares and somehow leads towards the understanding of unceasing prayer as "continuous desire", which is St. Augustine's understanding of it.

2. Origen thought that,

> "He prays 'constantly' *who unites prayer with the deeds required and right deeds with prayer.* For the only way we can accept the commandment to 'pray constantly' (1 Th 5:17) as referring to a real possibility is by saying that the entire life of the saint taken as a whole is a single great prayer. What is customarily called prayer is, then, a part of this prayer."[1000]

Origen thinks that the prayer which is supposed to be unceasing cannot be "what is customarily called prayer" i.e., understood as the formal activity of prayer;[1001] which, of course, cannot be unceasing. Therefore, according to him, the "prayer" which can be unceasing is the one taken in the broad sense, namely "a single great prayer",[1002] which is "the entire life of the saint taken as a whole".[1003]

---

[999] *On the Lord's Prayer,* 35-36. Quoted by RAMSEY, p. 167.

[1000] ORIGEN [2], XII, 2, p. 104. Emphasis ours. Origen's interpretation of unceasing prayer was perhaps inspired by SI 38:34: "[Craftsmen] who are not remarkable for culture and right judgement...their prayer is concerned with what pertains to their trade." The well-known Benedictine maxim: *ora et labora* (pray and work! Cf. Saint Benedict, *Rule*, 20,48, quoted by CCC, n. 2834) is akin with the Origenian formula.

[1001] RAMSEY, p. 167, comments: "Other Fathers seem to have understood prayer in the strict classical sense of conscious elevation of the mind and heart to God in the form of praise, thanksgiving and petitions." Whereas, in his interpretation of unceasing prayer Origen "succeeds in broadening the concept of prayer considerably."

[1002] RAMSEY, p. 168, translates this phrase of Origen: "a great synthesis of prayer".

[1003] Thomas a Celano made a similar remark when he wrote that St. Francis was "wholly not so much praying as transformed into prayer". *(Totus non tam orans quam oratio factus).*

The Origenian sequence of prayer both preceding and following good deeds implies that formal prayer should inspire all other Christian good deeds with saintly motivations and good deeds should resort to formal prayer in order to strengthen their motivation.

To be more explicit, prayer as worship ought to precede, accompany, and follow good deeds in order to offer them to God as spiritual oblations and sacrifices; prayer as communion ought to precede, accompany, and follow good deeds in order to infuse into them charity towards God and the neighbor.

Vatican II interprets unceasing prayer as prayer of worship preceding and accompanying the good deeds of Christians:

> "The baptized, by regeneration and the anointing of the Holy Spirit, are consecrated into a spiritual house and a holy priesthood... Therefore *all the disciples of Christ, persevering in prayer and praising God (cf. Acts 2:42-47), should present themselves as a living sacrifice, holy and pleasing to God" (cf. Rm 12:1).*[1004]
>
> "To those whom he (= Jesus Christ) intimately joins to his life and mission he also gives a share in his priestly office, *to offer spiritual worship for the glory of the Father and the salvation of man.* Hence the laity, dedicated as they are to the Christ and anointed by the Holy Spirit are marvelously called and prepared so that even richer fruits of the Spirit may be produced by them.
>
> For all their works, prayer and apostolic undertakings, family and married life, daily work, relaxation of mind and body, if they are accomplished in the Spirit - indeed even the hardships of life if patiently borne - *all these become spiritual sacrifices acceptable to God through Jesus Christ.* In the celebration of the Eucharist these may most fittingly be offered to the Father along with the body of the Lord. And so, *worshipping everywhere by their holy actions,* the laity consecrate the world to God."[1005]

These passages understand unceasing prayer as a spiritual worship, which carries on the celebration of Eucharist in all the good deeds of Christians.[1006]

[1004] LG, n. 10, FLANNERY, p. 360-361. Emphasis ours.

[1005] *Ibid.*, n. 34, FLANNERY, p. 391. Emphasis ours.

[1006] Such an unceasing spiritual worship is poetically put by GIBRAN, p. 124: "He whose worshipping is a window, to open but also to shut, has not yet visited the house of his soul whose windows are open from dawn to dawn."

A recent document of the Holy See seemingly joins together prayer as worship and prayer as communion in animating those good deeds:

> "*Inner habitual vigilance and asking for divine help,* which the New Testament calls "unceasing prayer', does not necessarily end, when, according to God's will, one performs the task of working and taking care of the neighbor, as the Apostle exhorts: 'Whatever you eat, whatever you drink, whatever you do at all, *do it for the glory of God"* (1 Co 10:31).
>
> In fact, *genuine prayer,* according to outstanding spiritual masters, *infuses praying Christians with a burning charity,* which pushes them to cooperate with the Church's mission and to minister to the brethren for the greater glory of God."[1007]

An early monk described how he used to practice unceasing prayer in a way which illustrates Origen's interpretation:

> "I pray without ceasing while working with my hands. For with God's help, I sit down, steeping my few palm fronds, and from them I make a mat, while I say: Have mercy on me, God, according to your great mercy, etc.[1008]...
>
> When I have spent the whole day at work, praying in my heart or with my lips, I earn about fifteen coins, and I put two of them at my door and I eat with what remains. Whoever finds these two denarii prays for me while I am eating or sleeping, and thus by the grace of God there is fulfilled in me what is written: Pray without ceasing."[1009]

Origen's idea that the obligation of unceasing prayer could be fulfilled by uniting prayer with good deeds and good deeds with prayer may have led some Fathers to overemphasize the performance of good deeds in order to fulfil the obligation of unceasing prayer. Most likely these Fathers wanted to curb the exaggerations of those Christians who took piety as an excuse for laziness, or claimed, as certain monks did, that they should dedicate their whole life to nothing else but praying.

> "Prayer does not consist so much in words as in good works, love and zeal for duty. Indeed, anyone who is inclined to good works, all his life

---

[1007] The *CDF Letter,* n. 30. Translations from the original Latin and emphasis ours.

[1008] This resembles the "Jesus prayer". We will talk about it.

[1009] *De vitis patrum,* 5, 12, 9. PL 73, 942, quoted by RAMSEY, pp. 170-171.

must needs to be in prayer, which is seen in his choice of these good works. Prayer is by necessity connected with good works, because a thing which is not good to be looked for is not good to be prayed for... a true prayer consists in good works, in love of God and diligence in the things which please him.[1010]

Meditation on the law (of the Lord day and night, as in Ps 1:2) consists not in reading but in doing. For it is said in another place: Whether you eat or drink, or whatever you do, do everything in the name of the Lord. If I give alms, I meditate on the law of God; if I visit a sick person, my feet meditate on the law of God; if I do those things that are commended, I meditate in my body what others meditate in their mouths... our meditation is our work."[1011]

Jesuits like to interpret unceasing prayer as a "being contemplative in action", which characterized St. Ignatius of Loyola's spiritual attitude. Some of them understand it as performing good deeds with a prayerful attitude, which resembles the joining of prayer and good deeds suggested by Origen:

"We are to pray always. A prayerful awareness should accompany our daily activities. We are to be contemplative in action."[1012]

But someone thinks that, for all practical purposes, to be contemplative in action means to replace contemplative prayer with an action performed for God's sake. And in this way Ignatius of Loyola would have given a "revolutionary" solution to the old problem of the relation between contemplation and action by

"Placing perfection no longer in a contemplative element, not even in religious contemplation, if by this is meant formal prayer, contemplation and other 'exercises', but essentially in the perfection of action undertaken purely for the sake of God, directed to Him and fulfilled in Him."[1013]

[1010] Theodore of Mopsuestia, *Ad Baptizandos,* 1, quoted by RAMSEY, p. 168-169.

[1011] St. Jerome, *Tractatus de Ps. 1,* quoted by RAMSEY, p. 168.

[1012] CARTER, p. 103 and 100.

[1013] CORETH, p. 195. It is worthwhile to remember that Ignatius of Loyola was a faithful daily practitioner of contemplative prayer (cf. his *Spiritual Journal*) from which, and not to the exclusion of which, he undoubtedly drew his being a

Such an interpretation of "contemplative in action" resembles the overemphasis of the early Fathers, quoted above, on the performance of good deeds in order to fulfill the obligation of unceasing prayer. It is, therefore, not so new as its author would like us to believe.

However, in another passage of his book *On Prayer* Origen offers also another interpretation of unceasing prayer. He suggests that the prayer implied by the obligation of unceasing prayer is the prayer which Christians can always offer to God within their hearts, where the kingdom and throne of God is established.

> "Let us suppose that the Scripture teaches us to say 'Our Father' at any appointed time of prayer. Rather, if we understand the early discussion of praying 'constantly' (1 Th 5:17), let ourwhole life be a constant prayer in which we say 'Our Father in heaven', before the throne of God, because the kingdom of God is established in all those who bear the inner image of the Man from heaven (1 Cor 15:49) and have thus become heavenly."[1014]

This other explanation of Origen for unceasing prayer is similar to that of St. Cyprian mentioned above and not too far from the "prayer of the heart" and the "unceasing prayer" of St. Augustine.

3. The so-called *prayer of the heart*[1015] is a method of prayer devised by the ancient monks. The "heart" is to be understood as,

> "The deep center of the human person as a whole. 'Prayer of the heart' means not just 'affective prayer' but prayer of the entire person."[1016]

"contemplative in action". A saying attributed to him can confirm that: "We ought to pray as if all depended on God, and act as if all depended on us." Quoted by CCC, n. 2834.

[1014] ORIGEN [2], XXI, 5, p. 125. Other Fathers think that "heaven", where the Father is, is the "heart" of Christians. E.g., St. Augustine *De Sermone Domini in monte,* 2, 11; PL 24, 1277. St. Cyril of Jerusalem, *Catecheses mistagogicae,* 5, 11; PG 33; 1117B. Both quoted by CCC n. 2794.

[1015] Cf. CCC, n. 2667 and 2668, 2613, 2616.

[1016] WARE [2], p. 246.

The identification of unceasing prayer with the prayer of the heart is another of the solutions to our problem. It was first practiced by monks who took prayer as an address which creates an interpersonal communion with God.

> "It is involved with the constant repetition of a particular phrase, which would eventually make its way into the heart of the one praying. It was possible so to interiorize one's prayer."[1017]

For the early monks such interiorized prayer consisted in the continuous remembrance of Jesus, that is, in always keeping the sense of his presence while working, talking with others, eating, etc. It took the subconscious state of prayer rather than a sequence of outward acts.[1018]

Several centuries later the conviction that "the prayer of the heart" is a form of continual prayer was still alive in the English spiritual tradition.

> "(It is) only in the heart, without speaking, and with great rest of body and soul", where the Christian "can pray in their hearts continually, glorifying and praising God."[1019]
>
> "(There are those) who love especially the name of Jesus, and honour it so that they never allow it to fall from their memory save in sleep."[1020]

The anthology of writings of the ancient monks entitled *Philokalia* contains important chapters on the "prayer of the heart". The author of *The Way of the Pilgrim* was inspired by the *Philokalia.*[1021] This unknown nineteenth-century Russian writer persistently practiced "the Jesus Prayer" in order to attain unceasing prayer.

[1017] RAMSEY, p. 171.

[1018] Cf. WARE [1], pp. 176, 180-181.

[1019] HILTON, I, ch. 32, pp. 102-103.

[1020] Richard Rolle, *Fire of Love,* I, 15. Quoted by KNOWLES, p. 58. "Indeed, the Name of Jesus is to him a kind of talisman, and the frequent repetition of it an exercise in the presence of God." *Ibid.,* p. 63.

[1021] E.g., "Sometimes I would spend the whole day in the forest conscientiously reading the *Philokalia...* my heart was becoming kindled toward union with God by means of the interior prayer which I was learning... When I began to pray with the heart, everything around me became transformed and I saw it in a new delightful way": *WAY OF THE PILGRIM,* ch. 2, p. 34.

4. To identify unceasing prayer with the *continuous desire of the heart* is to manifestly understand unceasing prayer as a permanent, prayerful state of communion with God.

St. John Chrysostom first described prayer as

> "Longing for God, love *(agape)* too deep for words, a gift not of man but by God's grace... one who tastes this food is set on fire with an eternal longing for the Lord: his spirit burns as in a fire of the utmost intensity."

Then he goes on to say that such "prayer of the heart and not of outside observance" should

> "Not be confined to fixed times or periods but continuous throughout the day and night. Our spirit should be quick to reach out towards God, not only when it is engaged in meditation; at other times also, when it is carrying out its duties, caring for the needy, performing works of charity, giving generously in the service of others, our spirit should long for God and call him to mind, so that these works can be seasoned with the salt of God's love, and so make a palatable offering to the Lord of the universe."[1022]

In sum, "In the marketplace or during a solitary walk too it is possible to pray frequently and fervently. It is possible even in your shop, both while buying and selling, or also while you are cooking."[1023]

Likewise, St. Augustine understood unceasing prayer as the constant desire of God,[1024] which permeates the whole Christian life:

> "The desire of your heart is itself your prayer. And *if the desire is constant, so is your prayer.* The Apostle Paul had a purpose in saying: 'Pray without ceasing'. Are we then ceaselessly to bend our knees, to lie prostrate,

---

[1022] Chrysostom quoted in LITURGY, vol. II, p. 69. This teaching is put forward by CCC, nn. 2742-2745 as an interpretation of St. Paul's "unceasing prayer", since it proves that "it is always possible to pray" (n. 2743) and that "prayer and Christian life are inseparable", as the same love is working in both (*Ibid.* n. 2745; cf. nn. 2668, 2752).

[1023] *Eclogae ex diversis homiliis,* 2,; PG 63, 585A. Quoted by CCC, n. 2743.

[1024] St. Augustine thought that "the whole life of a good Christian is a holy desire" *(In Epis. I Johannis, IV, 6).* This desire opens the human heart to the presence of God (cf. *Soliloquies,* 31).

or to lift up our hands? Is this what he meant in saying 'Pray without ceasing'? Even if we admit that we pray in this fashion, I do not believe that we can do so all the time.

Yet there is another, *interior kind of prayer without ceasing, namely, the desire of the heart.* Whatever else you may be doing, if you fix your desire on God's Sabbath rest, your prayer will be ceaseless. Therefore, if you wish to pray without ceasing, do not cease to desire."[1025]

So, "desire always prays, even if the tongue should be silent. If you are always experiencing desire you are always praying. When does prayer sleep? When desire has grown cold."[1026]

However, in another sermon St. Augustine also identifies unceasing prayer - understood as "praising God all day long" - with the "right deeds" performed by good Christians, as did Origen.[1027]

St. Augustine explains that the nature of the continual desire of God understood as unceasing prayer is the response given to God by the three theological virtues acting in concert:

"In faith, hope and charity themselves we pray always with a constant desire."[1028]

Aquinas reinterprets this Augustinian understanding of unceasing prayer by saying that the desire of charity does not really perform but rather

---

[1025] *Enarrationes in Psalmos,* Ps. 37, n. 13-14, in LITURGY, vol. I, p. 330 Emphasis ours. The same passage is quoted also by RAMSEY, p. 171, 172, in a slightly different translation.

[1026] *Sermo,* 80, 7. Quoted by RAMSEY, p. 172. Emphasis ours.

[1027] *Enarrationes in Psalmos,* Ps 34, 2, 16; EA n. 577, p. 307: "Et cuius lingua durat meditari tota die laudem Dei?... Tota die Deum laudare quis durat? Suggero remedium unde tota die laudes Deum, si vis. *Quidquid egeris, bene age, et laudasti Deum.* Quando cantas hymnum laudasti Deum... Cessasti ab hymno cantando, discedis, ut reficiaris? Noli inebriari... Noli fraudem facere... Noli litem movere, et laudasti Deum. *In innocentia operum tuorum praepara te ad laudandum Deum tota die."* See also: "Laudes vultis dicere Deo? Vos estote quod dicatis. Laus ipsius estis si bene vivatis."

[1028] *Epistula CXXX,* cap, 9, PL 33; 501. Translation from *The Fathers of the Church: St. Augustine,* vol. II, p. 390. Cf. *Enchiridion,* 3, PL 40; 232.

commands the acts of prayer.[1029] This explanation of Aquinas manifestly takes prayer in a strict sense as an act of worship elicited from the virtue of religion.[1030]

St. Thomas, however, often admits that Christians offer to God "interior worship" by believing, hoping, and loving him,[1031] which is hardly different from St. Augustine's understanding of unceasing prayer.[1032]

In fact, according to Aquinas, faith, hope and charity directly attain God himself, so that through these virtues Christians can enjoy the divine Persons in a manner analogous to the way the human intellect and will enjoy their known and loved objects.[1033] Therefore a form of unceasing prayer as communion can be brought about by the synergy of the three theological virtues, by whose "desire" praying Christians are always united with the Divine Persons, as Augustine thought.

Also St. Catherine of Siena shows herself to be a disciple of St. Augustine when from the very beginning of *The Dialogue* she continually asserts that:

[1029] "We may speak about prayer in two ways: first, in itself, secondly, in its cause. The cause of prayer is the desire of charity, and this desire ought to be with us continually, either actually or virtually. Virtually, this desire is present in all actions which are prompted by charity, and thus we ought *to do all things for the glory of God* (1 Cor 10:31). In this sense prayer ought to be continual, and hence Augustine says , *'Faith, hope and charity are a prayer of continual longing*'" (II-II, q. 83, a. 14, co.; BLACKFRIARS, vol. 39, pp. 87-89). Emphasis ours.

[1030] Cf. ST, II-II, q, 83, a. 3.

[1031] ST, I-II, q. 109, a. 3, co.; q. 101, a. 2, co.; q. 103, a. 3, co.; II-II, q. 101, a. 3, ad 1um.

[1032] "With regard to the worship of the heart, which is made up of prayer and devotion, man is led more by the prompting of the Holy Spirit" (II-II, q. 122, a. 4, co.; BLACKFRIARS, vol. 41, p. 303).

[1033] "...in whom (= intelligent being) God is said to be present as the known in the knower and the loved in the lover. And because by these acts of knowing and loving the intelligent being touches God himself, by reason of this equal way of being present we have the teaching that God is not merely in the intelligent creature, but dwells there as in his temple. No other effect but sanctifying grace, then, is the explanation of the divine person's being present to the intelligent being in this way" (I, q. 43, a. 3, co. Cf. ad 1um; BLACKFRIARS, vol. 7, p. 217).

> "A soul rises up, restless with *tremendous desire* for God's honor and the salvation of souls... in *continual humble prayer...* by such prayer the soul is united with God... *this desire of hers was great and continuous...*
>
> *Having a good and holy desire is continual prayer...* loving charity is continual prayer... The soul speaks to me (= God) with the tongue of holy and *constant prayer, that is the mouth of her holy desire.*"[1034]

She strongly emphasizes the permanence and firmness of this prayer of good and holy desire, particularly in Christians who have attained great perfection and are completely dead to their selfishness.

> "I (= God) am always at rest in their souls by grace and by feeling. For through their loving affection their desire has reached such union that nothing can separate it (from me). *Every time and place is for them a time and place of prayer.*"[1035]

To the Augustinian explanation of unceasing prayer as continuous desire, Catherine adds her own conviction that "when the soul is grounded in charity her desire must reach to the infinite"[1036] for it continues even after death, even when the soul reaches God, her final goal.

> *"Because desire has no end it cannot be satisfied in this life.* Rather, the more it loves, the less it seems to itself to love... But once the soul is separated from the body and has reached me (= God), her final goal, *she does not on that account give up her desire* so as to no longer desire me and the charity of her neighbor... What has ended is suffering, because if she longs for me she now possesses me in truth without any fear of being able to lose what she has long desired.
>
> This is how she feeds the flame (of desire), for the more she hungers the more she is filled, and the more she is sated, the more she hungers. But her satiety is far from boredom, and her hunger far from pain, for here she lacks no perfection. *So your desire is an infinite thing...*
>
> *For I who am infinite God want you to serve me with what is infinite, and you have nothing infinite except your soul's love desire... (In heaven) she*

[1034] Chs. 1, 2, 66, 76, pp. 25, 27, 126-127, 140. Emphasis ours.

[1035] *Ibid.,* ch. 78, p. 145. Emphasis ours. Until the very last day of her life Catherine was offering "sweet, loving and sorrowful desires, with tears, and with humble, continuous and faithful prayers". See in GILLET, p. 126.

[1036] *Ibid.,* ch. 11, p. 43.

(= *the soul) never ceases her constant offering of her desires,* blessed now and painlessly tearful. Hers are no physical tears now but the Holy Spirit's tears of fire."[1037]

Unceasing prayer, explained by Christian spiritual masters as continual spiritual worship and/or the heart's continuous desire was virtually identified with "the contemplative dimension" of Christian life by the following Document of the Sacred Congregation of Religious and Secular Institutes.

> "We describe the contemplative dimension fundamentally as the theological response of faith, hope and charity, by which the believer opens up to the revelation of the living God and to communion with him through Christ in the Holy Spirit...
>
> (It is) the unifying act of all human movements towards God, *the constant desire and search for God...* (from which) there results in the religious an attitude of *continuous and humble adoration of God's mysterious presence* in people, events, and things."[1038]

In fact, this document asserts that "the contemplative dimension" unifies both the constant desire and the continuous adoration of God.

CCC also unifies these two interpretations of unceasing prayer by virtue of the "untiring fervor of love", which in Christian life inspires and permeates both prayer and good deeds.[1039]

iii. *Unceasing Prayer and the Activity of Prayer*

Walter Hilton gives the following ample description of unceasing prayer:

> "I am nothing; I have nothing; I desire only one thing. You shall have the meaning of these words *continually in your intention and in the habit of your soul,* even though you may not always have their particular form in

---

[1037] *Ibid.,* ch. 92, pp. 170-171. Emphasis ours. Cf. The "limitlessness" of the human spirit's growth even in heaven was strongly emphasized by Gregory of Nyssa.

[1038] CDRL, n. 1. Emphasis ours.

[1039] Cf. CCC, n. 2742-2745.

your thought, for that is not necessary. Humility says, I am nothing; I have nothing. Love says, I desire only one thing, and that is Jesus.

These two strings, *well-fastened with mindfulness of Jesus,* make good harmony as the harp of the soul when they are skillfully touched with the finger of the reason."[1040]

Meister Eckhart writes that unceasing prayer is:

> *"Having only God, thinking only of God,* and all things are for him (= the prayerful Christian) nothing but God... (He) *regards, seeks and tastes nothing but God,* for God is united with that man in all his aims."[1041]
>
> "This true possession of God depends on the mind, on *inner mental turning and striving towards God* – but not in a continuous and equal thinking of Him, for that would be impossible for nature to strive for."[1042]

It is not easy to put such a "continual humility and charity well-fastened with mindfulness of Jesus" or such an habitual "having only God, thinking only of God by an inner mental turning and striving towards God" into simple and distinct intellectual categories. Perhaps the best way of elucidating the attitude of unceasing prayer described by these phrases is to compare it with the more understandable acts of prayer.

A contemporary author thinks that in every activity of true prayer an attitude of prayer, which is the common substratumm of all Christian prayerlife, is presupposed.

> *"All prayer begins with an invocation whose purpose is to signify the divine presence and to stir up accordingly the inner attitude of the praying person,* who has to render himself attentive to God... Whatever might be the forms that prayer takes, *the effort of putting oneself in the presence of God precedes and accompanies all the acts of prayer...*
>
> In the end, the essential element of prayer is the reciprocal presence of God and of the praying person. Unless one wants to sidestep *true prayer,* it is always necessary to end up with this presence in the heart."[1043]

[1040] HILTON, II, ch. 21, p. 228. The first is author's emphasis. Other emphasis is ours.

[1041] MEISTER ECKHART, vol. III, p. 177.

[1042] *Ibid.,* p. 17. Emphasis ours.

[1043] BERNARD C.A., p. 36, 362, 371. Translation and emphasis ours.

An inner attentiveness to the divine presence is essential to prayerlife. Actually, the divine presence and the inner responsive attitude toward it must precede, accompany, and conclude all acts of prayer. But such an inner attitude, which seems to be made of the same stuff as "unceasing prayer", can be either embryonic or fully grown.

a. The God-given seeds of unceasing prayer

We will first compare embryonic unceasing prayer with the acts of prayer.

There is in the baptized a fundamental and permanent union with Christ and an elevation to the divine sonship which precedes the fully lived experience. The baptized are permanently grafted onto Christ by the sacramental character, which makes them participants in Christ's priesthood, and their spirit is infused with sanctifying grace and the theological virtues, through which they become God's adopted children.

These supernatural gifts given by God are the seeds of the habitual attitude of unceasing prayer, which becomes fully developed through the practice of prayer. Fully grown unceasing prayer is the flowering of the ontological and psychological permanent union with Christ and God that all Christians receive by grace through baptism.

The participation in Christ's priesthood through the practice of prayer as worship produces a permanent attitude of spiritual worship, which permeates the whole life of the Christian. The union of love with the Divine Persons through the practice of prayer as communion produces a permanent attitude of loving awareness of God's presence, which pervades the whole life of the Christian.

These two permanent prayerful attitudes are not mutually exclusive but complementary as to reinform one another. Together they create in the Christian an orientation towards God which is both effective and affective.

When the participation in the priesthood of Christ, sanctifying grace and theological virtues are still at the beginning of their growth, they give Christians only an embryonic attitude, or better, a fundamental aptitude, for the fully grown attitude of unceasing prayer.

The recent CCC clearly states the rootedness of unceasing prayer in the grafting of the baptized onto Christ:

> "In the New Covenant prayer is the living relation of the children of God with their infinitely good Father, with his Son Jesus Christ and the Holy

> Spirit... Hence the life of prayer consists in being habitually in the presence of the thrice Holy God and in communion with him. *Such a communion of life is always possible, because, by means of Baptism, we became only one being with Christ.* Prayer is Christian insofar as it is communion with Christ and expands into the Church which is Christ's Body. Its dimensions are those of the Love of Christ."[1044]

André Louf does not hesitate to term *state of prayer* the beginning attitude or, better still, the aptitude, involved in the sanctifying grace infused into the Christian by means of baptism; although he acknowledges that it is still like a treasure hidden in our sleeping heart or like dry wood not yet set ablaze.

> "We received prayer along with grace, in our baptism.[1045] The state of grace, as we call it, at the level of the heart, actually signifies a *state of prayer.* From then on, in the profoundest depths of the self, we have a continuing contact with God. God's Holy Spirit has taken us over, has assumed complete possession of us; he has become breath of our breath and Spirit of our spirit. It takes our heart in tow and turns it towards God.
>
> He is the Spirit, Paul says, who speaks without ceasing to our spirit and testifies to the fact that we are children of God. All the time, in fact, the Spirit is calling within us and He prays, Abba-Father, with supplications and sighs that cannot be put into words but never for an instant cease within our hearts (Rm 8:15; Ga 4:6).
>
> This *state of prayer* is something we always carry about like a hidden treasure... we do not feel it. We are deaf to our praying heart, love's savour escapes us, we fail to see the light in which we live. For our heart, our true heart, is asleep... It must be brought to the surface of our consciousness... Prayer is nothing other than that unconscious *state of prayer* which in the course of time has become completely conscious...
>
> Little by little we must advance on the road to prayer. The technique is always the same. To rid our heart of its surrounding dross; to listen to it where it is already at prayer; to yield ourselves to that prayer until the Spirit's prayer becomes our own."[1046]

[1044] CCC, n. 2565. Emphasis ours.

[1045] This author does not mention the Christian participation in the priesthood of Christ through the sacramental character because he is entirely concerned with prayer as communion and, at least here, he does not pay any attention to prayer as worship.

[1046] LOUF, p. 18-19 and 22. Author's emphasis.

The formal activity of prayer develops the germinal *state of prayer* hidden in the heart and little by little it forms a fully grown attitude of unceasing prayer.

b. Gaining the fully grown attitude of unceasing prayer

Contemporary spiritual literature suggests various prayer exercises which should be practiced in order to form the full grown attitude of unceasing prayer. Some of these suggestions are:

> "The attitude of prayer originates in the act of prayer itself and consists in *introducing certain elements of contemplation into the routine of daily life.* For instance, if we frequently recollect ourselves and establish the consciousness of the presence of God, a series of 'stations of prayer' will be set up in the course of the day which will draw closer and closer together.
>
> From contemplation with its explicit focusing on God we may develop a *general attitude of reverence which permeates the day's activity,* imparting to it a religious character. We receive what happens as coming from the Father and offer our own work up to Him.
>
> Out of the general attitude of reverence which permeates the day's activity develops what is called *'moving in the presence of God' or 'life in the sight of God',* a permanent consciousness and feeling that God is at work in every event, and we see ourselves in a holy association with Him in the light of which we understand our life from hour to hour."[1047]
>
> *"A prayerful contemplation of the sanctifying word of God is called for,* so that we may be able to use God's good creatures according to his mind. And however much, in doing so, all our human powers come into play, our use of the creatures must always be 'of the truth' and 'in the truth', in *an attitude of prayer which has become habitual, an attitude of reverent worship of the divine truth, in which all the world's truth, even the most profane, is rooted.* Hence the admonition to *pray without ceasing* (1 Th 5:25 et passim)."[1048]

The authors implicitly suggest that the cause of the fully grown habitual attitude of prayer is the long practice of prayer which preceded it. Hassel puts it explicitly:

[1047] GUARDINI, pp. 123-124. Emphasis ours.

[1048] VON BALTHASAR, p. 80. Emphasis ours.

> *"That deep attitude developed gradually over many years of prayer,* contains one's deepest values and is the power behind all one's activities."[1049]

This happens because any repeated psychic activity stamps on the acting subject a habitual readiness to respond to the same object or to opt for the same value about which the activity is performed. Meister Eckhart illustrates this well-known psychic phenomenon by means of a simile and then applies the illustration to the life of prayer:

> "It is just like learning to write: truly if a man has to acquire an art, he must apply himself and practice hard, however heavy and bitter a task it seems to him, and however impossible. If he is prepared to practice diligently and often, he will learn and master the art.
>
> Of course, at first he has to remember every letter and fix it firmly in his mind. Later on, when he has acquired the art, he will be completely free of the image and will not have to stop and think, but will write fluently and freely - and the same with playing the fiddle or any other task that requires skill. All he needs to know is that he intends to exercise his skill, and even if he is not paying full attention, wherever his thoughts may stray, he will do the job because he has the skill.
>
> *Thus a man should be pervaded with God's presence, transformed with the form of his beloved God, and made essential by Him, so that God's presence shines for him without any efforts...* But first there must be thought and attentive study, just as with a pupil in any art."[1050]

Any activity of genuine Christian prayer suffices to form the attitude of unceasing prayer. Doubtless though, the so-called contemplative attitude of unceasing prayer is especially formed by acts of prayer as communion. For that attitude is the outcome of a communion with God by love which eventually becomes "a silent longing between the soul and God."[1051]

> "When your *stretching toward God becomes habitual and penetrates every thought, word and deed, you could be called a "contemplative"...* That consists fundamentally in standing before God, not with one faculty perceiving some facet of God. It is heart speaking to heart. It is the return of your whole being back to God as a gift that expresses *the attitude which we*

[1049] HASSEL, p. 131. Emphasis ours.

[1050] MEISTER ECKHART, vol. III, p. 19. Emphasis ours.

[1051] GUARDINI, p. 105.

> *could call worship-prayer, the ultimate point of true love which is called contemplation.*"[1052]

In order to form in himself the fully grown contemplative loving attitude of unceasing prayer, a Christian should be encouraged

> "To make, during his daily period of meditation and 'conversation', short pauses of *loving attention to God.* He must be reminded that moments of silence between friends can be as eloquent as any amount of chatter."[1053]

This prayer, through which we become

> "Open to the Holy Spirit's presence", is to be practiced "firstly by pausing frequently for a short time during the day, saying nothing and allowing our gaze to rest in God... *we are secure in the presence of God and we rejoice in his nearness...* standing silently in the presence of God."[1054]
>
> "Each of us can take time during prayer, whether only a few moments or much longer, *just to sit and be there quietly in the presence of God,* asking for nothing, saying nothing, thinking about nothing in particular, but *just aware of God's presence.*"[1055]

That is an activity of prayer which develops

> "Beyond thought, beyond imagination, and beyond all images. We simply rest with the Reality, *the realized Presence of God himself dwelling within our hearts.*"[1056]

All the authors quoted immediately above seem to speak of a form of prayer which has been called "prayer of presence", a prayer

---

[1052] MALONEY [2], p. 129-130. Emphasis ours. This author does not distinguish between what he calls "worship-prayer" and contemplative prayer. Certainly because at the highest stages of prayerlife prayer as communion and prayer as worship fuse into a single prayerful orientation towards God.

[1053] BUTLER, p. 131. Emphasis ours.

[1054] BOROS, p. 5, 7. Emphasis ours.

[1055] BONDI, p. 100. Emphasis ours.

[1056] MAIN, p. 16.

> "Acquired by certain means, under the assistance of ordinary grace, and (which) requires a transformation of one's personality and environment."[1057]

But, outside the concrete practice of a particular form of prayer, the presence of God in prayer

> "Will come sometimes in words and sometimes at a curious baffling level where there are neither words nor thought."[1058]

Perhaps, because of these non-conceptual prayer experiences, some authors think that the "prayer of presence" is a profound God-given awareness of him realized rather unexpectedly and hardly the result of human effort.

> "There are spontaneous moments of prayer when, indeliberately as it were, we are *aware of God's presence to us.* Such moments may occur, even in the life of a beginner in prayer."[1059]

The various moments of God's presence, acquired or infused, will eventually form a state of prayer, a spontaneous readiness, an attitude of loving awareness of God's presence in the Christian. By this means they have

> "learnt to respond to God habitually - to open themselves to an abiding experience of his presence in their lives."[1060]

This transforms the whole Christian existence into prayer for

> "Our prayer has become identical with *the essential attitude of our being in front of God. It is our whole being which is continually in prayer,* a prayer without form, but which takes all forms of our life and activity."[1061]
>
> "The words of the Lord that we ought 'always to pray and not to faint' (Lk 18:1) mean, in the first place, the earnestness with which the

[1057] VAN KAAM AND MUTO, p. 12.

[1058] HUME, p. 121.

[1059] GREEN, p. 104. Emphasis ours. Cf. RAGUIN, p. 29.

[1060] *Ibid,*. p. 105.

[1061] RAGUIN, p. 20. Emphasis ours.

> believer calls to the Father for help until his prayer is answered; but beyond this they mean the constancy of prayer in general, through which it should develop from a specific practice to an intrinsic part of our life and from an act to *an attitude or state of being... not an exceptional state but a permanent element of an existence which is directed towards God, extended to every aspect of his (i.e., the praying Christian's) daily life... Here life becomes prayer.*"[1062]

In fact, fully grown unceasing prayer "contains one's deepest values and is the power behind all one's activities."[1063]

> For "prayer makes sense only if it is lived. Unless they are 'lived', unless *life and prayer become completely interwoven,* prayer becomes a sort of polite madrigal which we offer to God at moments when we are giving time to him."[1064]

c. Feeding fully grown unceasing prayer

When the attitude of unceasing prayer is acquired by God's grace and through human practice, it must be fed continuously by repeated acts of prayer. The following will suffice to make this point quite clearly.

After writing of

> "Those men and women who by long labor of body and soul - or else by such sharp striking of love as I mentioned - come into rest of spirit, so that their affection is turned into spiritual savor, and so that they can pray in their heart continually, glorifying and praising God without great hindrance from temptations or vanities,"

Hilton adds:

> "I shall pray inwardly in my spirit, without labor, by feeling spiritual savor and sweetness in the love and sight of God, by which sight and love my soul shall be fed."

[1062] GUARDINI, p. 123-124. Emphasis ours.

[1063] HASSEL, p. 131.

[1064] BLOOM, p. 58. Emphasis ours.

But he also reminds us that whoever has attained this grade of prayer,

> "Shall nourish the fire of love in his heart with holy psalms, pure thoughts and fervent desires, so that it never goes out."[1065]

When unceasing prayer is still potential and dormant in the divine supernatural gifts granted to the Christian, the acts of prayer performed by him or her serve to stir and make it grow by their repetition. But when the attitude of unceasing prayer is fully grown, then the acts of prayer, which bob about on the consciousness of the Christian, serve both to express and to nourish that attitude.

Hence, the prayerful Christian who has a fully grown attitude of unceasing prayer can hardly dispense himself or herself from making enough time every day for concrete exercises of prayer. Neglecting often to act in this way would certainly make the Christian lose his or her fully grown attitude of unceasing prayer.

> "One cannot pray 'at all times' unless one is willing to pray at the set times when Christian prayer is more intensive and longer."[1066]

[1065] HILTON, II, ch. 39, pp. 102-103 passim.

[1066] CCC, n. 2697.

CHAPTER XII

THE ATTITUDE OF PRAYERFULNESS

Prayer becomes unceasing when its influence permeates the whole life of the praying Christian. The qualification "unceasing" directly refers to the continuity or permanence of prayer throughout the whole life of the Christian. But such a continuity cannot really occur unless prayer permeates the whole personality of the praying Christian, by reaching to his or her spiritual depths and remaining there as a permanent attitude of the spirit.

The persuasion that at a certain stage of its growth process prayer becomes a spiritual attitude of the praying Christian's personality is often expressed in contemporary literature on prayer. The ancient spiritual masters apparently said the same when they asserted that prayer becomes perfect when it sinks into the "heart". For by "heart" they meant that innermost unifying structure and principle of activity of the whole person that modern psychology is wont to call "personality".[1067]

i. *The Use and Meaning of "Attitude" in Prayerlife*

a. *"Attitude" in current literature on prayer*

Contemporary authors often use the word "attitude" when they write about prayer. Here is a sampling of how they employ that word.

> "(In) an existence which is directed towards God... (there is) the contemplative approach, *a general attitude* of reverence which permeates the day's activity."[1068]
>
> "Prayer is simply an inward grace of knowledge and love turned towards God... It is possible to remain in this *attitude* of loving attention to God even in the midst of the most absorbing occupations... Application to the

---

[1067] Cf. ŠPIDLÍK, pp. 266-271.

[1068] GUARDINI, p. 123-124.

task is perfectly compatible with a *permanent inward attitude of love for the beloved.*"[1069]

"Times of prayer set up *a frame of mind* which remains through all our activities, so that, as Herbert Waddams has expressed it, 'all our work and play is coloured by *a prayerlike attitude*'."[1070]

"The presence of God simply describes the principle of *the praying attitude, the inner attitude* of the praying person."[1071]

"Underlying each diverse manifestation of prayer is a *radical attitude.*"[1072]

"Prayer without ceasing, as a continuous state of soul, is primarily an *attitude* of heart and will... Love without ceasing is not a series of acts, but a *continuous attitude and state...* Prayer without ceasing is first of all an *attitude* of the will."[1073]

So, there is a prayer which

"has become identical with *the essential attitude of our being in front of God,*"[1074] "an *habitual attitude* of reverent worship of the divine truth,"[1075] "a *continuous state of being, a constant attitude.*"[1076]

But what do all these authors really mean when they speak of an "inward, inner, general, essential, radical, permanent, constant, continuous, habitual, prayerlike *attitude?"*

Before trying to give an answer to this question, it is in order to clarify the meaning of the word attitude.

1069 DUJAT, p. 116-117.

1070 MACQUARRIE, p. 38,

1071 BERNARD, C.A., p. 362. Translation ours.

1072 HASSEL [2], p. 1.

1073 WRIGHT, pp. 167, 168, 170.

1074 RAGUIN, [2], p. 20.

1075 VON BALTHASAR [2], p. 80.

1076 MALONEY [2], pp. 129-130. All emphasis in the preceding quotes is ours.

b. The meaning of psychological attitude

The easier way of explaining the meaning of the psychological attitude is to compare and contrast it with the similar better-known concept of *habitus.*

We will not translate the Latin word *habitus* as habit or habitude. Our reason for retaining the Latin is that a *habitus* is an active human disposition voluntarily acquired by the human person through his or her free, constant and energetic practice. But habits or habitudes are active human dispositions often involuntarily acquired by getting into a rut or routine, i.e., by more or less instinctively following the easiest way of doing things. The *habitus* is freely used by the person who has freely acquired it; whereas the habit or habitude results from routine reaction or unreflective behavior which can even create compulsiveness in some people.

Both the habitus and the attitude are enduring free responses and presuppose some aptitude for and inclination of the person towards reality. They differ because their extension and depth in the person's psyche is not the same, and they enable the person to give different responses to reality.

These differences originate in the fact that the *habitus* is caused by the repetition of the person's acts, whereas the habitual attitude is caused by the repetition of the person's options. Acts and options differ from one another because the person responds to different aspects of reality through them, and they spring forth from different sources within the person.

Acts reach specific objects. Objects meet specific needs of the person. Specific objects can be clearly conceptualized. The clarity of the objects is carried over into the acts so that the latter's nature can be clearly defined by their specific objects.

Options regard human values and receive their distinctiveness from the values toward which they are oriented. Values are determining factors of a life project, but do not allow such a clear conceptualization as the specific objects of the acts do. Thus options are not strictly definable by the values they choose and strive for as the acts are by their objects. Hence the intellectual clarity which makes acts understandable does not shine in the options.

Acts are elicited from the person's specific faculties. Options are made by the whole person in whom all faculties are unified in a single operative cluster. Therefore, options are more comprehensive, more profoundly embedded, more lasting in the person than acts; and so characterize the acting person more than acts.

Repetitions of the same acts and of the same options impress on the acting person firmly settled and lasting dispositions of readiness to act or to opt again in conformity with those acts or those options. The habitual disposition impressed on the acting person by the repetition of the same acts was termed *habitus* by Scholastic philosophers and theologians.[1077] The habitual disposition stamped in the acting person by repetition of the same options is called *attitude* by contemporary psychologists and moralists.

Here is a sample collection of contemporary psychologists' descriptions of attitude.

> "An attitude is a state of mind of the individual toward a value."[1078]
>
> "An attitude is a mental and neural state of readiness organized through experience, exerting a dynamic direct influence upon the individual's response to all objects and situations with which it is related... An enduring organization of motivational, emotional, perceptual and cognitive processes with respect to some aspect of the individual's world."[1079]
>
> "Attitudes are dispositions expressing a state of readiness to respond... (They) carry out an expressive function *in relation to the values* and serve as mediators between them and the behavior."[1080]
>
> (An attitude is) *"an habitually lived value,* which inspires and molds the activity flowing from it...developed gradually through many years of practice, *containing one's purest values* and is the power behind all one's activity. Nothing that one does escapes its influence."[1081]
>
> (An attitude is) "a mental and neural state of readiness to respond, organized through experience, exerting a directive and/or dynamic influence on mental and physical activity, and may have *a value-expressive function when the attitude is adopted in order to realize the values held by the subject."*[1082]
>
> The attitude is an "acquired reality: a selective manner of turning to certain objects; *the recognition in these objects of significant values for the*

[1077] CF. ST. I-II, qq. 49-54. Cf. TURIEL.

[1078] Allport, G. W. Quoted by JOHODA AND WARREN, p. 19. "A value is the objective counterpart of the attitude, and the attitude is the individual counterpart of the value.": *Ibid.,* p. 23. "Values are usually social in nature, that is to say, they are objects of common regard on the part of socialized men. Love of money, desire for fame, hatred of foreigners, etc., are values.": *Ibid.,* p. 19.

[1079] JOHODA AND WARREN, p. 23.

[1080] RULLA IMODA RIDICK, p. 32-33. Emphasis ours.

[1081] HASSEL, p. 76, 131. Emphasis ours.

[1082] RULLA, pp. 157-158. Emphasis ours.

subject... The attitude has to be confirmed by a commitment, for the meaning of the whole life requires a firm and stable position able to subtend every phase of existence in its intensity even more than its duration."[1083]

"By attitude I mean that it is a set or disposition of the whole person, a stance or posture which one takes up towards experience or sectors of experience, and from which one relates to such experience... (Attitudes) include some definite 'feel' for the world, and thus give some definite color or tone to experience. Such attitudes also promote some kind of behaviour rather than others, and encourage a measure of consistency in behaviour."[1084]

Hence, just as the repetition of acts causes the *habitus,* the persistence in a person of an option, stance or posture towards experience and reality beings forth an habitual attitude.

The *habitus* is a quality permanently disposing the person's operative capacity or faculty to specific acts. The Scholastic concept of *habitus* was articulated within the framework of the Aristotelian psychology of faculties. From that framework the concept of *habitus* derives both its usefulness and limitation.

The habitual attitude is a quality permanently disposing the whole individual personality to make general options. Therefore it encompasses all the capacities or faculties of the person.

The *habitus* gives the faculty of a permanent readiness to elicit acts and adds easiness and pleasantness to the performance of them. The habitual attitude similarly gives the individual personality a permanent readiness to make certain options and adds an analogous easiness and pleasantness to the actual making of them.

The total personality does not always need to be explicitly involved in each actualization of the *habitus,* because the *habitus* is rooted in a specific faculty, which is the only one directly actualized when the subject acts according to that *habitus*. On the contrary, the whole individual personality – viz., all the person's faculties united in only one operative cluster – is involved in each actualization of the habitual attitude, as the habitual attitude permeates the whole personality. Consequently, the very fact of having an habitual

---

[1083] PERRAULT, p. 55 and p. 60. Emphasis ours.

[1084] MACQUARRIE [3], p. 5.

attitude gives the whole personality of the individual a permanent readiness to easily and pleasantly opt again for the same value.[1085]

The differences between the *habitus* and the habitual attitude pointed out so far show that the gap between the acting person and reality can be bridged by two different psychic processes whose successive steps compound two distinct responses. Each step of both responses links up with the next, like links in the same chain.

The former response, whose central link is this *habitus,* joins the person to reality according to the following chain: person + faculty → *habitus* → act → object + reality.

The latter response, wherein the habitual attitude is the center, joins the person to reality according to the following chain: person + personality → *habitual attitude* → option → value + reality.

The notion of the persons' habitual attitude so far explained can help us to understand the habitual attitude of prayer.[1086]

ii. *The Spiritual Contents of the Attitude of Prayer*

Being a response of the praying person to reality, the attitude of prayer can be considered either from the side of its objective value, from which it receives its distinctiveness, or from the side of its subjective source from which it draws its spiritual consistence. We will begin to study the attitude of prayer from the side of its objective value.

[1085] According to Aquinas, the human faculties, each one of them perfected by its specific good *habitus,* are united as in a whole operative cluster by the virtue of prudence in the realm of natural Ethic and by the virtue of charity in the realm of supernatural Morality. See WILLIAMS. We believe that with this theory Aquinas virtually admits habitual attitudes of the individual personality.

In the New Testament the concept of attitude is seemingly expressed by the Greek verb *froneō.* A significant use of this verb can be found in St. Paul's exhortation: "Have among yourself the same *attitude* that is also yours in Christ Jesus." (Ph 2:5; translation of NAB. Emphasis ours).

[1086] The concept of "fundamental option" used today by moral theologians resembles our idea of habitual attitude. See, e.g., KEANE, p. 38: "Fundamental option is the stable orientation or life direction that exists in the core level of the human person." This concept is clearly distinct from that of *habitus* and cannot replace it for understanding the highly complex matter that makes up moral life. See CESSARIO, p. 62.

a. Opting for the divine presence

As the psychological attitude is a state of readiness or an habitual active disposition of the personality to opt for a value, it is in order to ask what value does the attitude of prayer make the praying Christian opt for? We think that the attitude of prayer creates in prayerful Christians the state of readiness to opt for Christ's and the Divine Persons' Presence as the most significant value of their existence.

St. Teresa of Avila, for one, often and in many ways describes her opting for God's Presence. Here are a few significant passages from her writings.

> "Although we are always in the presence of God, it seems to me that those who practice prayer are especially *(de otra manera)* so, because they can see *(estan viendo)* all the time that He is looking at them, whereas others may be in God's presence for several days without ever remembering that He can see."[1087]

This "seeing" all the time that God is looking at the praying Christian at times takes an imaginative form.

> "The soul can picture itself in the presence of Christ *(delante de Cristo)* and accustoms itself to become enkindled with great love *(enamorarse mucho)* for his sacred humanity and to have him ever with it *(traerle siempre consigo)* and speak with him, make complaints to him of its trials, rejoice with him in its joys.[1088]

When praying Christians reach the Teresian innermost "mansion" of the "interior castle" their enjoyment of the Divine Persons' marvelous company attains its climax. At that stage the Divine Persons clearly manifest their presence, commune and talk with praying Christians in the deepest recesses of their souls.[1089] This experience is also accompanied by an insightful inflamed

---

[1087] TERESA OF AVILA, vol. I, *Life,* p. 49.

[1088] *Ibid.,* p. 71.

[1089] *Moradas,* VII, ch. 1, n. 6 and 7: "Se le communican todas tres Personas, y la hablan y la dan a entender...en lo muy interior, en una cosa muy honda."

intellectual vision and profound understanding of the Divine Persons within a cloud of very bright clarity.[1090]

This living in the presence of Christ and the Divine Persons and communing with them does not remain confined within the self, but overflows from its depths and permeates the charitable encounters of the prayerful Christian with his or her brothers and sisters. Actually, a holy Christian, who really loves her neighbor for Jesus' sake, senses that Jesus, whom she experiences abidingly present within her, loves the neighbor through her:

> "Yes, I feel it, when I am charitable, it is Jesus alone who is acting in me; the more united I am with him, the more also do I love my sisters."[1091]

Besides, from their living in the presence of Christ in prayer good Christians draw their seeing, loving and serving Christ himself in all human beings.

> *"We try to pray through our work by doing it with Jesus, for Jesus, to Jesus.* That helps us *put our whole heart and soul into doing it.* The dying, the crippled, the mentally ill, the unwanted, the unloved – *they are Jesus in disguise...* You must make the poor feel loved and wanted. *They are Jesus for me.* I believe in that much more than doing big things for them"[1092]

These words uttered by Mother Teresa of Calcutta, about herself and on behalf of her Sisters, pointedly express her and their state of readiness to "see" Jesus and serve him in the poor, sick and needy. This is a state of readiness, an inner habitual attitude which overflows from their prayerlife into their daily activity. It has been called virtual prayer or prayer in action.

[1090] *Ibid.*, n. 6: "Por visión intellectual...con una inflamación...a manera de una nube de grandísima claridad...por una noticia admirable que se da al alma, entiende con grandisima verdad."

[1091] "Oui je le sens, lorsque je suis charitable, c'est Jésus seul que agit en moi: plus je suis unie à Lui, plus aussi j'aime toutes mes soeurs.": St. Therese of the Infant Jesus quoted by DALEY, p. 72. Translation ours. St. Catherine of Siena described this experience as an exchange of her heart with the heart of Jesus. Cf. GILLET, pp. 56-62.

[1092] DESMOND, p. 48. Emphasis ours. The words quoted contain the leit-motiv of all the instructions that Mother Teresa has been giving to her Sisters. See FELDMANN, p. 83.

> "Virtual prayer – prayer in action, whereby we express our love, faith, and devotion to God primarily by actions of loving service toward our fellow human beings. The emphasis is about purity of intention, i.e., *keeping the thought and will of God constantly in the forefront of our mind as we go about doing the work of the Lord and serving the needs of our brethren.*"[1093]

Caring for the poor and needy as if they were Jesus himself has always been a characteristic of good Christians. An ancient Father of the Church addressed the following words to the Christians of his time:

> "Servants of Christ, his brethren and coheirs, let us visit Christ whenever we may: let us care for him, feed him, clothe him, welcome him, honor him... Let us show him mercy in the persons of the poor!"[1094]

And the *Liturgy of the Hours* contains this petition:

> "Forgive us Lord, for failing to see Christ in the poor, the distressed and the troublesome, and for our failure to reverence your Son in their persons."[1095]

Not only the poor, sick and needy are "Jesus in disguise" for prayerful Christians, but also all brothers and sisters in Christ. Some early Christian writers attributed to Christ a maxim not recorded in the canonical Gospels:

> "Have you seen a brother? You have seen God!"[1096]

So, according to the Christian spiritual tradition the presence of Jesus and of the Divine Persons can be experienced and seen by prayerful Christians

---

[1093] CHESTER-MORRISEY, p. 185. Emphasis ours.

[1094] Saint Gregory of Nazianzus, *Oratio 14: De pauperum amore,* 38, 40 PG 35; 907-910. Translation of LITURGY, vol. II, pp. 266-267.

[1095] LITURGY, vol. II, p. 289. All Christian tradition of seeing Jesus and caring for him in the needy is founded in Mt 25:31-46.

[1096] St. Clement of Alexandria, *Stromateis,* I, 19; II, 15, 17. Tertullian, *De Oratione,* 26. The Greek Life of St. Pachomius, 22 and 48, reads: "because of the purity of his heart Pachomius could see the invisible God in a visible man, his temple." Quoted by ROUSSEAU, p. 130.

both in themselves and in all human beings. But what does the term "presence" really mean, particularly when it is applied to Christ and the Divine Persons?

b. The meaning of divine presence

Presence is a personal togetherness or intimacy which commands respect. On the one hand, it implies a personal closeness, particularly denoted by the word intimacy. On the other hand, it demands the personal distinctness of those who are intimate to one another, which is stressed by saying that it commands respect. In sum, a certain medley of and tension between spiritual closeness and personal distinctness constitutes and characterizes the mutual presence of persons.

This notion of presence can analogically serve to elucidate the relationship between praying Christians and God. When the term "presence" is referred to Christ and the Divine Persons it does not denote any particular attribute of theirs, but their very Personalities with all their attributes. In fact, the Presence of Christ and of the Divine Persons is experienced by prayerful Christians as the divine personal continuous loving care that Christ and the Divine Persons take of them. As such an experience stirs up and involves the Christian'ssurprised, humble and grateful acceptance of that continuous divine loving care, it brings forth the mutual interpersonal presence of prayerful Christians and Christ or the Divine Persons.

So, praying Christians who have the habitual attitude of prayer, by which they are enabled to always opt for and respond to the Divine Presence, approach Christ and the Divine Persons not as particular "objects" approached from the side of one or the other divine attribute, but as existential "values" including the whole divine personalities. We have said that any presence of persons commands respect for the other's distinctiveness, and this will also be the case with prayerful Christians when they recognize God's presence.

Actually, because of their infinite love and majesty Christ and the Divine Persons are, at one and the same time, the "closest" and the "remotest" partners to whom Christians can relate. Indeed, the presence of Christ and of the Divine Persons to Christians is so elusive[1097] that it can be termed presence-in-absence.[1098]

We must needs use such an oxymoron here to point out the apparently contradictory position of the Divine Persons as regards us. For the more we strive to penetrate into the Divine Persons perceived as present the more we discover that the core of their being eludes our spirit's grasp and is absent or far from us.

> "As the mind progresses and through an ever greater and more perfect diligence, comes to apprehend reality, as it approached more clearly to contemplation, *it sees more clearly what of the divine nature is uncontemplated.*
>
> For leaving behind everything that is observed, not only what sense comprehends but also what the intelligence thinks it sees, it keeps on penetrating deeper until by the intelligence's yearning for understanding it gains access to the invisible, and there it sees God.
>
> This is the true knowledge of what is sought: *this is the seeing that consists in not seeing,* because what is sought transcends all knowledge, being separated on all sides by incomprehensibility and by a kind of darkness."[1099]

But the very elusiveness or absence of Christ and the Divine Persons spurs praying Christians on to yearn more and more for the divine presence, for the yearning for the real presence of the beloved continually grows in the lover who suffers from the absence of the beloved. Of course, the lover would not yearn and seek for the beloved if the former could not somehow reach

---

[1097] Cf. TERRIEN.

[1098] St. John alludes to the disciples' experience of a divine presence-in-absence in Jesus Christ before his resurrection (Jn 14:7-11, especially 9-10): "How can you say, 'Letus see the Father'? Do you not believe that I am in the Father and the Father is in me?" The Augustinian confession: "contremui amore et horrore", which refers to the same experience, was developed by OTTO (cf. bibliography) in his theory of "the Holy" as a fascinating and frightening Mystery, *mysterium fascinosum et tremendum.*

[1099] GREGORY OF NYSSA, II, 162, p. 95. Emphasis ours. See also *Ibid.*, 165, p. 96: "Every concept which comes from some comprehensible image by an approximate understanding and by guessing at the divine nature constitutes an idol and does not proclaim God." *Ibid.*, 234, p. 115: "Who thinks God is something to be known does not have life, because he has turned from true Being to what he considers by sense perception to have being."

affectively the latter and, at the same time, sense that the mysterious being of the beloved is beyond whatever the lover already experiences of him.

> "Although lifted up through such lofty experiences, he (= Moses as the prototype of the perfect Christian) is still unsatisfied in his desire for more. He still thirsts for that with which he constantly fills himself to capacity, and he asks to attain as he had never partaken, beseeching God to appear to him, not according to his capacity to partake, but according to God's true being....
>
> The ardent lover of Beauty, although receiving what is always visible as an image of what he desires, yet longs to be filled with the very stamp of the archetype... The munificence of God assented to the fulfillment of his (= Moses') desire, but did not promise any cessation or satiety of the desire.... *Since the true sight of God never consists in this, that the one who looks up to God never ceases in that desire....*
>
> Thus, what Moses yearned for is satisfied by the very things which leave the desire unsatisfied .... *This truly is the vision of God: never to be satisfied in the desire to see him.* But one must always, by looking at what he can see, rekindle his desire to see more. Thus, no limit would interrupt growth in the ascent to God, since no limit to the Good can be found nor is the increasing of desire for the Good brought to an end because it is satisfied."[1100]

So the genuine experience of God's presence is more an experience of his absence than of his presence. Really, the ever-growing yearnings, which enable praying Christians to enjoy Christ's and the Divine Persons' presence, are a very poor response to the "divine touchings", which are infinitely beyond the human capacity to receive them. But, once again paradoxically, what of the divine presence Christians are unable to receive affects them no less than what they receive.

It is because of this essential elusiveness of the Divine Presence that in the selfsame passage of the Scripture we find that Moses spoke face to face with God and yet remained unable to see God's face.

> "Yahweh would speak with Moses face to face, as a man speaks with his friend... You (= Moses) cannot see my (= Yahweh's) face, for man cannot see me and live... You shall see my back: but my face is not to be seen."[1101]

[1100] GREGORY OF NYSSA, II, 230-235, 238-239, pp. 114-115, 116. Emphasis ours.

[1101] Ex 33:11, 20, 23.

A contemporary author describes an analogous experience in prayer:

> "Upon occasion during prayer God can seem so faraway, and I long for a closer union with him... Actually at such times God may be very close to me in prayer. God's seeming absence can mean a very special type of intimate presence.[1102]

c. Getting personally involved with the Divine Persons

It was explained above that the habitual inner attitude makes the subject'spersonality continuously opt for a value. Personality is taken here as meaning that comprehensive psychic structure which gives the person an enduring way of acting. The value for which praying Christians opt is the divine presence. Consequently, those Christians whose personalities are in a state of readiness to opt for the value of the divine presence can be said to have acquired a habitual inner attitude of prayer.

Having the status of virtues, that is, of a good *habitus* the theological virtues provide Christians with the habitual readiness to promptly, easily and pleasantly approach God as an object of supernatural knowledge and love. Such habitual readiness becomes a continuous opting for the Divine Persons' presence, when these virtues grow to the point of forming in praying Christians the attitude of prayer.

The Christian supernatural personality is essentially constituted by the theological virtues. These virtues form together only one operative center of spiritual activity, which embodies and carries out the options for God of praying Christians. So, praying Christians, who opt for the Divine Persons' presence by faith, hope, and charity, do it with their whole Christian personality.

Accordingly the attitude of prayer could also be termed "the prayer of the Christian personality", in a sense quite similar to "the prayer of the heart" of Eastern spiritual masters. In fact, the "heart" of which those masters speak means that innermost unifying structure and principle of activity of the whole person which we have termed "personality". This explains why the same spiritual master say that prayer becomes perfect when it sinks into the "heart", i.e., into the "personality".[1103]

[1102] CARTER [1], p. 5.

[1103] Cf. ŠPIDLÍK, pp. 266-271.

Bearing in mind that the "objective value" of the prayer attitude is the presence of the Divine Persons, and the "subjective source" of the same attitude is the whole supernatural personality of praying Christians, we must conclude that the attitude of prayer is an intensely interpersonal relationship. So contemporary authors who like to emphasize the interpersonal character of prayer, virtually identify prayer with the attitude of prayer –

> "Prayer is a sort of loving companionship, a form of personal presence – *God present to me in love, I present to God in love.*[1104]
>
> "Prayer that can be called contemplative is a prayer of relationship, of *conscious presence to one another.*"[1105]

Such interpersonal relationship with God is made possible by grace. Given the infinite distance between human creatures and their Creator, only supernatural grace can enable Christians to have a personal encounter with the Divine Persons and enjoy some togetherness and intimacy with them. As a matter of fact, God the Father by pure grace grants a very special presence of himself to Christians who through and in his Son Jesus Christ are his adopted children. And from the Holy Spirit Christians receive a supernatural gratuitous infusion of faith, hope, and charity which gives them that supernatural personality which enables them to opt for and reach out to the personal presence of the Divine Persons.

It is in order now to try to sum up the results of all the considerations we have made so far into an essential definition of the habitual inner attitude of prayer.

iii. *The Definition of the Attitude of Prayer*

a. *Loving awareness of God's presence*

The core of the attitude of prayer is the habitual readiness of praying Christians to opt for God's presence.

The subject in which the attitude of prayer inheres is the supernatural personality mostly constituted by the theological virtues of faith, hope, and charity. If we bear in mind that "spirit of prayer" is virtually synonymous with

---

[1104] CARTER [1], p. 4. Emphasis ours.

[1105] BARRY [1], p. 19. Emphasis ours.

"attitude of prayer", we can find this teaching implicitly suggested by Vatican II where it reads that seminarians,

> "Should learn ... to be firmly established in faith, hope and charity, so that the practice of these virtues may develop in them a spirit of prayer."[1106]

Therefore the state of readiness to opt for the divine presence, which the attitude of prayer creates within the supernatural personality of Christians is believing, hoping, and loving.

The divine presence for which the attitude of prayer opts, to which this believing, hoping, and loving responds, is the presence of the Divine Persons, each one of them playing a special role in the history of salvation. The Father plays the role of Creator, the Son the role of Saviour, the Holy Spirit the role of Sanctifier. Therefore the divine presence, that is, the objective side of the attitude of prayer, must be qualified as creating, saving, sanctifying.

Another phrase of the just quoted passage of Vatican II can be taken as confirmation of this:

> "The spiritual formation...should be conducted in such a way that the students (seminarians) may learn to live in intimate and unceasing union with God the Father through his Son Jesus Christ, in the Holy Spirit."[1107]

Finally, putting together the prayer attitude's subjective and objective sides, it is possible to sum up all its essential components into the following definition - The attitude of prayer is the *believing, hoping, loving state of readiness to respond to God's creating, saving, sanctifying presence.* In short, it is *the loving awareness of God's presence.*

A few comments about the shorter definition are in order. The centering of this definition on loving and knowing is inspired by Aquinas, who teaches that the Divine Persons are present in the good Christian "as the known in the knower and the beloved in the lover."[1108]

In our search for the definition of the attitude of prayer we started from praying Christians: an approach very natural to us. But in reality the Divine Persons are the first to irrupt into and to establish in the supernatural personality of praying Christians their Divine Presence, which the Christian

---

[1106] OT, n. 8, FLANNERY, p. 714.

[1107] *Ibid.*, FLANNERY, p. 713.

[1108] ST, I, q. 43, a. 3, co.

tradition based on the Scripture terms "indwelling". Hence the fundamental option for the value of the Divine Presence really is the opening up of the praying Christian's supernatural personality, i.e., chiefly of the human intellect and will elevated by the theological virtues, to the gratuitous self-communication of the Divine Persons.

When that fundamental option becomes habitual, it creates within praying Christians an attitude, an enduring readiness of their supernatural personalities to opt for the presence of the Divine Persons.

Since it is expedient to use a single word to express the contents of the above-given definition of the habitual inner attitude of prayer, we will suggest for this purpose the term *prayerfulness.*[1109]

St. John of the Cross may be considered a supporter of this definition. While describing the spiritual signs which evidence that a Christian has grown enough in prayerlife to be ready to abandon the exercises of meditation and venture safely into contemplation, he writes:

> "The third and surest sign is that the soul takes pleasure in being alone, and waits with *loving attentiveness upon God (atención amorosa a Dios),* without making any particular meditation, in inward peace and quietness and rest, and without acts and exercises of the faculties – memory, understanding and will – at least, without discursive acts, that is, without passing from one thing to another: the soul is alone, with *an attentiveness and a knowledge, general and loving, (atención y noticia general amorosa)* as we said, but without any particular understanding, and adverting not to that which it is contemplating."[1110]
>
> "God secretly and quietly infuses into the soul *loving knowledge and wisdom (sabidura y noticia amorosa)* without intervention of specific acts, although sometimes He specifically produces them in the soul for some length of time.
>
> And the soul has then to walk with *loving advertence to God (advertencia amorosa a Dios),* without making specific acts, but conducting itself, as we have said, passively, and making no effort of its own, but

---

[1109] According to one of his translators, Cassian thought that the ultimate aim of ancient monasticism was "prayerfulness": "Every monk aims at uninterrupted prayerfulness... Without the virtues no one can attain the continual serenity of prayerfulness which I am discussing.": *Conferences,* IX, n. 2. CHADWICK, p. 214. Cf. MALONEY [1], p. 63: "A person's 'prayerfulness' is determined by the degree to which his actions and prayerful attitude arise from the love of God."

[1110] CROSS [1], II, 13, 4; p. 221. Emphasis ours.

preserving this simple, pure and *loving advertence (advertencia amorosa)* and determination, like one that opens his eyes with the *advertence of love (advertencia de amor).*"[1111]

The mystical Doctor insistently uses three Spanish words - *atención, noticia, advertencia.* They are synonyms whose meaning can be cumulatively expressed by the English word *awareness,* which directly expresses the *advertencia* and implies some sort of *atención* and *noticia.* Our contention is that when praying Christians begin to yield silently and quietly to the "loving awareness of God's Presence" the habitual attitude of prayer is taking shape within them.

The prayer experience witnessed by members of the charismatic renewal movement who claim that they have received what they call "Baptism of the Spirit", apparently confirms our contention, since they describe their experience precisely in the same terms that we have used in our definition.

> "(One of these charismatics said that) for a few weeks he was overwhelmed with consolation: *an awareness of the presence of God...* (Others underwent) a change which made them *more deeply and more constantly aware of the presence of God* in the apostolic activity."[1112]

The phrase we have employed to define the attitude of prayer is widely used (even though sometimes put a little differently) by contemporary spiritual writers, not only when they deal with the attitude of prayer but also when they write about acts, exercises, habitual dispositions, etc., that one way or another have some connection with the attitude of prayer.

Frequently definitions are worded in ways that emphasize the component of knowledge without explicitly mentioning love, although it is certainly included. This seems to be the case of John Henry Newman writing of the protagonist of his covertly autobiographical novel.

[1111] CROSS [3], B, III, n. 33, p. 226.

[1112] SUENENS, pp. 77-78. Hence, SULLIVAN, p. 4, understands "Baptism in the Spirit" as a religious experience which initiates a decisively *new awareness of the powerful presence of God working in one's life."* All emphasis ours.

> "Charles' characteristic, perhaps above everything else, was an *habitual sense of the Divine Presence...* The pillar of the cloud before him and guiding him. He felt himself God's possession, not his own."[1113]

The same occurs to Guardini when he writes:

> "For contemplation to become prayer, the worshipper must reach out to the living God, must become *aware of his living presence:* must seek out his countenance and enter into his heart."[1114]

b. Loving or desiring awareness?

We have termed the praying response of the Christian personality to God's presence- "loving awareness", because it involves an inner perception of the divine presence, which is fittingly expressed with the word "awareness", and in it the "loving" of charity stands out from the believing of faith and the trusting of hope.

But, as charity on earth is always joined to faith, which does not see, and to hope, which does not obtain, the act of charity necessarily takes the form of desire, i.e., of a love whose object is not attained.[1115] That is why some Fathers employ the term "desire" to define the Christian attitude of prayer.[1116]

Obviously, such a desire is not a mere wish, but love striving for its growth and fulfillment.

[1113] NEWMAN [2], p. 161. Emphasis ours.

[1114] GUARDINI, p. 105.

[1115] Cf. 1 Co 5:6-7: "To live in the body means to be exiled from the Lord, going as we do by faith and not by sight."

[1116] St. Augustine, *Enarrationes in Ps. 37,* no. 13: "The *desire* of your heart is itself your prayer." In LITURGY, vol. I, p. 330. St. John Chrysostom, *De Precatione,* PG 64, 462. In LITURGIA, vol. II, p. 52: "Precationem siquidem dico, ne putes verba esse, *desiderium Dei est,* non ab hominibus praestita, sed a divina gratia effecta, de qua etiam dicit Apostolus: 'Spiritus intercedit pro nobis gemitibus ineffabilibus'... Qui [orat] Eum gustavit *desiderio aeterno.*" In the XVII century Augustine Baker will term this desiring prayer - "prayer of aspiration".

"Spiritual desire of God is to please him, love him, know him, see him and have him, here by a little feeling, and in the glory of heaven with a full being."[1117]

A contemporary author certainly had in mind the ancient Fathers' teaching when he described contemplative prayer as

"A *burning desire* within your heart, your consciousness infused by the Spirit's faith, hope and love, to stretch out in the totality of your being in self-surrendering love of God."[1118]

c. Is this the essence of prayer?

Several contemporary authors seemingly claim that the attitude of prayer or prayerfulness is the very essence of prayer.

"Prayer is *essentially* standing face to face with God, consciously striving to remain collected and absolutely still and *attentive in his presence.*"[1119]

"This is surely the *essence of prayer.* We need to have *an awareness of God and to respond to that awareness.*"[1120]

To be *"aware of God's presence in us"* means to have a *"personal encounter with God in love,"* which is *the very essence* of prayer at every stage of our development."[1121]

"Essential prayer... takes place when we become open to his (i.e., the Holy Spirit's) presence... *We now pray essentially* when we know that we are secure in the presence of God and rejoice in his nearness... standing silently in the presence of God.[1122]

[1117] HILTON, I, ch. 90, p. 159.

[1118] MALONEY [1], p. 129. Emphasis ours.

[1119] BLOOM [1], pp. 57-58. Emphasis ours.

[1120] HUME, p. 121. Emphasis ours.

[1121] GREEN [1], p. 104. Emphasis ours.

[1122] BOROS, p. 4-5, 7. All emphasis in the last four quotes is ours.

Other authors say virtually the same, even though they do not employ the terms "essence" or "essential".

> "*True prayer* is perhaps very rare, because of the lack of this necessary basis - the placing of oneself *in the presence of the Divine Person* whom we are addressing... The soul that prays enters into the upper room. It places itself *in the presence* of that Being who gives himself and enters into *communication* with him."[1123]
>
> "We call *prayer in the pregnant sense of the term* that speech to God, which whatever else is asked, ultimately asks for *the manifestation of the divine presence, for this presence becoming dialogically perceivable.*"[1124]

Doubtless, some embryonic "loving awareness of the divine presence" is always implied in any kind of true prayer. But most of the time this embryonic form of prayer is just the presupposed fundamental groundwork of prayerlife. Several authors do not fail to realize it.

> "The prayer of the heart (which is the inner attitude of the praying person toward the presence of God,) is, as it were, *the essential substratum of the other forms of praying activity.*"[1125]
>
> "It has to be strongly stressed that prayer is a state, *a habitual existential attitude,* a mode of being, a life. ...(This prayer is) *an existential substratum* on which life is embroidered, in many different ways."[1126]
>
> "Personal intimacy with God forms the *hidden foundation* of all prayer."[1127]
>
> "Essential prayer ... takes place when we become conscious of *the basis of prayer* and of the presence of the Holy Spirit in us.[1128]
>
> "It will be contended that *underlying each diverse manifestation of prayer is a radical attitude.* Thus prayer is here conceived to be basically

---

[1123] GUILLERAND, pp. 79, 85, 119. Emphasis ours.

[1124] BUBER, p. 163. Emphasis ours.

[1125] BERNARD, p. 362. Translation and emphasis ours.

[1126] ZARRI, p. 5, 196. Translation and emphasis ours.

[1127] FINLEY, p. 23. Emphasis ours.

[1128] BOROS, p. 4.

> attitude more than activity – though without activity prayer soon languishes... Nothing that one does escapes its influence."[1129]

But, as we have shown throughout all this book, prayerlife is such a vast and variegated spiritual phenomenon that the essence of prayer (if the word essence is taken in a strict sense) can hardly be limited to its groundwork or to the inner attitude resulting from the whole of prayerlife. Each and every prayer form, act, habitual disposition, etc., which develops on that groundwork has its own essence and proper definition. The many different definitions of prayer that are widespread throughout the history of Christian spirituality clearly demonstrate that there is not only one essence of prayer.

iv. *The Attitude of Prayerful Remembrance and Expectation*

a. Awareness, remembrance, expectation of God

Authors who admit the threefold distinction of intellect, will, and memory, make the attitude of prayer inhere to memory.

> "When you pray, keep your memory under close custody ... have it convey the awareness of your reaching out to God."[1130]

The memory mentioned here does not solely refer to the recollection of things past, but includes also the awareness of the present and the expectation of the future.

> *"Recollecting the generosity and the mercy of the Lord, past or present or future,* they are rapt into that spark-like prayer which no mortal can understand or describe."[1131]

Hence, the attitude of prayer which inheres to memory extends:
— to *the present:* with respect to which it involves the cognizance and affection properly called "loving awareness",

---

[1129] HASSEL, pp. 1 and 131. Emphasis in the last four quotes is ours.

[1130] EVAGRIUS, ch. 44, p. 62.

[1131] CASSIAN, IX, n. 15. CHADWICK, p. 221. Emphasis ours. Cf. HILTON, pp. 36 and 168 note 108.

— to *the past:* with regard to which an analogous cognizance and affection could fittingly be termed "nostalgic remembrance".
— to *the future:* in relation to which cognizance and affection become "foreseeing expectation".

Present, past, and future make up the entirety of human time and history, which Christian faith sees as a History of Salvation, in which God intervenes to forgive and sanctify his chosen ones.

Now, the History of Salvation includes many a salvific event. The most grand and central of all – the death-resurrection of Jesus Christ, is present with its saving power at every moment of history, and ought to be always kept in mind by Christians. In this sense, praying is equivalent to living in the present moment as the eternal *kairos* of God, who unceasingly saves us through the risen Christ.

> "Learning to pray is learning to live in the present moment. In meditation we seek to enter into the now, and in entering into the now to live as fully as possible with the now risen and ever-living Lord."[1132]

> "The time is in the hands of the Father: (when we pray) we meet him in the present moment: neither yesterday nor tomorrow, but today: 'If only you would listen to him today, do not harden your heart' (Ps 95:8). Praying in the events of each day and at any moment is one of the secrets of the Kingdom revealed to the 'little ones', the poor of the beatitudes... It is important 'to knead' the humble daily situations with prayer. All forms of prayer can be that yeast to which the Lord likens the Kingdom (Cf. Lk 13:20-21)."[1133]

But, when we look at the events of the History of Salvation from the viewpoint of our own temporal existence, several of those events, even though their consequences are still working in the present, have occurred in the past. Other events shall happen in the future, especially in the eschatological future, even though their pre-announcements already have an important influence in the present.

Therefore, besides the "loving awareness" of the Divine Persons' and the Risen Lord's eternal presence, the Christian attitude of prayer extends to the "nostalgic remembrance" which looks backwards at the saving events and

---

[1132] MAIN [1], p. 22.

[1133] CCC, nn. 2659-2660. Translation ours.

divine gifts of the past and the "foreseeing expectation" of the promised fulfillment of Salvation in events yet to come and gifts yet to be received.

b. Prayer as continual remembrance

When prayer is practiced within the context of the History of Salvation it becomes the continual remembrance of God: one prays remembering with gratitude God's mighty acts in favor of his People.

> "The Deuteronomic school pre-eminently emphasizes the necessity of recollecting God's mighty acts: the memory is to be stored in the heart to prompt proper prayer (Deut. 4:9; 32-39; 7:18-19; 8:2, etc.: cf. I Kings 8:23-27). Moses' own prayers start with a recollection, or anamnesis, claiming God's previous mercies (e.g., Deut. 9:25-29). The acts of thanksgiving in offering first fruits is to be so accompanied (26:5-11)."[1134]

An example of this form of prayer is the following psalm:

> "Bless Yahweh, my soul, bless his holy name, all that is in me! Bless Yahweh, my soul, and remember all his kindnesses: in forgiving all your offenses, in curing all your diseases, in redeeming your life from the Pit, in crowning you with love and tenderness, in filling your years with prosperity, in renewing your youth like an eagle's."[1135]

Christian spiritual writers often echoed this thankful mood of prayer. As early as the third century Tertullian wrote –

> "Of course, one will admit that it is fitting to bless God at any time and everywhere, for all human beings owe Him the remembrance of His benefits."[1136]

[1134] SMITH, p. 859 b.

[1135] Ps 103:1-5.

[1136] TERTULLIAN, *De Oratione,* ch. 3, PL 1; 1258: "Plane benedici Deum omni loco et tempore concedet, ob debitam memoriam beneficiorum eius ab omni homine." Translation ours. Tertullian seemingly refers to Ps 103.

The continual remembrance of God as the most generous of all our benefactors was the perfect prayer the early Christian monks aimed to achieve. The hermit, alone in the desert, tried to be

> "In constant remembrance of God and unflinching in attending to the inner presence."[1137]

St. Augustine often writes about a general "remembrance of God" *memoria Dei* as a subconscious state of the mind.[1138] In one of his homilies on prayer, St. John Chrysostom exhorts everyone to pray throughout all their daily occupations by a continuous "desire and remembrance of God."[1139]

St. Basil the Great exhorts his monks to a continuous grateful remembrance of God's benefits. Actually, he thought that God comes to dwell in a very special way in those who hold him continually in their thankful memory.[1140]

St. Gregory the Great is aware that not even contemplatives can continuously perform acts of formal prayer for they must attend to the performance of good deeds, too. However, during the latter they should keep feeding their spirit with the sweet remembrance and holy desire of God, which they concretely cultivated during their previous exercises of contemplation.[1141]

[1137] LE SAUX, p. 32. Confirmations can be easily found in biographies of monks. E.g., SOFRONIO, pp. 229-230: "Un monaco, preparandosi alla morte, aveva passato tutto il tempo in infermeria, tenendo gli occhi chiusi per non turbare la memoria di Dio con qualche immagine esteriore": Cf. BIANCHI, p. 206. DOROTEO, pp. 56-58: "lascia la preghiera (vocale): ricordati semplicemente di Dio e pensa che sta davanti a te." It is worth remembering that the ancient Greek poet Hesiod has written: "Prayer, a heart which remembers the gods, fits elderly people.": YOURCENAR, p. 45. Translation ours.

[1138] CILLERUELO, pp. 507-508.

[1139] "Precationem.... noctu diuque *continuo perficiatur....* oportet *desiderium et memoria Dei commiscere.*": quoted in LITURGIA, vol. II, p. 52. Emphasis ours.

[1140] LOUTH, pp. 164-165.

[1141] GREGORY THE GREAT, *Homilies in Ezechiel,* I, 5, n. 12. PL 76; 825-826.: "[Contemplativus] ad bona rursus opera deditus suavitatis *Dei memoria* pascitur et foris piis actibus intus vero *sanctis desideriis* nutritur...(contemplationis) *memoriam* student recolendo semper et loquendo eructare." The intertwining of remembrance and desire is clearly explained by Aquinas: "remembered pleasure (delectatio prout est in

Many centuries later Catherine of Siena repeats virtually the same teaching:

> "Affection is love's hand, and this hand fills the memory with thoughts of Me (= God) and of the blessings I have given. Such remembrance makes the soul caring instead of indifferent, thankful instead of thankless."[1142]

Yet, when the soul reaches the unitive stage,

> "Her *memory is filled with constant remembrance of me (= God)* as she lovingly drinks in my blessings. It is not so much my blessings in themselves, but my loving charity in giving them to her. Especially it is the blessing of creation, for she sees that she is created in my image and likeness...
>
> She knows the truth about me the eternal Father: that in love I have created her to give her eternal life. This is the truth, and I have revealed it to her in the blood of Christ crucified."[1143]

Very significant for the identification of continuous prayer of holy desires with the ceaseless keeping in mind the benefits of God is the following passage from one of her letters.

> "We should always be open above, that is, having holy desires and images and continuous prayer, and always keeping in mind the favors of God and especially the great favor of the blood with which we were ransomed."[1144]

Here is how Christian spiritual writers of the sixteenth century describe the remembrance of God's blessing in prayer.

---

memoria) is, of its nature, calculated to evoke thirst or desire for itself, for it takes a person back to that state of mind in which he found pleasure in the object now past.": ST, I-II, q. 33, a. 3, co.

[1142] DIALOGUE, ch. 51, p. 103. Cf. CATERINA [2], X, p. 108: "La memoria s'empie del continuo ricordamento de' benefici tuoi (= di Dio)."

[1143] DIALOGUE, ch. 96, p. 180. Emphasis ours.

[1144] Letter 23, vol. I, p. 74, quoted by GILLET, p. 183. Probably the teaching of Catherine on the remembrance of God is the source of the following statement: "The whole life of the [Dominican] Nuns is harmoniously ordered to preserving the continual remembrance of God." BCNOP, # 74, iv.

> "I will be asking for a deep knowledge of the many blessings I have received *(tanto bien recibido),* that I may be filled with gratitude for them *(enteramente reconociendo),* and in all things I love and serve the Divine Majesty."
>
> I will be calling to mind *(traer a la memoria)* the benefits which I have received from creation, redemption, and the particular gifts I have received... (and that) He dwells in me, giving me being, life, sensation, and intelligence, and making a temple of me, since He created me to the likeness and image of His Divine Majesty."[1145]

> "It is a very evident truth that we love a person most when we have a vivid remembrance of the kind actions he has done us. If, then, it is lawful, and indeed meritorious, for us *to remember* that it is from God that we have our being, and that He creates us from nothing, and that He preserves us, and also *to remember* all the other benefits of his death and of the trials which He had suffered for us now living long before any one of us was created, why should it not be lawful for me to understand, realize, and *consider again and again* that, though once I was wont to speak of vanities, the Lord himself has now granted me the desire to speak only of himself.
>
> Here is a jewel which, when *we remember* that it is given us, and that indeed we already possess it, invites and constrains us to love, and all this is the blessing that comes from prayer founded in humility...
>
> We must seek new strength with which to serve Him, and endeavour not to be ungrateful, for that is the condition on which the Lord bestows His jewels.... It is impossible, I think, taking our nature into consideration, that anyone who fails to realize that he is favoured by God should have the courage necessary for doing great things.... for it is through those gifts that the Lord bestows upon us the fortitude of which our sins have deprived us."[1146]

In short, as our charity towards God is always a response of gratitude to the infinitely generous and merciful love that God shows us through his innumerable gifts of nature and grace, the remembrance of God's gift is absolutely necessary to nourish our charity towards him as our greatest Benefactor.

De Caussade briefly suggests a very simple form of prayer of remembrance of God:

[1145] SE, IVth week, "Contemplation to attain love", pp. 103-104.

[1146] TERESA OF AVILA, vol. I, pp. 59-60. Emphasis ours.

> "Let us practice a *simple remembrance of God,* a profound forgetfulness of ourselves, and an humble loving acquiescence in God's will."[1147]

A contemporary author writes about meditation on God's benefits as follows:

> "The power to remember is part of the identity and continuity of the person and a means by which he comes to know God. The people of God has a long collective memory of all those events in which he has acted to save, revealing himself and his love. We call this long series of remembered events salvation-history: it forms the basis of the Church's response in prayer to God who is present now in all he has done in the past.
>
> But the same is true for the individual: you can look back on your personal salvation-history and recognize God's love in your life. This is the basis of friendship, for all friendship presupposes a history and some shared experience. To remember God like this is a springboard for prayer. You know him because he has shown his love in your history: he is present to you now in all the reality of that love; you do not begin from scratch but take a great deal for granted because you are his friend, and you go on from there. When you meet him face to face he will be no stranger, but the remembered lover you have known obscurely all along the road."[1148]

Besides quoting the major text of the New Testament about "unceasing prayer",[1149] the new *Catechism of the Catholic Church* insists on a prayer understood as "remembrance of God" which is as frequent as breathing.

> "Prayer is the life of the heart. It ought to animate us at any time. Instead, we forget him who is our Life and our All. For this reason the Fathers of the spiritual life, following the tradition of Deuteronomy and the Prophets, insist on prayer as 'remembrance of God,' the frequent awakening of the 'heart's memory': 'It behooves us to remember God more often than to breathe' (St. Gregory Nazianzus, *Orationes Theologicae,* 1,4 PG 36; 16B)."[1150]

[1147] DE CAUSSADE, p. 441. Emphasis ours.

[1148] BOULDING, p. 68.

[1149] Lk 18:1 in CCC n. 2098. 1 Th 5:17; Ep 5:8; 6:18 in CCC n. 2742.

[1150] CCC, n. 2697. Cf. n. 2626 where our recognition in prayer of the benefits with which God blesses us is called prayer of blessing.

c. Prayer as continual expectation

The words of prayer, "Come, Lord Jesus!", repeated as a refrain at the end of the Book of Revelation,[1151] and the petition of the Our Father, "Thy Kingdom come!", are the best-known expressions of Christian prayer as expectation.[1152]

Apparently, prayer as expectation has its source in the sanctifying grace poured out into Christians by the Holy Spirit, according to the words of Jesus to the Samaritan woman,

> "The water that I shall give will turn into a spring inside him, welling up to eternal life."[1153]

Similar words are repeated by Jesus in another passage of St. John's Gospel:

> "If any man is thirsty, let him come to me! Let the man come and drink who believes in me! As Scripture says: From his breast shall flow fountains of living water. He was speaking of the Spirit which those who believed in him were to receive."[1154]

Aquinas thinks that the water Jesus is talking about in these passages is sanctifying grace which is a certain beginning of eternal glory, which makes those Christians to whom grace is granted worthy of sharing eternally in the

---

[1151] Rv 22:17, 20.

[1152] Cf. CCC, nn. 2817-2818.

[1153] Jn 4:14.

[1154] Jn 7:37-39.

life of the Holy Trinity.[1155] So, sanctifying grace is the source of all yearning expectation of Life Eternal in Christian prayerlife.

In fact, this inner fountain of living water gushes forth in prayer like a spring incessantly bubbling up[1156] and leading praying Christians to the Father from whom they expect Life Eternal.[1157]

> "There is within me a stream of living water which murmurs and tells me - "Come to the Father!"[1158]

Contemporary authors speak of a prayerful "waiting expectation"[1159] and "trusting expectancy."[1160] What Christians expect by this form of prayer is an increase of sanctifying grace and of the divine presence resulting from this grace. But most of all their ultimate expectation is for eternal beatitude before the unveiled presence of the Divine Persons.

No less than the habitual awareness of God's presence and the habitual remembrance of God's blessings, the habitual expectation of the eternal beatitude is the result of many prayerful meditations upon the Last Things. The spiritual contents of such habitual prayer of expectation continue to reside actively in the depths of the spirit, where they create an ongoing advertence to God, who is coming as just judge of our sins and generous rewarder of our good works.

[1155] ESI, IV, lect. 2, n. 596, p. 112a: "Aqua autem spiritualis causam perpetuam habet, scilicet Spiritum Sanctum, qui est fons vitae, numquam deficiens... In vita autem gloriae, ubi beati perfecte bibunt *aquam divinae gratiae,* non sitient in aeternum." Emphasis ours. Cf. ST, II-II, q 24, a. 3, ad 2um: *"gratia nihil est aliud quam quaedam inchoatio gloriae in nobis."* See also I, q. 23, a. 3, co. Emphasis ours. I-II, q. 98, a 1, co.: "Quicumque gratiam habet, ex hoc ipso dignus est vitae aeternae."

[1156] According to ST. TERESA OF AVILA, *Life,* 30, 19: all infused prayer is "a bubbling spring water, which gushes up incessantly."

[1157] ESI, n. 587, p. 112 b.: "*Fiet in eo fons,* fons, inquam, perducens per bona opera ad vitam aeternam." *Ibid.,* c. VII, lectio 5, n. 1090, p. 207a: "Qui bibit credendo in Christum, haurit fontem aquae, quo hausto, vivescit conscientia, quae est venter interioris hominis..."

[1158] IGNATIUS OF ANTIOCH, *Letter to the Romans,* VII, 2. Several Christian mystics use the same imagery. Cf. JOHNSTON [1], p. 9.

[1159] DUPRÉ, p. 14.

[1160] HASSEL [2], p. 15.

It is a matter of spiritual experience that both remembrance of the past and expectation of the future instill into our spirit mixed feelings of joy and sadness. Perhaps nowhere are these feelings so beautifully described as in the following Psalm, whose words have been interpreted spiritually as descriptions of the ups and downs in the Christian journey towards the final eternal encounter with the Lord.

> *Yearning for:* "As a doe longs for running streams, so longs my soul for you, my God... When shall I go to see the face of God?...
>
> *Joyous remembrance:* "I remember, and my soul melts within me: I am on my way to the wonderful Tent, to the house of God, among cries of joy and praise and an exultant throng...
>
> *Sadness:* "Let me say to God my Rock, 'Why do you forget me? Why must I walk so mournfully, oppressed by the enemy?' Nearly breaking my bones my oppressors insult me, as all day long they ask me, 'Where is your God'?
>
> *Trustful expectation:* "Why so downcast, my soul, why do you sigh within me? Put your hope in God: I shall praise him yet, my saviour, my God... Send your own light and your truth, let these be my guide, to lead me to your holy mountain and to the place where you live. Then I shall go to the altar of God, to the God of my joy, I shall rejoice, I shall praise you on the harp, Yahweh, my God."[1161]

Christians cannot remember their past life without recalling both their sins and God's many gifts, without, at one and the same time, regretting their wicked ingratitude and rejoicing over God's infinite bounty. While the prayerful remembrance of sins heals the wounds left by them in the spirit, the prayerful remembrance of the innumerable divine graces received from God gives a joyful radiance to it.[1162]

All this remembering before God in prayer contributes to the reestablishment in Christians of the "stable memory, clear sight and pure burning love of God and spiritual things everlastingly,"[1163] which human beings enjoyed before original sin; but which, after original sin, only

---

[1161] Ps 42 and 43.

[1162] Cf. CLAIRE d'ASSISE, p. 112: "Cuius (Christ's) memoria lucescit suaviter."; p. 194: "Nec de tua mente unquam excidat eius memoria."

[1163] HILTON, II, ch. 5, p. 199-200.

> "Through length of time and great spiritual labor by perfect souls and contemplatives, in faith and gracious feeling,[1164] are brought into the soul through the working of the Holy Spirit with burning love and spiritual light."[1165]

v. *The Profound Seat of Prayerfulness*

a. *The subconscious and subliminal core of personality*

When in this book the various psychic levels of the mind and heart were analysed, we spoke of an unconscious level of the mind and of a subliminally deliberate level of the heart.[1166] Passing from the analysis of the mind's attentions and the heart's intention in the life of prayer, which was developed there,[1167] to a more synthetical approach we now contend that the subconscious being-aware-of-God merges and virtually identifies with the subliminally deliberate being-in-love-with-God, and comprises within it the "loving awareness of God's presence," which defines the radical and permanent attitude of Christian prayerfulness.

Indeed, it is clarifying to make real distinctions between the intentions and attentions involved in the practice of prayer at the level of the psyche where both full consciousness and explicit deliberation occur. But it becomes useless and virtually impossible to distinctively differentiate the intention and the attention of the prayerful person at the profound level of the psyche where consciousness flows into the subconscious and deliberation becomes subliminal.[1168]

[1164] Cf. HILTON, II, ch. 5, p. 199; cf. ch 17, pp. 219-220. In this work of Hilton "feeling" means "the fullest realization of God's presence in this life, short of the open vision *(species)* which belongs to heaven": p. 304, note 15. See also II, ch. 13, p. 213; ch. 17, p. 219.

[1165] HILTON, II, ch. 17, p. 219.

[1166] Cf. ch. II, iii; ch. III, iii.

[1167] Cf. the whole chapter II and III of this book.

[1168] Commenting on the "work" described by *The Cloud of Unknowing,* W. Johnston writes: "For the purpose of analysis it is possible to speak of knowledge and love in contemplation; but the activity the author speaks of is a blend of both, a completely simple experience in the depth of the contemplative's heart." CLOUD,

Therefore, summing up the results of the research made above[1169] we must now postulate the existence of a primary comprehensive power of both knowing and loving at those psychic levels, where the roots of intellect and will are intertwined and from which a continuous knowing-loving flux of spiritual life can be elicited. That primary comprehensive power is the proper seat of the habitual inner attitude of prayerfulness situated in the subconscious and subliminal core of the human personality.

Consequently, prayerfulness does not need to inhere and to be elicited from the distinct faculties of intellect and will as the mind's acts of attention and the heart's acts of intention do. Prayerfulness is a comprehensive attitude which inheres and is elicited from the subconscious and subliminal core of the human personality, wherein it finds the primary power of spiritual energy, as its proper seat and source.

At first, from the practice of prayer during which acts of knowing and loving are performed, certain "residues" of knowledge and love of God sink into the subconscious and subliminal core of the praying Christian's personality and create in it the comprehensive attitude of prayerfulness. But when the attitude of prayerfulness has been thus formed, then from the core of personality it influences the whole prayerlife and existence of Christians.

b. The nature of the seat of prayerfulness

In the core of the personality the roots of intellect and will coalesce, joining their energies into only one source of spiritual activity. How have theologians tried to understand the nature of this source?

St. Theresa of Avila called it the "extreme interior" of the human person, and confessed that she did not know how to explain it for lack of learning.[1170]

Tauler thinks that this profound center is the very essence of the soul from which the faculties flow toward God who abides there.

> "It is certain that God has selected for Himself a special place in the soul, which is the very essence from which the superior faculties flow... God

---

Introduction, p. 21. The blending of knowing and loving in the attitude of prayer was amply treated above in ch. IV, ii.

[1169] Cf. ch. IV, ii.

[1170] *Mansiones,* VII, 1, 7 and 2, 10.

is present most intimately in the depth of the soul, and there he continuously engenders His Word... He also engenders us that we may be His sons through the grace of adoption. From this depth of the soul, then, proceeds all of a man's life, action, and merit, which three things God works in man ...

But to be aware of this rebirth and the presence of God in a way that will produce abundant fruits, they (= Christians) must recollect the faculties of the soul at their very source, where they touch the naked essence of the soul. There they will discover the presence of God."[1171]

An English spiritual author of the last century seems to give a new version of Tauler's description:

> "Though God be everywhere present, yet he is only present to thee in *the deepest and inmost central part of thy soul.* The natural senses cannot possess God or unite thee to him: nay, thy inward faculties of understanding, will, and memory can only reach after God, but cannot be the place of his habitation in thee.
>
> But there is *a root or depth in thee, from whence all the faculties come forth,* as lines from a centre or branches from the body of the tree. This depth is called the Centre, the Fund or Bottom of the soul. This depth is the unity, the eternity, I had almost said the infinity of thy soul: for it is so infinite that nothing can satisfy it or give it any rest but the infinity of God."[1172]

To have a better understanding of this Centre, Fund, Bottom of the soul,[1173] we should remember what we wrote above[1174] about the human "spirit" and "heart". It is precisely to this innermost spiritual depth, whence the human faculties come forth and all their activity originates, that prayerfulness inheres. At that depth prayerful Christians respond with their whole personalities to God's indwelling presence.

In such a response, while the conscious intellect is baffled, blinded and silenced, and the deliberating will is as it were dormant, an elusive but real

---

[1171] Tauler, *Institutions,* ch. 34, quoted by ARINTERO, vol. I, p. 88, note 7.

[1172] William Law, *The Spirit of Prayer,* quoted by GRIFFITHS [2], p. 98. Emphasis ours.

[1173] ARINTERO, *Ibid.,* p. 116, note 42, reports many other terms used by spiritual authors to name this depth of the human soul.

[1174] Ch. I, i, b.

heart-knowledge of God deeply pervades prayerful Christians and from there influences all their life and activity.

The experiential insight and spontaneous impetus of this heart-knowledge immerse prayerful Christians into the unfathomable Mystery of God, and bring about within them a state of unceasing sensing of, yearning for, and waiting on God. The whole experience rests neither on any knowledge of him consciously grasped nor on any love toward him deliberately elicited, but on the subconscious awareness of and subliminally deliberate surrender to him melted together and recast into the single radical permanent attitude of prayerfulness.

As to illustrate this prayerfulness we have just referred to the explanation of mystical contemplation given by St. John of the Cross, before ending we must say that we do not think that prayerfulness is to be simply identified with mystical contemplation. What we do think is that such prayerfulness occurs at the same "center of the spirit" where mystical contemplation is elicited, and it is brought about in a "secret manner" (i.e., keeping the consciousness in darkness and the deliberating faculties of the person asleep) which is analogous to that which characterizes mystical contemplation.

Prayerfulness does differ from the mystical contemplation described by St. John of the Cross, for it is a lasting radical attitude of the prayerful person; whereas mystical contemplation is a more or less transitory or peak-experience. In comparison with the wonderful blooming of prayer which is reached in mystical contemplation, prayerfulness is the hidden sap of prayer pervading the whole existence of the prayerful person.

c. The characteristics of prayerfulness

By way of conclusion, we will indicate the more significant characteristics of the attitude of prayerfulness, which have been suggested throughout this whole chapter. They are:

1. *Comprehensiveness.* The attitude of prayerfulness contains all the spiritual riches of the active, responsive, and ecstatic grades through which the growth process of Christian prayerlife passes. Hence, prayerfulness involves an active-responsive-ecstatic, continuous response of Christians to their being first known and loved by God. The absolute gift of being known and loved by God penetrates into the depths of the human spirit, where prayerfulness resides

and becomes within it a spring of loving awareness "welling up to eternal life."[1175]

So, prayerfulness represents between prayerful Christians and God a two-way flow of knowing and being known, loving and being loved, caring and being cared about, which is distinctive of intimate lovers.[1176]

2. *Deep-rootedness.* By its very nature the attitude of prayerfulness penetrates into and abides within the profound recesses of the praying Christian's supernatural personality at the root of its life.

3. *All-pervasiveness.* Since the whole supernatural activity of praying Christians is, as it were, soaked through and through by such an attitude, the influence it exerts in their existence is all-pervading: it penetrates every thought, word, and deed, and nothing that one does escapes its notice.

4. *Essentiality.* Being a permanent and radical response to and option for the Divine Presence, in its embryonic state prayerfulness plays the role of the primary and solid foundation or substratum from which all praying activity springs forth.

5. *Finality.* The attitude of prayerfulness in its full-grown state is the goal which all praying Christians crave and strive for by virtue of the divine infusion of faith, hope, and charity into their spirit. Actually, it is the exercise of the theological virtues in the practice of prayer which imprints in the depths of Christians the full-grown attitude of prayerfulness.

6. *Permanence.* Precisely because it is an habitual attitude prayerfulness is enduring. It is that state of readiness to opt for God's Presence which results in prayerful Christians from all their practice of prayer.

[1175] Jn 4:14.

[1176] Cf. ODEN.

POSTSCRIPT

We trust that the reader drew from this book many clarifications about the life of Christian prayer. However, we cannot consider our task completely concluded unless the light which has been cast on prayer is shown to have consequences for the practice of it. For Spiritual Theology, to which field this study belongs, cannot limit itself to being "faith seeking for understanding." It must also aim at construing spiritual experience and helping to expand its positive values into Christian existence. Undoubtedly, most of the preceding clarifications may look rather abstract. But the whole effort that motivated them was aiming at a very practical purpose: to find convincing answers to some crucial questions, whose practical bearings on the life of prayer cannot be overlooked. To point out the relevant and practical usefulness of our speculations we will draw some consequences which should help Christians to reassess and bring a sharper focus to their prayer life.

In our hectic society prayer is also often among the things caught up into the activistic trend, as if a pragmatic and utilitarian spell were cast over it. Paradoxically enough, prayer, whose specific function is to cultivate and develop the contemplative dimension of Christian existence, is twisted instead into another opportunity to get something done for the personal satisfaction of the one praying. In this way prayer's specific efficacy in remembering God's constant love and care and in bringing the praying person into contact with God's presence wanes and eventually gets lost. Errors and prejudices about prayer, clumsiness and ineffectiveness in its practice inevitably follow whenever prayer falls a prey to an activistic, pragmatic, utilitarian and sentimental cast of mind.

These biases and misunderstandings about prayer can be spelled out as follows.

- A quantitative bias: prayer is looked upon as mostly a matter of specific acts and exercises – so many rosaries, so many novenas, so many psalms, etc. Acts and exercises of prayer and the amount of time and psychic energy spent in performing them are viewed as the whole story.
- A legalistic bias: prayer is approached mainly as an obligation – something to be done to fulfill our obligations and appease our conscience. What is essentially a joyous communication and

intimacy with a God who hears and loves us becomes distorted into an oppressive burden to be carried in submission to a cold and severe Taskmaster, who abides in heaven while we struggle on earth.

- A sentimental bias: prayer is practiced in order to make the pray-er feel good – its fruitfulness is measured according to the pleasurable emotions which one can get from it.

All these outlooks render prayer spiritually sterile and futile, because they overlook or deny the possibility of a deeply personal communion between God and the human creature. How could such an attitude accept the mysterious interplay between God's wisdom and love and the human person's freedom and surrender to him in prayer? Is it not about such prayer that God complained through Isaiah, *"This people approaches me only in words, honors me only with lip-service, while its heart is far from me"* (29:13)? These "prayer prejudices" are rooted in faulty views of who God is, who the Christian is, and what kind of communication is possible between them.

In other words, a merely quantitative, legalistic, sentimental outlook towards and evaluation of prayer takes interest only in the length of its acts, whether one's debts to God are being satisfactorily paid, and what its spiritual delights are. No wonder that such prayer is so well characterized by the many different methods that facilitate its performance. Yet not even the most sophisticated and efficient methods can ever do justice to the innermost elusive nature of prayer. Whenever this quantitative, legalistic and sentimental outlook intrudes, it risks creating a distorted image of prayer as if the latter were a sort of currency exchange through which we can buy special "graces" which are precisely apportioned by God (as if he were some "certified accountant") according to the measure of time and psychic energy that one has invested in the exercises of prayer.

Authentic Christian prayer can by no means be measured, evaluated, and enjoyed in terms of investment and returns, of time and psychic energy spent and "consolations" received. However, by saying that, we do not wish in any way to depreciate the importance, even the necessity of acts and exercises of prayer. Without sustained effort in making such explicit acts and exercises the union of the pray-er with God would have never been established and, when established, would soon diminish to the vanishing point.

The desire of attaining an intimate union with God is the *sine qua non* of prayerful living. Yet the desire without acts and exercises of prayer becomes mere wishful thinking and reverie. Acts and exercises of prayer are absolutely necessary to acquire, feed, and renew the union of the pray-er with

God; so that the pray-er eventually succeeds in discovering union with God in the very depths of his or her spirit.

Indeed, the very core of Christian prayer is essentially a deep experience of the inner encounter of the Christian with God. The expressions of prayer clothe this mysterious intimate encounter with thoughts, images, affections, words, gestures, etc.; and such a "clothing" rebounds into deep inner prayer. On the other hand unless the "expressions" used by the Christian at prayer manifest his or her inner encounter with God they are spiritual "lies."

Prayerfulness is the continued and expanded experience of that encounter. Consequently the inner experience of prayerfulness and the outer acts and exercises of prayer, although differentiated from each other as the two sides of a coin, like those sides are not mutually exclusive but instead complementary to each other. To adhere together is for both of them the only way of being genuine. So the final plea of this book for prayerfulness by no means excludes the acts and exercises of prayer, but rather aims at adding to them a fresh and higher goal and motivation. It intends to infuse every activity of prayer with the earnest desire of imprinting the attitude of prayerfulness in the depths of the praying person.

ABBREVIATIONS

ASIAN *The Asian Journal of Thomas Merton* (New York: New Direction Books, 1975).

AG *Ad Gentes*

BC *Basic Catechism of Christian Doctrine,* Revised Edition (London: Catholic Book Society, 1971).

BCNOP *Book of the Constitutions of the Nuns of the Order of Preachers,* Private edition.

BLACKFRIARS St. Thomas Aquinas, *Summa Theologiae,* Latin text and English translation, etc. (Blackfriars, in conjunction with MacGraw-Hill Book Co., New York, and Eyre and Spotteswoode: London, vols. I-60, 1963).

CCC *Catechism of the Catholic Church.*

CCL *The Code of Canon Law,* in English translation (London-Grand Rapids, MI: Collins-William B. Eerdmans Publ. Co., 1983).

CDF: LETTER Congregation for the Doctrine of Faith *Epistula ad Totius Ecclesiae Catholicae Episcopos: Orationis Formas,* in L'Osservatore Romano, 15 December, 1989.

CDRL Sacred Congregation of Religious and Secular Institutes, *The Contemplative Dimension of Religious Life,* January 1981.

CLOUD *The Cloud of Unknowing and the Book of Privy Counsel,* newly ed. with introd. by William Johnston (Garden City, NY: Image Books, Doubleday and Co., 1973).

CP *Christian Prayer: The Liturgy of the Hours,* (Boston: St. Paul Editions, 1976).

CRUZ *Vida y Obras de San Juan de la Cruz,* edit. Crisogono de Jesús, Licinio del SS. Sacramento, Matias del Niño Jesús, tercera edición (Madrid: Biblioteca de Autores Cristianos, MCMLV).

CSB *The Catholic Study of the Bible,* gen. ed., Donald Senior (New York-Oxford: Oxford University Press, 1990).

CT Thomas Aquinas, *Compendium Theologiae ad Fratrem Reginaldum Socium Suum Carissimum,* in *Opuscula Theologica,* cura et studio P. Doct. Fr. Raymundi A. Verardo (Taurini, Romae: Marietti, 1954).

DBT *Dictionary of Biblical Theology,* ed., Xavier Léon-Dufour (Montreal: Palm Publishers, 1967).

DIALOGUE St. Catherine of Siena, *The Dialogue,* transl. and introd. by Suzanne Noffke (New York-Ramsey-Toronto: Paulist Press, 1980).

DNT *Dictionary of the New Testament,* Xavier Léon-Dufour (San Francisco: Harper and Row Publ., 1983).

DNTT *Dictionary of New Testament Theology,* gen. ed., Colin Brown (Grand Rapids, MI: Zendervan Publ. House, 1978).

DO *The Divine Office: The Liturgy of the Hours according to the Roman Rite* (London: Collins-Sydney: E.J. Dwyer-Dublin: Talbot, 1974).

DV *Dei Verbum.*

EA *Enchiridion Asceticum,* ed., M.J. Rouet de Journel and J. Dutilleul (Barcinone-Friburgi Brisg.,-Romae: Herder, MCMLVIII), editio quinta.

ESI S. Thomae Aquinatis, *Super Evangelium S. Joannis,* cura P. Raphaelis Cai, edit. V revisa (Taurini-Romae: Marietti, 1952).

ESP S. Thomae Aquinatis, *Super Epistolas S. Pauli,* cura P. Raphaelis Cai, edit. VIII revisa, Vol. I and II (Taurini-Romae: Marietti, 1953).

FRANCIS *Opuscula Sancti Patris Francisci Assisiensis,* edidit C. Esser (Romae: Editiones ad Claras Aquas, Grottaferrata, 1978).

GELNT *A Greek-English Lexicon of the New Testament and the Early Christian Literature,* transl, and adapt. of Walter Bauer's.... (Chicago- London: University of Chicago Press, 1979).

GS *Gaudium et Spes*

IC *The Imitation of Christ.*

IDB *The Interpreter's Dictionary of the Bible* (Nashville: Abingdon Press, 1982, 13th printing).

JB *The Jerusalem Bible* (Garden City, NY: Doubleday and Co., 1966).

JBC *The Jerome Biblical Commentary,* ed. by Raymond E. Brown, Joseph A. Fitzmeyer and Roland E. Murphy (Englewood Cliffs, NJ: Prentice Hall International, 1968).

LG *Lumen Gentium.*

NA *Nostra Aetate*

NAB *The New American Bible* (Nashville, TN: Thomas Nelson Publ., 1971).

NJBC *New Jerome Biblical Commentary* (Englewood Cliffs, NJ: Prentice Hall, 1990).

NW *The Nine Ways of Prayer of St. Dominic,* ed. and transl. by Simon Tugwell (Dublin: Dominican Publications, 1978).

M Aristotle, "*Metaphysics*", in Aristoteles Graece, ex recensione Bekkeri (Berolini: Academia Regia Borussica, 1831).

OF *An Outline of the Faith,* reprinted from *The Book of Common Prayer* (New York: Church Hymnal Co., 1979).

OT *Optatam Totius*

RM *The Roman Missal,* revised by decree of the second Vatican Council and published by the authority of Pope Paul VI. *The Sacramentary,* English translation (New York: Catholic Book Publ. Co., 1974).

SC *Sacrosanctum Concilium.*

SCG St. Thomas Aquinas, *Summa Contra Gentiles* trans. with introd. and notes by Charles J. O'Neill (Notre Dame-London: University of Notre Dame Press, 1975).

SE *The Spiritual Exercises* of St. Ignatius, trans. by Anthony Mottola, Ph. D., with an introd. by Robert W. Gleason, S.J. (Image Books, Garden City, NY: Doubleday and Co., 1964).

SM *Sacramentum Mundi* (New York: Herder and Herder, 1968).

SS *The Study of Christian Spirituality,* ed. by Cheslyn Jones, Geoffrey Wainwright and Edward Yarnold (New York-Oxford: Oxford University Press, 1986).

ST Thomas Aquinas, *Summa Theologiae* (Alba-Roma: Edit. Paulinas, 1962).

TDNT *Theological Dictionary of the New Testament,* ed. by Gerhard Kittle, trans. by Geoffrey W. Bromley (Grand Rapids, MI: William B. Eerdmans Publ. Co., 1964).

WDCT *Westminster Dictionary of Christian Theology,* ed. by Alan Richardson and John Bowden (Philadelphia: Westminster Press, 1983).

SELECT BIBLIOGRAPHY

AMBROSE ST., *Treatise on Cain and Abel*, PL 14, 334-379.

———, *De Officiis Ministrorum*, PL 16, 26-194.

ANGELA OF FOLIGNO, *The Book of Divine Consolation of Angela of Foligno,* revised, adapted and modernized by Msgr. Wm J. Doheny, C.S.C. (Rome: Private Edition, 1978).

ARINTERO JOHN G., *The Mystical Evolution in the Development and Vitality of the Church,* Vol. I-II, transl. by Jordan Aumann, O.P. (St. Louis, MO-London: B. Herder Book Co., 1950).

ASSAGIOLI ROBERT, *Psychosynthesis: A Manual of Principles and Techniques* (Wellingborough, Northhampshire: Turnstone Books, 1980).

ATHANASIUS ST., *De Virginitate,* PG 28, 251-282.

———, [2] *The Life of Anthony and Letter to Marcellinus,* Trans. and introd. by Robert C. Gregg (New York-Ramsey-Toronto: Paulist Press, 1988).

AUGUSTINE ST., *Confessiones,* PL 32, 659-868.

———, *Soliloquiorum Libri,* PL 32, 869-904.

———, *Epistolae*, PL 33, 1-1094.

———, *Ennarrationes in Psalmos,* PL 37, 67-1966.

———, *Enchiridion*, PL 40, 231-290.

———, *De Civitate Dei*, PL, 41, 13-804.

———, *De Trinitate,* PL 42, 819-1098.

———, *The Trinity,* transl. by Stephen McKenna, Washington, DC: Catholic University of America Press, 1963)

AUMANN JORDAN, *Spiritual Theology* (Huntington, IN: Our Sunday Visitor, 1980).

AVILA TERESA OF, *The Interior Castle,* trans. by Kieran Kavanaugh and Otilio Rodriguez, O.C.D. (New York-Ramsey-Toronto: Paulist Press, 1973).

BARILE RICCARDO, *La Fatica di uno Scriba: Riflessione sulla Preghiera* (Bologna: Edizioni Studio Domenicano, 1988).

BARRY WILLIAM A., [1], *God and You: Prayer as a Personal Relationship* (New York-Mahwah: Paulist Press, 1987).

———, [2], *Seek My Face: Prayer as Personal Relationship in the Scripture* (Ibid., 1989).

BARTH KARL, *The Awakening of Conversion,* in *Conversion,* ed. by Walter E. Conn (Staten Island, NY: Alba House, 1978).

BASIL ST., *Regulae Fusius Tractatae,* PG 31.

BAUDELAIRE CHARLES, *Les Fleurs du Mal* (Milano: Feltrinelli Editore, 1964).

BENSON HERBERT, *The Relaxation Response* (New York: Avon Books, 1976).

BERGANT DIANNE, *The World is a Prayerful Place* (Wilmington, Delaware: Michael Glazier, Inc., 1987).

BERGSON HENRI, *The Two Sources of Morality and Religion* (New York: Henry Holt, 1935).

BERNARD ST., *Sermones in Cantica*, PL, 183, 786-1198.

———, *Sermones de Diversis,* PL 183, 538-747.

BERNARD CHARLES ANDRE, *Theologie Affective* (Paris: Edit. du Cerf, 1984).

BIANCHI ENZO, *Vivere la Morte* (Torino: Gribaudi, 1983).

BLOOM ANTHONY [1], *Living Prayer* (London: Longman and Todd, 1966).

———, [2], *Courage to Pray* (New York: Paulist Press, 1973).

BOASE LEONARD, *The Prayer of Faith* (Chicago: Loyola University Press, 1985). A reprint of the original 1950 edition with a foreword by Thomas Green.

BOLAND VIVIAN, "Dominic's Ways of Prayer" in *Dominican Ashram,* 8 (1989), pp. 176-188.

BORTON JOHN, "The Old Testament", in SS.

BOUCHET JEAN-RENÉ, "La Prière du Coeur dans l'Orient Chrétien", in *La Vie Spirituelle,* 142 (1988)

BONDI ROBERTA C., *To Love as God Loves* (Philadelphia: Fortress Press, s.d.).

BOROS LADISLAUS, *Christian Prayer* (New York: The Seabury Press, s.d.).

BORROWS RUTH, *To Believe in Jesus* (Denville, NJ: Dimensions Books, 1981).

BOULDING MARIA, *Prayer: Our Journey Home* (Ann Arbor, MI: Servant Books, 1980).

BROK SEBASTIAN, "The Syrian Tradition", in SS, pp. 199-215.

BROWN RAYMOND E., *The Gospel according to St. John,* intr., trans., notes by Raymond E. Brown, S.S. (Garden City, NY: Doubleday and Co., 1987).

———, [2], "The Pater Noster as an Eschatological Prayer", in *New Testament Essays* (Garden City, NY: Doubleday and Co., 1968), pp. 275-320.

BUBER MARTIN, *Eclipse of God: Studies in the Relation between Religion and Philosophy* (New York: Haper and Row, 1952).

———, [2] *The Way of Response,* Selections from his writings ed. by N.N. Glatzer (New York: Schocken Books, 1972).

BUTLER BISHOP B.C., *Prayer: An Adventure in Living* (Wilmington, Delaware: Michael Glazier Inc., 1983).

CARRETTO CARLO, *Summoned by Love* (London: Darton, Longman and Todd, 1977).

CARTER EDWARD [1], *Prayer Is Love* (St. Meinrad, IN: Abbey Press, 1975).

———, [2], *Prayer Perspectives* (Staten Island, NY: Alba House, 1987).

CASSIAN JOHN, *Collationes,* PL 49.

CASSIODORE, *Expositio in Psalterio,* PL 70, 9-1056.

CATERINA DA SIENA, *Teologia dell'Amore* (Roma, 1968).

———, [2], *Orazioni,* a cura di G. Cavallini (Roma: Edizioni Cateriniane, 1978).

CESSARIO ROMANUS, *The Moral Virtues and Theological Ethics* (Notre Dame-London: University of Notre Dame Press, 1991).

CHADWICK OWEN (ed.), *Western Asceticism,* Selected transl. with introd. and notes (Philadelphia: Westminster Press, 1958).

CHENU MARIE-DOMINIQUE, "Spiritus: le vocabulaire de l'ame au XIIe siècle", in *Revue des Sciences Philosophiques et Théologiques,* 41 (1957), especially pp. 226-227.

CHESTER MICHAEL P. and MORRISEY MARIE C., *Prayer and Temperament* (Charlottesville, Virginia: The Open Door, Inc., 1984).

CHRYSOSTOM JOHN, *Homilia VI: De Precatione,* PG 64.

CILLERUELO L., "La memoria Dei según San Augustin", in *Augustinus Magister.*

CLAIRE D'ASSISE, *Ecrits,* introd., text latin, trad., notes and index par Marie-France Becker, Jean-Francois Godet, Thaddée Matura (Paris: Les Edit. du Cerf, 1985).

CLEMENT OF ALEXANDRIA, *Paedagogus,* PG 8, 247-684.

———, *Stromata,* PG 8, 85-1382.

CLIMACUS JOHN, *Scala Paradisi,* PG 88, 31-1164.

———, [2], *The Ladder of Divine Ascent,* transl., notes and introd. by Colm Luibheid, Norman Russell, Kallistos Ware (New York-Ramsey-Toronto: Paulist Press 1982).

CONGAR YVES, *Credo nello Spirito Santo, vol. II, Lo Spirito come Vita* (Brescia: Queriniana, 1982).

CORETH E., "Contemplative in Action", in *Contemporary Spirituality,* ed. by R. Gleason (New York: MacMillan, 1967).

CROSS JOHN OF THE [1], *Ascent to Mount Carmel,* trans. and ed. by E. Allison Peers (Garden City, NY: Image Books, Doubleday and Co., 1958).

———, [2], *Dark Night of the Soul,* idem, 1959.

———, [3], *Living Flame of Love,* idem, 1962.

CYPRIAN, *De Oratione Dominica,* PL, 519-544.

DALEY JACQUES DE PAUL, *The Problem of Combining Spiritual Direction and Personal Friendship Shown in the Monastic Life of Saint Therese of the Infant Jesus and of the Holy Face* (Romae: Pontificia Studiorum Universitas a S. Thoma Aq. in Urbe, 1991).

DALRYMPLE JOHN, *Simple Prayer* (Wilmington, Delaware: Michael Glazier, Inc., 1984).

DAMASCENE JOHN, *De Fide Orthodoxa,* PG 94, 783-1228.

DE CAUSSADE JEAN PIERRE, *Self-abandonment to Divine Providence* (Templegate, IL: 1961).

DESMOND EDWARD W., "A Pencil in the Hand of God", in *Time (Magazine),* Dec. 4, 1989.

DE SAINT-EXUPERY ANTOINE, *The Little Prince* (New York: Hartcourt Brace Janovich, 1971).

DOROTEO DE GAZA, *Scritti e Insegnamenti Spirituali* (Alba: Edizioni Paoline, 1980).

DUBAY THOMAS, *Fire Within: St. Teresa of Avila, St. John of the Cross and the Gospel – on Prayer* (San Francisco: Ignatius Press, 1989).

DUJAT JEAN, *Prayer* (New York: Hawthorn Books, 1964).

DUNNE S. JOHN, *The Reasons of the Heart* (New York: MacMillan, 1978).

DUNNE, T., *Lonergan and Spirituality* (Chicago: Loyola University Press, 1985).

DUPRÉ LOUIS, *The Deeper Life: Introduction to Christian Mysticism* (New York: Crossroad, 1981).

DURRWELL FRANCIS X., *In the Redeeming Christ* (London: Sheed and Ward, 1963).

EDWARDS DENNIS, *Human Experience of God* (New York-Ramsey: Paulist Press, 1983).

ELDERS LÉON, *Autour de Saint Thomas d'Aquin* (Paris: Fac-éditions - Brugge: Uitgeverij TABOR, 1987).

EVAGRIUS PONTICUS, *The Prakticos and Chapters on Prayer,* trans., introd. and notes by John Eudes Bamberger, OCSO (Spencer, Mass: Cistercian Publ., 1972).

EVANS C.F., *The Lord's Prayer* (London: SPCK, 1963).

EVDOKIMOV PAUL, *The Struggle with God* (Glen Rock, NJ: Paulist Press, 1966).

FARRELLY JOHN, "Notes on Mysticism in Today's World", in *Spirituality Today,* 43, (1991).

FELDMANN CHRISTIAN, *Les Fous de l'Amour* (Montreal: Editions Paulines, 1987).

FERNALD JAMES C., Funk and Wagnall's *Standard Handbook of Synonyms, Antonyms and Prepositions* (New York: Harper and Row, 1947).

FINLEY JAMES, *The Awakening Call: Fostering Intimacy with God* (Notre Dame, Ind.: Ave Maria Press, 1984).

FITZMEYER JOSEPH A.[1], *The Letter to the Romans,* in NJBC.

———, [2], *Pauline Conception of Man,* in JBC, pp. 820-821.

FLANNERY AUSTIN (gen. ed.), *Vatican Council II: The Conciliar and Post Conciliar Documents* (Northport, New York: Costello Publ. Co., 1975).

FRANKL VICTOR, *Man's Search for Meaning: An Introduction to Logotherapy* (New York: Pocket Books, 1972).

FROMM ERICH, *The Art of Loving* (New York-San Francisco: Harper and Row, Perennial Library, 1974).

GANDHI MOHANDAS K., "Prayer" in *The Encyclopedia of Religion,* ed. in chief Mircea Eliade, vol. II (New York: MacMillan Publ. Co., 1987).

GASTER T.H., "Sacrifice and Offerings, OT" in IDB, Vol. IV.

GIARDINI FABIO [1], *Loving Awareness of God's Presence in Prayer* (Staten Island, NY: Alba House, 1978).

———, [2], *St. John of the Cross, Master of Charity,* in *Angelicum,* 68 (1991), pp. 535-552.

———, [3], *Prayerfulness: A Psychotheological Search into the Spirit of Prayer,* Studia Universitatis S. Thomae in Urbe No. 24 (Milano: Edit. Massimo, 1984).

GIBRAN KAHLIL GIBRAN, *Il Profeta* (Milano: Guanda, 1983).

GILLETT LAURA, *Heart of Jesus – Heart of Catherine: A Theological Study of Catherine of Siena's Teaching on the Heart of Jesus* (Romae: Dissertatio ad Lauream in Facultate S. Theologiae apud Pontificiam Universitatem S. Thomae de Urbe, 1992).

GOOD E.M., "Love in the OT", in IDB, vol. III.

GREEN THOMAS H. [1], *Opening to God: A Guide to Prayer* (Notre Dame, Ind: Ave Maria Press, 1979).

———, [2], *When the Well Runs Dry: Prayer Beyond Beginnings* (Notre Dame, In: Ave Maria Press, 1979).

GREGORY OF NYSSA, *Life of Moses,* trans., introd. and notes by Abraham J. Malherbe and Everett Ferguson (New York-Ramsey-Toronto: Paulist Press, 1978).

GREGORY THE GREAT, *Moralia in Job,* PL 75, 509-1162; PL 76, 9-782.

———, *Homiliae in Ezechiel,* PL 76, 785-1072.

———, *Homiliae in Evangelia,* PL 76, 1077-1314.

GRIFFITHS BEDE [1], *The Marriage of East and West* (London: Font Paperbacks Collins, 1982).

———, [2], *Return to the Centre* (London: Font Paperbacks Collins, 1984).

GROESCHEL BENEDICT, *Listening at Prayer* (New York-Ramsey: Paulist Press, 1984).

GUARDINI ROMANO, *Prayer in Practice* (Garden City, NY: Image Books, Doubleday and Co., 1963).

GUIGUES II, *Lettre sur la Vie Contemplative,* ed. by E. Colledge and J. Walsh (Paris: éditions du Cerf., Sources Chrètiennes, vol. 163, 1970).

GUIGO II, *The Ladder of the Monks and Twelve Meditations,* transl. and introd. by Edmund Colledge, O.S.A. and James Walsh S.J. (Garden City, NY: Doubleday and Co., 1978).

GUILLERAND AUGUSTIN, *The Prayer of the Presence of God,* (Wilkes Barre, PA: Dimension Books 1966).

HALL THELMA, *Too Deep for Words: Rediscovering Lectio Divina* (New York-Mahwah: Paulist Press, 1988).

HANEMAN MARY ALPHONSETTE, *The Spirituality of St. Teresa of Avila* (Boston: St. Paul Editions, 1983).

HAPPOLD F.C., *Mysticism: A Study and an Anthology* (New York: Penguin Books, 1979).

HARDING M.E., *The "I" and the "Not-I": A Study in the Development of Consciousness* (Princeton: Princeton University Press, 1973).

HARDON JOHN A., *Theology of Prayer* (Boston: St. Paul Editions, 1979).

HASSEL J. DAVID, [1], "The Fourth Level of Prayer: Mystery", in *Review for Religious,* 1980 (39).

———, [2] *Radical Prayer* (New York-Ramsey: Paulist Press, 1983).

HAUSSHERR IRENÉ, *Penthos: La Doctrine de la Componction dans l'Orient Chrètien,* (Roma: OCA, 1944).

HERRIGEL EUGEN, *The Zen in the Art of Archery* (New York: Vintage Books, 1971).

HILL WILLIAM J., *The Three-Personed God: The Trinity as a Mystery of Salvation* (Washington DC: The Catholic University of America Press, 1982).

HILTON WALTER, *The Scale of Perfection* (New York: Paulist Press, 1990).

HOSTIE RAYMOND, *Depth Psychology,* in SM, vol. V.

HUME BASIL, *Searching for God* (London-Toronto: Hodder and Stoughton, 1997).

HURNARD HANNAH, *Wayfarer in the Land* (London: Olive Press, 1970).

IGNATIUS OF ANTIOCH, *Letter to the Romans*,(*Patres Apostolici,* ed. Funk, Tubingen,1901)

———, *Letter to Polycarp*,(*Ibid.*)

IRENAEUS ST., *Adversus Haereses,* PG 7, 433-1224.

ISIDORE ST., *Etymologiarum Libri,* PL 82, 72-728.

JAMES WILLIAM, *The Varieties of Religious Experience* (New York: Collier Books, 1961).

JARRETT BEDE, *Life of St. Dominic* (Washington-Chicago: Dominican Publications, s.d.)

JEROME ST., *Epistulae,* Pl 22.

JOHN XXIII, *Inde a Primis,* AAS 52 (1960).

JOHN PAUL II [1], *Christifideles Laici* (Vatican City, Rome: Libreria Editrice Vaticana, 1988).

———, [2], *Redemptoris Missio* (Boston: St. Paul Books and Media, 1991).

———, [3], *Address to Cardinals and the Roman Curia,* December 22, 1986, in AAS 79 (1987).

———, [4], *Dominum et Vivificantem,* in AAS, 78 (1986).

———, [5], *Pastores Vobis Dabo,* in *L'Osservatore Romano,* April 8, 1992).

JOHNSTON G., "Love in the OT", in IDB, vol. III.

JOHNSTON WILLIAM [1], *The Inner Eye of Love: Mysticism and Religion* (San Francisco: Harper and Row Publ., 1978).

———, [2], *The Wounded Stag* (San Francisco: Harper and Row Publ., 1984).

JOHODA MARIE and WARREN NEIL (ed.), *Attitudes: Selected Readings* (Baltimore, MD: Penguin Books, 1966).

JONES C.P., "The New Testament", in SS.

JUNG KARL GUSTAV [1], *Memories, Dreams, Reflections* (New York: Vintage Books, 1965).

———, [2], *The Undiscovered Self* (New York: The American Library, 1964).

KANT IMMANUEL, *Critique of Pure Reason,* William Benton publisher (Chicago-London-Toronto: Encyclopecia Britannica Inc., 1952).

KÄSEMANN ERNST, *Commentary on Romans,* trans, and ed. by Geoffrey W. Bromiley (Grand Rapids, MI: William B. Eerdmans Publ. Co., 1980).

KAVANAUGH KIERAN, St. Teresa of Avila, *Interior Castle,* trans. by Kieran Kavanaugh and Otilio Rodriguez OCD (New York-Toronto: Paulist Press, 1979).

KEANE PHILIP, *Sexual Morality: A Catholic Perspective* (New York: Paulist Press, 1977).

KNOWLES DAVID, *The English Mystical Tradition* (London: Burns and Oates, 1961).

KRAPIEC MIECZYLAW A., *I-Man: An Outline of Philosophical Anthropology* (New Britain, Connecticut: Mariel Publ., 1983).

LAWRENCE (BROTHER) OF THE RESURRECTION, *The Practice of the Presence of God,* newly trans. by John J. Delaney (Garden City, NJ: Image Books, Doubleday and Co., 1977).

LECLERCQ JEAN, *The Love of Learning and the Desire of God: A Study of Monastic Culture* (New York: A Mentor Omega Book - the New American Library, 1962).

LEECH KENNETH, *True Prayer: An Invitation to Christian Spirituality* (San Francisco: Harper and Row Publ., 1980).

LE SAUX HENRI (Abhishiktananda), *Prayer* (Philadelphia: The Westminster Press, 1967).

LEWIS C.S., *The Screwtape Letters* (London: Geoffrey Bles, The Centenary Press, 1942).

Liturgia Horarum Iuxta Ritum Romanum (Typis Polyglottis Vaticanis, MCMLXXII).

Liturgy of the Hours (New York: Cath. Book Co., 1975).

LONERGAN BERNARD, *Method in Theology* (New York: Herder and Herder, 1972).

LOSSKY VLADIMIR, *The Mystical Theology of the Eastern Church* (London: James Clark and Co., 1973).

LOUF ANDRÉE, *Teach Us to Pray: Learning a Little about God* (Chicago: Franciscan Herald Press, 1975).

LOUTH ANDREW, "The Cappadocians", in SS.

———, [2] "Maximus the Confessor", in SS.

Love, ed. by Jane Lahr and Lena Tabori (New York: Stewart, Tabori and Chang Publishers, s.d.)

MACQUARRIE JOHN, *Paths of Spirituality* (New York-London: Harper and Row, 1972).

———, [2], "Prayer and Theological Reflection", in SS.

———, [3], *Christian Hope* (New York: The Seabury Press, 1978).

MAIN JOHN [1], *Words into Silence*(Ramsey, NY: Paulist Press, 1981).

———, [2], *Moments of Christ: The Path of Meditation* (New York: Crossroad, 1984).

MALONEY A. GEORGE [1], *The Prayer of the Heart* (Notre Dame, IN: Ave Maria Press, 1981).

———, [2], *Journey to Contemplation* (Locust Valley, NY: Living Flame Press, 1983).

MARITAIN JACQUES [1], *Creative Intuition in Art and Poetry* (Washington: The A.W. Mellon Lectures, Pantheon Books, 1953).

———, [2], *Approaches to God* (New York: Collier Books, 1962).

———, [3], *Existence and the Existent* New York: Vintage Books, 1966).

McCASLAND S.V., "Spirit", in IDB, vol. IV.

MEISTER ECKHART, *Sermons and Treatises,* transl. and ed. by M. O'C. Walshe (Shaftesbury, Dorset: Element Books Ltd., Longmead, 1987).

MEREDITH ANTHONY, "Greek Philosophy, Wisdom Literature, and Gnosis". in SS.

———, [2], "Clement of Alexandria", in SS.

MERTON THOMAS [1], *Contemplative Prayer* (New York: Herder and Herder, 1969).

———, [2], *The Role and Meaning of Love* (London: Sheldon Press, 1953).

———, [3], *The New Man* (New York: Farrar, Straus and Giroux, 1979).

METZ JOHN BAPTIST, "Religious Act", in *Sacramentum Mundi: An Encyclopedia of Theology* (New York: Herder and Herder, 1970).

MOUROUX JEAN, *L'Experience Chrètienne: Introduction a une Théologie* (Paris: Aubier edit. Montaigne, 1952).

———, [2], *The Meaning of Man* (Garden City, NY: Doubleday and Co., 1961).

NARDINI CARLO, "'Affectio' e 'ratio' nell'itinerario mistico del 'Benjamin minor' de Riccardo di San Vittore", in *Annali della Facoltà di Lettere e Filosofia dell'Università degli Studi di Perugia,* vol. XXIV, nuova serie, X, 1986-1987.

NEWMAN JOHN HENRY [1], "Moral Effects of Communion with God, in *Parochial and Plain Sermons,* 1938.

———, [2], *Loss and Gain: The Story of a Convert* (Oxford: University Press, 1986).

NICOLAS JEAN HERVÉ, *Contemplation et Vie Contemplative en Christianisme* (Fribourg, Suisse: Éditions Universitaires, 1980).

NOUWEN HENRI J.M., [1], *Clowning in Rome* (Garden City, NY: Doubleday and Co., 1979).

———, [2], *With Open Hands* (Notre Dame, Ind: Ave Maria Press, 1972).

ODEN THOMAS C., *Game Free: A Guide to the Meaning of Intimacy* (San Francisco-New York: Harper and Row, 1974).

O'DONNELL JOHN J., *The Mystery of the Triune God* (New York-Mahwah: Paulist Press, 1990).

OECHSLIN RAPHAEL-LOUIS, "Divinization: Ecole Rhénane et Flamande", in *Dictionaire de Spiritualité - Doctrine et Histoire* (Paris: Beauchesne, 1957), vol. III.

OLDROYD DAVID, *The Arch of Knowledge* (New York: Methuen, 1986).

ORIGEN, *De Oratione,* PG 11, 415-562.

———, [2], *On Prayer,* trans. with introd. by Rowan Greer (New York-Ramsey-Toronto: Paulist Press, 1979).

OTTO RUDOLF, *The Idea of the Holy* (London: Oxford University Press, 1958).

PATFOORT ALBERT, "Ista cognitio est quasi experimentalis" and "Missions divines et expérience des Personnes Divines selon St. Thomas d'Aquin", in *Angelicum,* 1986 (63), pp. 3-13: 545-559.

PEGUY CHARLES, *Le Mystère des Saints Innocents* (Paris: NRF, s.d.)

PENNINGTON M. BASIL [1], "Centering Prayer - Prayer of Quiet", in *Cross and Crown,* 1977 (29).

———, [2], *Centering Prayer: Renewing an Ancient Prayer Form* (Garden City, NY: Image Books, Doubleday and Co., 1982).

———, [3], "Centering Prayer: Refining Rules", in *Review for Religious,* 1986 (46).

PERRAULT GEORGES, "Belonging to a Community: Meaning and Support", in *Dominican Ashram,* 8 (1989).

Philokalia, transl. by E. Kadloubovsky and G.E. Palmer (London: Faber and Faber, 1951).

PIEPER JOSEPH, *Leisure: The Basis of Culture* (New York and Scarborough, Ontario: New American Library, 1963).

PILCH J. JOHN, "Romans", in *The Collegeville Bible Commentary,* Dianne Bergant and Robert J. Karris eds., (Collegeville, MN: The Liturgical Press, 1989).

PINCKAERS SERVAIS, *La Prière Chrètienne,* (Fribourg, Suisse: Editions Universitaires, 1989).

PIUS XII, *Mediator Dei,* AAS 39 (1947).

PORTEOUS N.W., "Soul", in IDB, vol. IV.

POZO CANDIDO, *Teologia dell'Aldilà* (Roma: Edizioni Paoline, 1972).

PRINCIPE WALTER H., *Thomas Aquinas' Spirituality* (Toronto, Ontario: Pontifical Institute of Mediaeval Studies, 1984).

PRZYWARA = *An Augustine Synthesis,* arranged by Erich Przywara (New York: Harper and Brothers Publ., Harper Torchbooks, Cathedral Library, 1958).

PSEUDO-DYONISIUS, *De Divinibus Nominibus*, PG 3, 693-984.

RABANUS MAURUS, *De Universo,* PL 111, 9-614.

RAGUIN YVES [1], *How to Pray To-day* (Saint Meinrad, Ind: Abbey Press, 1973).

———, [2], *Ways of Contemplation: East and West* in *Asian Religious Tradition and Christianity,* ed. by Fausto Gomez (Manila, Philippines: University of Santo Tomas Press, 1983).

RAHNER KARL [1], *Foundations of Christian Faith: An Introduction to the Idea of Christianity* (New York: Seabury Press, 1978).

———, [2], *The Practice of Faith: A Textbook of Contemporary Spirituality* (New York: Crossroad, 1986).

———, [3], *I Remember: An Autobiographical Interview with Meinold Krauss* (New York: Crossroad, 1985).

———, [4], *On Prayer* (New York-Toronto: Paulist Press, Deus Books, 1958).

RAMSEY BONIFACE, *Beginning to Read the Fathers* (New York-Mahwah: Paulist Press, 1985).

RICHARDSON ALAN, "Prayer, Theology of", in WDCT.

RINKER ROSALIND, *Prayer: Coversing with God* (Grand Rapids, MI: Zondervan Books, 1970).

ROBINSON LILLIAN H., "Psychoanalysis and Religion: A Comparison", in *Psychiatry and Religion Overlapping Concern* (Washington DC: American Psychiatric Press, 1986), ed. by Lillian H. Robinson.

ROLLE RICHARD, *The Fire of Love and the Mending of Life,* transl. with an introd. by M.L. Del Mastro (Garden City, NY: Image Books, Doubleday and Co., 1981).

ROSAGE DAVID E., *Discovering Pathways of Prayer* (Locust Valley, NY: Living Flame Press, 1975).

ROUSSEAU PHILIP, "The Desert Fathers: Anthony and Pachomius", in SS.

RULLA L.M., *An Anthropology of Christian Vocation: Interdisciplinary Bases* (Rome: Gregorian University Press, 1986), vol. II.

RULLA L.M., IMODA F., RIDICK J., *Psychological Structures of Vocation: A Study of the Motivations for Entering and Leaving Religious Life* (Dublin: Villa Books, 1978).

SALES FRANCIS OF [1], *Treatise on the Love of God* (Rockford, IL: Tan Book Publ. Inc., 1975).

———, [2], *Introduction to the Devout Life,* transl, and ed. by John K. Ryan (Garden City, NY: Image Books, Doubleday and Co., 1972).

SANDERS J.N., "Word, The", in IDB, vol. IV.

SCHMAUS MICHAEL, *Dogma VI: Justification and the Last Things* (Westminster, Maryland: Christian Classics, 1984).

SCHNACKENBURG RUDOLF, *The Gospel According to St. John* (New York: Crossroad, 1982).

Scritti (gli) di Francesco e Chiara d'Assisi (Padova: Edizioni Messaggero, 1982).

SIMON YVES R., *Free Will* (New York: Fordham University Press, 1987).

SLADE HERBERT, *Exploration into Contemplative Prayer* (London: Darton, Longman and Todd, 1975.

SMITH C.W.F., "Prayer", in IDB, vol. III.

SOFRONIO ARCIVESCOVO, *Silvano del Monte Athos: Vita, Dottrina, Scritti* (Torino, 1978).

SOMMERFELDT JOHN R., "The Monk and Monastic Life in the Thought of Bernard of Clairvaux", in *Word and Spirit,* 12, (1990), pp. 43-52.

ŠPIDLÍK TOMAS [1], *La Doctrine Spirituelle de Théophane le Reclus: Le Coeur et l'Esprit* (Roma: OCA, 172, 1965).

———, [2], *La Spiritualité de L'Orient Chrètien: 11. La Prière* (Roma: Pont. Inst. Studiorum Orientalium, 1988).

———, [3], "Il Dono delle Lacrime nella Tradizione della Chiesa Orientale", in *Communio,* (Italian Edition), no. 119, sett. - ott. 1991).

SPLETT IORG, "Consciousness", in SM, vol. 1.

STEEL C.G., *The Changing Self: A Study of Soul in Later Neoplatonism* (Brussel, 1978).

STEINGRAEBER JOHN, *Love Is Prayer: Prayer Is Love* (Liguori, MO: Liguori Publ., 1973).

STOPP ELISABETH, "Francois de Sales", in SCS.

SUENENS LEON J., *A New Pentecost* (New York: The Seabury Press, 1975).

SULLIVAN F.A., "Baptism in the Holy Spirit", in *Gregorianum,* 55 (1983), p. 4.

TANQUEREY ADOLPHE, *The Spiritual Life: A Treatise of Ascetical and Mystical Theology* (Tournai, Belgium: Desclée and Co., s.d.)

TERESA DE JESÚS, *Obras,* edición y notas del P. Silverio de Santa Teresa, cuarta edición (Burgos: Editorial de "El Monte Carmelo", 1949).

TERESA OF AVILA, *The Complete Works of St. Teresa of Jesus,* trans. and ed. by E. Allison Peers (London: Sheed and Ward, 1975).

TERRIEN SAMUEL, *The Elusive Presence: The Heart of Biblical Theology* (San Francisco: Harper and Row Publ., 1978).

TERTULLIAN, *De Oratione,* PL 1, 1249-1304.

———, *Apology,* in *The Anti-Nicene Fathers,* Alexander Roberts and James Donaldson editors - *Latin Christianity: Its Founder, Tertullian,* American Reprint of the Edinburgh Edition (Grand Rapids, MI: Wm. E. Eerdsmans Publ. Co., 1986).

TILLICH PAUL, *Systematic Theology* (Chicago: Chicago University Press, 1951).

TRETHOWAN ILLTUD, *Mysticism and Theology* (London: G. Chapman, 1975).

TUGWELL SIMON [1], *The Nine Ways of Prayer of Saint Dominic,* ed. and transl. by Simon Tugwell (Dominican Publications: Dublin, 1978).

———, [2], "A Dominican Theology of Prayer" in *Dominican Ashram,* I (1982).

———, [3], *Ways of Imperfection* (London: Darton, Longman and Todd, 1984).

———, [4], "The Nine Ways of Prayer of St. Dominic: A Textual Study and Critical Edition", in *Mediaeval Studies,* 47 (1985), pp. 1-124, Offprint.

———, [5], *Albert and Thomas: Selected Writings* (New York-Mahwah: Paulist Press, 1988).

———, [6], *Prayer,* vol. I, *Living with God* (Dublin: Veritas Publ., 1974).

TURIEL BIENVENIDO, *El Habito-Qualidad* (Madrid: Convento de San Pedro Mártyr, 1961).

ULANOV ANN AND BARRY, *Prayer and Personality: Prayer as Primary Speech,* in SS.

———, [2], *Primary Speech: A Psychology of Prayer* (Atlanta: John Knox Press, 1982).

UNDERHILL EVELYN [1], *Mysticism: A Study of the Nature and Development of Man's Spiritual Consciousness* (New York: E.P. Dutton, 1961).

———, [2], *Worship* (New York: Crossroad, 1985).

———, [3], *The Spiritual Life: Five Broadcasts* (London: Hodder and Stroughton, 1937).

VAN KAAM ADRIAN and MUTO SUSAN, *Practicing the Prayer of Presence* (Denville, NJ: Dimension Books, 1980).

VON BALTHASAR HANS URS [1], *Love Alone* (New York: Herder and Herder, 1969).

———, [2], *Prayer* (San Francisco: Ignatius Press, 1986).

VON HILDEBRAND ALICE, *Introduction to the Philosophy of Religion* (Chicago: Franciscan Herald Press, 1971).

WALSH LIAM, *The Sacraments of Initiation: Baptism, Confirmation, Eucharist* (London: Geoffrey Chapman, 1988).

WALTER WILLIAM GREY, *The Living Brain* (New York: W.W. Norton and Co., 1963).

WARD BENEDICTA, "The New Orders", in SS.

WARE KALLISTOS, "The Origin of Jesus Prayer: Diadochus, Gaza, Sinai", in SS.

———, [2], "The Hesychasts: Gregory of Sinai, Gregory Palamas, etc.", in SS.

———, [3], "The Spirituality of the Icon", in SS.

Way (the) of the Pilgrim and the Pilgrim Continues His Way, a new translation by Helen Bacovcin (Garden City, NY: Doubleday and Company, 1978).

WEIL SIMONE, *Waiting for God* (London: Fontana Collins, 1963).

WILLIAMS C., *De multiplici virtutum formam iuxta doctrinam S. Thomae Aquinatis expositio synthetico-speculativa.* (Romae: Pont. Athenaeum Angelicum, 1954).

WILBER K., *The Atman Project* (Illinois: The Theosophical Publ. House, 1985).

WIJNGAARDS JOHN, *Experiencing Jesus* (Notre Dame, Ind.: Ave Maria Press, 1981).

WOLFF PIERRE, *Is God Deaf?* (Waldwick, NJ: Arena Letters, 1984).

WRIGHT ADDISON G., "Ecclesiastes (Qoheleth)", in *The New Jerome Biblical Commentary,* ed. by Raymond Brown et al. (Englewood Cliffs, NY: 1990).

WRIGHT JOHN H., *A Theology of Christian Prayer* (New York: Pueblo Publ. Co., 1979).

YOURCENAR MARGUERITE, *La couronne et la lyre: poèmes traduits du grec* (Paris: Gallimard, 1979).

YUSHI NOMURA, *Desert Wisdom: Sayings from the Desert Fathers* (Garden City, NY: Image Books, Doubleday and Co., 1984).

ZARRI ADRIANA, *Nostro Signore del Deserto: Teologia e Antropologia della Preghiera* (Assisi: Cittadella Editrice, 1978).

ZORELL FRANCISCO, *Lexicon Graecum Novi Testamenti* (Parisiis: Lethielleux, 1961).